THE SOLZHENITSYN FILES

THE SOLZHENITSYN FILES

SECRET SOVIET DOCUMENTS REVEAL ONE MAN'S FIGHT AGAINST THE MONOLITH

Edited and with an Introduction by
Michael Scammell

Translated from Russian under the supervision of
Catherine A. Fitzpatrick

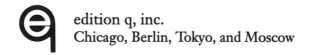

edition q, inc.
Chicago, Berlin, Tokyo, and Moscow

Translators

Catherine A. Fitzpatrick • Alex Cigale • Lev Dykhno
Elena Kolesnikov • Vladimir Kolesnikov • Alexei Serebrennikov
Alexander Sumerkin • Laura E. Wolfson

© 1995 edition q, inc.
© Introduction 1995 Michael Scammell

edition q, inc.
551 N. Kimberly Drive
Carol Stream, IL 60188-1881

Library of Congress Cataloging-in-Publication Data

The Solzhenitsyn files: secret Soviet documents reveal one man's fight against the monolith / edited and with an introduction by Michael Scammell; translated from Russian under the supervision of Catherine A. Fitzpatrick.
    p.   cm.
    Includes bibliographical references and index.
    ISBN 1-883695-06-6
    1. Solzhenitsyn, Aleksandr Isaevich, 1918– —Sources. 2. Authors, Russian—20th century—Biography. 3. Soviet Union—History—1953–1985—Sources. 4. Political persecution—Soviet Union—History—20th century—Sources. I. Scammell, Michael.
PG3488.04Z8864 1995
891.73'44—dc20

        95–31827
        CIP

Printed in the United States of America

CONTENTS

Introduction xvii
Preface to the Russian Edition xxxvii

PART I
1963–1969 EARLY STRUGGLE 1

1963
1. Report from V. Lebedev. 22 March 1963. 3

1965
2. Report of the Committee for State Security of the USSR Council of Ministers. No. 2275–S. 5 October 1965. 7
3. Report of the Committee for State Security of the USSR Council of Ministers. No. 2285–S. 5 October 1965. 26

1966
4. Memorandum of the Committee for State Security of the USSR Council of Ministers and the USSR Public Prosecutor's Office. No. 6–S. 4 January 1966. 29
5. Report of the Committee for State Security of the USSR Council of Ministers. No. 81–S. 14 January 1966. 32
6. Report of the Central Committee Culture Department. 29 January 1966. 33
7. Letter from Konstantin Simonov, "On Solzhenitsyn's Novel *The First Circle*." 1 February 1966. 36

1967

8. Excerpts from a Transcript of a Meeting of the Secretariat of the Central Committee of the USSR Communist Party. 10 March 1967.   41

9. Report of the Committee for State Security of the USSR Council of Ministers. No. 1197–S. 17 May 1967.   43

10. S. Toka's Letter to the Central Committee. No. 63. 1 June 1967.   44

11. Report of the Committee for State Security of the USSR Council of Ministers. No. 1740–B. 5 July 1967.   51

12. Report of the Committee for State Security of the USSR Council of Ministers. No. 1756–A. 5 July 1967.   54

13. Memorandum from the International Department of the Central Committee. No. 25–S–1014. 10 July 1967.   55

14. Resolution of the Politburo of the Central Committee, "Instructions to the Soviet Ambassador to Italy." No. P47/95. 17 July 1967.   56

15. From a Transcript of a Meeting of the Central Committee Secretariat. 18 July 1967.   58

16. Report of the Committee for State Security of the USSR Council of Ministers. No. 2338–A. 14 September 1967.   60

17. Report of the Culture Department of the Central Committee of the Communist Party of the Soviet Union, "On the Discussions in the Soviet Writers' Union Regarding Solzhenitsyn's Conduct." 4 October 1967.   63

18. Memorandum of the Secretariat of the USSR Writers' Union. No. 812. 12 December 1967.   68

1968

19. Report from the Committee for State Security of the USSR Council of Ministers. No. 218–A. 31 January 1968.   75

20. Memorandum from the USSR Foreign Ministry and the Central Committee Department of Relations with Communist and Workers' Parties of Socialist Nations. No. 1506/GS. No. 15–D–887. 16 June 1968.   79

21. Politburo Resolution, "On a Verbal Communication to the Secretariat of the Ministry of Foreign Affairs of the Republic of Yugoslavia in Connection with the Publication of Solzhenitsyn's *Cancer Ward* in the Yugoslav Newspaper *Delo*." No. P87/7. 21 June 1968.   81

1969

22. Memorandum from the Central Committee Culture Department, "On the Writer A. Solzhenitsyn Regarding the Publication of His Works Abroad." 22 January 1969.   83

23. Report of the Central Committee Culture Department, "Writers' Responses to the Expulsion of Solzhenitsyn from the Soviet Writers' Union." 13 November 1969.   85

24. Report of the Central Committee Culture Department, "On the Responses of Writers to Solzhenitsyn's Antisocial Activities." 18 November 1969.   87

25. Report of the Moscow City Party Committee. No. 328. 20 November 1969.   89

PART II
1970–1971 NOBEL PRIZE   93

1970

26. Central Committee Secretariat Resolution, "On Measures in Connection with the Act of Provocation of Awarding the 1970 Nobel Prize for Literature to A. Solzhenitsyn." No. St–112/gs. 9 October 1970.   95

27. Report of the Chief Directorate for the Preservation of Government Secrets in the Press [Glavlit] of the USSR Council of Ministers. No. 988s. 13 October 1970.   97

28. Letter from A. Solzhenitsyn to M. Suslov. 14 October 1970.   100

29. Report of the Central Committee Culture Department, "On the Reaction of the Writers' Community to the Awarding of the Nobel Prize to Solzhenitsyn." 15 October 1970.   102

30. Memorandum from the Culture Department of the Central Committee, "On Solzhenitsyn's Letter." 27 October 1970.   104

31. Memorandum from the Committee for State Security of the USSR Council of Ministers. No. 2945–A. 29 October 1970.   107

32. Report from M. Zimyanin, Editor-in-Chief of *Pravda*. No. GL–124.   110

33. Letter to the Central Committee from A. Chakovsky, Editor-in-Chief of *Literaturnaya Gazeta*. 11 November 1970.   114

34. Memorandum from the Culture Department of the Central Committee, "On Solzhenitsyn." 11 November 1970.   117

35. Memorandum from the Committee for State Security of the USSR Council of Ministers. No. 3125–Ts. 14 November 1970.   124

36. Telegram from the USSR Embassy in Sweden. Special no. 694. 15 November 1970 Stockholm.   125

37. Memorandum from the Central Committee Department of Relations with Communist and Workers' Parties of Socialist Nations and the Culture Department, "On Instructions to the USSR Ambassador to the Democratic Republic of Vietnam." 17 November 1970.   126

38. Politburo Resolution, "On Instructions to the USSR Ambassador to the Democratic Republic of Vietnam." No. P183/134. 18 November 1970.   127

39. Memorandum from the Culture Department of the Central Committee, "On the Publication of Materials on Solzhenitsyn." 20 November 1970.   129

40. Memorandum from the Committee for State Security of the USSR Council of Ministers and the Public Prosecutor's Office. No. 3181–A. 20 November 1970.   138

41. Memorandum from the International Department of the Central Committee and the USSR Ministry of Foreign Affairs. No. 2147/GS. No. 25–S–1993. 23 November 1970.   141

42. Politburo Resolution, "On Instructions to the Soviet Ambassador in Stockholm in Connection with Awarding the Nobel Prize to Solzhenitsyn." No. P 184/159. 27 November 1970.   142

43. Report from the Committee for State Security of the USSR Council of Ministers. No. 3249–tsv. 28 November 1970.   144

44. Telegram from the USSR Embassy in Sweden. Special no. 742. 1 December 1970 Stockholm.   146

45. Memorandum from the USSR Minister of Foreign Affairs. No. 2235/GS. 3 December 1970.   147

46. Report from the Committee for State Security of the USSR Council of Ministers. No. 3271–A. 3 December 1970.   148

47. Politburo Resolution, "On the Statement Made to Sweden's Ambassador to the USSR in Connection with Awarding the Nobel Prize to Solzhenitsyn." No. P185/7. 4 December 1970.   150

48. Report from the Committee for State Security of the USSR Council of Ministers. No. 3511–A. 28 December 1970.   151

1971

49. Politburo Resolution, A Question from the Committee for State Security and the USSR Public Prosecutor's Office (On Solzhenitsyn). No. P187/XI. 7 January 1971.   153

50. Letter from Solzhenitsyn to the Chairman of the Council of Ministers of the USSR. 18 February 1971.   154

51. Report from the Committee on State Security of the USSR Council of Ministers. 1630–A. 25 June 1971.   156

52. Memorandum from the Committee of State Security of the USSR Council of Ministers. No. 2067–A. 16 August 1971.   158

53. Memorandum from N. Shchelokov, "On the Solzhenitsyn Question." No later than 7 October 1971.   161

54. From the Minutes of a Meeting of the Secretariat of the Central Committee of the Communist Party. 7 October 1971.   164

55. Report from the Committee for State Security of the USSR Council of Ministers. No. 3720–A/OV. 27 October 1971.   165

56. Memorandum from the Committee on State Security of the USSR Council of Ministers and the USSR Ministry of Foreign Affairs. No. 1924/gs. 16 November 1971. 168

57. Politburo Resolution, "On the Instructions to be Given to the Soviet Ambassador in Stockholm Regarding Solzhenitsyn's Nobel Prize." No. P26/44. 19 November 1971. 169

58. Report from the Committee for State Security of the USSR Council of Ministers. No. 2953–A. 23 November 1971. 170

59. Report from the Committee for State Security of the USSR Council of Ministers of the USSR. No. 3256–Ts. 25 December 1971. 177

60. Report from the Committee for State Security of the USSR Council of Ministers. No. 3318–A. 31 December 1971. 180

PART III
1972–1973 APPROACHING CRISIS 183

1972

61. From the Minutes of a Politburo Session. 7 January 1972. 185

62. From Minutes of a Meeting of the Central Committee Secretariat. 16 February 1972. 185

63. E. Furtseva's Letter to the Politburo. 17 February 1972. 186

64. Memorandum of the Committee for State Security of the USSR Council of Ministers. No. 421–A. 20 February 1972. 189

65. Report from the Committee for State Security of the USSR Council of Ministers. No. 438–A. 22 February 1972. 191

66. Report from the Committee for State Security of the USSR Council of Ministers. No. 601–A. 11 March 1972. 192

67. Memorandum from the Committee for State Security of the USSR Council of Ministers and the USSR Public Prosecutor's Office. No. 778–A. 27 March 1972. 194

68. From the Minutes of a Politburo Session. 30 March 1972. 199

69. Politburo Resolution. No. P37 per minutes. 30 March 1972. 212

70. Report of the Committee for State Security of the USSR Council of Ministers. No. 854–A. 3 April 1972. 212

71. Telegram from the USSR Embassy in Sweden. Special No. 285. 8 April 1972 Stockholm. 214

72. Report of the Committee for State Security of the USSR Council of Ministers. No. 942–A/OV. 10 April 1972. 215

73. Memorandum from the USSR Foreign Ministry. No. 739/GS. 12 April 1972. 217

74. Resolution of the Central Committee's Politburo, "On the Verbal Statement to the Swedish Embassy in Moscow." No. P40/60. 13 April 1972. 218

75. Report of the Committee for State Security of the USSR Council of Ministers. No. 969–A. 13 April 1972. 219

76. From the Minutes of the Central Committee Meeting. 221

1973

77. Memorandum of the Committee for State Security of the USSR Council of Ministers. No. 1707–A. 17 July 1973. 223

78. Report of the Committee for State Security of the USSR Council of Ministers. No. 1902–A. 10 August 1973. 230

79. Memorandum of the Committee for State Security of the USSR Council of Ministers. No. 2036-A. 26 August 1973. 232

80. Memorandum of the Committee for State Security of the USSR Council of Ministers. No. 2045–A. 27 August 1973. 236

81. From the Minutes of a Politburo Meeting. 30 August 1973. 241

82. Telegram from the USSR Embassy in France. Special No. 2232. 30 August 1973 Paris. 243

83. Telegram from the USSR Embassy in France. Special No. 2256. 1 September 1973 Paris. 244

84. Report of the Committee for State Security of the USSR Council of Ministers. No 2114–A. 4 September 1973. 246

85. Letter from A. Solzhenitsyn to L. Brezhnev. 5 September 1973. 248

86. Memorandum of the USSR Ministry of Foreign Affairs and the Central Committee's International Department. No. 2175/GS. 7 September 1973. 250

87. Report of the Committee for State Security of the USSR Council of Ministers. No. 2176/CH. 8 September 1973. 251

88. Report of the Committee for State Security of the USSR Council of Ministers. No. 2180/Ch. 10 September 1973. 252

89. Politburo Resolution, "Regarding a Representation to the Government of France in Connection with the Anti-Soviet Campaign in the French Media." No. P103/138. 13 September 1973. 254

90. From the Transcript of a Politburo Session. 17 September 1973. 256

91. Politburo Resolution, "Regarding Sakharov and Solzhenitsyn." No. P104/VIII. 17 September 1973. 258

92. Memorandum of the Committee for State Security of the USSR Council of Ministers. No. 2239–A. 17 September 1973. 259

93. Memorandum of the Committee for State Security of the USSR Council of Ministers. No. 2487–A. 19 October 1973. 264

94. Report of the Committee for State Security of the USSR Council of Ministers. No. 2654–A. 2 November 1973.   267
95. Memorandum of the Committee for State Security of the USSR Council of Ministers. No. 3079–A. 12 December 1973.   269

PART IV
1974 EXPULSION   275

1974

96. Memorandum from the Committee for State Security of the USSR Council of Ministers. No. 2–A. 2 January 1974.   277
97. Memorandum from the Committee for State Security of the USSR Council of Ministers. No. 4–A. 2 January 1974.   279
98. Resolution of the Secretariat of the Central Committee, "On Exposing the Anti-Soviet Campaign of Bourgeois Propaganda Regarding the Publication of *The Gulag Archipelago* by Solzhenitsyn." No. St–108/4s. 4 January 1974.   280
99. From Minutes of Politburo Meetings. 7 January 1974.   283
100. Politburo Resolution, "On Solzhenitsyn." No. P120/1—transcript. 7 January 1974.   292
101. Memorandum from *Pravda* Political Commentator Yuri Zhukov. 11 January 1974.   293
102. Report from the Moscow City Party Committee. 11 January 1974.   297
103. Memorandum from Central Committee International Department, "On Information for Fraternal Parties Regarding the Anti-Soviet Activity of Solzhenitsyn." No. 25–S–90. 15 January 1974.   301
104. Report from the Central Committee's Departments of Propaganda, Culture, and Science and Educational Institutions. 15 January 1974.   302
105. Report of Committee for State Security. No. 119–A. 15 January 1974.   304
106. Report of the Committee for State Security. No. 139–A. 16 January 1974.   306
107. Report from the General Department of the Central Committee, "On Workers' Letters in Regard to the Anti-Soviet Activities of A. Sakharov and A. Solzhenitsyn." 16 January 1974.   308
108. From the Minutes of a Politburo Session. 17 January 1974.   311
109. Politburo Resolution, "On a Report to Fraternal Parties Regarding the Anti-Soviet Activities of Solzhenitsyn." No. P122/XVII. 17 January 1974.   312

110. Report of the Committee for State Security of the USSR Council of Ministers. No. 147–A. 17 January 1974. 319

111. Report from the Moscow City Party Committee, "On Responses of Moscow Workers to the Article 'The Path of Treason' by I. Solovyev, Published in *Pravda* on 14 January 1974." No. 18. 17 January 1974. 320

112. Report of the Committee for State Security of the USSR Council of Ministers. No. 150–A. 17 January 1974. 323

113. Report of the Committee for State Security of the USSR Council of Ministers. No. 157–A. 18 January 1974. 325

114. Report of the Committee for State Security of the USSR Council of Ministers. No. 174–A. 19 January 1974. 327

115. Report of the Department of Organizational and Party Work of the Central Committee, "On the Attitudes of Soviet People to the Publication Abroad of the Slanderous Writings of A. Solzhenitsyn." 21 January 1974. 330

116. Report of the Committee for State Security of the USSR Council of Ministers. No. 266–A. 29 January 1974. 335

117. Report of the Committee for State Security of the USSR Council of Ministers. No. 300–A. 1 February 1974. 336

118. Memorandum of the Committee for State Security of the USSR Council of Ministers and the USSR Public Prosecutor's Office. No. 348–A. 6 February 1974. 339

119. Memorandum of the Committee for State Security of the USSR Council of Ministers. No. 350–A/OV. 7 February 1974. 340

120. Letter from Y. Andropov to L. Brezhnev. 7 February 1974. 342

121. Memorandum of Committee for State Security of the USSR Council of Ministers. No. 388–A. 9 February 1974. 346

122. Memorandum of the Committee for State Security of the USSR Council of Ministers and the USSR Ministry of Foreign Affairs. No. 389–A. 9 February 1974. 349

123. Politburo Resolution, "Report of Committee for State Security of the USSR Council of Ministers, 9 February 1974, No. 388–A." No. P125/112. 11 February 1974. 350

124. Politburo Resolution, "On Instructions to the Soviet Ambassador to Bonn." No. P125/113. 11 February 1974. 352

125. Decree of the Presidium of the USSR Supreme Soviet, "On the Revocation of A.I. Solzhenitsyn's Soviet Citizenship and His Deportation from the USSR." No. 5494–III. 12 February 1974. 354

126. From Minutes of a Meeting of the Politburo of the Central Committee. 14 February 1974. 355

127. Politburo Resolution, "On Informing Our Friends Concerning the Actions Against Solzhenitsyn." No. P125/7—To be minuted. 14 February 1974.   356

128. Decree of the Central Committee Secretariat, "On Informing Leaders of Fraternal Communist and Workers' Parties on the Solzhenitsyn Matter." No. St–114/51gs. 14 February 1974.   356

129. Telegram from the USSR Embassy in Sweden. Spec. No. 129. 14 February 1974 Stockholm.   361

130. Report from the Central Committee of the CP of the Ukraine. No. 1/25. 14 February 1974.   365

131. Report from the Committee for State Security of the USSR Council of Ministers. No. 444–A. 14 February 1974.   369

132. Report of the Central Committee Department for Organizational and Party Work, "On Workers' Responses to the Deportation of Solzhenitsyn from the USSR." 15 February 1974.   372

133. Memorandum from the Central Committee International Department, "On Instructions to the Soviet Ambassador to Sweden." No. 25–S–371. 22 February 1974.   374

134. Report from the Committee for State Security of the USSR Council of Ministers. No. 553–Ts. 23 February 1974.   376

135. Politburo Resolution, "On Instructions to the Soviet Ambassador to Sweden." No. P127/103. 28 February 1974.   379

136. Memorandum from USSR Ministry of Foreign Affairs and the Committee for State Security of the USSR Council of Ministers. No. 536/GS. 1 March 1974.   382

137. Politburo Resolution, "On Solzhenitsyn's Royalties." No. P128/23. 5 March 1974.   383

138. Memorandum from the Presidium of the USSR Supreme Soviet. No. 154cc. 20 March 1974.   384

139. Report from the Committee for State Security of the USSR Council of Ministers. No. 1168–A. 2 May 1974.   387

140. Report from the Committee for State Security of the USSR Council of Ministers. No. 2035–A. 24 July 1974.   388

PART V
1975–1980 EXILE   391

1975

141. Memorandum from the Committee for State Security of the USSR Council of Ministers, "On *The Oak and the Calf* and the Further Compromising of Solzhenitsyn." No. 1437–A. 6 June 1975.   393

142. Report of the Committee for State Security of the USSR Council of Ministers, "On the Publication of an Open Letter by V.A. Tvardovskaya to Solzhenitsyn in the Italian Newspaper *L'Unita*." No. 1812–A. 11 July 1975.   399

143. Memorandum from the Committee for State Security of the USSR Council of Ministers, "On Publishing Yakovlev's Article 'The Calf with a Blade' on Solzhenitsyn in *Golos Rodiny* (Voice of the Motherland)." No. 2337–A. 30 August 1975.   409

144. Memorandum from I. Chernoutsan, Consultant, the Central Committee Culture Department, to M. Suslov. 9 September 1975.   427

1976

145. Report from the Committee for State Security of the USSR Council of Ministers, "On Solzhenitsyn's Hostile Activities and the Decline of Interest in His Person Abroad and in the USSR." No. 7–A. 4 January 1976.   431

146. Memorandum of the Committee for State Security of the USSR Council of Ministers, "On the Revocation of N.D. Solzhenitsyna's Soviet Citizenship." No. 2302–A. 12 October 1976.   436

147. Politburo Resolution, "On Revoking N.D. Solzhenitsyna's Soviet Citizenship." No. P3O/8. 17 October 1976.   438

1977

148. Report from the Committee for State Security of the USSR Council of Ministers, "On the Publication of a Manuscript About Solzhenitsyn." No. 87–Ts. 17 January 1977.   441

149. Memorandum of the Committee for State Security of the USSR Council of Ministers, "On Publication of the Decree of the Presidium of the USSR Supreme Soviet on the Revocation of N.D. Solzhenitsyna's Soviet Citizenship." No. 423–A. 2 March 1977.   446

150. Politburo Resolution, "On Publication of the Decree of the Presidium of the USSR Supreme Soviet on the Revocation of N.D. Solzhenitsyna's Soviet Citizenship." No. P49/23. 5 March 1977.   447

151. Memorandum of the Committee for State Security of the USSR Council of Ministers, "On Publication of a Book on Solzhenitsyn in the Russian Language." No. 1432–A. 5 July 1977.   448

152. Politburo Resolution, "On Publication of a Book on Solzhenitsyn in the Russian Language." No. P63/31. 11 July 1977.   449

153. Report from the Committee for State Security of the USSR Council of Ministers, "On Solzhenitsyn's Attempt to Found a So-Called 'All-Russian Memoir Library.'" No. 2439–A. 11 November 1977.   449

1978

154. Memorandum from the USSR State Committee for Publishing, Printing, and the Book Trade and from Novosti Press Agency. No. 0500. 8 August 1978.   451

155. Memorandum of the Central Committee Propaganda Department and of the Department for Political Propaganda Abroad, "On Rezac's Book *Solzhenitsyn's Spiral of Treason*." 18 September 1978.   452

1979

156. Telegram from A. Solzhenitsyn to K. Chernenko. 20 December 1979 Moscow.   455

1980

157. Memorandum of the USSR Ministry for Internal Affairs, "On the Matter of Solzhenitsyn's Telegram." No. 1/703. 6 February 1980.   457

List of Documents Included in the Book

I.   Minutes of Politburo Meetings   459

II.   Politburo Resolutions   459

III.   Minutes of the Central Committee Secretariat Meetings   461

IV.   Central Committee Secretariat Resolutions   461

V.   The Decree of the Presidium of the USSR Supreme Soviet   461

VI.   Memorandums from Ministries, State Committees, Central Committee Departments, and Officials   462

VII.   Reports from Ministries, State Committees, Central Committee Departments, and Officials   464

VIII.   Telegrams from the USSR Embassies in Sweden and in France   467

IX.   Letters and a Telegram from Solzhenitsyn and Other Persons   467

Index   468

INTRODUCTION

Michael Scammell

Imagine the President of the United States conferring with his advisors on whether to allow an American novelist to accept the Nobel Prize for Literature or to live in Washington; or the Security Council sitting down to discuss stripping that same author of his citizenship and deporting him from the country for his opposition to the government's policies. Picture, if you will, the Secretary of State and the Attorney General holding meetings with their staff members, and the CIA and the FBI devoting millions of dollars and huge numbers of agents to wiretapping the novelist's home, tracking his friends and relatives, reading his mail, analyzing his books, commissioning their own articles and books to discredit him, and orchestrating a disinformation campaign on an international scale.

That would convey some notion of what was occupying the time and resources of the world's other superpower during the late sixties and early seventies when the Cold War was still at its height—and is the subject of the present book. The novelist in question was Alexander Solzhenitsyn, and the book before you consists of secret Soviet government documents chronicling the handling of "the Solzhenitsyn case" by Soviet leaders (up to and including First Secretary Leonid Brezhnev, effectively the Soviet president) over a twenty-year period, beginning in 1965. The documents were declassified by President Yeltsin in the summer of 1992, and were published in Russia the following year.

Collected here is formerly confidential evidence about the entire Solzhenitsyn operation, ranging from the minutes of Politburo sessions and meetings of the Central Committee Secretariat at the top; through memos and reports from ministries, state committees, departments, and of course the ubiquitous KGB in the middle; down to intercepted letters, transcripts of bugged conversations, records of interrogations, and all the paraphernalia of the spy trade at the lowest level. Together they constitute a treasure trove of information about the inner workings of the Politburo (the Soviet "cabinet"), the Ministry of Foreign Affairs, the Committee for State Security (KGB), the Communist Party's Central Committee, the Writers' Union, the Censorship (Glavlit), and of course the KGB's "kitchen." All these items were faithfully recorded and stored away by Soviet bureaucrats who never dreamed that one day their painstaking records would be made public and used in evidence against them—though, interestingly enough, Solzhenitsyn himself had predicted something of the sort after his expulsion from the Writers' Union in 1969 (Documents 23 and 24).

Quite apart from their scholarly and historical interest, however, these documents recount an enthralling story of the entrapment, persecution, and expulsion of one of the greatest Russian writers of modern times, and provide a record of one of the most significant recent episodes in the continuing conflict between political power and moral principles that has been fought out in western culture at least since the death of Socrates. From the second document in this collection (containing a transcript of Solzhenitsyn delivering himself of some breathtakingly prophetic political remarks about the Soviet regime in a bugged conversation with a friend) through to the Politburo resolution decreeing his arrest and expulsion from the country and beyond, we are able to watch the tentacles of the KGB coiling around his person, tightening to exert their irresistible pressure—and continuing to reach out after him even after his deportation to the West.

We are also able to see, if we read these documents carefully, and despite the KGB's strenuous efforts to conceal the fact, that their entire efforts and the millions of rubles they expended went for nought. Solzhenitsyn not only succeeded in publishing all the novels, short stories, and plays the KGB sought to suppress, but he also brought out his unique, crushing chronicle of the monstrosities of Stalinist totalitarianism, *The Gulag Archipelago*, that the KGB strove so mightily to stop at any price. Indeed, as he himself observed after the fact, it was the KGB's relentless determination to obtain a copy of that book that triggered its early publication, thus contributing to the KGB's—and the regime's—demise.

It is true that, thanks to the KGB's efforts, this and other works by Solzhenitsyn were forced to appear first abroad, and reached the Soviet public only in small numbers or via western radio broadcasts (and we see in these documents what strenuous exertions were made by the KGB to neutralize their effects abroad, as well as in their own country). But that only added to Solzhenitsyn's authority and increased his mystique: the KGB served to attract not less, but more attention to his books and statements, which only reinforced their influence at home. Moreover, Solzhenitsyn lived to see the day—as he had also predicted he would—when the entire edifice of Soviet communism would come crashing down, and when not only his books, which had helped to prepare the way for the debacle (about this, at least, the KGB was right), but he himself would return to Russia.

■

These documents, then, have a fascinating story to tell, and arranged as they are in strictly chronological order, they reveal events in the Solzhenitsyn saga unfolding with the inevitability of a Greek tragedy. Alone they already contain much of the information a reader needs to form his or her own judgments, but to get the most out of them, it helps to know a little about the personalities involved and about the political context in which these events unfolded.

The first thing that needs to be said is that the fall of Solzhenitsyn was intimately connected with the fall of First Secretary Nikita Khrushchev, and with the reversal by Khrushchev's successor, Brezhnev, of Khrushchev's policy of de-Stalinization. De-Stalinization itself had begun almost immediately after Stalin's death in 1953, and had been given new impetus by Khrushchev at Party congresses in 1956, 1959, and 1961. This period, known informally as the period of "the Thaw," saw the dismantling of nine tenths of Stalin's system of labor camps (the Gulag), the mass freeing of prisoners, a switch of economic resources from heavy industry to consumer goods, and a general relaxation in the hitherto draconian discipline that had bound Soviet society to communist ideals.

One of the immediate beneficiaries of these policies was the then-unknown writer Alexander Solzhenitsyn, who had a sheaf of unpublished manuscripts not so much in his desk drawer as buried in the earth for safekeeping. The inspiration and the impetus for those manuscripts had come from the trauma he had experienced when, as a young officer at the front during World War II, he had been arrested for "anti-Soviet propaganda" on the basis of letters to a friend criticizing some of Stalin's policies. Although not a Party member, Solzhenitsyn was a loyal Marxist at the time, who blamed Stalin only for "backsliding," so the shock of his arrest, and of being flung into the labor camps without a trial, was all the greater. It was during eight years in the camps that he had slowly come to understand the larger iniquities of Stalin's purges and of the collectivization of the peasantry, and it was in the camps that he had become a writer, composing a long autobiographical poem, *Volunteers' Highway*, two plays, *The Republic of Labor* and *Feast of the Victors*, and a great deal of lyric poetry.

None of these works could be offered for publication. Although

Solzhenitsyn completed and polished them while in administrative exile in southern Kazakhstan (between 1953 and 1956), they were too bitter for general consumption, and had been shown only to a handful of close friends. They dealt with his experiences as a student during the thirties, as an officer in the Red Army toward the end of the war, and as a prisoner in the labor camps at various stages in his confinement. In Kazakhstan he also started a big novel about his years as an inmate in a prison research institute outside Moscow. Provisionally called *Sharashka* (see Document 2, Note 6), it was not intended for publication at the time either; the political situation in the late fifties was still too repressive.

Only after Solzhenitsyn had been released in 1956, as a result of Khrushchev's policies, and had returned to the city of Ryazan in Central Russia (where he worked as a teacher of physics and mathematics) did he begin to dream of publication. It was there that he wrote a "lightened" version of some of his labor camp experiences in the shape of a short novel, *One Day in the Life of Ivan Denisovich*, but he didn't dare show even that to any editors until after Khrushchev's second big de-Stalinization speech in the fall of 1961. Eventually he was persuaded to offer the novel to Alexander Tvardovsky, editor of Moscow's most liberal journal *Novy Mir* (New World), and Tvardovsky was so enraptured by it that, despite its controversial tone and subject matter, he went all the way up to Khrushchev personally to secure its publication. The middleman for this operation was Khrushchev's personal secretary, Vladimir Lebedev (see Document 1), and it seems that Khrushchev glanced at the book only superficially before giving his assent. For him it was a weapon with which to beat his pro-Stalinist adversaries, and he little suspected the enormous reverberations this little book would have both inside the Soviet Union and throughout the rest of the world. (In his memoirs Khrushchev lamented his decision and suggested that it had contributed to his subsequent downfall. This may be true.)

When the book was published in November 1962, Solzhenitsyn skyrocketed from being an obscure provincial schoolteacher to author of a world-famous book. So cleverly did *Ivan Denisovich* camouflage its subject matter that it managed to convey an incredible amount of the truth about the unprecedented cruelties of Stalin's regime and the extraordinary tragedy of the average Soviet citizen's life. Many Russian readers, especially ex-prisoners (of whom there were millions) wept over its pages, while foreigners gaped at its stark revelations. It represented the climax of Khrushchev's Thaw: after *Ivan Denisovich*, many believed that censorship would be abolished and Khrushchev would sweep away the last vestiges of Stalinism.

This was not to be. Although journals and publishing houses were inundated with manuscripts about life in the labor camps and the rigors of Stalin's purges, all were rejected, and not another word about the camps was allowed to creep into print, except in government-commissioned and sanitized stories that were deliberately designed to neutralize the effects of Solzhenitsyn's novel. Worse still, the liberal tide had in fact reached its high point with *Ivan Denisovich*, and within weeks of the book's publication it began to ebb. Khrushchev himself sanctioned a government counterattack on liberal intellectuals and let it be known that Party discipline over the arts would be reinforced rather than relaxed.

Until this time Khrushchev had ruled without too much difficulty as undisputed leader of both Party and country. By 1963, however (the date of the first document in this book), Khrushchev was in trouble. His industrial and agricultural reforms had not worked. He had antagonized the Party apparatus by weakening its power. He had offended the KGB by reforming its structure, reducing its numbers and trying to make it more answerable to the politicians for its actions. Worst of all, his foreign policy had brought about the debacle of the Cuban missile crisis in October 1962, badly undermining both his own prestige and that of the Soviet Union as a whole.

In October 1964, Khrushchev was overthrown in a palace revolution that placed Brezhnev at the head of the Party and state. For about a year afterward it was unclear whether the Brezhnev administration would continue Khrushchev's reforms, halt them, or try to reverse the reforms and return to a version of Stalinism. By the fall of 1965 (when the second and a very important document in this collection was produced), it was becoming clear that Khrushchev's reforms were being reversed; and we now know that the events of that weekend of September 11 and 12, 1965, when Solzhenitsyn's manuscripts were confiscated by the security services (Documents 2 and 3), signalled the effective end of the Thaw, at least in cultural matters, and the start of a high-profile policy of preemptive activism on the part of a resurgent KGB.

Solzhenitsyn was thus caught up in a major change of political policy that had nothing to do with him personally, but was a consequence of the Brezhnev regime's determination to change direction. Since he was in a sense "Khrushchev's man," and profoundly associated with the attack on Stalinism, his reputation with the authorities, as chronicled in these documents, can be read as a barometer of the creeping re-Stalinization introduced between 1965 (the date of the confiscation of his manuscripts) and 1979 (the date of the last document in this collection). This is not entirely unjust, for Solzhenitsyn was indeed a "political" writer in the fullest sense of that word (which the authorities understood very well); from the moment of its inception his career had borne a political dimension.

During the brief window of opportunity opened up by his success with *Ivan Denisovich*, Solzhenitsyn had managed to publish just two more short stories, but had failed to get *The Republic of Labor* staged (Document 1).

Instead of being awarded the Lenin Prize for Literature in 1964, for which he was the overwhelming literary favorite, he had been passed over in favor of a hack novelist from the Ukraine.

Meanwhile, still unaware of the major change that was impending, he had revised his big novel about the prison institute, altered its name from *Sharashka* to *The First Circle*, and shown it to Tvardovsky, who had declared his desire to publish it. Solzhenitsyn had then delivered a copy to the offices of *Novy Mir*, but when Khrushchev was toppled, he fell into a sudden panic, took the novel back again, and dropped it off at the apartment of his friend, Veniamin Teush. It was by sheer chance that the KGB stumbled across the novel when they raided Teush in connection with another case, and by chance that they found Solzhenitsyn's early manuscripts, for they evidently had no idea what they were looking for. Their search was part of a Moscow-wide sweep of dissident intellectuals that weekend. It was during that same sweep that the KGB arrested Andrei Sinyavsky and Yuli Daniel on charges of publishing anti-Soviet stories abroad (see Document 6, Note 7), and set in motion a case that was to rival Solzhenitsyn's own in its reverberations and unpleasant consequences for the government.

From the point of view of the KGB, the politically rash and bitterly outspoken early plays and poems by Solzhenitsyn were an unexpected windfall, which they soon put to excellent use with their tendentious summaries and selective quotations. In this way, they were able to set the stage and establish the context for all future discussions of Solzhenitsyn's work, and the documents show that they continued to use the same quotations and the same incendiary passages in their memos year after year, right up to the time of Solzhenitsyn's expulsion. Meanwhile, the wide but secret distribution of *Feast of the Victors* to selected authors for review and comment (Documents 5, 6, 8, 10, and 17) served to discredit Solzhenitsyn among waverers and to strengthen the hostility of Party loyalists, while his own efforts to disown the play (Documents 10 and 16) were only partially successful. Finally, the inclusion of *The First Circle* into the list of seized manuscripts (although it had been accepted by Tvardovsky for publication and in principle was quite respectable) and the summary of its contents in the context of the earlier works also defined it as "clandestine," and almost certainly doomed its chances of publication before it had been properly considered.

From Solzhenitsyn's point of view, the confiscation was a tragic accident and abominably bad luck. The galling thing was that if he hadn't panicked and removed the typescript of *The First Circle* from *Novy Mir*, the KGB would never have found it at Teush's and would have had less chance to characterize it as politically unacceptable. He would also have had a much easier time getting his other big novel, *Cancer Ward* (Document 10), into print, for that work received its first reviews not from the KGB but from other authors and was much less controversial. But in the end it too was blackened by association with Solzhenitsyn's earlier works and was banned.

The other instance of bad luck, which Solzhenitsyn knew nothing about at the time, was the KGB's success in eavesdropping on, and recording, his unbuttoned conversation with Teush in the latter's apartment. But it is also clear from that conversation that "luck," bad or otherwise, operated only on a relatively superficial level, for the conflict between Solzhenitsyn and the Brezhnev regime was a fundamental one. Solzhenitsyn represented the best hopes and aspirations of the liberal intelligentsia, and of that progressive element in Soviet society that had backed Khrushchev's reforms. Had those reforms succeeded and been followed by others, it is possible that there would have been no "Solzhenitsyn case" at all. The problem was that, although Khrushchev did not know it, the reforms carried within them the seeds of a complete revolution in Soviet society. Solzhenitsyn, Sakharov, and the other dissidents accepted these reforms and very much wanted to see them pushed through, but Khrushchev's Party colleagues did not.

Indeed, when Brezhnev and his colleagues understood the revolutionary implications of Khrushchev's reforms, they applied all their strength to putting on the brakes and reversing them. While Brezhnev was at the helm they succeeded. In that sense, the persecution of Solzhenitsyn was but a by-product of a larger process. It was not until Gorbachev came to power and attempted to complete Khrushchev's work that the momentum of reform was resumed. By that time Solzhenitsyn was already in the West, Sakharov was near death, the dissidents were dispersed, and it was too late for reform. As de Tocqueville would have been able to predict, reform led to collapse; Gorbachev was swept from power and the revolution came after all.

Among the many revelations afforded by the documents is the news that Solzhenitsyn had gone much further in his critique of Soviet communism at an earlier stage in his career than was hitherto apparent. Already in Document 2 of this collection, for instance, we find Solzhenitsyn delivering himself of some astonishingly prophetic comments about the bankruptcy of the Soviet regime:

> This is a government without prospects. They have no conveyor belts connecting them to ideology, or the masses, or the econo-my, or foreign policy, or to the world communist movement—nothing. The levers to all the conveyor belts have broken down and don't function. They can decide all they want sitting at their desks. Yet it's clear at once that it's not working. . . .

Even more prophetic were his statements about the nationalities:

> I'm amazed that liberal Russian people don't understand that
> we have to separate from the republics. . . . I tell them it's all
> over for the Ukraine, it has to go. . . . And how could there be
> any question about the Caucasus, the Baltics! On the very first
> day if you want—whoever wants to leave, for God's sake, do so!

All this was in the spring of 1965, twenty-five years before the rest of the
world caught up with Solzhenitsyn's assessment, and well before even the other
liberals understood what was happening. No wonder the secret policemen's
hair stood on end, or that the KGB hastened to inform members of the
Central Committee about what they had found. Equally disquieting must have
been the news that all Solzhenitsyn's early works were already in the West and
would automatically be published in the event of his arrest or early death, and
that he was hard at work on a new book, tentatively entitled *Archipelago*, that
would make both *Ivan Denisovich* and *The First Circle* "look innocuous."

The fascinating thing about this document is not only its vivid
confirmation of Solzhenitsyn's political hostility to the regime and of his love
of conspiratorial methods, but also the revelation that the KGB knew all
these things far earlier than was ever suspected—least of all by Solzhenitsyn
himself. As it happens, we know a great deal about Solzhenitsyn's side of the
conflict from his vivid memoir *The Oak and the Calf*, published in 1975 after
his exile to the West (the full Russian title, by the way, was "The Calf Butted
the Oak," which gives a better sense of the adversarial nature of the
relationship than the English title does). If Solzhenitsyn's account represents
the view of the "calf," this collection presents a rather different version of the
same events as seen from the point of view of the "oak," ie, the government.

What *The Oak and the Calf* showed us, *inter alia*, was that "the calf" was by
no means as innocent and helpless as Solzhenitsyn's ironic title implied; one
of the most absorbing features of these documents is their demonstration that
the oak was not entirely immovable either. Indeed, the most surprising
revelation here is that of the government's endless dithering and indecision
about what steps, if any, to take to put a stop to Solzhenitsyn's insub-
ordination, and the repeated procrastination of the Politburo when faced
with the decision to take concrete action. After all, they had a convincing
corpus delicti (in the form of his early manuscripts and the self-incriminating
tapes) as early as the fall of 1965, and according to his account in *The Oak*,
Solzhenitsyn himself was convinced that after the raid on Teush the game
was up. He went into hiding immediately after the raid and writes that he
even contemplated suicide for a while, so sure was he of his impending arrest.

Yet nothing happened to him at the time. That this was no manifestation of softness or liberalism on the part of the authorities is demonstrated by the fact that just a few months afterward, in January 1966, the two other offending writers, Sinyavsky and Daniel, were made the objects of a big show trial and sentenced to seven and five years in the labor camps, respectively. Their sentences, and the protests they provoked, were a huge stimulus to the nascent dissident movement, whose protests led in turn to a whole series of arrests and trials of Soviet intellectuals, many of them members of the literary world. But Solzhenitsyn remained untouched.

What seems to have spared him initially was the circumstance that, since he had been raised to eminence by a former First Secretary of the Communist Party, he retained a vestigial respectability as a member of the "loyal opposition" long after he deserved the description, and hence was given the benefit of the doubt even in the face of overwhelming evidence of his political unreliability.

The documents show that even the then-head of the KGB, Vladimir Semichastny (he who had persecuted Pasternak and compared the poet to "a pig who has fouled the place where he eats") and the Public Prosecutor, Roman Rudenko, were unwilling to take concrete action after the raid, and referred the whole matter to the Writers' Union for confirmation of what they already knew (Documents 3–6). It took eighteen months for the Writers' Union to send out copies of *Feast of the Victors* and *The First Circle* to trusted readers and gather the requisite denunciations, and for the matter to be referred to the Secretariat of the Central Committee (Document 8). But by that time, heartened and emboldened by the government's immobility (and by the growing activity of other dissidents), Solzhenitsyn had completed and sent to the West both volumes of his new novel, *Cancer Ward*, and had almost completed work on the first draft of *The Gulag Archipelago*. He had started touring scientific institutes to give readings from his works that, from the official point of view, were still banned and therefore illegal.

In the face of this activity, all that Semichastny could find to propose was that Solzhenitsyn be expelled from the Writers' Union (Document 8), while the other members of the Politburo contented themselves with wringing their hands. The interesting exception was Yuri Andropov, the former ambassador to Hungary and the man in charge of bloodily suppressing the Hungarian Revolution of 1956. Andropov was for sterner measures:

> The question of Solzhenitsyn goes beyond working with writers. He has written certain things, like *Feast of the Victors* and *Cancer Ward* that are anti-Soviet in nature. We should take decisive measures to deal with Solzhenitsyn, for he is involved in anti-Soviet activities.

Andropov was helpless to move on his own, however, until in the summer of 1967 he succeeded Semichastny as head of the KGB, by which time Solzhenitsyn himself had gone over to the offensive. In May that year he had written and distributed a massive indictment of the Writers' Union and the Soviet censorship in the form of an "open letter" to the Fourth Congress of Soviet Writers (see Document 10). More significantly from the point of view of the KGB, Solzhenitsyn had for the first time publicly played the Western card by deliberately sending copies of his open letter abroad, whence it was broadcast back to the Soviet Union by Western radio stations.

For the next couple of years the matter was allowed to rest with the Writers' Union, while Solzhenitsyn brought out book after book in the West and forged an international reputation as Russia's greatest living writer. Documents 16–19 offer rich material on the pathetic writhings of that Byzantine institution in its attempt to come to terms with so determined an opponent, while Documents 22 and 23 reveal that a year elapsed from the time the Central Committee proposed Solzhenitsyn's expulsion from the Union until the deed was finally done in November 1969. Less than a year after that, Solzhenitsyn was awarded the Nobel Prize for Literature, and from then on it was virtually open warfare between the famous writer and the security organs of the world's second most powerful state.

■

A curious aspect of this struggle was the way it developed into a sort of duel between Solzhenitsyn and the new head of the KGB, Yuri Andropov. Andropov was widely credited by observers with being the most intelligent and capable head of the security services for many years. Immediately after his appointment in 1967, he set about expanding and professionalizing the KGB and increasing its powers of clandestine operation, for which he was rewarded, in 1973, with a place in the Politburo (the first time the security chief had sat there since Beria in Stalin's time). After his experiences with the Hungarian Revolution, which he blamed on "the intellectuals," Andropov was particularly hostile to the intelligentsia, and he was notorious for his zeal in clamping down on the writers, artists, teachers, and scientists who made up the bulk of the dissident movement.

It was no surprise, then, that he personally should lead the charge against the most dangerous writer of them all. What is newly revealed in these documents, however, is that as early as November 1970, only one month after the announcement of the Nobel Prize, Andropov was arguing to his colleagues that Solzhenitsyn was a "political enemy," and was drafting a decree for the Politburo to deprive Solzhenitsyn of his citizenship and expel him from the Soviet Union (Document 40). The initial impulse for this was the rumor that Solzhenitsyn would actually go to Stockholm to receive his prize, and so could be barred from returning by the passage of such a decree. It is true that, for a while, Solzhenitsyn considered the possibility of going to Stockholm. He was prevented by, among other things, his tangled domestic situation: although he was already living with the woman who was to become his second wife, Natalia Svetlova, his wife of long standing, Natalia Reshetovskaya, was still his legal spouse, and the KGB was already learning how to exploit that fact. Should Solzhenitsyn ask to be accompanied by "his family," there was little doubt that the KGB would make it as difficult as possible for him, or would try to insist on him taking the "wrong" wife.

In the end, Solzhenitsyn decided not to go and the Politburo balked at expulsion. Instead it formed a special commission, with Andropov as one of its members, to study the matter (Document 49). It turned out to be the first of several such commissions, and it would take Andropov three more years to persuade his colleagues of the correctness of his point of view. But from this time on Andropov appears to have taken an intensified interest in pursuing this affair. Thus we find his agents tapping the telephones of Solzhenitsyn's friends to find out who was reading his new novel, *August 1914*, and what they thought of it; lifting Solzhenitsyn's notes for the next volume in the series; and sending a team of agents to burgle Solzhenitsyn's summer cottage, where they were surprised by a luckless friend of Solzhenitsyn's (Alexander Gorlov), whom they half-killed before they realized their mistake (Documents 51, 52, and 55).

It was at this juncture that Solzhenitsyn seems to have realized the identity of his main antagonist. Having earlier written a more or less conciliatory letter to the Chairman of the Council of Ministers, Alexei Kosygin, concerning receipt of his prize money, he now turned with full fury on Andropov:

> For many years I have borne in silence the lawlessness of your employees: the inspection of all my correspondence, the confis-cation of half of it, the tracking down of my correspondents. . . the spying around my house, the shadowing of visitors, the tap-ping of telephone conversations, the drilling of holes in ceil-ings, the placing of recording equipment in my city apartment and my country cottage, and a persistent slander campaign against me from the platforms of lecture halls when they are put at the disposal of officials from your ministry. But after your raid yesterday I will no longer be silent (Document 52).

Solzhenitsyn concluded with a demand for punishment of the intruders.

He sent a copy of this letter to Kosygin, and in the covering note he wrote:

> I enclose a copy of my letter to the Minister of State Security. I
> consider him personally responsible for all the illegalities men-
> tioned. If the government of the USSR does not approve these
> actions of Minister Andropov, I shall expect an investigation
> into the matter (*Oak*, p. 498).

Andropov responded by himself forwarding a copy of the letter to the
Politburo and lying about the nature and the purpose of the raid on the
cottage, while making it quite clear that he would also lie to Solzhenitsyn and
his supporters (Document 52). The battle lines were now drawn and no
quarter would be given until the struggle was over.

Another revelation contained in this volume is that by this time (the
summer and fall of 1971), members of the Politburo were reading KGB
summaries of Solzhenitsyn's novels, while the Central Committee was
discussing such weighty matters as whether or not to allow Solzhenitsyn a
permit to live in the capital. But the most interesting tidbit of all is that
within the Politburo, the Minister of the Interior, Nikolai Shchelokov, was
taking a completely different line from Andropov and disputing the latter's
whole approach to Solzhenitsyn and other dissident writers.

In a special memo to the Politburo (Document 53) Shchelokov argued (in
opposition to the jeering tone that was already being adopted by the KGB)
that Solzhenitsyn was undoubtedly a major talent, and that in treating him so
cavalierly the government was "repeating the same glaring errors that we
committed with regard to Boris Pasternak." Shchelokov cited similar errors
in the harsh treatment of Daniel and Sinyavsky, pointing out that they had
been turned into martyrs, and adding that the problem in that instance "had
not been removed, but rather aggravated." The best course, he wrote, was
"not to execute our enemies publicly but to smother them with embraces."
Solzhenitsyn should be allowed to go abroad to receive the Nobel Prize, and
"under no circumstances should the issue of depriving him of his citizenship
be raised." Solzhenitsyn "should be given an apartment without delay. He
needs to receive a residence permit and have his needs catered to. . . . In a
word, we need to fight *for* Solzhenitsyn and not against Solzhenitsyn."

Interestingly, this memo was retained by Brezhnev for several days, and
returned with the passages about Pasternak, and Sinyavsky and Daniel,
underlined. However, there was no underlining of the places where
Shchelokov urged a softer treatment of Solzhenitsyn, and when the Central
Committee met to discuss the matter, they decided to postpone a decision on
the residence permit and refer it to the KGB (Document 54)—in other words
to remit the whole thing back to Andropov.

Had Shchelokov's proposals been adopted, the history of the Solzhenitsyn affair might have ended quite differently, but as it turned out, he had few allies in the Politburo and Andropov was able to make the running. He also gained a powerful supporter in the form of Foreign Minister Andrei Gromyko. The Nobel Prize and the international attention it attracted to Solzhenitsyn, together with Solzhenitsyn's increased use of Western publishers, Western reporters, and Western radio stations to propagate his views, had turned his writings from a more or less domestic matter into a foreign policy issue. Gromyko now entered the fray directly on the side of Andropov, and his ministry expended more and more time instructing ambassadors on what to say abroad, contacting friendly communist parties to enlist them in the Kremlin's propaganda campaign, browbeating the Swedes to stay out of the affair, and doing everything it could to ensure that the Nobel Prize was not handed over at any kind of official ceremony.

The extraordinary thing shown by these documents is that Andropov was still not able to get his way. In March 1972, he and Rudenko repeated the arguments he himself had made in 1970 about Solzhenitsyn being "a political enemy" and submitted a third draft of the decree to deport Solzhenitsyn and deprive him of his citizenship (Document 67). At a meeting of the Politburo to discuss the memo (Document 68), Brezhnev waffled at great length about dissidents and nationalism and the "healthy moral and political condition of our society," which was "dynamically moving forward toward the cherished goal of communism." But he was loath to recommend any concrete action. The meeting ended with Podgorny suggesting the formation of yet another commission to investigate the Yakir and Solzhenitsyn questions, consisting of himself, Andropov, and "comrades from the Public Prosecutor's Office, the Ministry of Internal Affairs, the Ministry of Justice, and other organizations."

And so it continued. Each time Andropov pressed the Politburo for Solzhenitsyn's deportation, he was fobbed off with excuses for doing nothing. He was obliged to collect yet more wiretapping evidence and provide yet more commentaries on Solzhenitsyn's open letters and statements. In mid-1973, Solzhenitsyn and Sakharov upped the ante by their public opposition to the burgeoning policy of détente between the Soviet Union and the West, and by their open calls to the US Senate to deny the Soviet Union most-favored nation status. This brought them into direct conflict with one of the government's most important foreign policy initiatives, and because of their growing celebrity in the West posed a real political threat to the Soviet leaders. Andropov's men tracked this process carefully, documenting the two dissidents' meetings with foreign correspondents and dutifully forwarding copies of their incendiary statements to the Politburo. Andropov even knew, through eavesdropping, that the two men did not agree on many matters and that their alliance was an uneasy one (Solzhenitsyn wrote his *Letter to the*

Soviet Leaders that summer partly as a response to Sakharov's ideas). And yet still no action was taken, until that same summer Andropov scored a coup by getting his hands on a copy of *The Gulag Archipelago*.

The documents provide valuable new information on this operation as well. It was known that KGB agents had worked on the case for many years and had achieved their breakthrough by brutally interrogating one of the book's typists, Elizaveta Voronyanskaya, until she divulged where a copy of the book was hidden. She committed suicide in despair over what she had done and was buried secretly and in great haste. Documents 77, 78, and 84, however, reveal that it was through the indiscretions of a friend of Voronyanskaya's that the KGB learned of her role as typist, and that through this friend they had reason to believe that Solzhenitsyn had already decided to publish his book, come what may. In fact this was not so, and things might still have turned out differently had the KGB known Solzhenitsyn's true position. But they didn't. Nor did they foresee that their scramble to obtain a copy of the book would accelerate, rather than delay, the book's publication.

After the capture of the Gulag, Andropov moved into top gear, bombarding the Politburo with memos throughout the fall and winter of 1973 and into the early months of 1974. Yet as the transcripts show, he still found it impossible to get his way. At a session of the Politburo in September 1973 (Document 90), Brezhnev at last agreed that "we have been tolerating their [Solzhenitsyn's and Sakharov's] anti-Soviet activities for far too long," and commented that he had received a copy of Solzhenitsyn's *Letter to the Soviet Leaders*, which exhibited a different tone from earlier writings but was still "nonsense." When it came to action, however, all he would agree to was the formation of yet another commission to "carefully study all these issues and make specific proposals."

Andropov was again a member, of course, and it was at this juncture that he developed a new thesis, namely, that Solzhenitsyn and Sakharov were either being manipulated by "foreign intelligence agencies," or were directly in collusion with them (Documents 92–94). He also introduced a cunning variation on his earlier idea of deporting Solzhenitsyn and stripping him of his citizenship. Why not, he argued, institute criminal proceedings against Solzhenitsyn, but at the same time secretly inform selected Western governments of this and ask if they'd be willing to grant asylum to Solzhenitsyn to avert his arrest and imprisonment? In that way Solzhenitsyn could be sent abroad, or perhaps even provoked into choosing to go himself, and the government saved from having to take difficult and unpopular measures. It was a type of moral blackmail in which the Soviet security services excelled, and it sounded as if it might work. In the meantime, Andropov revised the KGB's earlier bill of indictment against Solzhenitsyn, rehearsed all the wiretapped conversations and juicy quotations the KGB had amassed since 1965, and painted Solzhenitsyn as the active leader of a fully fledged "political opposition" (Document 95).

Meanwhile the KGB's capture of a copy of *The Gulag Archipelago* brought about what it had been intended to forestall, namely, the publication of the work in the West. There it created a furor surpassing all earlier scandals associated with Solzhenitsyn's name. At a session of the Politburo in January 1974, Andropov revealed that Solzhenitsyn had more support within the country than had been admitted before, and again demanded that he be deported:

> Comrades, since 1965 I have been raising the issue of Solzhenitsyn. Today he has gone to a new, higher stage in his hostile activities. He tries to create an organization within the Soviet Union made up of former convicts. He opposes Lenin, the October Revolution, and the Socialist system. His *Gulag Archipelago* is not a work of fiction; it is a political document. This is dangerous. There are tens of thousands of supporters of Vlasov, OUN [the Ukrainian Liberation Movement], and other hostile elements. In general there are hundreds and thousands of people among whom Solzhenitsyn will find support. . . .
>
> We should take all the measures I wrote about to the Central Committee, ie, deport him from the country. . . .
>
> I propose that we expel Solzhenitsyn from the country using administrative measures. We should instruct our ambassadors to make the appropriate inquiries in a number of countries, as I stated in my memo, with the goal of having them accept Solzhenitsyn. If we don't take these measures, then all our propaganda work will lead to nothing. If we publish articles in the press, speak about him on the radio, but don't take measures, it will be idle talk. It is necessary to clarify what we do about Solzhenitsyn (Document 99).

Andropov was strongly supported by Suslov, Gromyko, and Kosygin, and less enthusiastically by Podgorny, Shelepin, and some of the other speakers, but Brezhnev still wouldn't go along. The "issue of Solzhenitsyn" was difficult, he said, since it was being linked by Western governments with negotiations over European security and the peace process, and even if Solzhenitsyn were deported, "nobody would accept him." Then, surprisingly, Brezhnev seemed to opt for a criminal investigation and trial. "At one time we were not afraid to stand up against the counterrevolution in Czechoslovakia. We were not afraid to let Alliluyeva [Stalin's daughter] out of the country. We have endured everything. I think we will survive this case too."

A resolution was drafted instructing the KGB and the Public Prosecutor's Office to investigate the possibility of instituting legal proceedings against Solzhenitsyn, but it too was neutralized by another resolution "not to go beyond the exchange of views at the meeting of the Politburo on this issue" (Document 100). Andropov was again checked.

This Politburo discussion also confirms the enormous importance attached by Brezhnev and his colleagues to propaganda matters. In 1970 already, after the award of the Nobel Prize to Solzhenitsyn, the KGB, the Central Committee, and the Ministry of Foreign Affairs had devoted considerable resources to combatting Western views of the matter, and to ensuring that the official line on Solzhenitsyn was published and promoted both at home and abroad. Then, in 1973, when Solzhenitsyn and Sakharov started to give statements and press conferences to Western reporters, the propaganda war escalated; and, with the publication of *The Gulag Archipelago* at the end of that year, it reached a crescendo.

It is amazing to see how many of the documents in this book concern brainwashing of the public with the government's version of events and ascertaining whether the process is working. It is as if the leaders were completely in the dark as to what Soviet citizens (not to speak of foreign public opinion) were really thinking, and were terrified to take a single step without bolstering their action with a barrage of ideological explanations and interpretations. Every proposal was accompanied by a recommendation that it be explained and promoted by press and media commentaries, and these commentaries were followed by surveys of public opinion purporting to show that the overwhelming majority of the population supported the government's actions.

The process is revealed in a particularly naked form in the documents relating to January 1974, when *Pravda* responded to the appearance of *The Gulag Archipelago* abroad with a huge article called "The Path of Treason." The article was preceded and followed by a barrage of memos and reports from *Pravda* itself, from the Moscow Party Committee, from various departments of the Central Committee, the KGB, local Party committees, and so on (Documents 101, 102, 104, and 110–113), all designed to show that Soviet citizens "are unanimous in appraising Solzhenitsyn as a traitor to the motherland and betrayer of the Soviet people, as a slanderer of Soviet reality, and as a paid lackey of the enemies of Socialism and the Soviet Union" (Document 104). A similar process was put into operation on an international scale (Documents 103, 108, and 109) with the dispatch of communiqués and instructions to "fraternal" parties and organizations in other countries, all coordinated from Moscow. Meanwhile the KGB was also eavesdropping on diplomats and journalists in Moscow to ascertain if they too were being influenced by the official propaganda (Documents 105 and 106).

It was a means both of softening up public opinion to prepare it for stricter measures and of reassuring the leaders of the Politburo that they were moving in the right direction, and it is clear that both Brezhnev and his eventual successor, Konstantin Chernenko, to name but two, set great store by these letters (Document 107). Yet to the Western reader, the whole operation has a surreal quality to it, for the procedure emerges as completely circular. First the catchphrases ("traitor," "lackey," "writer of lampoons," "betrayer of the motherland," "we unanimously reject," etc) invented by the KGB, appear in virtually identical form from letter to letter. Then the exact same phrases and formulas show up in the article in *Pravda*. They appear for a third time in a batch of letters supposedly responding to the article in *Pravda*, and these are in turn relayed back to the Politburo by the same KGB that has manufactured them in the first place.

All this is supposed to represent a faithful picture of "public opinion," and it is difficult to know who was kidding whom. Did Andropov really believe in the sincerity of the letters that his organization was gathering and collating for the benefit of the Politburo? And did he think they represented the true state of public opinion in the country? If so, what does that say about his celebrated intelligence and ability to defeat the dissidents at their own game? On the other hand, if he did not believe in the genuineness of the letters, was he deliberately playing a cunning game to deceive his own colleagues about the true state of affairs in the country? Or simply manipulating the evidence to bring about his desired goal of expelling Solzhenitsyn from the country?

And what about Brezhnev and the rest of them? Were they also incapable of recognizing the emptiness and fraudulence of all those pat formulas, and the disinformation inherent in the KGB's (and Central Committee's) reports? Or were they too deluding themselves because the alternative explanation was too painful to bear? Either way, the portrait of the Soviet leadership that emerges is highly unflattering, and Solzhenitsyn is shown to be completely correct in his contempt for the government's abilities. In fact, some of the leaders' speeches about the loyalty of the people and their devotion to communism could themselves be taken for parodies written by Solzhenitsyn, if we did not know they were genuine. It is little wonder that the regime eventually collapsed under the weight of its own ignorance and inertia.

But that did not happen for another ten years. In the meantime, the government's grip was still sufficiently firm for the propaganda campaign to achieve its goal. On February 7, 1974, Andropov submitted his draft decree on deportation for the *fourth time* and followed it up with a personal letter to Brezhnev, hinting that influential members of the military and the Party were growing restive over the Solzhenitsyn issue and demanding action (Documents 119 and 120). He also pointed out that West German Chancellor Willy Brandt was agreeable to receiving Solzhenitsyn and that failure to act now might embarrass the Chancellor and create a serious international incident.

∎

At long last the Politburo was ready to act. On February 11 it met to "agree upon the proposals of Comrade Andropov," and to approve the decree stripping Solzhenitsyn of his citizenship and deporting him. An interesting addition to our existing knowledge of this decision is the text of the briefing sent to the Soviet ambassador in Bonn, and precise details of the deal that was to be struck with the West German government. The next day Solzhenitsyn was arrested and incarcerated in Lefortovo Prison in Moscow while the ambassador went to work. And the day after that, on January 13, 1974, Solzhenitsyn was forcibly placed on a commercial Soviet flight to Frankfurt and deported to West Germany.

The last part of this volume is devoted to the renewed propaganda blast that the Soviet authorities launched to cover and justify their action, and to the continuing attempt to discredit Solzhenitsyn as he pursued his writing in the West and kept up his public criticisms of the Soviet regime. Of particular note in these pages are the attempts to neutralize the impact of Solzhenitsyn's memoir, *The Oak and the Calf*, published in 1975, in which he gave his own account of the preceding twenty years' conflict with the Soviet government. Also noteworthy is the KGB effort to enlist the authority of Solzhenitsyn's first wife, Natalia Reshetovskaya, and of Tvardovsky's daughter, Valentina Tvardovskaya, to blacken the author in the eyes of the West. We also learn new details about the KGB's penetration of Czech emigré circles in Zurich and how they were able to continue their surveillance of Solzhenitsyn even when he was in the presumed safety of Switzerland.

Paradoxically, the efforts of the Soviet government to undermine Solzhenitsyn's influence bore more fruit once he was in the West than they ever had while he was under their noses. This was partly because, as both he and his opponents were aware, Solzhenitsyn derived an immense amount of his authority from his physical presence in the Soviet Union and his status as a witness. Once deported, he was transformed into an "emigré" (however unwilling), and lost the cachet of being a participant in the life of the country. Indeed, Andropov had predicted as much. However, the documents show that Andropov continued to delude himself (and his colleagues) as to how quickly this would come about. He was crowing about Solzhenitsyn's insignificance at the very moment when millions of copies of *The Gulag Archipelago* were pouring from the presses, and when presidents and prime ministers (with the notable exception of Gerald Ford) were lining up to be photographed in Solzhenitsyn's presence.

It was in fact the publication of *The Oak and the Calf*, with its boastful portrayal of his achievements and his denigration of former allies, that began the process of disenchantment among his Russian supporters, while the increasingly shrill tones of his denunciations of Western foreign policy brought about a similar decline in his influence on the West. Needless to say, the KGB continued to fish energetically in these troubled waters, and to do whatever it could to further this process. Witness the distribution of Tvardovskaya's riposte to the *Oak* (Document 142) and of critical statements by Solzhenitsyn's former friends such as Nikolai Vitkevich and Pyotr Yakubovich.

But these were sideshows compared with the drama of the events leading up to Solzhenitsyn's expulsion and the expulsion itself. This drama will continue to have an enduring fascination—not only for those who lived through that time and watched events unfold, but for all future generations who wish to understand the life and importance of one of the most outstanding writers of the second half of the twentieth century.

PREFACE TO THE RUSSIAN EDITION

Starting in 1965, when Alexander Solzhenitsyn's anti-Soviet literary works were confiscated by state security agencies, the writer became an object of intense scrutiny by the Central Committee. The Politburo, the highest body of the Communist Party and the superpower Soviet Union, not only actively collected information on Solzhenitsyn, it acted as the chief organizer and director of all propaganda measures and public political campaigns in the USSR and abroad against the undesirable writer. Not a single matter regarding Solzhenitsyn was decided without the proper instructions and recommendations of the Politburo. This was to be expected, since according to the precept of Lenin's famous article,[1] literary activity was like many other things in our recent lives, Party business, a constant "paternal concern" of the Central Committee. The documents published in this collection once again make this point self-evident.

Intended only for an elite group of persons within the highest Party leadership, the documents provide a fairly full and detailed account of the events described by Solzhenitsyn in his book *The Oak and the Calf*. In fact, these materials could quite appropriately be seen as an appendix of documents to *The Oak and the Calf*, a series of sketches of Soviet literary life in the 1960s and 1970s, with the only difference being that these events of "literary life" are seen through the eyes of the powerful "oak," which has a view of things and events completely different from that of Solzhenitsyn, the "calf".

Almost all the documents discovered in the former Politburo archives have been included here. Most of them were unknown to researchers and are being published here for the first time. The documents have been organized in chronological order, which enables the reader to follow the course of events and see the immediate perceptions and evaluations of them by Party and state bodies, the reactions of the public, and their influence on subsequent actions and events. As a result of this strict chronological order, the internal logical connection between documents is sometimes broken. This connection has been restored with appropriate notes and cross-references.

The documents are published in full, without editorial summaries or deletions, except for the minutes of the Politburo session of March 30, 1972, where speeches not related to Solzhenitsyn have been cut.[2]

The minutes of the Politburo and Central Committee Secretariat meetings should not be viewed as complete transcripts of the matters discussed. A memo from Konstantin Chernenko, who was head of the Central Committee's General Department at the time (responsible, among other things, for organizing Party meetings), notes that "brief minutes of the sessions were made by me personally, chiefly in order to preserve the sequence of each speech on individual issues, and also some of the thoughts characterizing the content of the speeches of Politburo members."

The documents are reproduced as they appeared in the original, with all the particularities of their drafting. Only obvious spelling mistakes and misprints in the Russian have been corrected. Mistakes of a substantive nature, for example, incorrect spelling or distortion of last names and first initials, the names of works of literature, inaccurate dates, etc, have been left without change, with explanations in the footnotes. Resolutions, notes, and marks on the documents that relate to the content as a whole are also included in the notes. Notations of an administrative nature such as "to file" or "file in the Politburo archive" and so on were removed by the editors on publication. Our own editorial headings of documents are placed in quotation marks. The filing number and date of the document are noted immediately after our heading. At the end of each document, the call numbers are shown in the Russian abbreviations (*fond* [fund] (*f.*), *opis* [register] (*op.*), *delo* [file] (*d.*), *listy* [pages] *l.*) as well as information about the documents' authenticity.

We felt it was possible to limit ourselves to brief annotations of the documents containing the minimum of information for an accurate understanding of the text, the particularities of their preparation, and their logical connection with other documents. All notes (textual and on substance) are indicated with arabic numerals and grouped after each document.[3]

All documents were declassified on the basis of Russian Presidential Decree No. 658 of June 23, 1992, "On the Removal of Restrictive Classifications on Legislative and Other Acts that Served as the Basis for Mass Persecutions and Violations of Human Rights."

The discovery and preparation of the documents for publication, the commentary, and the compilation of the list of documents were done by a literary collective made up of A. Korotkov, S. Melchin, and A. Stepanov.

Notes

1. In his article "Party Organization and Party Literature" (1905), Lenin coined the concept of *partiinost* ("partymindedness"), indicating the obligation of all party members to write their political commentaries from a Party (ie, Bolshevik) point of view. This concept later became a cornerstone of the theory of Socialist Realism and a pretext for the subordination of all forms of literature to ideological control.

2. Additional cuts have been made in the English-language edition of some summaries of Solzhenitsyn's best-known works, and of some letters from "indignant workers" repeating points made in earlier letters. All cuts are indicated in the text.

3. The Russian editors' notes have been merged with the American editor's notes, but are printed in italics for ease of identification.

PART I
1963–1969
EARLY STRUGGLE

1963

1 Report from V. Lebedev[1]

22 March 1963

To Comrade N. S. Khrushchev:
After the meeting in the Kremlin of Party and government leaders with the creative intelligentsia and after your speech,[2] Nikita Sergeyevich, I was telephoned by the writer Alexander Solzhenitsyn, who said the following:

> I am deeply touched by the speech of Nikita Sergeyevich Khrushchev and would like to convey to him my profound gratitude for his exceptionally kind attitude toward us writers and to me personally, and for the high value accorded my humble work. My call to you is explained by the following: Nikita Sergeyevich has said that if our writers and other artistic figures get carried away by the theme of the labor camps, it will provide ammunition for our enemies, and huge, fat flies will fall on such materials like dung.
>
> Having made your acquaintance and recalling our conversation in the Vorobyov Hills during the first meeting of our leaders with the creative intelligentsia, I would like to ask your kind advice. But I ask you to view this not as a request for an official ruling, but for the comradely advice of a Communist whom I trust. Nine years ago I wrote a play on labor-camp life entitled *The Tenderfoot and the Tramp*.[3] It does not duplicate *A Day in the Life of Ivan Denisovich*; it has a different grouping of images: the prisoners in it do not oppose the labor-camp administration, but unscrupulous elements from among their own ranks. My 'literary father,' Alexander Trifonovich Tvardovsky,[4] after reading this play, recommended that I not give it to the theater. However he and I somewhat differed in our opinions, and I gave it to O. N. Yefremov, the Chief Director of the Sovremenik Studio Theater, to read.

"Now I am tormented by doubts," Solzhenitsyn went on to say, taking into account the particular attention and warning that was expressed by Nikita Sergeyevich Khrushchev in his speech at the meeting regarding the use of labor-camp materials in art. Conscious of my responsibility, I would like to ask your advice as to whether I and the theater should work further on this play.

Solzhenitsyn also urged me to read his play.

I would like to check my opinion again: was I right or was Alexander Trifonovich Tvardovsky right when he advised me not to present this play. If you say the same thing as Tvardovsky, I will immediately withdraw this play from the Sovremenik and will work on it some more. I would be very pained if I were not to act as required of us writers by the Party and by Nikita Sergeyevich Khrushchev, who is very dear to me.

When I received the play, I asked Oleg Nikolayevich Yefremov, chief director of the Sovremenik, with whom I am acquainted, whether it was true that he was intending to stage this play. Yefremov informed me that they were not planning to stage this play yet, although in his opinion the play was suitable for their theater. Only a small group of theater workers were familiar with the play, and only he had a copy of the text, as chief director.

It appears that the Agence France Press correspondent Mazankin learned from one of the Sovremenik staff that the theater was supposed to put on a play by Solzhenitsyn called "The Criminals." However, in his dispatch of 21 March, not only did he distort the name of the play, he made up all the rest, since there were no rehearsals of the play at the theater, and no set designs being prepared. Yefremov said there had only been an author's reading of the play, when Solzhenitsyn read his play *The Tenderfoot and the Tramp* to a group of theater actors. Moreover, as Comrade Yefremov assured me, all the actors who were present at the reading were warned not to speak of this play, since the question of its staging had not been decided either by the author or the theater directors.

After reading *The Tenderfoot and the Tramp*, I informed Comrade Solzhenitsyn that it was my profound conviction that this play in its current form was not suitable for staging in the theater. It would bring critical acclaim neither to the author nor the theater. In my view, the play was precisely the kind of material to which, as Nikita Sergeyevich Khrushchev said in his recent speech to the creative intelligentsia, clouds of "huge, fat flies" would fly at the theater. These "flies" would be correspondents from foreign newspapers and wire services and all sorts of common people.

I expressed the same thought in a conversation with Yefremov.

Both Solzhenitsyn and Yefremov agreed with these conclusions and said that they would not prepare the play for staging.

The writer Solzhenitsyn asked me, if the opportunity presents itself, to send his heartfelt greetings and best wishes to you, Nikita Sergeyevich. Once again he would like to assure you that he very well understood your paternal concern for the development of our Soviet literature and art and would try to be worthy of the high calling of a Soviet writer.

V. Lebedev

F. 3, *op.* 80, *d.* 194, *l.* 104–107. Original.

Notes

1. *On page one a note reads: "Comrade Khrushchev has reviewed. To the archive. 23–Sh–63 (signature illegible)." Vladimir Lebedev was Khrushchev's personal secretary and was instrumental in persuading Khrushchev to approve the publication of* One Day in the Life of Ivan Denisovich.

2. The meeting between Khrushchev and selected writers and artists was the second of such gatherings and took place on 7–8 March 1963 in the Kremlin's Sverdlovsk Hall. Khrushchev gave a long speech entitled "High Ideals and Artistic Mastery—the Great Strength of Soviet Literature and Art," in which he excoriated writers and artists who had gone "too far" in exploiting his de-Stalinization campaign and invoked "partymindedness" to justify reversing this policy. He also referred specifically to *One Day in the Life of Ivan Denisovich:* "Take my word for it, this is a very dangerous theme. It's the kind of 'stew' that will attract flies like a carcass, enormous fat flies; all sorts of bourgeois scum from abroad will come crawling all over it."

3. This is an idiomatic rendering of Solzhenitsyn's original title, *Olen' i shulashovka,* which is expressed in labor-camp slang. The published version of the play translated into English is called *The Love-girl and the Innocent* (Farrar Straus, 1969).

4. A reference to the fact that it was Tvardovsky, as editor of the liberal literary journal *Novy Mir* ("New World"), who had succeeded in getting *One Day in the Life of Ivan Denisovich* published (it was also Tvardovsky who had enlisted the help of Lebedev).

2 Report of the Committee for State Security of the USSR Council of Ministers[1]

No. 2275–S
5 October 1965
Top Secret

To the Central Committee:
The KGB is presenting a memorandum on surveillance materials[2] concerning the attitudes of the writer Solzhenitsyn, and also a commentary on the manuscript of his book *The First Circle* and other unpublished works seized during a search 11 September 1965 at the home of his close acquaintance V.L. Teush.

KGB Chairman
V. Semichastny

Enclosure 1
2 October 1965
Top Secret

Memorandum on Surveillance Materials Concerning the Attitudes of the Writer Alexander Solzhenitsyn

The KGB has tracked down V.L. Teush[3] as the author of an anonymous manuscript of anti-Soviet content.

In the course of seeking him out, it emerged that the writer Solzhenitsyn maintains regular contact with Teush. As can be seen from the surveillance materials, Solzhenitsyn indulges in politically damaging statements and disseminates slanderous fabrications.

Some of Solzhenitsyn's statements are cited below:

Did I tell you about Fischer's book? . . . I was brought a book by the American journalist called *The Life of Lenin*.[4]. . . Despite the fact that I had long had no great opinion of Lenin during the period of the revolution . . . It took me two months to read, every day for five hours. On the whole, I think it saved me several years, because I had been intending to juxtapose Lenin's quotations with one another and study his books. Now I don't have to do that, it's all been done. On any question, he'll tell you: Lenin said this, Lenin said that. Lenin was nothing but a serpent, a man totally without principles. He would literally tell you he was on your side, but when you went to the door, he would shoot you in the back. Totally unprincipled.

. . . Listen, your hair stands on end when you read it. . . . Really, from the moment of the revolution, Lenin was simply reborn, he became another person. . . . He was an opportunist. We don't properly understand this word. It's somebody who seizes his opportunities. He was like an eagle who sees a mouse in a field. He was a genius. He would at once see all the opportunities. He saw the opportunity for victory or defeat of the enemy and that was it, he didn't care whether it corresponded to the theory or not; or whether it had any moral worth. Maybe he would take it. He would grab whatever he could, and nothing more. Therefore, when he constructed one theory and then later discovered it was pointless, that things shouldn't be done that way, he would do it a completely different way, but like a genius. He recognized that he was a genius. He [Fischer] acknowledges that he was a genius.

. . . There are some stunning things [in the book]. He knows how to highlight such simple things. The fact that rule by the soviets ceased to exist on 6 July 1918. . . . That's completely understandable, my friends. . . . The rule of the soviets ended. . . . The dictatorship of the Party [began]. . . . How was it all done? First, our people systematically falsified the results of the elections. . . . Then in 1918 . . . in a totally brazen fashion, all the elections to the Third, Fourth, and Fifth Congresses of the soviets were falsified. Everything was falsified, and more and more Bolsheviks got elected. For example, starting in January 1918, the Bolsheviks along with the "left" socialist revolutionaries forced the "right-wing" socialist revolutionaries out of the soviets. And immediately began to put them in jail.

In early 1918. You see? They immediately suppressed both them and the anarchists. But the "left" socialist revolutionaries remained. Then the elections at the Fifth Congress were fabricated. The peasantry was for the "left" socialist revolutionaries. The peasantry was seething with discontent. . . .

I once knew a Latvian woman. . . . She told me herself. . . . She was one of Lenin's security guards. The men weren't working [when they were supposed to] on voluntary work days. Lenin came, they surrounded him so that nobody knew he had come, they called in a secret policeman disguised as a worker and photographed him with Lenin, and then Lenin left. And where six of them are shown—that's a drawing. But there was one snapshot. Lenin is prominently shown with the policeman, and he is standing with the pistol. Lenin then left and that was that. . . . Fischer doesn't know this. I'm telling you this. . . .

. . . You know, some day we'll take this up more thoroughly. I have lots of people who are simply yearning to type things up for me. I'll take these notes of mine and have them retyped. Just in order to keep them. Then you can read them. . . .

In response to the idea advanced in the conversation that "at one time there was the truth, but evil people concealed it and then it became a lie," Solzhenitsyn said: "Such a conception is possible, but not with the Bolsheviks. . . . The people possessed the truth, not the Bolsheviks." Speaking about the Soviet government, Solzhenitsyn said:

This is a government without prospects. They have no conveyor belts connecting them to ideology, or the masses, or the economy, or foreign policy, or to the world communist movement—nothing. The levers to all the conveyor belts have broken down and don't function. They can decide all they want sitting at their desks. Yet it's clear at once that it's not working. You see? Honestly, I have that impression. They're paralyzed.

Sharing his impressions about a recent trip to Obninsk in the Kaluga Region and meetings with scientists there, Solzhenitsyn said:

. . . There's a fashion there now—not to join the Party. Timofeyev-Ressovsky (department head at the Institute of Medical Radiology of the Academy of Medicine, Solzhenitsyn's former "cell-mate," in his words) said: 'We don't have a single Party member among 725 junior researchers. Then two joined. The moment they joined, they were somehow hopelessly cut off from the collective—everyone scorned and ridiculed them. "One on probation and one member. Everyone cut them off, and moved away from them!' "

Expressing his opinion on the nationalities question, Solzhenitsyn said:

I'm amazed that liberal Russian people don't understand that we have to separate from the republics; they don't understand that we have to face this. . . . Liberal people. I tell them it's all over for the Ukraine, it has to go. 'No, no,' [they say]. Well, the Ukraine is a controversial issue. But about the western territories of the Ukraine, of course, there's no question, we must let them go. As for the eastern part, a plebiscite should be held in each region and it should be divided up according to the numbers of the population. But how could there be any question about the Caucasus, the Baltics! On the very first day, if you want—whoever wants to leave, for God's sake, do so! Just resolve the question of financial settlements. What's in store for us? It will be terrible if things start to collapse in the West and infect the central territories. I really don't know what's going to happen. It will be a complete collapse. It's interesting that the Armenians and Georgians, too. . . . This republic [Armenia] is under the same harsh control as many others. For instance, the Baltics or the Ukraine. Nevertheless, it's fairly autonomous and could choose a semi-Romanian route. The Armenians have a tendency, a wish to emancipate themselves like the Romanians. . . .

On the publication of his works abroad, and possible complications and troubles in this regard, Solzhenitsyn said:

. . . So, *Encounter*, the British journal,[5] published my 'Essays' in a place of honor. . . . Do you know how I made the decision of what to do with the 'Essays?' I sometimes happen to be in public places, where in some undesirable group where I am asked if those are my 'Essays.' I reply with an inconsequential remark: 'I usually give my works to *Novy Mir* to publish.' I evade a direct answer. For example, I'm summoned to some Party

office. I could just as well not go there. Do I work for them or
something? Why should I go just because they summon me? I
could just as well not go. But let's say that one way or another,
I'm told to. I've decided not to acknowledge fully my authorship of the 'Essays.'. . . I'll say: 'I really did write some poems
in prose. I submitted them to *Novy Mir*, true, with some delay,
but that's not important. You can find them there. What about
the others? Well, all sorts of things are going around.' As for
the works that I deny are mine—the Ryazan pieces, which
show a great familiarity with Ryazan and the surrounding district: 'A clever forgery; maybe a provocation; maybe a sincere
imitation. I don't know.' And that's it. And if they still pressure
me and somehow prove it to me then I'll say: 'Why do I have
to begin by telling you? Am I a high school student? Why
should I answer you? Maybe I have three times as many
more? . . .'

. . . Now I will have indirect information about what plans
have been made, where it will be kept, who will be in charge of
this, and under what circumstances it will be released. I gave
them a detailed testament. I intend to deal all of them the first
blow, so that *Sharashka*[6] will be published in the form in which
it is presently. But not right away. . . .

To the question: "Perhaps it should be sooner?" Solzhenitsyn gave the
following reply:

Perhaps. But it will happen automatically, that is, if I lose communication with them, they'll publish it anyway. . . . Then the
entire long poem, all the poetry and plays. . . . In the event of
my death, publish it all together at once. From the time I'm
arrested, start releasing my works at the rate of one every three
months. All automatically. If they unleash a heavy, all-out campaign against me in the newspapers, release them less often,
with six months or a year in between.

Solzhenitsyn claimed that he was ready for the following ultimatum as well:

If they seriously come after me or summon me for a serious
explanation and say: 'We'll do such-and-such to you,' I'll say:
'Gentlemen! That's going to cost you more than it will me. I
warn you that for the time being, as you see, I have not pub-

lished abroad. But the moment you arrest me, things will come out that will make *Ivan Denisovich* look pale in comparison.'

But for now I have to gain time in order to write *Archi-pelago*. . . . I'm writing frantically now, on a binge, I've decided to sacrifice everything else. . . . I'll unleash an entire avalanche. . . . I've set the time for its appearance, you know, somewhere between 1972 to 1975. When the time comes, I'll fire a simultaneous and crushing salvo.

To the question: "And if events happen much faster than that?" Solzhenitsyn replied:

Then thank God, if it's earlier it's earlier. But for myself I have scheduled this deadline in the sense that even if nothing happens, if events are unfavorable, than no later than 1975 I will fire this terrible salvo. . . .

. . . I'll hand everything around and will publish over there (laughs). I don't know what will happen. Myself, I'll probably go to the Bastille, but I'm not despondent.

Of his new work, Solzhenitsyn said:

I look a little desperate now. I submitted something now that makes *Sharashka* look innocuous. . . . You see, I feel that soon the time will come when people will want to hear about the October Revolution, when it will have to be explained. And I feel that I will be able to provide this explanation in a literary form. And I must provide it. That is now my main task. . . . *Archipelago* will murder them. It will be devastating!

To the question: "Is it an artistic work?" Solzhenitsyn replied:

I define it this way: an experiment in literary investigation. That means that where scholarly research can't be carried out, owing to the absence of all the necessary documents, I'll apply the methods of literary investigation, ie, there's a great deal of logic in it, a very clear outline and a clear construction, but many of the missing links will have to be filled in through the use of intuition and linguistic imagery.

. . . I have been restricting myself. I start with 1921. I haven't covered the Civil War at all. . . . Of course, you can't fit in everything. . . . The material is such that people will not take a liberal attitude to it. I don't know how it will turn out.

. . . The first part is called 'The Prison Industry.' I've finished, fifteen signatures.[7] The second part is called 'Perpetual Motion.' That's the prison convoys and transit prisons. . . . I finished that, too. Besides that, I've also written the fifth part, 'Penal Servitude'—twelve chapters. Everything's written. . . . Now I have to go back to the third part. . . . I don't have enough cases on the liquidation of the kulaks.[8]. . . I went to Tambov,[9] that was great! The things I saw there! Participants in all those events! . . . After all, Tambov was behind the October Revolution by four and a half months. The October Revolution was over, and Tambov had no Whites and no Reds. It was the most ordinary democratic local government, mostly Mensheviks and social revolutionaries. An ordinary, elected democratic government that didn't know of any revolution, and didn't need one. And there month after month they reported on everything that was happening in the country, as seen through their own eyes. It's absolutely incredible. I've never seen anything like it. We've gotten used to the idea of either Red or White. But in Tambov they still had a city council and a district authority. They had almost no power, true, but Tambov lasted four and a half months. The Bolsheviks were shouting 'Hurrah,' whistling, trying to jump on the tables in order to disrupt meetings. Things like that. . . . I was there and found such material in the archives! . . .

. . . I use myself at only the most climactic moments in vivid little episodes that I witnessed myself. I did that well. . . . The historical, and the ideological, the economic, and the psychological setting. A complete picture of the archipelago. . . . It's like lava flowing when I'm writing the *Archipelago*, it's impossible to stop. I think I'll finish the *Archipelago* by next summer.

To the idea expressed in the conversation about the possibility of sending his manuscripts abroad, Solzhenitsyn replied:

That's how it is over there. But you see the problem. For some reason they say over there that they don't accept galleys, as if there isn't such a form of safekeeping. But I can't go over there and go around and push things. . . .

. . . We have to see to a number of things, who will send it to the Russian publisher, when, who will give the order, and how the translation will be managed. The Russian publisher can't cover his own costs. It's a very small press run, and it is not profitable for them to reprint. I accepted the terms that 10 percent be paid for each translation, that each foreign publisher pay the Russian publisher 10 percent. Then it will be very profitable for the Russian publishing house and it will do all the work. It's such a simple thing, but it has to be seen to. In what order, which publishing houses in other countries have the right to get it. It turns out that there's a lot of questions like that starting to come up, which we had no idea of here. I don't have all the information yet, I'm still waiting for it.

In the part about receiving royalties for works published abroad, Solzhenitsyn replied: "Not a damn thing is coming through yet, but I've taken measures through several channels. They were told in Italy and France not to hold it up and to send the money. . . ."

Claiming that he was being "boycotted" in the Soviet Union, Solzhenitsyn expressed his readiness to make a public statement:

It has to be made where it will strike an echo in the West. . . . I have several moves ready. First, I have to make sure that my play *Candle in the Wind* is delayed. That'll be a good sign as well. . . . It's not important what they say, the main thing is that they don't release it. Then I'd have more excuses. First one play was suppressed then another. . . . And then I need to talk about it in the right place, like dropping a bomb, so that they immediately know about it in the West, I will answer questions. There'll be an interview. . . . When some foreigner will be present. We don't need a Soviet! And when they ask the question I can answer: 'It's like this. They're shutting me up every which way! They don't let me publish. My novel's being held up there, and other things too.'

Deputy Head of Second Chief Directorate of the Committee for State Security of the USSR Council of Ministers
Shcherbak[10]

Enclosure 2
30 September 1965

Commentary on A.I. Solzhenitsyn's Novel *The First Circle*

The author sets the actions and events described in the novel in December 1949.

In the village of Mavrino outside Moscow, a scientific research center has been established within the Ministry of State Security's system to develop a "secret telephone" for Stalin's use. In addition, an assignment has been given to develop within a certain time period an apparatus that would enable the state security agencies to identify voices covertly in telephone conversations in order to expose new innocent victims.

The staff of the institute is made up of prisoners serving sentences under "Article 58."[11] Although they are entirely without rights, as in other numerous penal institutions here, the food is somewhat better and some trivial items for everyday use are allowed, thus creating the illusion of a privileged position. Using Dante's well-known classifications, the author compares these prisoners with the sinners in the highest circle of hell, where suffering is not as severe as it is for the other "denizens." Hence the title of the novel, *The First Circle*. In the language of the novel's prisoner characters, the institute is called a *sharashka*, whereas in the terminology of the workers of the penal institution, it is a "special prison."

The novel opens with an episode in which Innokenty Volodin, an official of the Ministry of Foreign Affairs, learns of a provocation being prepared by the Ministry of State Security against Professor Dobroumov at a time when he will attempt to transmit a non-classified patent to foreigners. Although terribly frightened, Volodin musters the courage to warn Dobroumov of this over the telephone.

The *sharashka* in fact operates in order to catch such "criminals;" the story of its founding is outlined in the subsequent chapters. The laboratories and their purposes are described; the author acquaints the readers with the basic characters of the novel among the prisoners (Nerzhin, Rubin, Sologdin, Pryanchikov, Doronin, and others) and describes how they ended up in the *sharashka*. Meanwhile attention is not so much devoted to the development of the plot lines as to the content of the prisoners' conversations and their assessments of various aspects of Soviet society.

The director of the *sharashka*, State Security Col. Yakonov, suffers an oppressive fear of punishment for not fulfilling the assignment by the deadline. Along with other officials from the Ministry, he reports on the progress of the work to Abakumov. In expectation of the inevitable reprisal for failing to perform the assignment, Yakonov usually dodges the truth, just as Abakumov himself lies when he reports on the same matter to Stalin.

The author devotes several of the novel's chapters to Stalin as an individual: "The Birthday Hero," "Language is a Tool of Production," "Give Us Back the Death Penalty!" and "Emperor of the Earth." In exaggerated, grotesque fashion, numerous details are cited here characterizing Stalin's manner and work style, the atmosphere at his country dacha, his reception of Abakumov, and the personality of [his secretary] Poskrebyshev.

Parallel to the description of the prisoners' life in the *sharashka* and their relations with the administration and the nonimprisoned staff, the author establishes a category of characters who have a kind of indirect relationship to the *sharashka*. These include Public Prosecutor Makarygin; his daughters Dinera (named for the Russian phrase *Ditya novoy ery*, [Child of the New Era]), Dotnara (*Doch trudovogo naroda* [Daughter of the Working People]); and Clara; their husbands, Volodin and the writer Galakhov; the Public Prosecutor Slovuta; and others. All the characters among the "free" people are in two categories: the morally depraved "brazenly fattening wealthy" and the rest of the Soviet people, disenfranchised and barely making ends meet.

This contrast is particularly vivid in the chapters on the family of Prosecutor Makarygin and in the scenes of visits with the prisoners' relatives. These meetings bring no relief to the prisoners since they learn that on the outside, their relatives are being subjected to various types of persecution due to their arrest.

Finally, the Ministry of State Security agents track down the person who has called Dobroumov. The voices of suspects are "researched" in the *sharashka*. In order to accelerate the process of "identifying the criminal," a decision is made to arrest all those whose voices are on tape.

Volodin gets a telephone call from his director, who invites him to the Ministry of Foreign Affairs in order to coordinate some details before Volodin's trip abroad. On the way there Volodin is arrested. . . . Then the author describes in great detail the process of throwing the arrested man "into the Lubyanka."[12]

The novel ends with scenes of some of the prisoners being sent from the *sharashka* to labor camps, "where once again the pickaxe and the wheelbarrow were awaiting them, the starvation rations of uncooked bread, the hospital, and death." Prison vans travel the streets of the city disguised as meat or bread vans, and a foreign correspondent notes in his dispatches: "Trucks with produce, quite neat and impeccably clean, are often encountered on the streets of Moscow. It must be admitted that the capital is excellently provided for."

As can be seen from a note in the text, the novel was written between 1955 and 1963. It consists of eighty-six chapters and the length of the manuscript is 839 typescript pages.

The absence of a coherent plot does not mean the author does not have aims to which the entire narrative and contents of the novel are essentially subordinated. In trying to explicate them, we can come to the following conclusions, which evidently reflect those that Solzhenitsyn himself came to.

1. He attempts to demonstrate the existence of "slave labor" in the Soviet Union, and perhaps prove that the building of socialism is above all a ruthless exploitation of people, a system of labor camps, the forced labor of prisoners. Moreover, this is not an abuse, but a deliberate and organized system of exploitation of a work force by the government.

On page 91, in explaining the nature of the scientific research institute called a *sharashka*, the author writes:

> All these *sharashkas* were started in 1930 when they sentenced the Promparty engineers on a charge of conspiring with the British,[13] and then decided to see how much work they would produce in prison. The leading engineer of the first *sharashka* was Leonid Konstantinovich Ramzin. The experiment was successful. Outside prison it was impossible to have two big engineers or two major scientists in one design group. They would fight over who would get the name, the fame, the Stalin Prize, and one would invariably force out the other. That's why outside prison all design offices consist of a colorless group around one brilliant head. But in the *sharashka*? Neither money nor fame threatens anyone. Nikolai Nikolaich gets half a glass of sour cream and Pyotr Petrovich gets the same ration. A dozen academic lions live together peacefully in one den because they've nowhere else to go. It's a bore to play chess or smoke. What about inventing something? Let's. A lot has been created that way. That's the basic idea of the *sharashka*.

The *sharashka* is a privileged camp. It's been created according to the principle: ". . . high yields of wool from sheep depend on how well they are watered and fed." There are many kinds of *sharashkas*: this one, run by the Security Service, is also an artillery camp, where German prisoners of war also work, but everyone in it is required to provide intellectual goods in return for half a glass of sour cream. Apart from these places, there are many unprivileged places of detention, where harsh physical labor is required (construction sites, canals, logging camps, etc). It is the labor of these prisoners that has created the wealth of the country, conquered the heights of science, erected dams, built new cities, dug canals. The fact that people have been arrested because of the necessity to satisfy the demands for a larger work force can be seen in the efforts of the camp administrations to keep hold of their "useful" prisoners, extend their sentences, and augment the numbers of prisoners every now and then by arresting innocent people still at large, such as Volodin and his colleagues.

2. The labor camp system is a state within a state ("the country of the Gulag"), but if we read the novel carefully, we can easily determine that labor camps are already an organized state, or an ideal state, so to speak. The "outside," or the state itself, is a kind of appendage to the Gulag system, since there are no freedoms on the outside. The only advantage a person who is not imprisoned in a labor camp has is access to women (p. 100)—everything else is the same. A prisoner is even less afraid for his future.

The oppression is irrespective of whether you are an official in the labor camp or a hired hand from the outside, a diplomat or a prosecutor, an old communist or a Party worker—everyone lives in fear. And even Stalin, who is in the innermost sanctum, does not trust anyone. The only person whom he once trusted was Hitler. In fact, the comparison with fascism does not stop there. Bits and pieces of comparisons are scattered throughout the novel, which are supposed to provoke associations in the reader between our state and a fascist regime.

3. On the nation's victims:

Throughout the entire book, the author attempts to maintain a thread that the whole history of the Soviet state, beginning with October, has produced unjustified and unnecessary victims (the Civil War, collectivization, the first five-year plans, World War II). And here it is 1949, and there are victims once again. It turns out the victims are of the cultural revolution, and one of the characters in the novel, Prosecutor Makarygin (p. 531) says: "When Vladimir Ilyich [Lenin] told us that the *cultural* revolution will be much harder than the October Revolution, we could not imagine it! And now we understand how farsighted he was."

The author's conclusion that these victims are sacrificed in the name of world domination is interesting. Each time the context dictates the mention of the victory of communism throughout the world, Solzhenitsyn uses the expression "world dominion." Furthermore, this is not the yearning of the masses. One man goes his way, subordinating everyone to his will, "traversing a path known only to him, capable of bringing mankind to happiness."

This system does not bring anything new to the people and state, but on the contrary, revives all the old ways, which Stalin found very much to his liking. For example:

> . . . there should be not 'school managers' but directors; not 'command staff' but the officer corps; not the All-Union Central Executive Committee but the 'Supreme Soviet' (supreme was an excellent word); the officers would have to have orderlies; high school girls should study separately from the boys, wear pinafores and pay tuition; and like all Christians, the Soviet people should rest on Sundays and not on impersonal numbered days; and only legal marriages should be recognized as in the tsar's time (even though he himself had had a hard time because of it in his day), no matter what Engels thought about it while out to sea.

For what reason was the revolution made? Apparently, according to the author's conclusion, because the existence of an "Emperor of the World" does not contradict world communism in the slightest.

4. The idea that the October Revolution has not justified itself is expounded by the author from other positions as well: from the position of the rebirth of the Party of Communists, and the people who took part in the October Revolution.

> What was the Revolution against?" argues the prisoner Doronin. . . . It was against *privileges* (the author's italics)! What were the Russian people sick of? Privileges: some being dressed in overalls and others in furs, some trailing on foot and others riding in carriages, some listening for the factory whistle while others filled their faces in restaurants. . . . Then why is it that people don't shun privileges now but run after them? . . . I saw enough of them. I live in a small town in Kazakhstan and what do I see? Were the wives of the local bosses ever seen in the shops? Never! They sent me personally to deliver a case of macaroni to the First Secretary of the District Committee. A whole case. Unopened. It was easy to figure out that this wasn't the only case and not the only delivery. . . . And this is what we see from childhood on: they spout lots of pretty words in school, but once you get out you can't move an inch without greasing palms, and wherever you go there's another one. . . . (pp. 330–331)

Or:

> The prosecutor's first wife, now dead, who had gone through
> the Civil War with her husband, was an excellent shot with a
> machine gun, had always worn a leather coat and had lived by
> every last decree of the Party cell, not only would have been
> incapable of bringing Makarygin's home up to its present stan-
> dard of luxury, but if she had not died in 1925 while giving
> birth to Clara, it is hard to imagine how she would have adapt-
> ed to the new era. (p. 505)

The leaders of the state, who virtually turn the state into a farce,
demonstrating its successes with "Potemkin villages," understand this as well.
No wonder the rumor spreads through the camp that Stalin and Beria have
fled to China, and Molotov and Kaganovich have converted to Catholicism.
As a result, a provisional democratic government has taken power and
everyone is awaiting elections to the Constituent Assembly.

5. What, then, is the author calling for? Most likely for the restoration of
private property and the unleashing of petty bourgeois elements. That is
what the simple Russian peasant wants.

The author depicts such peasantry in the person of the prisoner Spiridon,
who works honestly as a janitor at the *sharashka*. Spiridon has had peace and
quiet twice in his life: during the time of the "glorious seven-year period of
Russia, during NEP[14] and before the collective farms," and under the
Germans, when they gave him back a piece of his own land.

6. The reader is struck by the author's obsessive desire to slander literally
everything having to do with Soviet reality. Morning in Moscow is the time
"when there is nobody in the streets who takes your coat and nobody to take
the coat from." People will not be able to imagine how their ancestors got
around the country during the years of the first five-year plans and the war.
There is the people's lack of culture, not to mention the ugly depiction of
state and Party workers and secret police officials.

It was good in the old Russia, in the quiet world of the churches, in
religion, in that popular truth that has been destroyed, among the honest and
decent old intelligentsia, the world into which a man armed with a hand
grenade once ventured.

7. Finally, are there any signs of light in this state, can we hope for
anything better?

The last chapters of the novel provide an answer to this question. The
labor camps are filling up with new, innocent victims, whom the symbol "to
be preserved forever" [stamped on their files] hounds everywhere and
reconciles them to the reality of prison. Only now, instead of "black marias"

[black police vans], buses now travel through the streets of Moscow painted a different color, with signs saying "Meat," "Bread," and so on.

Seeing this scene on the street, a correspondent from the newspaper *Libération* makes a note: "Trucks with produce, quite neat and impeccably clean, are often encountered on the streets of Moscow. It must be admitted that the capital is excellently provided for." The farce goes on.

Besides the novel *The First Circle*, a number of other unpublished works by Solzhenitsyn have been discovered:

1. The plays *Feast of the Victors* and *The Republic of Labor* (the author wrote these under the pseudonym Stepan Khlynov).[15] These plays essentially reflect the same views that the author cites in the novel reviewed above, therefore there is no need to make a detailed commentary on them.

The play *The Republic of Labor* is from the life of the tribe of convicts. As the author writes, the scene takes place in the country "Gulag" in the fall of 1945. Here are two excerpts from the stage directions:

> The audience will walk from a brightly lit foyer into the darkened auditorium. In here the only light comes from a number of tinplate hooded lanterns which are placed, almost like crowns, on a semicircle of posts right along the edge of the orchestra pit. The posts are quite low, so as not to interfere with the audience's view of the stage. They are wrapped with barbed wire which vanishes down into the orchestra pit. The center post carries an indicator to mark the dividing point in the field of observation from the two nearest watchtowers.
>
> There are two camp watchtowers standing to the right and left of the proscenium arch. Throughout the play the towers are manned by sentries.
>
> The curtain parts. It is an ordinary theater curtain, but is not used again until the end of the play. Behind it there is a second curtain—a length of fabric crudely painted with a poster-like industrial landscape, depicting cheerful, apple-cheeked, muscular men and women working away quite effortlessly. In one corner of the curtain a joyful procession is in progress complete with flowers, children, and a portrait of Stalin.[16]
>
> High up and out of sight, a loudspeaker relays a powerful choir of young voices lustily singing:

We shall raise the banner,
Comrades! Over here!
Come join us in constructing
A republic of labor!

When this curtain also parts, the audience sees a labor camp in which the whole of the succeeding action unfolds, interrupted from time to time (at the end of each scene) by the closing of the abovementioned jolly curtain.[17]

Scene II ('The Bonus Awards'). (A small conference hall. Sitting on benches with their backs to the audience are about fifty foundry workers. At the far end of the hall is a raised stage, decorated with standard slogans, a small bust of Lenin and a large portrait of Stalin. There are five men seated at the table on the stage, all of them typical "leading comrades," including Chief Engineer Kaplyuzhnikov and Lieutenant Ovchukhov. To the left of the stage a lecturer is painfully reading his report from notes that he is keeping out of sight. The hall is filled with the hum of indifferent listeners.)

The lecturer: . . . still more mechanization, still more ore, we've *exceeded* our pre-war levels. The fuel industry is the linchpin. Of our industry, if we didn't have our own coal and lumber, our factories would grind to a halt, along with our mills, steamers, and locomotives, transpiring . . . transporting the guns, tanks, and armaments of our gore-covered army. If it weren't for the world-shattering, historic victory of the Soviet Union under the direction of our inspired (at this moment four of the leaders on the stage, excluding the chairman, who have been completely immobile up until now, half rise from their chairs in unison and draw their hands back an identical distance in readiness to clap, thus demonstrating that they are puppets) leader, teacher, and best friend of fuel industry workers, Comrade Stalin.

(The puppets stand up to their full height, the chairman and the audience rise. Loud applause. The puppets clap in unison and then cease clapping in unison before sitting down) . . . in the West and the East, otherwise the whole world would have been plunged into the pitched darkness of enslavement and production. Or take the defeat of the brazen quantitative army of Japanese metallarism. What the Americans couldn't accomplish with their much-vaunted but completely undangerous atom bombs, our highly motivated Soviet infantry accomplished in less than a dozen days. Let the social regenerates and their suppositors not forget on our twenty-eighth anniversary that we stand ready to defend our grape victories! (Applause.) Fraternal greetings to the *Eastern Democracies*, which are joining us in cerebrating the glorious anniversary of the October Revolution. Long live our dear Communist Party and its perspiring, deeply beloved. . . !!! (The puppets stand, followed by the entire audience. The speaker's slogans are drowned with applause. He also applauds and leaves the lectern. The puppets all sit in unison, while the chairman remains standing.)[18]

The play *Feast of the Victors* is taken from the life of soldiers fighting at the front. Only one excerpt needs to be cited from it:

The USSR! Its impenetrable forest! A forest. It has no laws. All it has is power—power to arrest and torture, with or without laws. Denunciations, spies, filling in of forms, banquets and prizewinners, Magnitogorsk and birchbark shoes. A land of miracles! A land of worn-out, frightened, bedraggled people, while all those leaders on their rostrums—each one's a hog. The foreign tourists who see nothing but well-organized collective farms, Potemkin style. The schoolchildren who denounce their parents, like that boy Morozov. Behind black leather doors there are traps rather than rooms. Along the rivers Vychegda and Kama there are camps five times the size of France. Wherever you look you see epaulettes with that poisonous blue stripe; you see widows whose husbands are still alive, who surreptitiously wipe away their tears; and you see all those invented *Matrosovs* and silly *Zoyas* who fulfill their plans one hundred percent. Applause! For a land of miracles, where hymns and odes are sung to hunger and misfortune. For the miracles of Communism when whole peoples are transported into the depths of Siberia overnight. And Rokossovsky. Wasn't it only yesterday that he was in a labor camp, a slave, not a man at all, felling trees in Siberia, loading them onto barges, but who today is summoned, he is needed, he's made a marshal. But tomorrow perhaps he'll be back in Siberia.[19]

2. Sketches and short stories.

These are individual sketches from the life of our society.

The most interesting thing about them is that all of them, except one, have already been published in the NTS journal *Grani*, no. 56, 1964.

3. There is also a story in verse, "A Sad Tale," which reflects the same sentiments and views on the part of the author as in the previous works.[20]

In this poem, as in his other works, Solzhenitsyn once again tries to prove the pointlessness of collectivization and the contrived nature of the thesis of the class war against the kulak. The author claims that the kulak was actually the hardest-working person in the village, who had responded to the state's call to develop agriculture intensively. It was this "intensive worker" who was "dekulakized."

> Are you from the moon? Nineteen thirty? Don't you know what happened? They called me a kulak. Okay . . . liquidate them. As a class. Was it because I built myself a stone house? Because I didn't kowtow to them? Was it because I produced too much? Anyway, I had too many sins to count. . . .
>
> Yet from the time, brother, when they read us the decree on the land, we had kicked out the Czechs and beaten back Kolchak for the sake of that land, and so as to have our freedom and our own people in power![21] They gave us the land and we toiled day and night to earn our callouses. But the bastards called me a kulak! But who can fail to get rich from tilling the soil if he works hard enough? It's the state you see, though why does it get up its nose when the peasant has a couple of horse teams?

The poem contains another interesting idea: only the young believe in Marx; ordinary people are interested only in vodka.

And again there is "slave labor" under the conditions of socialism, the charms of the "much-abused NEP" and the kingdom of Stalin.

F. Bobkov
V. Strunin

F. 3, *op.* 80, *d.* 643, *l.* 1–22. Original.

Notes

1. *The document has been initialled by N. Podgorny, D. Polyansky, A. Mikoyan, G. Voronov, M. Suslov, P. Demichev, B. Ponomarev, I. Kapitonov, F. Kulakov, A. Shelepin, D. Ustinov, Y. Andropov, A. Kosygin, and K. Mazurov.*

2. "Surveillance materials"—a euphemism for the transcripts of wiretaps, intercepted letters, confiscated documents, and other materials obtained by the KGB through its clandestine operations.

3. Veniamin L. Teush was a retired high school teacher whom Solzhenitsyn had gotten to know when both taught at the same high school in Ryazan. He was Solzhenitsyn's only confidant in the city, and one of the very few people who had been allowed to read all the writer's early works.

4. *The Life of Lenin* by Louis Fischer (Harper & Row, 1964).

5. The reference is to Solzhenitsyn's "Miniature Stories." See *Encounter* (London), March 1965, pp. 3–9.

6. Solzhenitsyn's shorthand term for his novel *The First Circle*, set in a special prison institute that was colloquially called a *sharashka*, a term of unknown origin and etymology.

7. A common unit of measure in Russian publishing equal to 16 printed pages.

8. "Kulak" was the traditional Russian term for a successful peasant or small farmer. In order to promote collectivization in the early thirties, the Soviet government decided to destroy the kulaks as a class by a mixture of judicial execution, imprisonment in labor camps, or exile to remote regions of Siberia.

9. Chief city of the province of the same name in south central Russia. It was a center of White resistance during the Civil War.

10. By an interesting coincidence, Shcherbak was also the name of Solzhenitsyn's maternal grandfather.

11. Article 58 of the Soviet Penal Code was a catch-all article directed against "anti-Soviet propaganda." It was applied particularly widely in the years after World War II.

12. The Lubyanka, on Petrovsky Street in Moscow, was the largest and most notorious of the KGB's investigation prisons. Solzhenitsyn was held there himself for a while after his arrest in February 1945.

13. The Promparty or "Industrial Party" Trial in 1930 was one of the first big show trials of the early Soviet period. A group of "bourgeois" engineers, of whom the most prominent was Leonid Ramzin, was falsely accused of sabotaging industrial progress. Ramzin's death sentence was later commuted to ten years, which he served in labor camps. Solzhenitsyn later devoted considerable space to this trial in *The Gulag Archipelago*.

14. The NEP (New Economic Policy), introduced by Lenin in 1921, allowed for a controlled admission of market forces into the Soviet economy after the rigors of War Communism had led to a drastic fall in the popularity of the Bolsheviks. It led to a real increase in prosperity, but was abolished by Stalin in 1925.

15. Both plays were started when Solzhenitsyn was a labor-camp prisoner in Ekibastuz, Northern Kazakhstan, from 1950–1953, and completed when he was in administrative exile in Southern Kazakhstan from 1953–1956. *Feast of the Victors* is the name by which the first play was known in English for many years, but when finally published in translation it was called *Victory Celebrations* (Farrar Straus, 1983). *The Republic of Labor* was an early draft of *The Tenderfoot and the Tramp* (see Document 1, Note 2). Stepan Khlynov was one of several pseudonyms used by Solzhenitsyn as a prisoner and in exile.

16. These are the opening stage directions for the play (see *The Love-girl and the Innocent*, p. ix).

17. This part of the stage directions does not appear in the text of *The Tenderfoot and the Tramp*.

18. This scene does not appear in *The Tenderfoot and the Tramp*.

19. See *Victory Celebrations*, pp. 28–29.

20. This long narrative poem, composed by Solzhenitsyn in the labor camps and written in exile, has never been published in its entirety, although a few excerpts have appeared in journals. Other titles used by Solzhenitsyn for the poem are *The Road* and *Volunteers' Highway*.

21. The reference is to the decree of 1917 granting land to the peasants immediately after the establishment of the Soviet regime. The Czech Legion and Admiral Kolchak fought for the Whites, with the restoration of land to the landowners as one of their goals.

3 Report of the Committee for State Security of the USSR Council of Ministers

No. 2285–S
5 October 1965
Secret

To the Central Committee (for the Cultural Department):
The KGB is sending you one copy of the manuscript of Solzhenitsyn's novel *The First Circle*, the plays *The Republic of Labor* (written under the pseudonym Stepan Khlynov) and *Feast of the Victors*, the long poem *A Sorrowful Tale*, and also sketches and miniature stories: "Breathing," "Lake Segden," "The Duckling," "A Poet's Ashes," "The Elm Log," "A Reflection in the Water,"

"The City on the Neva," "Sharik," "Mode of Transport," "The Old Bucket," "In Yesenin's Homeland," "The Collective Farm Rucksack," "The Campfire and the Ants," "*We* Shall Never Die," "Starting the Day," "Travelling Along the Oka," and "Prayer."

All these materials were confiscated on 11 September 1965 from Solzhenitsyn's close acquaintance V.L. Teush.

KGB Chairman
V. Semichastny

F. 3, *op.* 80, *d.* 651, *l.* 1. Original.

4 Memorandum of the Committee for State Security of the USSR Council of Ministers and the USSR Public Prosecutor's Office[1]

No. 6–S
4 January 1966
Classified

To the Central Committee:
The Committee for State Security and the USSR Public Prosecutor's Office are reporting on the results of an investigation of a criminal case concerning the dissemination of an anonymous document entitled "On the Artistic Mission of A.I. Solzhenitsyn" and "Some Features of the Rhythm System and Composition of the Poem on Ivan Denisovich."[2]

Praising the mastery of the writer Solzhenitsyn and the artistic qualities of the short novel *One Day in the Life of Ivan Denisovich*, the author of these documents concludes that in this work, small in size, Solzhenitsyn managed to depict the fundamental features of the Soviet state, which in the recent past, because of a crisis in the spiritual life of society, was like a concentration camp with all its attributes, and calls on representatives of the arts to lead a campaign for the renewal of human dignity and freedom.

It has been established that the author and distributor of these documents is Veniamin Lvovich Teush, born 1898, a Jew, non-Party member, candidate of technical sciences, holder of a state prize, now retired and living in Moscow.

Teush testified at the investigation that he wrote these works between 1963 and 1964, apparently under the influence of profound disenchantment and an enormous spiritual upheaval caused by the violations of socialist legality and other distortions exposed at the Twentieth and Twenty-Second Party Congresses and described subsequently in the Soviet periodical press and in literature.

Teush denies any anti-Soviet orientation in his works or any intent to undermine and weaken the Soviet government and explains that in his work "On the Artistic Mission of A.I. Solzhenitsyn," he allowed himself to express to people close to him his negative attitude toward the consequences of the personality cult and to redeem his guilt, as it seemed to him, for his justification of Stalin's policies in the past. That is why he showed this work to several of his acquaintances and friends in 1964–1965.

As for the work "Some Features of the Rhythm System and Composition of the Poem on Ivan Denisovich," Teush stated that he wrote it as literary criticism of Solzhenitsyn's short novel and intended to publish it in the Soviet press. For that purpose he showed the work to certain persons well-versed in literature.

It was established that Teush typed five copies of his work, of which three copies were confiscated during searches, and the rest destroyed by the persons who had been keeping them.

A number of witnesses have confirmed that Teush is the author and distributor of these documents, and this has been corroborated by forensic tests, material evidence, and other case materials.

Taking into account Teush's advanced age and poor state of health, his admission of guilt, and the limited publicity received by these works, the decision was made not to bring criminal charges against Teush, but to limit ourselves to having officers of the Committee for State Security, with the participation of the Public Prosecutor's Office, conduct a comprehensive prophylactic discussion with him based on the investigation materials.

We surmise that the very opening of a criminal case over the dissemination of slanderous documents, and the interrogations of Teush and his friends have already exercised a certain influence on them and will facilitate the termination of their ideologically flawed activity. Moreover, the investigation's materials may be used in the press if necessary.

As has already been reported, in the course of investigating this case we confiscated certain manuscripts of unpublished works by A.I. Solzhenitsyn— the novel *The First Circle*, the plays *The Republic of Labor*, and *Feast of the Victors*, and other works.

Taking into account the fact that Solzhenitsyn's works, by virtue of their hostile content, cannot be published in the USSR and are banned from distribution, and also bearing in mind the possibility that these works might be sent for publication abroad, which could damage the Soviet Union's international prestige, we have made a decision to confiscate them and place them for safekeeping in the KGB's archive. At the present time, several writers (see list), with the consent of the Central Committee's Secretariat, are reviewing these works.

We consider that it would be advisable:

—to assign the USSR Writers' Union to review these works and organize a discussion of them with the participation of Solzhenitsyn, after which, together with the Central Committee's Culture Department, the Union could determine the expediency of publishing the results of this discussion in the press;

—to conduct a conversation with Solzhenitsyn in the USSR Public Prosecutor's Office with the participation of an officer of the Committee for State Security on the reasons for the confiscation of his manuscripts.

Please review.

Chairman
Committee for State Security
V. Semichastny

USSR Public Prosecutor
R. Rudenko

F. 3, *op.* 80, *d.* 643, *l.* 23–25. Original.

Notes

1. *Page one of the document bears the resolution [sic]: "Comrade Shauro. M. Suslov," and the last a notation: "Note: A number of prominent writers have been acquainted with the manuscripts of Solzhenitsyn. The matter of the discussion with him at the USSR Writers' Union will be decided later. Comrades Semichastny and Rudenko have been briefed and have approved. Deputy Director, Culture Department, Y. Melentiev," and the stamp of V. Shauro.*

2. A shortened version of the article was published in Russian in the Frankfurt-based emigré journal *Grani* ("Facets") Nos. 64 and 65, 1967. The author's name was given as D. Blagov, and the title as "A. Solzhenitsyn and the Writer's Spiritual Mission."

5 Report of the Committee for State Security of the USSR Council of Ministers[1]

No. 81–S
14 January 1966
Classified

To the Central Committee:
I enclose photocopies of Solzhenitsyn's play entitled *Feast of the Victors*, confiscated during the search of the apartment of Teush. As has already been reported in memorandum No. 6–S of 4 January 1966, the investigation of his case has been completed and prophylactic measures are being taken.

A group of prominent Soviet writers is being acquainted with this and other works of Solzhenitsyn confiscated during the course of the investigation, with the consent of the Central Committee Secretariat, in order to discuss them at the USSR Writers' Union with Solzhenitsyn's participation.

Enclosure: Twenty-Four copies of the text.[2]

Chairman
Committee for State Security
V. Semichastny

F. 3, *op.* 80, *d.* 643, *l.* 27. Original.

Notes

1. *Sent to Central Committee Presidium members and candidate members, and Central Committee Secretaries, 21 January 1966 under No. P118.*
2. *The photocopies are missing from the file.*

6 Report of the Central Committee Culture Department[1]

29 January 1966

To the Central Committee:
In accordance with instructions, the Central Committee Culture Department is acquainting a number of prominent writers with the manuscripts of the writer Solzhenitsyn confiscated from a certain Teush.

The following have already reviewed the manuscripts: Secretaries of the USSR Writers' Union Board, Comrades Brovka, Surkov, Gribachev, Kozhevnikov, Chakovsky, Voronkov; RSFSR Writers' Union Board Secretary, Comrade Alexeyev; and Editor-in-Chief of the journal *Inostrannaya Literatura* ("Foreign Literature"), Comrade Ryurikov. The following are studying the manuscripts: USSR Writers' Union Board Secretaries, Comrades Fedin, Tikhonov, Markov, and director of the Gorky Institute of World Literature, Comrade Anisimov. Comrades Leonov and Tvardovsky *did not take* the manuscripts; the latter made reference to the fact that he had read almost all these works except the play *Feast of the Victors*, which, however, he also *refused to read*. Comrade Simonov read only the novel *The First Circle*, and *categorically refused* to read the remaining works.

For information purposes, we are enclosing Comrade Surkov's review of Solzhenitsyn's works.[2]

Deputy Director
Central Committee Culture Department
Y. Melentiev

Department Section Head
Y. Barabash

Enclosure

I managed to read only the plays, poems, and short stories by Solzhenitsyn. I only read parts of the novel—there was not enough time, and it was typed in such a way that my eyes refused to read it.[3]

What is my impression of what I have read? It is very sad. I am not an apologist for *One Day in the Life of Ivan Denisovich*, but it contained much of life's bitter truth, although overlaid with the philosophy of "existentialism" which I find unacceptable. Moreover, I could not help taking into account that for a person who innocently suffered from our very specific "justice system" of that time, it seemed natural to me that he would have feelings of personal bitterness and trampled human dignity, which comes through the lines of this short novel. I was in the position in which Solzhenitsyn found himself in 1919, when I was in a White Estonian prisoner-of-war camp, and I know from my own experience that what happens to people in such conditions remains with them for their entire lives. Moreover, Solzhenitsyn was still a non-Party member of the intelligentsia, and what is more, as it seems to me, had stayed out of the Party "on principle."

Nevertheless, reading these works by Solzhenitsyn upset me, because everything I have read tells me that this unquestionably talented person is, not only by virtue of his rightful feeling of bitterness, but, as it seems to me, *organically* opposed to our entire way of life. The Promparty Trial (see the sections of the poem on Ramzin), a vivid example of class warfare during NEP, seems to him to be our crime.[4] In this same poem he speaks of Bukharin as a person who wanted the people to live well, that NEP should not have been exchanged for industrialization and collectivization, which he hates. According to everything I read, all the years of the existence of our system are years when Russia was turned into some kind of universal labor camp, and the people into "convicts." The fact that for Solzhenitsyn there is not a single bright spot in our history since the October Revolution is as vividly demonstrated by the play *Feast of the Victors*. In it, our army is portrayed as a bunch of looting officers and time servers, a bunch of robbers and rapists, which the author's favored "heroine," Galina, calls "your" army. Paradoxically, the only "attractive" officer in this army, Nerzhin, undertakes to lead this bitch and traitor across the front lines to her fiancé, an officer in Vlasov's army.[5]

On the whole, everything I read was dictated by some kind of visceral hatred and scorn of everything to which I have dedicated three-fourths of my life, and I do not want to understand this, and I cannot accept this either as literature in general, or more particularly, as Soviet literature. No matter how great Solzhenitsyn's talent, his malice and scorn blind his eyes, and what I have read is not serious literature, no matter who tries to prove the opposite to me. Error cannot prevent a genius from being a genius (Tolstoy, Dostoevsky) but malice always, even in the greats, produces weak or not very strong works (Dostoevsky's *The Possessed*), and the antinihilistic works of the talented Pisemsky and Leskov. The same thing happens with Solzhenitsyn, although I did not note signs of genius even in his previous works.

The image of Lenin in the writings I read I regard as blasphemy. The entire perception of life expressed in these writings is opposed to Lenin, just as the Socialist revolutionaries were opposed to Bolshevism.

Reading Solzhenitsyn and recalling Tarsis,[6] Sinyavsky,[7] Daniel,[7] Remezov [sic],[8] and their ilk, I have concluded with sorrow that in the era of open class warfare phenomena (in the 1920s) such as Zamyatin's *We* or Pilnyak's *Mahogany*[9] were fairly liberal in comparison with these "opuses." Even *Doctor Zhivago*, again against the background of these "opuses," seems loyal to some aspects of our life.

How can this all be reconciled with the fact that we no longer have class warfare now in the "common national" state of the workers? And where in our literature interpreting literary processes can the explanation for this "phenomenon" be found?

F. 3, *op.* 80, *d.* 643, *l.* 29–30 ob. Original.

Notes

1. *A separate sheet bears the instruction: "Brief Central Committee Secretaries," and the signatures of M. Suslov, Y. Andropov, I. Kapitonov, B. Ponomarev, F. Kulakov, D. Ustinov, P. Demichev, A. Shelepin, and A. Rudakov.*

2. Alexei Surkov, a minor poet, was a Party loyalist of long standing, who had risen to become a member of the Supreme Soviet and had been a Candidate of the Central Committee for a while. From 1953 to 1959 he was also General Secretary of the Writers' Union, in which capacity he had played a leading role in the persecution of Boris Pasternak for publishing *Doctor Zhivago* in the West.

3. In order to conserve paper and make his manuscripts easier to conceal, Solzhenitsyn had typed his early works with virtually no spaces between the lines and with no margins. It was these manuscripts (or copies of them) that Surkov had been given to read.

4. The Promparty or "Industrial Party" Trial in 1930 was one of the first big show trials of the early Soviet period. A group of "bourgeois" engineers, of whom the most prominent was Leonid Ramzin, was falsely accused of sabotaging industrial progress. Ramzin's death sentence was later commuted to ten years, which he served in labor camps. Solzhenitsyn later devoted considerable space to this trial in *The Gulag Archipelago*.

5. General Andrei Vlasov was captured by the Germans in 1942 and persuaded to organize and lead a division of ex-Soviet prisoners who fought on the German side. Soviet propaganda elevated him into a monster of depravity in order to counter the popularity of his forces when they first appeared on Soviet territory. Solzhenitsyn's attitude to Vlasov was ambivalent, but he was fascinated by the psychological

dilemma faced by Soviet prisoners of war caught between their patriotic opposition to the Germans and their bitter loathing of Stalinism.

6. Valery Tarsis was arrested in 1962 after publishing two of his stories abroad. Interned in a psychiatric hospital, he wrote a highly successful novella, *Ward No. 7*, about his experiences, which was also published abroad. Shortly after Surkov's report was written, Tarsis became the first dissident to be "encouraged" to emigrate.

7. Andrei Sinyavsky, a literary scholar, and Yuli Daniel, a translator, were arrested the same weekend that Solzhenitsyn's archive was confiscated, and accused of publishing stories and articles abroad under the pseudonyms of Abram Tertz and Nikolai Arzhak, respectively. Their case was still under investigation when Surkov's report was written. The following month (February) the two writers were publicly tried and sentenced to seven and five years' imprisonment in hard labor camps on charges of conducting anti-Soviet propaganda.

8. This appears to be a misprint for (Alexei) Remizov, a novelist and poet of the pre-revolutionary period, who emigrated in 1921.

9. Yevgeny Zamyatin's celebrated dystopian novel *We* (one of the inspirations for Orwell's *1984*) was published in the West in 1927, leading to a campaign of vilification against him and his virtual expulsion from the Soviet Union in 1931. Pilnyak's novel *Mahogany*, published in Berlin in 1929, led to a similar hate campaign against the writer, but he recanted and survived for a while. He was eventually arrested and shot during the purges of 1937.

7 Letter from Konstantin Simonov[1] "On Solzhenitsyn's Novel *The First Circle*"[2]

1 February 1966

To the Central Committee:

I spent three days at the Central Committee reading this novel with a deep sense of pain, trying to carry out a task I was charged with as a Party member.

At one time, after reading Solzhenitsyn's short novel *One Day in the Life of Ivan Denisovich* in *Novy Mir*, I thought it was good it had appeared in our journal. I stated my opinion in *Izvestia*[3] regarding both the story and what in my view was the author's extraordinary talent. Even today, I would subscribe to everything I said in my review. I continue to believe that the dark and tragic aspects of our society must be truthfully covered in our literature, so that nothing like this could ever happen again.[4]

I have always believed that our society in all its many-faceted truth could be best described by a writer who would address all aspects of its life and all their inner connections and conflicts, and who at the same time would avoid dwelling on just one aspect of this life, and avoid dealing exclusively with the description of life in prisons and camps, although it was an integral part of our society during those years.

However, I continue to believe that a writer who spent a number of years in prisons and camps himself has the moral authority to focus on this essential and tragic aspect of our life at that time. I think that he described this essential and tragic aspect truthfully and with a lot of talent. At the same time, he described it in such a way that the reader in general, and I in particular, did not feel only indignation over such a thing happening in a socialist society, but was left with confidence that nothing like this could ever happen again.

In this I have continued to see a great objective usefulness in Solzhenitsyn's story, although I did not think at the time, nor do I now, that all the opinions expressed by the author are the ultimate truth.

Why, then, was I reading *The First Circle* with a deep sense of pain?

Was it because it was written with less talent than the author's first work?

No. In fact, its most powerful chapters are written with even greater talent.

The reason I read it with a deep sense of pain is that in this new novel, Solzhenitsyn tries to cover more or less fully the life of our society during the first five years after World War II, and in so doing draws a biased and unfair picture.

As a reader, I happen to believe that the novel provides a truthful description of the *sharashka*, the secret research institute within the NKVD system headed by Beria and Abakumov,[5] where the main characters of the novel conduct their work while imprisoned.

The very system that entrusts imprisoned persons who are pronounced spies and enemies of the people with carrying out important and sensitive tasks for the state seems obnoxious to me and fills me with feelings of disgust. At the same time, I feel proud of our society which, after Stalin's death, found enough internal resolve to do away with this disgraceful system.

The focus of the narrative does not strike me as forbidden material, because, unfortunately, this was indeed part of our history during Stalin's day. If we are to tell the whole truth about our history, we must also be truthful about this—whether we like it or not.

But Solzhenitsyn passes from a description of this aspect of society to other aspects and other people. Here we discover that, with a few extremely rare exceptions, he seems unable to see in the society of that time anything other than two categories of people. He writes on the one hand about characters who are related to the prisoners and to people in camps who are therefore victims to some extent, while his other category contains the people who find the *status quo* convenient and profitable, and who in the final analysis lend either actual or moral assistance to the oppressors, or at the very least provide a moral basis for the stable existence of all the terrible injustice described in the novel.

If we believe that this is an accurate portrayal of our society in those days, it will be totally incomprehensible why, after Stalin's death, this society did not follow in his footsteps, or continue with Stalin's punitive policies. Instead, it went on to dismantle the camps, free their inmates, and restore the good names of many hundreds of thousands of people, living or dead.

While reading Solzhenitsyn's novel, it is impossible to understand who could have done all that after Stalin's death. The society he portrays in his novel takes no interest in restoring justice. The people he describes outside the prison walls are incapable of fighting for justice. At the same time, his novel offers almost no other characters outside the prison walls, except those who cannot even wish for justice, let alone restore it.

This is an inaccurate portrayal of the people living at the time described in the novel, and it is certainly an untrue historical depiction of our society.

If we assume that this novel was written back in 1950, in the days when the events described took place, and that it was written by a prisoner, a person who was slandered, deeply humiliated and who had lost faith in justice, who was in despair and who, by force of circumstances, perceived the whole of society through the distorting keyhole of a prison cell, then I would at least be able to understand the mentality behind such a view of society. However, objectively the book would not gain in fairness because of that.

But today, after the Twentieth and the Twenty-First Party Congresses,[6] after all that our society has done to rectify Stalin's mistakes and crimes, after it has displayed its great moral strength in this enormous work, conducted under psychological adversity, I cannot accept the view of our society of the late forties expressed in Solzhenitsyn's novel.

Thus, I do not accept the very premise of this novel, which consists of a lack of faith in the sane inner core of our society that it has always possessed, even during the hardest periods of its evolution in the last years of Stalin's life.

For me, this is the most important factor.

It is a secondary consideration that some chapters of the novel are written with blind fury and for this reason display an almost total loss of talent, like, for instance, the chapters about Stalin. After all, the author could easily eliminate these chapters from the novel himself if he were to discern the lack of artistic talent in them.

His general view of the people who lived at that time and of our society is another matter. Here, if the author had lent me the manuscript to read and later sought my opinion, I would have told him everything I have said above. If I failed to convince him that the general concept of our society as described in his novel is unfair, I would have become one of the opponents of the novel as a whole—despite a great measure of talent characteristic of its many chapters, in particular the chapters about prison life.

If the novel were published in its present form, I would convey in the press everything I have said here from beginning to end (except of course the first and the last paragraphs of this letter). As far as I know, Solzhenitsyn himself contacted the Central Committee with regard to his novel. I have read his novel at the request of the Central Committee. I would be very glad if it were deemed useful to convey my opinion of the novel to its author.

Konstantin Simonov

F. 3, *op.* 80, *d.* 643, *l.* 31–34. Original.

Notes

1. Konstantin Simonov, a novelist, poet, and war correspondent during World War II, was the recipient of six Stalin prizes for literature, as well as a Lenin Prize, and was a Hero of Socialist Labor. His attempt to become more liberal during Khrushchev's de-Stalinization campaign (when he had written a laudatory review of *One Day in the Life of Ivan Denisovich*) began to fade after 1963, although Document 6 (see above) shows that he still "categorically refused" to read Solzhenitsyn's early works confiscated by the KGB. His review of *The First Circle* for the Central Committee gains extra piquancy from the rumor, later circulated around Moscow, that the figure of the faint-hearted novelist Galakhov portrayed in the novel was based by Solzhenitsyn on Simonov himself.

2. *The reverse side of the last page reads: "To the Central Committee. Memo. 4 October 1967. The Culture Department reported to the Central Committee on the work and decision of the Special Meeting of the USSR Writers' Union Board Secretariat on 22 September this year which discussed the unpublished works of A. Solzhenitsyn. K. Simonov was present at this meeting of the USSR Writers' Union Board Secretariat. G. Diakonov, Head of the Central Committee Culture Department."*

3. Simonov's article, "About the Past in the Name of the Future," appeared in *Izvestia* on November 18, 1962.

4. The subject of *One Day in the Life of Ivan Denisovich* was the everyday life of the prisoners in one of Stalin's labor camps.

5. Lavrenty Beria was head of the Secret Police from 1938 until Stalin's death in 1953. Viktor Abakumov was the Minister of State Security from 1946 until Stalin's death. Both men were executed after Stalin died. Abakumov is also portrayed in *The First Circle*.

6. The Twentieth and Twenty-First Party Congresses, held in 1959 and 1961, were the two congresses that took the strongest line against Stalinism and the personality cult.

8 Excerpts from a Transcript of a Meeting of the Secretariat of the Central Committee of the USSR Communist Party

10 March 1967
Chairman: Comrade Suslov
Present: Comrades Andropov, Demichev, Kapitonov, Kulakov, Ponomarev, Solomentsev, Shelepin, and Pelshe

Discussion of Agenda Items
XVI. On the writer Solzhenitsyn:

Semichastny: No one has talked with this writer seriously. At present he is touring different agencies and writers' organizations reading excerpts from his works. He also gave an interview to a Japanese newspaper.[1] *Sovietskaya Zhenshchina* [Soviet Woman] magazine is about to publish an excerpt from his novel *Cancer Ward*. Solzhenitsyn is rearing his head; he thinks he is a hero.

Andropov: The question of Solzhenitsyn goes beyond working with writers. He has written certain things, like *Feast of the Victors* and *Cancer Ward* that are anti-Soviet in nature. We should take decisive measures to deal with Solzhenitsyn, for he is involved in anti-Soviet activities.

Solomentsev: The Moscow organizations should be made responsible for Solzhenitsyn's actions. It is here that art shows are organized. Can these people be called to order? Things are not going well with the artists' organizations in Moscow.

Semichastny: The Kurchatov Institute Party Committee has invited Solzhenitsyn to read excerpts from his novel.

Shauro: Solzhenitsyn has been very active lately. His place of residence is Ryazan, but he spends most of his time in Moscow. Incidentally, he gets help from well-known scientists such as Kapitsa[2] and Sakharov. We spoke with Solzhenitsyn twice at the Culture Department. We are planning another meeting at which our leading writers will take part in a discussion of Solzhenitsyn's work.

Demichev: Solzhenitsyn is a crazy writer with anti-Soviet attitudes. He should be resolutely opposed.

Grishin: He spreads slander against everything Russian, including all our cadres.

Demichev: The Culture Department should decide on the requisite measures and report to the Central Committee.

Semichastny: First of all, Solzhenitsyn should be expelled from the Writers' Union. That is the first measure.

It was decided not to take this matter beyond discussion at the level of the Secretariat.

From transcripts of the Central Committee Secretariat meetings in 1967. Original.

Notes

1. See Solzhenitsyn, *The Oak and the Calf: Sketches of Literary Life in the Soviet Union*, Appendix 1, pp. 457–458 for the text of this interview.
2. Academician Pyotr Kapitsa, who had worked with the English scientist Rutherford between the two world wars, was the most distinguished nuclear physicist in the Soviet Union. In 1966, together with a group of leading Soviet intellectuals, he had petitioned the Central Committee to grant Solzhenitsyn an apartment in Moscow. The request was turned down, but Solzhenitsyn did receive a larger and more modern apartment in Ryazan than the one he had been living in up until then.

9 Report of the Committee for State Security of the USSR Council of Ministers[1]

No. 1197–S
17 May 1967
Classified

To the Central Committee:
The Committee for State Security reports that the writer Solzhenitsyn has initiated a massive distribution of a document addressed to the Fourth Writers' Congress[2] (in lieu of a speech), to the presidium members, to delegates to the Congress, to members of the Writers' Union, and to the editorial boards of newspapers and magazines (see enclosed photocopy).[3]

On 17 May 1967, Solzhenitsyn is known to have sent the document to Writers' Union members Comrades P.S. Boriskov (of Petrozavodsk), A.E. Makayenko (of Minsk), A. Veyan (of Riga), A. Abu-Bakhara (of Makhachkala), and to the magazine *Literaturnaya Armenia* ["Literary Armenia"].

Chairman of the Committee for State Security
V. Semichastny

F. 3, *op.* 80, *d.* 643, *l.* 41. Original.

Notes

1. *Sent to Politburo members and candidate members, and Central Committee Secretaries.*
2. The Fourth Writers' Congress, which took place a year later than scheduled in May 1967, was designed to celebrate the fiftieth anniversary of the October Revolution. The attendance and agenda were carefully screened. Solzhenitsyn was not invited and his open letter never discussed.
3. *The photocopy is missing from the file.*

10 S. Toka's Letter to the Central Committee[1]

No. 63
1 June 1967

I am sending you a "letter" from a certain A.I. Solzhenitsyn addressed to the Fourth Writers' Congress, a copy of which was mailed to me as a delegate. In my view, the so-called "letter," both in content and form, is full of slander concerning our Soviet reality.

The Tuva Republic is living proof of the flourishing state of all aspects of culture, art, and literature which is the result of the wise Leninist policy pursued by the Central Committee of our Party and by the government. Before 1930, the Tuva people were totally illiterate. Now the Republic has become a land of universal literacy. Our children of school age are all enrolled in a compulsory eight-year educational system. We have a considerable number of local experts in all branches of the economy and workers in the arts. It has not been long since Tuva people knew nothing of what a writer was, nor did they have any idea of writing, books, and newspapers. Now, however, thanks to the Soviet government and the Communist Party, more than fifty writers work in Tuva. Their names are known far beyond the boundaries of our Republic; for instance, Stepan Saryg-ul, Oleg Sagan-ul, Aldyn-ul Darzhaa, Anton Kalzan, and Oleg Suvakpit, to name just a few.

Solzhenitsyn's slander and indiscriminate disparagement of the great achievements of the Soviet people in the cultural revolution show the true colors of the author of the said "letter." As a member of the Soviet Writers' Union, I totally reject Solzhenitsyn's hostile pronouncements as unsubstantiated, indiscriminate, and maliciously anti-Soviet.

It is obvious that Solzhenitsyn's mailing of this "letter" is an act of provocation. I request the Central Committee to assign appropriate persons to deal with this matter and draw the necessary conclusions.

The "letter," which I received after returning from the Writers' Congress, is dated 16 May 1967. Due to this fact I am sending it to you a little belatedly.

Member of USSR Writers' Union
S. Toka

Enclosure

Letter to the Fourth Congress of Soviet Writers[2]
(In Lieu of a Speech)

To the Congress Presidium and Delegates:

To Members of the Writers' Union:

To the Editorial Boards of Literary Newspapers and Magazines:

Not having access to the platform, I ask the congress to discuss:

I. The no longer tolerable oppression to which our literature has been subjected for decades by the censorship, and to which the Writers' Union can no longer submit.

The censorship, which is not provided for in the constitution and is therefore illegal—a fact that is never publicly mentioned—broods over our literature, using the name of Glavlit[3] as its smoke screen, and gives people completely ignorant of literature arbitrary powers over writers. A survival of the Middle Ages, censorship has managed, Methuselah-like, to drag out its existence almost to the twenty-first century. Perishable, it attempts to arrogate to itself the prerogative of imperishable time—that of separating good books from bad.

Our writers are not supposed to have the right, are not allowed the right, to express their cautionary judgments about the moral life of man and society, or to expound in their own way our social problems, or the historical experience that our country has acquired at the cost of so much suffering. Works that might express what the people urgently need to express, writers who might have a timely and salutary influence in the realm of the spirit or on the development of a social awareness, are banned or mutilated by the censorship on the basis of considerations that are petty, egotistical, and—from the national point of view—short-sighted.

Excellent manuscripts by young authors, as yet entirely unknown, are nowadays rejected by editors solely on the ground that they "won't get through." Many members of the Union, even some who are delegates at this congress, know how they themselves have bowed to the pressures of the censorship and made concessions affecting the structure and message of their books—changing chapters, pages, paragraphs, or sentences, giving them innocuous titles—just for the sake of seeing them finally in print, and by doing so have done irreparable damage to the content and to their artistic procedures. It is an understood quality of literature that talented works suffer most disastrously from all those distortions, while untalented works are not

45

affected by them. Indeed, it is the best of our literature that is published in mutilated form.

Meanwhile, the censor's labels—"ideologically harmful," "corrupt," and so forth—are proving ephemeral and unstable; in fact, are changing before our very eyes. Even Dostoevsky, the pride of world literature, was at one time not published in our country (and his works are still not published in full); he was excluded from the school curriculum, made inaccessible to readers, and reviled. For how many years was Yesenin[4] considered "counter-revolutionary?" People were even sent to jail for reading his books. Wasn't Mayakovsky[5] called "an anarchistic political hooligan?" For decades the imperishable poetry of Akhmatova[6] was considered anti-Soviet. The first timid printing of the dazzling Tsvetaeva[7] ten years ago was declared a "gross political error." Only after a delay of twenty to thirty years were Bunin, Bulgakov, and Platonov returned to us. Inevitably, Mandelstam, Voloshin, Gumilev, and Klyuev will follow in their turn, and at some time or other we shall be forced to "recognize" even Zamyatin and Remizov. The decisive moment in this process comes with the death of a troublesome writer, after which he is sooner or later returned to us with an "explanation of errors." It is not so very long since the name of Pasternak could not be spoken aloud; but then he died, and ever since, his books have been published and poems by him are quoted even at ceremonial occasions.

Pushkin's words proved truly prophetic: "They are capable of loving only the dead."

But the belated publication of books and "authorization" of names does not make up for either the social or the artistic losses suffered by our people as a consequence of these monstrous delays and the suppression of artistic consciousness. (In fact, there were writers in the 1920s—Pilnyak, Platonov, Mandelstam—who called attention at a very early stage both to the beginnings of the "personality cult" and to the peculiar traits of Stalin's character; but these writers were silenced and destroyed instead of being listened to.) Literature cannot develop in the categories of "permitted" and "not permitted," "this you can write about, that you can't." A literature that is not the breath of life for the society of its time, that dares not communicate its own pain and its own fears to society, that does not warn in time against threatening moral and social dangers does not deserve the name of literature; it is only a facade. Such a literature loses the confidence of its own people, and its published works are pulped instead of read.

Our literature has lost the leading position it occupied at the end of the last century and the beginning of this one, and it has lost the brilliance of experimentation that distinguished it in the 1920s. To the entire world the literary life of our country now appears immeasurably more colorless, trivial, and inferior than it actually is—than it would be if it were not confined and hemmed in. Not only does our country lose by this—in world opinion—but world literature is the poorer for it too. If the world had unrestricted access to all the fruits of our literature, if it were enriched by our spiritual experience, the whole artistic evolution of the world would move in a different way, acquiring a new stability and rising indeed to new artistic heights.

I propose that the congress demand and ensure the abolition of all censorship, open or hidden, of imaginative literature and release publishing houses from the obligation to obtain clearance for every printed page.

II. The duties of the Union toward its members.

These duties are not clearly formulated in the statutes of the Soviet Writers' Union (under "Protection of Copyrights" and "Measures for the Protection of Other Rights of Writers"), and at the same time, in the course of a third of a century it has become lamentably clear that the Union has not defended either the "other" rights or even the copyrights of persecuted writers.

Many writers have been subjected during their lifetime to abuse and slander in the press and from the platform without being afforded the physical possibility of replying. More than that, they have been exposed to violence and personal persecution (Bulgakov, Akhmatova, Tsvetaeva, Pasternak, Zoshchenko, Andrei Platonov, Alexander Grin, Vasily Grossman). Not only did the Writers' Union not make its own publications available to these writers for purposes of reply and justification, not only did it not spring to their defense, but its leaders were always first among the persecutors. Names that will be the glory of our twentieth-century poetry found themselves on the list of those expelled from the Union or not even admitted to it in the first place. *A fortiori*, the leadership of the Union cravenly abandoned to their distress those for whom persecution ended in exile, labor camps, and death (Pavel Vasilyev, Mandelstam, Artem Vesely, Pilnyak, Babel, Tabidze, Zabolotsky, and others). The list must be curtailed at "and others." We learned after the Twentieth Congress of the Party that there were more than six hundred completely innocent writers whom the Union had obediently handed over to their fate in prisons and camps. However the roll is even longer, and its curled-up end cannot be and will never be read by our eyes. It contains the names of young prose writers and poets whom we may have known only accidentally through personal encounters, whose talents were destroyed in camps before they could blossom, whose writings never got further than the offices of the state security service in the days of Yagoda, Yezhov, Beria, and Abakumov.

There is no historical necessity for the newly elected leadership of the Union to share responsibility for the past with its predecessors.

I propose that all guarantees provided by the Union for the defense of members subjected to slander and unjust persecutions be clearly formulated in Paragraph 22 of the Union statutes, so that past illegalities will not be repeated.

If the congress does not remain indifferent to what I have said, I also ask that it consider the interdictions and persecution which I myself have endured.

1. It will soon be two years since the state security authorities took from me my novel *The First Circle* (comprising thirty-five signatures), which has held up its submission to publishers. Instead, in my own lifetime, against my will, and even without my knowledge, this novel has been "published" in an unnatural "closed" edition for reading in an unidentified select circle. I have been unable to obtain a public reading and open discussion of the novel, or to prevent misuse and plagiarism. My novel is shown to literary bureaucrats, but concealed from most writers.

2. Together with this novel, my literary archive dating back fifteen to twenty years, and containing things that were not intended for publication, was taken from me. Now, heavily slanted excerpts from these papers have also been covertly "published" and are being disseminated within the same circles. The play *Feast of the Victors*, which I wrote in verse and memorized in a prison camp (where I wore a four-digit number, and where, condemned to die by starvation, we were forgotten by society, *no one* outside the camps spoke against repressions)—this long-abandoned play is being ascribed to me as my very latest work.

3. For three years now, an irresponsible campaign of slander has been conducted against one who fought all through the war as a battery commander and received military decorations. It is being said that I served time as a criminal, or surrendered to the enemy (I was never a prisoner of war), that I "betrayed" my country and "served the Germans." That is the interpretation being put now on the eleven years I spent in camps and exile for having criticized Stalin. This slander is being spread in secret briefing sessions and meetings by people holding official positions. I have tried in vain to stop the slander by appealing to the board of the Writers' Union of the RSFSR and to the press. The board did not even reply, and not a single paper printed my answer to the slanderers. On the contrary, slander against me from official platforms has intensified and become more vicious within the last year, making use of distorted material from my confiscated archive, while I have no way of replying.

4. My novel *Cancer Ward* (comprising twenty-five signatures), the first part of which was approved for publication by the Prose Section of the Moscow writers' organizations, cannot be published by chapters (rejected by five magazines), still less in its entirety (rejected by *Novy Mir*, *Prostor*, and *Zvezda*).

5. The play *The Tenderfoot and the Tramp*, accepted in 1962 by the Sovremenik Theater, has so far not been approved for performance.

6. The screenplay *Tanks Know the Truth*, the stage play *The Light That Is in You*,[8] the short stories "The Right Hand," "What a Pity," and my series of "Miniatures" cannot find a producer or a publisher.

7. My stories published in *Novy Mir* have never been reprinted in book form, having been rejected everywhere (by the Sovietsky Pisatel and the State Literary Publishing Houses, and by the *Ogonyok* Library). They thus remain inaccessible to the general reading public.

8. I have also been prevented from having any other contacts with readers, through public readings of my works (in November 1966, nine out of eleven scheduled meetings were canceled at the last moment), or through readings over the radio. Even the simple act of giving someone a manuscript for "reading and copying" has now become a criminal act (ancient Russian scribes were permitted to do this five centuries ago).

Thus my work has been completely suppressed, locked away, and slanderously misrepresented.

Faced with these flagrant infringements of my copyright and "other" rights, will the Fourth Congress defend me or will it not? It seems to me that the choice is not without importance to the literary future of some of the delegates themselves.

I am of course confident that I shall fulfill my duty as a writer in all circumstances—from the grave even more successfully and incontrovertibly than in my lifetime. No one can bar the road to truth, and to advance its cause I am prepared to accept even death. But may it be that repeated lessons will finally teach us not to stay the writer's pen during his lifetime?

This has never yet added luster to our history.

A. Solzhenitsyn
16 May 1967

F. 3, *op.* 80, *d.* 643, *l.* 42–47. Original.

Notes

1. *The first page bears the signature of P. Demichev, and on the last page there is the following notation: "Central Committee. Solzhenitsyn's letter was discussed at a meeting of the Secretariat of the Writers' Union Board. Literaturnaya Gazeta will publish the results of this discussion in the near future. Comrade Toka has been informed accordingly. Deputy Head of Central Committee Culture Department, I. Chernoutsan. Instructor A. Galanov. 27.10.67."*
2. See Appendix 2 of Solzhenitsyn's *The Oak and the Calf*, pp. 458–462. The translation, by Harry Willetts, is reprinted with permission.

3. An acronym for the Chief Directorate for the Preservation of State Secrets in the Press, the official name of the Soviet censorship office. The name and functions of this body were themselves state secrets, although well known to editors, writers, and critics.

4. Sergei Yesenin (1895–1925) was an outstandingly talented peasant poet whose lyrical verse enjoyed enormous popularity before, during, and after the Revolution. In the early twenties he was fiercely attacked by Communist critics and committed suicide at the age of thirty.

5. Vladimir Mayakovsky (1893–1930), a Futurist poet who had become the "bard of the Revolution" (and who was one of those who criticized Yesenin for committing suicide), himself came under attack after Stalin's ascent to power and committed suicide in 1930.

6. Anna Akhmatova (1889–1966) one of Russia's greatest lyric poets of the twentieth century, virtually stopped writing for a decade after harsh criticism of her work soon after the Revolution. She resumed writing in the 1930s, but was able to publish only a handful of poems until a few years before her death in 1966.

7. Marina Tsvetaeva (1892–1941), another great lyric poet, emigrated to Paris shortly after the Revolution and worked there in obscurity for seventeen years. She returned to the Soviet Union in 1939 and committed suicide two years later. Most of her work was banned until the 1960s.

8. The original title of *Candle in the Wind*.

11 Report of the Committee for State Security of the USSR Council of Ministers[1]

No 1740–B
5 July 1967
Classified

To the Central Committee
(Central Committee Culture Department):
We are forwarding this report on writer A. Solzhenitsyn at the request of
comrade Y.S. Melentiev.

Deputy Chairman for the Committee of State Security
Bannikov

Enclosure
3 July 1967
Classified

Report on A.I. Solzhenitsyn

Alexander Isaevich Solzhenitsyn was born on 11 December 1918 in the city
of Kislovodsk. He spent his childhood and youth in the city of Rostov-on-
the-Don. From 1927 to 1936, he attended a secondary school there. In 1936,
he entered the Department of Physics and Mathematics at Rostov University,
from which he graduated in 1941. At the same time he took a correspondence
course in literature. While at the university, he was a member of the Young
Communist League.

As can be seen from the documents, in his autobiographical information
Solzhenitsyn says practically nothing about his parents, nor does he even
provide their first and last names or patronymics. To obtain more details we
conducted an investigation, in the course of which we went to Solzhenitsyn's
birthplace and the places where he lived, studied, and worked. Files, archives,
and other official documents were also reviewed.

From his personal file at Rostov University it appears that before the war Solzhenitsyn lived with his mother. The only thing he says about her is that she was a stenographer. In his autobiography currently in his personal file at the Writers' Union, he says that he was born into a family of office workers, that his mother worked as a typist and a stenographer, and that he lost his father before he was born.

The 1918 archives in Kislovodsk have not been preserved, which is why it was impossible to obtain any information on Solzhenitsyn's parents at his birthplace.

There is no information about Solzhenitsyn's parents in the investigation and prosecution archives concerning Solzhenitsyn's case in the USSR Ministry of Defense.

Solzhenitsyn's wife, Natalia Alexeyevna Reshetovskaya, was born in 1919 in the city of Novocherkassk; Russian; non-Party member; and he married her in 1940. She graduated from Rostov University in 1941, and obtained a PhD in chemistry after the war. In her personnel form she says that her father, Alexei Nikolaevich Reshetovsky, born 1888, was engaged in literary activities before the Revolution and died in 1919. Her mother, Maria Konstantinovna Reshetovskaya, born 1890, was a teacher by training and at present resides in the city of Ryazan.

According to current data, Reshetovskaya's father used to be a chief of a Cossack squadron in Novocherkassk. He was killed during the Civil War, in circumstances that the Reshetovskys have not disclosed.[2]

In 1941, Solzhenitsyn was called up for military service. Until March 1942 he was a private in the 74th Horse-Drawn Transport Battalion; from April to November 1942, he was a trainee officer at the Third Leningrad Artillery School. From December 1942 to February 1945, he saw active service in the army as commander of a sound-ranging battery on the North-West, Bryansk, Central, and First and Second Byelorussian fronts. He was awarded the Order of the Patriotic War, second class, the Order of the Red Star, and two medals.

In February 1945, Solzhenitsyn was arrested and later sentenced by a decree of the Special Board of the USSR NKVD, under Articles 58–10, part II, and 58–11 of the Russian Federation Penal Code,[3] to eight years of hard labor. According to the information available to us, he indulged in anti-Soviet outbursts and slanderous allegations against Stalin. When under investigation he at first rejected the charges against him, but then admitted he was guilty of engaging in anti-Soviet agitation and in an attempt to establish an anti-Soviet group.[4]

While serving his sentence, Solzhenitsyn was, from 1946 to 1950, a research associate in various scientific institutes of the USSR Ministry of Internal Affairs and the Ministry for State Security.[5] From 1950 to 1953, he worked for the Irtysh Coal Combine in the city of Ekibastuz in the Pavlodar District.[6] After his release he was exiled, and from February 1953 to April 1956, he worked as a teacher of mathematics in the Kirov Secondary School in the town of Berlik in the former Kok Terek District of the Dzhambul Region.[7]

The Military Collegium of the USSR Supreme Court exonerated Solzhenitsyn by a decree of 6 February 1957. From the place of his exile he came to live in the Kurlovsky District of the Vladimir Region. In 1956–1957, he worked there as a teacher of mathematics in the Mezinovsk Secondary School.

In June 1957, Solzhenitsyn moved to the city of Ryazan where he currently resides at the following address: Yablokov proyezd, building No. 1, apartment 11.

Solzhenitsyn is not a Party member. He has been a member of the Writers' Union since December 1962.

Deputy Head of the Second Chief Directorate of the Committee for State Security of the USSR Council of Ministers
Bobkov

F. 3, *op.* 80, *d.* 643, *l.* 48–51. Original.

Notes

1. *A note on the document reads: "Report. Staff members of the Central Committee Culture Department, Comrades Shauro, Melentiev and Belyaev have read it. G. Diakonov, Chief of Secretariat of the Central Committee Culture Department. 6 October 1967."*
2. Reshetovsky was not killed. He had fought on the side of the Whites during the Civil War and left Russia in 1919. The Reshetovsky family naturally concealed those details and pretended that he was dead.
3. Article 58, paragraph 10, part 2 was directed against "propaganda or agitation containing an appeal to overthrow, undermine, or weaken the Soviet regime, or to commit individual counterrevolutionary crimes, and also the preparation, distribution, or conservation of literature of this nature. . . ." Paragraph 11 referred to "any type of organizational activity directed toward the preparation or commission of [such] crimes. . . ."
4. Solzhenitsyn's "organization" was found to consist of himself and his best friend, Nikolai Vitkevich.
5. One of these institutes formed the setting for *The First Circle*.
6. The setting of *One Day in the Life of Ivan Denisovich*.
7. Kok Terek was in southern Kazakhstan.

12 Report of the Committee for State Security of the USSR Council of Ministers

No. 1756–A
5 July 1967
Classified

To the Central Committee:
We are forwarding an NTS[1] leaflet and a clipping from *Russkaya Mysl* [Russian Thought], an anti-Soviet newspaper published by emigrés in Paris. Also, please find attached the text of the letter by A.I. Solzhenitsyn, a Soviet Writers' Union member, entitled "To the Fourth Congress of Soviet Writers (in Lieu of a Speech)," which was sent throughout the USSR by mail.

We confiscated the documents noted above.

Chairman of the Committee for State Security
Andropov

F. 3, *op.* 80, *d.* 643, *l.* 67. Original.

Notes

1. NTS—*Narodno-Trudovoi Soyuz* (Popular Labor Union), an emigré organization based in Frankfurt, Germany, provided the most active and vigorous opposition to the Soviet system from the time of the end of World War II to the collapse of the communist government. It was loathed by the Soviet authorities and its name became a bogy in Soviet propaganda. NTS was the publisher of the literary journal *Grani* in which Teush's article on Solzhenitsyn had appeared (see note to Document 2 above) and was a zealous supporter of Solzhenitsyn's work from the moment of his first appearance.

13 Memorandum from the International Department of the Central Committee[1]

No. 25–S–1014
10 July 1967
Classified

To the Central Committee:
On 5 July of this year, *L'Unita*, the central newspaper of the Communist Party of Italy, published an article by its Moscow correspondent A. Guerra entitled "Solzhenitsyn's Appeal Cannot Remain Unanswered." The author extols Solzhenitsyn's letter addressed to the Fourth Congress of Soviet Writers and at the same time criticizes the way the Party supervises literature and the procedure by which works of literature are published in the Soviet Union.

We deem it necessary to draw the attention of the leaders of the Communist Party of Italy to the unfriendly tone of the article written by *L'Unita*'s Moscow correspondent A. Guerra. We would also like to request that A. Guerra be instructed not to submit any such publications in the future. We regard it as advisable to invite Comrade Guerra for an interview at the International Department and the Culture Department of the Central Committee to discuss with him the questions addressed in his article.

A draft resolution by the Central Committee is enclosed.

B. Ponomarev

F. 3, *op.* 68, *d.* 515, *l.* 50. Original.

Notes

1. *The memo was sent to Politburo members on 11 July 1967 as No. 47–40.*

14 Resolution of the Politburo of the Central Committee

"Instructions to the Soviet Ambassador to Italy"

No. P47/95
17 July 1967
Top Secret

The text of instructions to the Soviet Ambassador for an interview with Comrade Longo[1] is approved (see attachment).

Secretary of the Central Committee

Enclosure
Re: Item 95, minutes No. 47
Classified

Rome
To the Soviet Ambassador:
You are to meet with Comrade Longo and discuss the following matters with him, mentioning that you are acting on instructions from the Central Committee.

An article by *L'Unita*'s Moscow correspondent A. Guerra entitled "Solzhenitsyn's Appeal Cannot Remain Unanswered," published in *L'Unita* on 5 July this year, did not go unnoticed in Moscow. In this connection we would like to share certain considerations with Comrade Longo in a comradely fashion.

The article is obviously unfriendly towards us. Its author extols Sozhenitsyn's letter and criticizes the way the Party supervises literature and the existing procedure for publishing works of literature in the USSR. In our opinion, the fact that the article was published runs counter to the fraternal relations established between the Communist Party of the Soviet Union and the Communist Party of Italy. The Voice of America broadcast of 6 July this year proves that *L'Unita*'s publication is being used by our opponents to pursue their anti-communist goals, and especially, in connection with the forthcoming fiftieth anniversary of the October Revolution, to disseminate hostile and provocative conjectures regarding relations between our parties.

In the course of your discussions, you are to stress that Solzhenitsyn obviously wrote his letter as an act of provocation and drew a totally distorted picture of the real situation of Soviet literature, ignoring or distorting the true facts. It is fundamentally wrong to portray Solzhenitsyn's isolated case as proof that the Soviet Union has yet to resolve the problem of the "relationship between the revolution and culture," as Guerra writes in his article. There is no such problem. It has been resolved during the fifty years of socialist construction in our country, resulting most importantly in the creation of a Soviet intelligentsia devoted to the ideals of communism and actively participating in its construction, as well as the acquisition by the broad masses of our people of all the riches of culture.

We believe that an article like the one written by Guerra leads Italian intellectuals to conclude falsely that socialism has been unable to resolve cultural problems in fifty years, whereas in reality these problems have been resolved in the Soviet Union. It is true that the constant evolution of socialist culture poses ever new tasks for our Party to fulfill. In this context, certain discussions may arise, to which our Party will not erect barriers, so long as they are held in the spirit of communist construction. As Comrade Longo is aware, our Party has accomplished a great deal in this area, and we will continue to strive to perfect our methods for the Party's supervision of culture.

We in Moscow expect the leaders of the Communist Party of Italy to display an understanding of the considerations that we have here set forth in a frank manner, and to instruct A. Guerra accordingly.

Telegraph confirmation that this has been done.

F. 3, *op.* 80, *d.* 643, *l.* 52–54. Excerpt from the minutes.

Notes

1. Luigi Longo (1900–1980) was the leader of the Italian Communist Party, having been elected Secretary-General in 1964.

15 From a Transcript of a Meeting of the Central Committee Secretariat

18 July 1967
Chairman: Comrade M.A. Suslov
Present: Comrades Demichev, Kapitonov, Kirilenko, Kulakov, Solomentsev, Ustinov, and Shelepin

On the conduct and views of A. Solzhenitsyn

Ustinov: I am not certain if we need to forward the memo on this question to all Party organizations.[1]

Kulakov: If we do send such a memo, won't it look as if we are justifying our actions to the Party because of Solzhenitsyn's conduct?

Demichev: Let me tell you why the question of sending such a memo to local Party organizations emerged at all. The point is that foreign radio stations and the foreign press are providing extensive coverage of Solzhenitsyn's conduct and discussing his letter to the Writers' Congress. Our local Party leaders often find themselves in a situation where they are unable to answer questions about Solzhenitsyn's conduct when they are asked at Party meetings and during discussions. We intended to circulate such a memo in order to orient our Party cadres on this question.

Tumanova: We believe that the circulation of such a memo is a way to provide information to Party activists.

Kirilenko: I do not think we should issue a document like this. We could ask the Writers' Union to consider Solzhenitsyn's conduct and to pass an appropriate judgment on the subject. If required, we could get appropriate materials published in the press. However, we should not circulate any such document among Party organizations.

Demichev: Solzhenitsyn is a well-known person. We cannot rely on the Writers' Union Secretariat to provide the relevant information on the subject. We may want to provide information to Party activists in one way or another. What we could do is send a memo from the Central Committee Culture Department instead of directly from the Central Committee.

Kapitonov: I do not think it would be appropriate to send a memo. If we send such a memo on Solzhenitsyn it could meet with a negative response. Let me remind you that when Sinyavsky and Daniel were sentenced it produced an extremely negative reaction.[2] Solzhenitsyn should be debunked in the press. Let the Writers' Union do this in an appropriate fashion.

Solomentsev: No doubt Solzhenitsyn should be debunked. But will the Writers' Union be up to the task? I do think we should inform local Party organizations in an appropriate manner.

Ustinov: I am against sending the memo to Party organizations. We should not draw too much attention by Party activists to this question. It will not work out the way we want it to. Maybe we should entrust this matter to the Writers' Union.

Suslov: Let's perhaps do this: we could ask the Writers' Union to expedite their review of all the questions bearing on Solzhenitsyn's conduct and to evaluate it in a substantive manner. After that we will return to this question and see how best to proceed.

The proposal was approved.

From transcripts of meetings of the Central Committee Secretariat in 1967. Original.

Notes

1. *A memorandum by the Central Committee Culture Department dated 13 July 1967 "On Solzhenitsyn's Conduct and Views." Reference is made to it in Document 34. The memo is missing from the files.*
2. This was an understatement. The trial and sentencing of Sinyavsky and Daniel led to a storm of protests from intellectuals from all over the world, including many prominent leftists. It also spawned an unprecedented wave of protests inside the Soviet Union from intellectuals who rightly saw the trial as signaling the end of "the Thaw" in Soviet politics and culture. The leading protesters later formed the core of the Dissident Movement, which dates its inception from the trial of these two writers.

16 Report of the Committee for State Security of the USSR Council of Ministers¹

No. 2338–A
14 September 1967
Classified

To the Central Committee:
We are forwarding you copies of letters from A.I. Solzhenitsyn to the Board Secretariat of the Soviet Writers' Union and A.T. Tvardovsky.

As can be seen from the text he is circulating these letters among all the Secretaries of the Writers' Union Board, demanding that they assist him in getting *Cancer Ward* published.

Chairman of the Committee for State Security
Andropov

Enclosure 1
12 September 1967

Dear Alexander Trifonovich [Tvardovsky],
I spent all day waiting for you at *Novy Mir* but unfortunately you were out. I wanted your advice on a certain matter. The people from the Writers' Union Secretariat have been dragging their feet, and time is slipping away in an inexcusable manner. I think it is necessary to prod them toward making a decision. However, in my view three or four Secretaries do not represent the entire Secretariat, and for this reason I am circulating my letter among all the Writers' Union Secretaries. It is addressed to them, and them alone. They have to say "yes" or "no" to publishing my novel.

I do not list you among the Secretaries present at the meeting on 12 June. Do not consider this a discourtesy. The thing is, I could not bring my pen to include your name. I cannot help seeing every line from the perspective of bygone years. Anyway, that day you were not, strictly speaking, "the master of the palace," so it is quite fair.

I am informed that Markov and Voronkov were part of the effort aimed at distorting certain events. Markov is spreading rumors that at the meeting on

12 June we allegedly "had a big fight," and Voronkov is adding fantastic details to the story of the confiscation of my archive.

Accept my firm handshake.

With very best wishes.

A. Solzhenitsyn

Enclosure 2

To the Soviet Writers' Union Board Secretariat:
To all Secretaries of the Board:
To A.T. Tvardovsky:

Although it had the support of more than a hundred writers, my letter to the Fourth Writers' Congress has been neither published nor answered. All that has happened is that rumors—all along the same lines and evidently from a single source—have been spread to pacify public opinion: rumors that my archives and my novel have been returned to me and that *Cancer Ward* and a book of stories are on press. But this, as you know, is all lies.

In an exchange of views with me on 12 June 1967, Secretaries of the Board of the Union of Writers of the USSR G. Markov, K. Voronkov, S. Sartakov, and L. Sobolev declared that the Board of the Union of Writers considered it a duty to refute publicly the base slander that has been spread about me and my military record. However, not only has no refutation followed, but the slanders continue; at confidential briefing sessions, at meetings of activists, and at seminars for agitators, more fantastic nonsense is being disseminated about me—that I have defected to the UAR, for instance, or to England. (I would like to assure the slanderers that I am less likely to run away than they are.) Prominent persons persistently express their regret that I did not die in the camp, that I was ever liberated. (However, the same regret was voiced by some people as soon as *One Day* was published. This book is now being secretly withdrawn from circulation by public libraries.)

These same Secretaries of the Board promised at least to "look into the question" of publishing my latest long story, *Cancer Ward*. But in the space of three months—a quarter of a year—no progress has been made in this direction either. During these three months, the forty-two Secretaries of the Board have been unable to make an evaluation of the story or to make a recommendation as to whether it should be published. The story has been in this same strange and equivocal state—no direct prohibition, no direct permission—for over a year, since the summer of 1966. While the journal *Novy Mir* would now like to publish the story, it still awaits permission to do so.

Does the Secretariat believe that my story will silently disappear as a result of these endless delays, that it will cease to exist, so that the Secretariat will not have to take a vote as to whether to include it in or exclude it from the literature of this country? While this is going on, the book is being read avidly, especially by writers. On the initiative of readers, it has already been circulated in hundreds of typewritten copies. At the 12 June meeting I warned the Secretariat that we must make haste to publish the story if we wished to see it appear first in Russian; that under the circumstances we could not prevent its unauthorized appearance in the West.

After the senseless delay of many months, the time has come to state that if this does happen, it will clearly be the fault (or perhaps the secret wish?) of the Secretariat of the Board of the Union of Writers of the USSR.

I insist that my story be published without delay!

Solzhenitsyn
12 September 1967[2]

F. 3, *op.* 80, *d.* 643, *l.* 63–65. Original.

Notes

1. *A notation on a separate sheet reads: "Distribute to Central Committee Secretaries as well as Comrades V.F. Shauro and V.I. Stepakov" and also has the signatures of M. Suslov, I. Kapitonov (twice), P. Demichev, A. Kirilenko, F. Kulakov, D. Ustinov, B. Ponomarev, V. Shauro, and V. Stepakov.*
2. See *The Oak and the Calf: Sketches* . . . , Appendix 3. Reprinted with permission.

17 Report of the Culture Department of the Central Committee of the Communist Party of the Soviet Union

"On the Discussions in the Soviet Writers' Union Regarding Solzhenitsyn's Conduct"[1]

4 October 1967
Top Secret

To the Central Committee:
As has already been reported, in May this year the writer A. Solzhenitsyn forwarded a letter to the Fourth Congress of Soviet Writers. The presidium of the Congress directed the newly elected Secretariat of the Writers' Union to review this letter. A considerable amount of time was spent on the preparation for the discussion, because the Secretaries decided to familiarize themselves more closely with Solzhenitsyn's unpublished works in order to make a more accurate appraisal of the ideological tendencies of his creative work as a whole.

They read the following works: his plays *Feast of the Victors* and *The Republic of Labor*, his novel *The First Circle* (839 pages), the novel *Cancer Ward* (500 pages), and selected short stories. (According to Solzhenitsyn, he wrote *Feast of the Victors* while a prisoner).

On 12 September, Solzhenitsyn forwarded another letter to the Soviet Writers' Union in which he categorically demanded that the question of the publication of *Cancer Ward* be decided without further delay. He claims that the manuscript of this novel has been reproduced in hundreds of typewritten copies, and it is not excluded that it may soon be published abroad. He tries to put the blame for this on the Secretariat of the Soviet Writers' Union.

On 22 September this year, the Secretariat held a meeting where Solzhenitsyn's letters were reviewed in his presence. Out of twenty-six Secretaries in attendance, twenty-one spoke at the meeting, including K. Fedin, I. Abashidze, T. Abdumonunov, S. Baruzdin, P. Brovka, K. Voronkov, B. Kerbabaev, V. Kozhevnikov, A. Korneychuk, G. Markov, G. Musrepov, L. Novichenko, V. Ozerov, B. Ryurikov, A. Salinsky, S. Sartakov, K. Simonov, A. Surkov, A. Tvardovsky, A. Sharipov, and K. Yakshen. The meeting lasted more than six hours and was chaired from beginning to end by K. Fedin.[2]

Secretaries of the Board M. Sholokhov, B. Polevoy, and S. Mikhalkov were unable to attend the meeting. However, they sent letters in which they expressed their views on the question under discussion. Their letters were read out loud. Sholokhov,[3] in particular, gave an appropriate assessment of the anti-Soviet nature of *Feast of the Victors* and proposed expelling Solzhenitsyn from the Writers' Union.

Speaking about Solzhenitsyn's letters, the participants of the meeting held a broad and substantive discussion on the ideological orientation the writer assumes in his works, pointing out his mistakes and erroneous concepts.

In their statements, the Secretaries examined in painstaking detail the entire gamut of questions concerning Solzhenitsyn's creative and civic positions. The exchange of views was outstandingly frank, principled, and ideologically rigorous. Solzhenitsyn's works and conduct were discussed in the context of the Soviet writer's responsibility for his work in a situation characterized by the ideological struggle of two systems, and in light of the writer's duty to serve the cause of socialism honestly. The Secretaries were decisive and uncompromising in their condemnation of Solzhenitsyn's unworthy conduct, which provides fodder for the whipping up abroad of anti-Soviet hysteria on the eve of the Fiftieth Anniversary of the Great October Revolution.

In opening the meeting K. Fedin noted that Solzhenitsyn's letters in both tone and content were offensive to the Writers' Union, and that the Secretariat rejected the categorical demands set forth in them. Fedin called upon participants in the discussion to go beyond a mere analysis of Solzhenitsyn's works and to give their opinions of his social conduct.

After that Solzhenitsyn made a "statement" in which he said that he disassociated himself from *Feast of the Victors* and therefore requested that participants no longer discuss it.

The participants took due note of his statement. However, they found it impossible to ignore this play in their remarks because, as B. Ryurikov put it, "traces" of the profoundly anti-Soviet *Feast of the Victors* were to be found in one form or another in Solzhenitsyn's later works as well, including *Cancer Ward*.

Thus, addressing Solzhenitsyn directly, A. Surkov said: "The underlying idea of *Feast of the Victors* is 'To hell with all of you!' I wouldn't mention this right now if I had not discerned something similar while reading *Cancer Ward*."

It was noted that all the writer's unpublished works, including those he insisted should be published, were shot through with themes of vengefulness, bitterness, and a lack of faith in the vital strength of the Soviet system.

At the same time, noting Solzhenitsyn's literary gift, the participants thought it was not excluded that he could return to correct positions, stressing that the decision as to whether he was prepared to reconsider his unhealthy and erroneous concepts depended on Solzhenitsyn himself.

The Secretariat of the Writers' Union suggested that Solzhenitsyn first of all define his attitude to the fact that his name and his works were being used abroad for anti-Soviet purposes. K. Fedin suggested that Solzhenitsyn make a press statement with a resolute rebuttal of his foreign "defenders," thus demonstrating that he did not disassociate himself from Soviet society and Soviet literature. Such a step, in the view of Fedin and other Secretaries of the Writers' Union, would meet with the favorable response of the Soviet public and would help Solzhenitsyn escape the vicious circle in which he found himself through his own fault. Writers' Union Secretaries (Comrades Markov, Korneychuk, Ryurikov, Kozhevnikov, Sharipov, Surkovy, and others) supported Fedin's idea and stressed that an appropriate response to foreign anti-Soviet circles was the immediate duty of a Soviet writer if he sensed his responsibility to his country and his people.

Solzhenitsyn chose not to comment on this question. In a demagogical fashion he stated that he did not understand why views expressed abroad were held in such "esteem," that it was supposedly quite unnecessary to "be so sensitive to what was being said abroad," that he was totally indifferent to what was being said about him abroad, and that, allegedly, he did not know what they were writing or saying about him. When somebody proposed to read translations of foreign publications about him, he refused to listen and said that he was pressed for time.

At the end of the meeting Solzhenitsyn took the floor again and said that he would respond to the "West" only if at least half of the demands set out in his letter to the Writers' Congress were met. "Then I will accept the proposal of Konstanin Alexandrovich [Fedin] and the other speakers," he said.

The Secretariat of the Writers' Union rejected outright Solzhenitsyn's attempts to dictate his conditions.

Since Solzhenitsyn insisted on hearing the Secretariat's views on *Cancer Ward*, the participants discussed this work and commented on it in a frank fashion. It was noted that the story was permeated with ill will towards our society, and that its ideological premise was unacceptable. A. Surkov, L. Novichenko, and others pointed out that Solzhenitsyn's story was "dragging us back" to the idealistic ideas of Vladimir Solovyov, Mikhailovsky, and Kropotkin,[4] and that his story, according to Surkov, had "a distinct flavor of SR-ism" [Socialist Revolutionarism].[5] Responding to this criticism, Solzhenitsyn stated that, in his view, "the writer's task was not confined to defending a certain way of distributing the national product, or a certain 'social system.'" In his opinion, the writer's duty was to raise "eternal" questions of human existence.

The overwhelming majority of the Secretaries came to the conclusion that it was not advisable to publish the novel in its present form.

Tvardovsky was of a different opinion. He stated, as did other Secretaries, that Solzhenitsyn's letter to the Writers' Congress, phrased in categorical terms and actually addressed to the public abroad, should be condemned, and that such actions were not permissible for a Soviet writer. At the same time, Tvardovsky stressed more than once that he personally admired Solzhenitsyn's talent, and that in order to save this writer for the benefit of Soviet literature, *Cancer Ward* should be published without delay. Here Tvardovsky ignored the main question under discussion, which was Solzhenitsyn's public position and the erroneous concepts underlying his works.

K. Simonov and A. Salinsky also avoided the most important question, which was to evaluate Solzhenitsyn's public position. They also spoke in favor of immediate publication of *Cancer Ward*, albeit with certain reservations.

The participants in the discussion stated that Solzhenitsyn's letter to the Fourth Congress of Soviet Writers was a political statement used by the bourgeois media to discredit our country and the Soviet system. They also condemned Solzhenitsyn's defiant conduct. The Secretariat demanded that Solzhenitsyn react to the bourgeois media's attempts to use his name in pursuit of anti-Soviet goals. Comrades Marshak and Yashen proposed that if Solzhenitsyn refused to do this, they should consider the question of expelling him from the Writers' Union.

This discussion showed that an overwhelming majority of the Secretaries of the Soviet Writers' Union were united in their ideology and strict adherence to the Party line, and that they would not tolerate any actions discrediting the name of a Soviet writer. The participants in the discussion explained to Solzhenitsyn that they criticized his work and conduct so harshly with only one goal in mind, which was to help him understand his mistakes.

The Secretariat decided to issue a statement about the discussion. This statement is to be published in *Literaturnaya Gazeta*.[6]

Head of the Culture Department of the Central Committee
V. Shauro

F. 3, op. 80, d. 643, l. 57–61. Original.

Notes

1. *This memorandum was circulated among Politburo members and candidate members, and Central Committee Secretaries, on 5 October 1967 as No. P1590.*

2. Konstantin Fedin was a novelist of the older generation who had come to prominence soon after the Revolution with his modernist novel *Cities and Years* (1924). After that he became increasingly orthodox, both politically and esthetically, and wrote his later novels according to the formula of Socialist Realism. When he replaced Alexei Surkov as First Secretary of the Writers' Union it was seen as a mildly liberal development, but Fedin's conformism disappointed the hopes placed in him.

3. Mikhail Sholokhov was of the same post-revolutionary generation as Fedin. His epic novel *The Quiet Don* (1928–1940), modelled on Tolstoy, is a fine neorealist novel, and was the reason for the belated award to Sholokhov of the Nobel Prize in 1965. Politically, however, Sholokhov was a reactionary Stalinist, who publicly attacked both Pasternak and Solzhenitsyn for their "anti-Soviet" writings.

4. Vladimir Solovyov (1853–1900) was an idealist religious philosopher of the late nineteenth century. Nikolai Mikhailovsky (1842–1904) was a political thinker of the same period and the chief theorist of Russian Populism. Pyotr Kropotkin (1842–1921), a contemporary of these two figures, was a proponent of Anarchist Communism.

5. The Socialist Revolutionary Party was founded in 1901 and at the time of the Revolution was by far the biggest socialist party in Russia. Its leaders were outmaneuvered by Lenin, however, and soon after the Revolution, the party was outlawed and many of its leading members arrested or shot.

6. *See Document 35.*

18 Memorandum of the Secretariat of the USSR Writers' Union

No. 812
12 December 1967

To the Central Committee:
The Secretariat of the Soviet Writers' Union Board has discussed the questions raised by Solzhenitsyn's letter to the Fourth Writers' Congress. In our view, we could approach this situation in one of two ways.

The first way would be to publish a report on the meeting held by the Secretariat, at which Solzhenitsyn's attitude was condemned. The draft prepared by the Secretariat Bureau is enclosed. However, a statement like this needs to be further improved, and it could only be published after it has been approved by all the Secretaries of the Board.

A second option is also possible due to some recent developments. After the discussion in the Secretariat, the editorial board of *Novy Mir* signed an agreement with Solzhenitsyn. As of now, they consider *Cancer Ward* ready for publication. This would take care of some of our most serious proposals for establishing relations between publication agencies and Solzhenitsyn on a proper basis. This also signals a substantial change in the position of *Novy Mir*'s editors, who are now in solidarity with the writer.

At the same time, there is reason to believe that at present Solzhenitsyn may be prepared to reconsider some of his views. In particular, in his recent letter to the Secretariat (copy attached) he sounds less militant than in his previous letters and raises less global issues. However, most of his statements still do not conform with reality.

In view of this, it seems appropriate to make another attempt to persuade Solzhenitsyn to condemn the foreign media in the press for using his name for anti-Soviet purposes. It may be worth inviting him for another discussion to explain to him that he can only expect a writers' organization to accommodate him if he acts accordingly.

If another discussion yields no positive results, then stricter measures should be taken, such as publishing something similar to the proposed draft statement.

Since this problem as a whole is very complex and is not an internal literary problem, but rather a political and state problem, we would be extremely grateful for advice on what methods and tactics to use in its resolution. We therefore request that the Central Committee Secretaries receive us together with the leadership of the Culture Department of the Central Committee.

As requested by the Bureau of the Secretariat and the Board of the Soviet Writers' Union.

K. Voronkov
S. Sartakov

Enclosure 1
Draft

Regarding Solzhenitsyn's Letters

The letters *Literaturnaya Gazeta* has received from its readers harshly condemn Solzhenitsyn's act in sending a letter to the Fourth Congress of Soviet Writers, since it has been used for some time now by a number of foreign broadcasting stations as calculated anti-Soviet propaganda, to which the writer himself has not provided an appropriate response. In this connection, readers are wondering what the attitude of the Writers' Union is to Solzhenitsyn's letter.

The editorial board of *Literaturnaya Gazeta* contacted the Soviet Writers' Union, which has provided the following information.

Solzhenitsyn sent a letter to the Fourth Congress of Soviet Writers using the right of a member of the Writers' Union, as stipulated in its Charter, to address the Congress directly. However, contrary to established norms, he sent this letter to 250 different addresses before the Congress opened, obviously expecting that, as a sensational event in literature, it would be further copied and circulated. No wonder under the circumstances that Western propaganda immediately started playing up some of his statements that blatantly distorted the history of Soviet literature and of the public position of Soviet writers.

Since Solzhenitsyn's letter contained references to his manuscripts with which it would take a significant amount of time to become acquainted as well as to check every statement he made in his letter thoroughly, his letter was submitted by the Presidium of the Congress to the Secretariat of the newly elected Board of the Writers' Union for review. At the same time, Solzhenitsyn was informed about the status of the case during a personal interview. However, in early September he sent a second letter to the Writers' Union demanding in a categorical manner that *Cancer Ward* be published immediately. He also stated that otherwise "we would be unable to do anything to prevent it from appearing in the West."

Despite the defiant tone of Solzhenitsyn's letters and his actions, the Secretariat of the Writers' Union Board approached this case from a position of concern for the creative future of one of its members. At the meeting it convened on 22 September this year, these letters were discussed in a calm and objective manner in the presence of Solzhenitsyn.

The meeting was chaired by K. Fedin. An absolute majority of the Secretaries of the Board representing the literatures of all the Soviet Republics took part in the meeting. The Secretaries who were unable to attend for one reason or another expressed their views in writing.

At the meeting it was noted that Solzhenitsyn had exaggerated the violations of socialist legality which had taken place in the past and which had already been condemned by the Twentieth and Twenty-First Party Congresses. In his letter, Solzhenitsyn portrays the evolution of Soviet literature as a neverending process of subjugation by the state agencies responsible for overseeing publishing, thereby slanderously reducing writers to a bunch of miserable time servers and simply nullifying the achievements of Soviet literature that have been recognized by the entire world. He demands that "any censorship of works of art, explicit or hidden, be abolished." In other words, he advocates granting writers unlimited opportunities for publishing their books irrespective of their contents, in the form presented by the writer to the publishing house. In other words, side by side with works of high ideological value, he wishes to open the door to the uncontrolled publication of works of utterly low artistic quality, which would create favorable conditions for the publication of the vilest anti-Soviet ravings. Thus Solzhenitsyn speaks out against the Party's supervision of literature as well as against its ideological and educational importance, striving to disassociate the goals that should be pursued by literature from our national goal, which is the construction of a communist society.

The literary public thinks that when problems arise from time to time between writers, on the one hand, and editors or Glavlit, on the other, they should be resolved by raising the professional and political responsibility of the authors for the work they submit to publishing houses, and staffing with qualified personnel the agencies that are engaged in creative work with writers.

Solzhenitsyn proposes to amend the Writers' Union Charter by including a separate paragraph that would stipulate "all the guarantees of protection that the Union provides to its members who have been subjected to slander and unfair persecution to avoid a repetition of lawlessness in the future." In other words, he wants to place the Charter of the Writers' Union above state laws that guarantee protection for all Soviet citizens against slander and unfair persecution. What he wants to do is grant writers a privileged place in Soviet society.

In his letter Solzhenitsyn attempted to show that he was persecuted, and that some of his manuscripts had been "confiscated by the security services."

As was discovered during the investigation, these statements were untrue. At the request of the Secretariat of the Writers' Union, the Prosecutor's Office stated that Solzhenitsyn's apartment in Ryazan had never been searched, nor had his manuscripts been seized. What did happen was that some typed copies of Solzhenitsyn's manuscripts, whose authorship was unknown, together with other materials, were found in the possession of a certain citizen Teush, and were removed during a search in connection with an investigation initiated by the relevant agencies after a foreign tourist was stopped by customs officers while carrying manuscripts with slanderous statements about life in the Soviet Union.

Equally untrue is Solzhenitsyn's claims that his works were rejected by publishers without reason, in particular, *Cancer Ward*, submitted in turn to the magazines *Novy Mir*, *Zvezda* [The Star], and *Prostor* [Expanse]. Editors-in-Chief of the abovementioned magazines state that they had serious criticisms regarding his work, but that these were made in accordance with the established procedure between writers and publishers. *Novy Mir*, for one, even proposed signing an agreement with Solzhenitsyn, while needless to say requesting he should amend his manuscript substantially. At that time Solzhenitsyn rejected *Novy Mir*'s proposals (now, since the meeting held by the Secretariat, they have signed an agreement with him).

According to the publishing house *Sovietsky Pisatel* [Soviet Writer], Solzhenitsyn did ask them to publish his selected stories previously published in periodicals, but he never submitted a manuscript. The Secretariat sees no grounds for opposing this publication.

In his letter Solzhenitsyn claims that while he "fought during the entire war as a battery commander and has numerous decorations for his service in action," at present rumors were being spread about him to the effect that he "had served his term on criminal charges or had been a POW," "betrayed his motherland" or "served the Germans." He goes on to say that in reality he had been confined to labor camps "for criticizing Stalin." The Secretariat took note of the information received from the relevant agencies that Solzhenitsyn's imprisonment in labor camps was acknowledged as unfounded for lack of evidence by the Military Collegium of the USSR Supreme Court.

The discussion of Solzhenitsyn's letter at the Secretariat was held in a comradely fashion in an atmosphere of genuine concern for the writer's creative future. The participants in the discussion expected Solzhenitsyn to react to instances of political provocation perpetrated by hostile Western media using his name. Regretfully, Solzhenitsyn's conduct at the meeting simply confirmed the demagogic nature of his public statements. Claiming that he was pressed for time, Solzhenitsyn refused even to look at statements the Secretariat had in its possession by anti-Soviet foreign publications applauding his writings. The Secretariat advised Solzhenitsyn to reflect on all that had taken place and then comment on the remarks and proposals he had heard whatever way he wished. After two months had elapsed the Secretariat reminded Solzhenitsyn of this. In response he repeated his complaints in the usual categorical terms. Thus, while addressing sonorous declarations to the Writers' Union in reality Solzhenitsyn ignores it.

When Solzhenitsyn submitted an application for membership to the Soviet Writers' Union, he thereby agreed to act in conformity with the Charter of the Union and the principles of the active involvement of writers in the construction of communism through their creative work. Now he rejects these same principles in his letters. Speaking at the meeting convened by the Secretariat, he went so far as to state that a writer's ideals should not be confined to a certain social system.

Solzhenitsyn's categoric demand that the Secretariat should take a special decision on the immediate publication of *Cancer Ward* met with opposition.

It was stressed that publishers had every right and were competent enough to resolve this question themselves. The Secretariat had no reason to interfere in the work of editorial boards, who would decide for themselves and in a responsible fashion whether a book was ready for publication, and would carry out the necessary negotiations with writers.

Without determining the future of *Cancer Ward* in advance, the participants in the meeting expressed some serious criticisms of the manuscript and stated their hope that Solzhenitsyn would take them into consideration and would approach his work with due responsibility. His future relations with publishers will depend entirely on his own actions. Is he ready to accept the norms of life that are common for us all?

As for Solzhenitsyn's warning that his story might first be published abroad, it is worth noting that hostile Western propaganda has long since developed a knack for appropriating everything that could be directed against the Soviet Union. If foreign publishers display similar interest in *Cancer Ward* as well, which is not yet ready for publication, they will reveal once again their unworthy tricks. It is clear that the writer himself has the right and ability to prevent anyone from publishing his unfinished book, especially when that publication might serve nefarious purposes.

In a frank and substantive discussion, many outstanding Soviet writers reiterated once again the responsibility an artist has to his era and his people. Solzhenitsyn will do well to reflect on this.

It is the duty of every Soviet writer to march in the ranks of his people as they engage in a collective effort to build communism.

Enclosure 2
1 December 1967

To the Secretariat of the USSR Writers' Union, Ryazan:
From your letter No. 3142 of 25 November 1967 I am unable to understand:

1. Whether or not the Secretariat intends to protect me from a three-year-old uninterrupted campaign of slander against me in my own country (unfriendly would be too mild a word for it). (New facts: On 5 October 1967, in the House of the Press in Leningrad, the chief editor of *Pravda*, Zimyanin, repeated in the presence of a large audience the tired lie about my having been a prisoner of war, and he also tried out the possibility of using against me a hackneyed recipe for dealing with awkward customers—declaring me a schizophrenic, and my past in the camps an *idée fixe*. While lecturers from the Moscow Party organization have put forward new lying tales of my "trying to knock together" in the army what they sometimes call a "defeatist" and sometimes a "terrorist" organization. It is difficult to understand why the Military Panel of the Supreme Court failed to spot this in the records of my case.)

2. What measures were taken by the Secretariat to end the illegal prohibition on the use of my published works in libraries, and the instructions issued by the censorship that any mention of my name must be removed from critical articles? In *Voprosy Literatury* [Questions of Literature] even an article translated from Japanese has been treated in this way. In the University of Perm, disciplinary measures have been taken against a group of students who tried to discuss my published works in one of their academic symposia.

3. Whether the Secretariat wants to prevent publication of my book *Cancer Ward* abroad, where we have no control of it, or whether it remains indifferent to this danger. Are any steps being taken to publish excerpts from this novel in *Literaturnaya Gazeta*, and the whole novel in *Novy Mir*?

4. Whether the Secretariat intends to petition the government to adhere to the International Copyright Convention. This would provide our authors with an effective means of protecting their works from illegal publication abroad and from the shameless commercial race between rival translations.

5. During the last six months since I wrote my letter to the Congress, has distribution of the illegal "edition" of excerpts from my archives been stopped and has this "edition" been destroyed?

6. What measures have been taken by the Secretariat to get my sequestered archives and my novel *The First Circle* returned to me, apart from public assurances (by Secretary Ozerov, for instance) that they have already been returned?

7. Has the Secretariat accepted or rejected K. Simonov's suggestion that a collection of my short stories should be published?

8. Why have I not yet received the verbatim transcript of the meeting of the Secretariat on 22 September so that I can study it.

I would be very grateful for clarification of these points.

A. Solzhenitsyn[1]

F. 3, *op.* 80, *d.* 643, *l.* 77–87. Original.

Notes

1. See *The Oak and the Calf*, Appendix 6.

19 Report from the Committee for State Security of the USSR Council of Ministers[1]

No. 218–A
31 January 1968
Classified

To the Central Committee:
According to information we have received, in January 1968 Tvardovsky addressed a letter to K. Fedin calling for measures in support of Solzhenitsyn and for the publication of his new opus, *Cancer Ward*.

The following are excerpts from the letter, obtained through surveillance operations:

> Solzhenitsyn is an extraordinary figure in our literature. I want to remind you of the publication history of *Ivan Denisovich*: the venerable dean of our literature, Chukovsky, entitled his review of it 'A Literary Wonder.'[2] I also remember your high appraisal. I referred to it in my own letter requesting permission to publish *Ivan Denisovich*. I further recall that Sholokhov, although he did not put it in writing, asked me to convey to the author his warmest regards. One prominent leader declared at that time, 'I must note that Solzhenitsyn is acquiring a growing international following. This can't be explained away by 'sensational material.' Dyakov's novel is based on the same sensational material. However, it is as if Dyakov didn't even exist.'[3] As an editor, I am firmly convinced that Zalygin's and Aitmatov's themes are to a great extent responsible for Solzhenitsyn's prose.[4] Not in the sense that these subjects are in fashion, or something of that sort, but their principle is the same: truthfulness. They may still want to write in the old way, but the narrative won't let them; and because no one wants to read them any longer in the old way.
>
> Literary life has become more complex with Solzhenitsyn's appearance. I do not accept Solzhenitsyn whole, without a recognition of his flaws. However, by now, Solzhenitsyn no

longer stands just for himself, but as a portent of a tendency—
do we go backwards or forwards. 'The Solzhenitsyn Affair'
does no honor to the Secretariat [of the Writer's Union] nor,
in the words of Chekhov, "to those on whom this thing
depends." The form of Solzhenitsyn's letter indeed is worthy
of censure. But its contents are so clear and accurate: I do not
remember, in the long series of considerations, a single attempt
to refute its contents. Everyone only talks about the way it was
circulated. And why? Because the contents are indisputable. I
would sign it with both hands. And I am no exception to the
rule, though I have not yet written or signed any documents in
connection with this letter. I myself have addressed the Central
Committee on the subject of censorship on more than one
occasion and even more caustically than Solzhenitsyn. And
regarding Solzhenitsyn's personal fate, if I may say so, I have
already spoken everywhere. It is hopeless to decide this matter
by arguing only. One way or another, we must admit that
Solzhenitsyn has completely overshadowed the shallow bab-
blings of the congress. 'The Solzhenitsyn Affair' has become
the most significant question currently facing the Writers'
Union. What is most disturbing and shocking is that Solzhenitsyn is willing to air his complaints against the Writers' Union
in any auditorium or in the press, whereas the Union can allow
itself neither the one nor the other. . . .

Your position deeply upsets me, you, the friend of Gorky,
the perpetuator of his tradition. And Sholokhov? He recently
wrote: 'We ought not to let Solzhenitsyn near a pen.' Neither
access to a pen nor to the printing press! Like Shevchenko,
who was forbidden to write or paint in exile.[5] . . . This is particularly depressing in light of the well-known literary and political statements by [Sholokhov] the author of *And Quiet Flows the
Don*, who has so demeaned himself in the eyes of the reading
public. To rebuke! Dissociate yourself! Serebryakov and Voz-
nesensky have dissociated themselves. These dissociations
cause us great harm. They engender an image of writers as
people who are undiscriminating in the moral and ethical
sense, who lack a sense of self-dignity and who are entirely
dependent on orders.

. . . It was proposed to me that I use my influence with
Solzhenitsyn. In the first place, there is no point in exaggerat-
ing my influence on him. He is not at all a young author under
apprenticeship to me. This year, by the way, he will turn 50

years of age. He's a grownup. And secondly, what am I to
advise him to do? Should I tell him to castigate those Western
writers who have supported his letter and who want to publish
his *Cancer Ward*? And how about the communists? Do communist comrades in the West also support his letter and also want
to publish *Cancer Ward*? And what should he do with them,
castigate them or not?

Some ancient writer said, if a book elevates the spirit, if a
book inspires some noble impulse, then it is already a good
book. And Solzhenitsyn's book is precisely of this kind. . . . Our
interest in having this novel published is greater than that of
the author himself. It is criminal to conceal such an important
work. The novel has already circulated, perhaps in thousands
of copies. In the coming days it may be published in France
and, according to my information, it is being prepared for publication in Italy. The last thing we need is a repetition of the
Pasternak affair. And then there are domestic considerations. If
this novel is delayed during typesetting it will go to the head of
a list of all those books delayed, but not yet forbidden by anyone. For example, Simonov's *One Hundred Days* and Bek's *New
Assignment*—a bottleneck is created.[6] And in order to free it up
we must use our brainpans. And it all depends on you, entirely
on you. The Secretariat would support you if you agreed. To
have this matter decided by the editorial board of *Novy Mir* is
what I am asking of you. . . .

What do you have to gain from this whole affair now? I
don't think that you will be able to polish the final pages of
Bonfire[7] with a clear conscience after having been directly
involved in burying the completed work of a comrade. . . . I am
not so naive as to presume that you will suddenly burst into
tears and change your point of view, but circumstances will
oblige you to. 'Necessity will force you to eat humble pie.' I
call upon you to act in a manner consonant with reason and
conscience. I cannot suppose that you are burdened by outside
pressures or motives. Thank god those times are past! It is we
who must decide the problems of literary life. We are not
going to receive direct orders. Do you fear to make a decision
in case it is the wrong decision? But you know, an incorrect
decision is better than none at all. You are facing a double-
edged sword—to affix your name to a shameful decision or to a
no less shameful non-decision. And besides, just between you
and me, the history of world literature knows no instance when

the persecution of talent met with success.

You have heard me, Fedin—you are a person of honor, a noble person. You defended me in 1954 at the very top, when I was removed.[8] You will understand my letter correctly. The dog's bark is worse than his bite. I am incapable of back-stabbing. My caustic manner at the last meeting of the Secretariat was due to your inexplicable irritability with respect to Solzhenitsyn. Solzhenitsyn has paid for every written line in a way none of us have. He has endured war, prison, and terminal illness, and is now being unofficially subjected to political ostracism. I understand the degree of his desperation and find it humanly impossible to cast stones even over the form of his letter. . . . I know that you are busy and I do not expect an answer, but I await your decision.

This report is provided for information purposes.

Chairman of the Committee for State Security
Andropov

F. 3, op. 80, *d.* 643, *l.* 72–75. Original.

Notes

1. *Distributed to Politburo members and candidate members, and Central Committee secretaries, on 13 February 1968 as P238.*
2. Kornei Chukovsky (1882–1969), a well-known poet and writer of books for children, was the doyen of Soviet literature. The review referred to by Tvardovsky was one of several internal reviews of *One Day in the Life of Ivan Denisovich* that Tvardovsky commissioned before approaching Party officials with the book. When Solzhenitsyn's novel and early works were seized by the KGB, Chukovsky offered him refuge for a while at his dacha in Peredelkino (the writers' colony just outside Moscow).
3. *Endurance*, a feeble and unconvincing novel about camp life by Party loyalist Boris Dyakov, was widely thought to have been specially commissioned by the authorities to counterbalance Solzhenitsyn's novel. Dyakov later appeared as an "expert witness" at meetings of the Writers' Union held to discredit Solzhenitsyn.
4. Sergei Zalygin was a controversial exponent of so-called "village prose," who set many of his stories and novels in Siberia. Zalygin denounced the negative impact of collectivization on the Russian peasants and the folly of the Party's agricultural policies. Chingiz Aitmatov, a writer from Kirghizia, also contrasted the evils of collectivization with an idyllic picture of Kirghizian nomadic life in its traditional forms.

5. Taras Shevchenko (1814–1861), the romantic poet and finest writer ever produced by the Ukraine, was arrested and exiled in 1847 for writing in the Ukrainian language, which was officially banned at the time.

6. Simonov's *One Hundred Days* was based on the diaries and notebooks he had kept as a correspondent during World War II, and gave a more truthful picture of wartime Russia than was contained in his novels and stories. Its publication was announced and postponed several times. Alexander Bek's novel *The New Appointment*, an unorthodox account of Stalin's dealings with his Minister of Steel Production I. Tevosyan, was blocked by censorship and eventually appeared in the West in 1972.

7. *The Bonfire*, an enormous trilogy of novels in Socialist Realist style, was Fedin's last and longest work.

8. In 1954 Tvardovsky's first stint as editor of *Novy Mir* was ended by his dismissal for publishing a number of works that were too liberal for the times. He was restored to the editorship in 1958 and remained until he was forced out again in 1970, one year before his death.

20 Memorandum from the USSR Foreign Ministry and the Central Committee Department of Relations with Communist and Workers' Parties of Socialist Nations[1]

No 1506/GS
No. 15–D–887
16 June 1968
Classified

To the Central Committee:
According to a communiqué from the Soviet Ambassador in Belgrade, the Yugoslav newspaper *Delo*[2] in June of this year printed a positive review of Solzhenitsyn's slanderous book, *Cancer Ward*, and began publishing excerpts from it.

The Yugoslav government is aware that this book has not been published in the USSR, that it was delivered to the West illegally, and that even American publishers have refused to print it.

Accordingly, this department of the Central Committee and the USSR Foreign Ministry consider it advisable to direct the Soviet Ambassador in

Belgrade to visit the Yugoslav Foreign Ministry and to express our bewilderment in regard to the said unfriendly publications in the Yugoslav press.

A draft resolution is enclosed.[3]

Please review.

A. Gromyko

K. Rusakov

F. 3, *op.* 68, *d.* 838, *l.* 133. Original.

Notes

1. *Sent to Politburo members for a vote on 17 June 1968 under No. 86–22.*
2. *Delo* [Work] was the daily newspaper of the Slovenian Communist Party published in Ljubljana, the capital of Slovenia.
3. *The Politburo passed resolution P87/7 on 21 June 1968 (see Document 21).*

21 Politburo Resolution "On a Verbal Communication to the Secretariat of the Ministry of Foreign Affairs of the Republic of Yugoslavia in Connection with the Publication of Solzhenitsyn's *Cancer Ward* in the Yugoslav Newspaper *Delo*"

No. P87/7
21 June 1968
Top Secret

To approve the draft of instructions to be given to the Soviet Ambassador to Yugoslavia regarding this question (enclosed).

Central Committee Secretary

Enclosure
Re: point 7 of minutes No. 87
Classified

Belgrade
To the Soviet Ambassador:
Visit the Minister of Foreign Affairs of Yugoslavia or his deputy and tell him the following:

> The Yugoslav newspaper *Delo*—an organ of the Socialist League of Working Peoples of Slovenia—printed on 1 and 3 June of this year a positive review of the so-called novel by Solzhenitsyn, *Cancer Ward*, and on 4 June began publication of excerpts from it.
>
> The Yugoslav government is aware that this book has not been published in the USSR, that it was delivered to the West illegally, and that even American publishers have refused to print it.

While directing your attention to these publications by *Delo*, I would like to express our bewilderment over the fact that a newspaper of a friendly nation has considered it possible to make its pages available to the publication of materials that slander the Soviet Union.

For our part, we have more than once drawn the attention of official representatives of the Republic of Yugoslavia to the fact that such publications in the Yugoslav press do not correspond to the friendly nature of relations between our two countries.

We expect our Yugoslav comrades to understand our appeal correctly and to undertake appropriate measures to prevent publications that damage the development of neighborly relations between the Soviet Union and the Union of Federated Republics of Yugoslavia.

Telegraph confirmation.

F. 3, *op.* 80, *d.* 643, *l.* 88–89. Excerpt from transcript.

1969

22 Memorandum from the Central Committee Culture Department "On the Writer A. Solzhenitsyn Regarding the Publication of His Works Abroad"[1]

22 January 1969
Classified

To the Central Committee:
According to available information, the publication of certain of Solzhenitsyn's manuscripts sent abroad through illegal channels is being actively pursued in a number of foreign countries. Several publishers in the United States, West Germany, Italy, England, and France have already brought out the novel *The First Circle* and the novel *Cancer Ward*. Excerpts from these works are also being published in the periodical press of Yugoslavia.

As has already been reported to the Central Committee, these works by Solzhenitsyn contain serious ideological and artistic shortcomings and have antisocialist tendencies. It is entirely clear that the publication of these works abroad is accompanied by a noisy, propagandistic campaign on the "suppression" of artistic freedoms in the USSR and is being used as the basis for routine anti-Soviet attacks.

The Secretariat of the Soviet Writers' Union has repeatedly drawn Solzhenitsyn's attention to the errors in his ideological and artistic positions and in his civic conduct. In September 1967, the Secretariat of the Board of the Soviet Writers' Union, under the chairmanship of K.A. Fedin, resolutely condemned Solzhenitsyn's letter to the Fourth Congress of Soviet Writers; gave a responsible, critical evaluation of the works that he insisted be published; and demanded from Solzhenitsyn that he publicly dissociate himself from the anti-Soviet uproar that has been raised abroad in connection with his name.

Solzhenitsyn failed to comply with the demands of the Secretariat of the Soviet Writers' Union. Moreover, when it became known that some bourgeois publishers were preparing to print *Cancer Ward*, Solzhenitsyn, instead of making a public declaration of his attitude, addressed to *Literaturnaya Gazeta* a short letter containing only a formal objection against the publication of his manuscripts abroad without his permission.

Since Solzhenitsyn has persisted in maintaining his mistaken positions, the Secretariat of the Board of the Writers' Union considered it essential to accompany the aforementioned letter with an article entitled "The Ideological Struggle: The Responsibility of the Writer" (*Literaturnaya Gazeta* of 26 June of last year), in which it proffered a responsible evaluation of the work and conduct of this writer. The article pointed out that Solzhenitsyn's creative future depends on himself, and on his attitude to the criticisms expressed at the meeting of the Secretariat of the Writers' Union.

Solzhenitsyn's conduct in recent months indicates that he has not drawn the requisite conclusions.

Voices in the Writers' Union are beginning to say that the time is ripe to consider the question of Solzhenitsyn's continuing presence in the ranks of the Union. At the same time, it has been noted that his expulsion from the Writers' Union should be carried out in the Ryazan Section of the Russian Writers' Union, where this writer is enrolled as a member, with subsequent confirmation of the decision by the Secretariat of the Russian Writers' Union.

We find ourselves able to agree with the opinion of the Soviet Writers' Union.

Please review.

Head of the Culture Department of the Central Committee
V. Shauro

F. 3, op. 80, d. 643, l. 90–91. Original.

Notes

1. *On the first page of the resolution is the note: "Politburo. To be circulated. For agreement. M. Suslov (also ask Comrade Demichev)" and the signatures of D. Polyansky, K. Mazurov, N. Podgorny, A. Shelepin, G. Voronov, A. Pelshe, A. Kosygin, and P. Demichev; on the last page is the notation: "Comrade V.F. Shauro has been informed. N. Solvyev."*

23 Report of the Central Committee Culture Department "Writers' Responses to the Expulsion of Solzhenitsyn from the Soviet Writers' Union"[1]

13 November 1969

To the Central Committee:
The decision regarding the expulsion of Solzhenitsyn from the Writers' Union[2] has been actively supported by influential authors in our country.

"Solzhenitsyn had long ago placed himself outside the Union. This final solution is a logical conclusion to what took place at the meeting of the Writers' Union Secretariat in September 1967," said Konstantin Fedin.

"My opinion is contained in my letter to the Writers' Union Secretariat," said Sholokhov. "At that time already I insisted on the expulsion of Solzhenitsyn from the Writers' Union."

"The fact that such an uproar has been raised around Solzhenitsyn in the West," said Alexander Chakovsky,[3] "convinces me even more that the decision to expel him from the ranks of the Writers' Union is correct and timely."

"I am an implacable ideological opponent of Solzhenitsyn in every respect," declared Alexei Surkov.[4] "This question had to be decided sooner or later."

"Even though this action will provoke another wave of anti-Soviet propaganda abroad," said Boris Polevoy,[5] "he had to be expelled. It all became clear after the Fourth Congress of Soviet Writers, where Solzhenitsyn essentially appealed for support from bourgeois propagandists."

"Our Union," said Sergei Smirnov,[6] "is an organization that brings together people who think alike politically. The writer is obligated to fulfill the demands of membership. Solzhenitsyn did not do so."

"A person who resolves to use his creativity in the service of the enemy, of anti-Soviet propaganda," said Antonina Koptaeva, "cannot continue in our ranks."

"I already said at the meeting of the Writers' Union that I do not wish to be a member of the same organization as Solzhenitsyn," declared Vadim Kozhevnikov.

"The problem of Solzhenitsyn had to be resolved, and resolved without delay. The writers of Ryazan acted appropriately," said the poet Yegor Isaev.

The same opinion is held by Petrus Brovka, Mustay Karim, Georgy Berezko, Sergei Vasilyev, Elizar Maltsev, Vasily Ardamatsky, Vladimir Firsov, and many others.

There is also evidence of negative attitudes to the expulsion of Solzhenitsyn from the Writers' Union.

Alexander Tvardovsky, in a conversation with one of the Secretaries of the Writers' Union, Konstantin Voronkov, called the resolution of the Ryazan writers' organization and of the RSFSR Writers' Union Board inadmissible and incorrect. He declared that Solzhenitsyn was "an outstanding writer of our times," and that his expulsion from the Writers' Union would not be approved by Soviet and foreign intellectuals.

The poet Semyon Kirsanov said that it may have been better not to expel Solzhenitsyn from the Writers' Union, but to force him to resign from the organization.

The RSFSR Writers' Union Board and local writers' organizations are carrying on the work of clarifying questions arising in connection with the expulsion of Solzhenitsyn from the Writers' Union.

Reported for information purposes.

Head of the Culture Department of the Central Committee
V. Shauro

F. 3, *op.* 80, *d.* 643, *l.* 93–94. Original.

Notes

1. *A separate page bears the directive: "Inform the Central Committee Secretaries and also V.I. Stepankov" and the signatures of B. Ponomarev, K. Katushev, D. Ustinov, I. Kapitonov, M. Suslov, P. Demichev, A. Kirilenko, and V. Stepankov.*

2. Solzhenitsyn was expelled from the Writers' Union at a hastily called meeting of the Ryazan Branch of the Union on 4 November 1969.

3. A prominent loyalist and mediocre novelist who was editor of the *Literaturnaya Gazeta*.

4. See Document 6, Note 2.

5. Editor of the formerly liberal journal *Yunost* [Youth].

6. The rest of the writers cited here (with the exception of Tvardovsky and Kirsanov) are or were nonentities.

24 Report of the Central Committee Culture Department "On the Responses of Writers to Solzhenitsyn's Antisocial Activities"[1]

18 November 1969

To the Central Committee:

The anti-Soviet uproar that has been raised by bourgeois propaganda in connection with the expulsion of Solzhenitsyn from the Writers' Union and his subsequent antisocial activities (sending information abroad on the meeting of the Ryazan Writers' Organization and publishing a so-called "transcript" of this meeting in the bourgeois press, etc)[2] has provoked the just indignation of many Soviet writers.

Leonid Leonov, Lenin Prize laureate and Hero of Socialist Labor,[3] declared that "Solzhenitsyn has gone too far, has lost any true notion of his place in society. The writer can, of course, portray negative phenomena in his work, but to pour salt into the wound is not permissible and is irresponsible."

Nikolai Tikhonov, Hero of Socialist Labor,[4] fully approved Solzhenitsyn's expulsion from the Writers' Union as a measure that was timely and justified.

The poet Sergei Narovchatov emphasized that Solzhenitsyn was behaving "like an open anti-Soviet. It is shameful for a Russian writer to appeal to the enemies of his motherland."

Boris Suchkov, director of the A.M. Gorky Institute of World Literature, deems Solzhenitsyn's anticivic conduct worthy of the most severe censure.

The Secretary of the RSFSR Writers' Union Board, Daniil Granin, who, as was reported earlier, abstained from voting on the question of expelling Solzhenitsyn from the Writers' Union,[5] reconsidered his position and officially addressed a request to the RSFSR Writers' Union Board to consider the Secretariat's decision to expel Solzhenitsyn as unanimous.

At the same time, various writers (S. Antonov, G. Baklanov, B. Okudzhava, B. Tendryakov, B. Mozhaev)[6] verbally requested the Soviet Writers' Union to review the Solzhenitsyn affair before a plenum of the Union. A similar request was contained in a telegram sent by A. Arbuzov, Y. Yevtushenko, and A. Shtein from the Writers' Retreat in Gagra.[6]

A discussion with some of these writers was held at the Central Committee Culture Department, at the Moscow District Party Committee, and at the Soviet Writers' Union. After being properly informed, the writers S. Antonov and G. Baklanov retracted their requests.

The Moscow City Party Committee has scheduled a meeting of the Party Committee and the Secretariat of the Moscow Writers' Organization together with the Party cell leaders, to hear reports from Comrades L. Sobolev and K. Voronkov and adopt an appropriate resolution.

On 5 November of this year, the American newspaper *The New York Times* published Solzhenitsyn's so-called "open letter" to the Secretariat of the RSFSR Writers' Union.[7] It should be noted that the original of this letter was not received by the RSFSR Writers' Union until 17 November. This fact again underscores the premeditated nature of Solzhenitsyn's actions and his efforts to appeal to bourgeois propaganda.

The contents of Solzhenitsyn's letter caused indignation among members of the RSFSR Writers' Union Secretariat. The chairman of the Board, Leonid Sobolev, announced that Solzhenitsyn's letter left no doubt that its author had conclusively adopted the position of an overt opponent of our social order. In the name of his comrades in the Secretariat, Leonid Sobolev expressed the opinion that Solzhenitsyn's conduct was incompatible with the status of a Soviet citizen.

The USSR and RSFSR Writers' Unions propose to publish an article in the literary press that will issue a sharp rebuttal to Solzhenitsyn and will provide a responsible assessment of his antisocial activities.

A detailed account of Solzhenitsyn's conduct and opinions will be placed in the newsletter of the Soviet Writers' Union, which is distributed to local writers' organizations throughout the country.

Reported for information purposes.

Deputy Head of the Culture Department of the Central Committee
Y. Melentiev

F. 3, *op.* 80, *d.* 643, *l.* 96–97. Original.

Notes

1. *Sent to Politburo members and candidate members, and Central Committee Secretaries, on 19 November 1969 as No. P1985.*
2. Solzhenitsyn had made his own record of the proceedings of the meeting at which he was expelled and had sent his transcript abroad, from where it was transmitted back by Western radio stations.

3. A talented older novelist of the twenties and thirties who had been worn down by Party pressures and became a conformist in his later years. Same generation as Fedin and Sholokhov, but not as venial as either of them.

4. Another writer of the older generation who had shown talent in the twenties but lost his nerve later. Closer to Fedin than to Leonov in his conformism.

5. A cautiously liberal novelist of the middle generation who wrote about the idealistic aspirations of engineers and scientists.

6. Writers of the middle generation who espoused generally liberal positions but stopped just short of dissidence.

7. In his letter Solzhenitsyn accused the Union of violating its own statutes and deciding on his expulsion in advance of the Ryazan meeting. He also protested against the refusal to give him a proper right of reply, and continued: "Blow the dust off the clock. Your watches are behind the times. Throw open the heavy curtains that are so dear to you—you don't even suspect that day has already dawned outside. . . . The time is near when each of you will seek to erase his signature from today's resolution. Blind leading the blind! You don't even notice that you are wandering in the opposite direction from the one you announced yourselves. At this time of crisis, you are incapable of suggesting anything constructive for our grievously sick society—only your malevolent vigilance and your 'hold tight and don't let go' attitude."

25 Report of the Moscow City Party Committee[1]

No. 328
20 November 1969

To the Central Committee:
We consider it essential to inform the Central Committee of the responses and statements of Moscow writers in connection with the publication of V. Kochetov's novel *What Do You Want?*,[2] and the expulsion of Solzhenitsyn from the Writers' Union.

In total, the Moscow Writers' Organization has in excess of 1,600 members and leads a full-blooded creative and political life. The overwhelming majority of the writers are involved in sociopolitical work, actively participate in artistic discussions, and take part in the political education network.

The writers are striving to commemorate the centennial of V.I. Lenin's birth with new productions of the highest ideological and artistic merit. The mood among the writers is good; they comment that they highly value the attention paid to writers by the Central Committee and the awarding of medals to numerous writers for their services to the development of Soviet literature.

The writers of the capital enthusiastically endorse the domestic and foreign policies of our Party and its program of widening the struggle against bourgeois ideology, and they express a lively interest in current political and international events.

The expulsion of Solzhenitsyn from the Soviet Writers' Union has attracted a great deal of attention from writers. The majority of Moscow writers approve the simple fact of Solzhenitsyn's expulsion. At the same time, it is noted that Solzhenitsyn's conduct is openly anti-Soviet and provocative, and that Solzhenitsyn rudely ignored the Writers' Organization, removed himself from its activities, and provided the bourgeois press with slanderous materials.

However, some writers express doubt whether the appropriate time was chosen for the expulsion of Solzhenitsyn. The writers P. Sazhin and N. Aroseva have posed the questions: "Why was he not expelled earlier? The facts of Solzhenitsyn's improper conduct have been known for a long time. What occurred that was new?" Writers appearing publicly in recent days have told us that similar questions are being posed during lectures and discussions.

The brief notices in *Literaturnaya Gazeta* and *Literaturnaya Rossia* about Solzhenitsyn's expulsion from the Soviet Writers' Union did not satisfy all writers. Individual writers, who in principle support the decision on Solzhenitsyn, think that the expulsion was rushed, that this will, so to say, reflect poorly on the attitudes of the intelligentsia of foreign countries towards the Soviet Union.

A group of writers—the non-Party members Y. Trifonov, S. Antonov, and B. Mozhaev; the Communists V. Tendryakov, G. Baklanov, and B. Okudzhava—have appealed to the Writers' Union Secretariat with a proposal to convene a plenum of the Board of the Soviet Writers' Union, at which the question of Solzhenitsyn would be re-examined.

The Moscow Writers' Organization, the Moscow City Party Committee, the Krasnopresnensk and Zhdanov District Party Committees have held discussions with the aforementioned writers (except for Okudzhava, who is away from Moscow), in the process of which Baklanov and Antonov retracted their requests.

Meanwhile, Tendryakov[3] and Mozhaev[4] continue to insist on their proposal, and have even declared that the expulsion "of the most visible representative of Russian literature" is an "insult to every honest writer," and that they will seek the convocation of a special plenum of the Writers' Union where, as Tendryakov declared, "it is not yet clear who will be in the majority." If a plenum of the Writers' Union is not convened, they will consider other measures to express their protest against the expulsion of Solzhenitsyn from the Writers' Union.

The playwrights A. Arbuzov and A. Shtein; the poet Y. Yevtushenko, who is now on vacation in Gagra; and the writers L. Kopelev[5] and L. Chukovskaya[6] hold analogous opinions.

Some communist writers believe that the expulsion of Solzhenitsyn from the Soviet Writers' Union and the appearance of Kochetov's novel create complications for the Moscow Writers Organization's party election meetings and for the meeting to select the delegates to the Third Congress of Writers of the RSFSR.[7]

The Moscow City Party Committee has scheduled a joint meeting of the Party committee and the Secretariat of the Moscow Writers' Organization with the Party cell leadership, which will decide on measures for intensifying work among Moscow writers in support of the decision of the Board of the RSFSR Writers' Union Secretariat on Solzhenitsyn.

We will redouble our efforts in preparing for pre-election meetings in the Writers' Organization and the press, and insure that meetings of writers to select delegates to the RSFSR Writers' Congress are thoroughly prepared.

Secretary of the Moscow City Party Committee
V. Grishin

F. 3, op. 80, d. 643, l. 99–101. Original.

Notes

1. *A separate page bears the directive: "Inform Central Committee Secretaries, and also Comrades V.F. Shauro and V.I. Stepankov" and the signatures of B. Ponomarev, D. Ustinov, K. Katushev, I. Kapitonov, A. Kirilenko, M. Suslov, F. Kulakov, P. Demichev, and V. Stepankov; on the last page there is the notation: "Comrade V.F. Shauro has been informed. G. Dyakonov 18.12.69."*

2. Vsevolod Kochetov was the editor of the conservative journal *Oktyabr* [October] and a notorious Party hack ever willing to write works to order. His novel *What Do You Want?* was expressly directed against Solzhenitsyn and other dissidents and made the author a laughing stock in Soviet literary circles.

3. Vladimir Tendryakov, the finest short story writer of the middle generation, had come to prominence during Khrushchev's "Thaw" and was a precursor of the "village prose" writers of the sixties and seventies.

4. Boris Mozhaev was a contemporary of Tendryakov and also wrote about village life. His preferred genre, however, was the novel rather than the short story. He also lived not far from Ryazan and had recently become a personal friend of Solzhenitsyn's.

5. Lev Kopelev, a critic and scholar of German literature, had been arrested at about the same time as Solzhenitsyn toward the end of World War II and had become friends with him when they were both prisoners in the *sharashka*. It was Kopelev who had introduced Solzhenitsyn to Tvardovsky and the *Novy Mir* board.

6. Lydia Chukovskaya was the daughter of Kornei Chukovsky (see Document 19, Note 2) and a talented novelist and journalist in her own right. She had become friendly with Solzhenitsyn when the latter stayed for a while at her father's dacha in Peredelkino.

7. *The Third RSFSR Writers' Congress was held in March 1970.*

PART II
1970–1971
NOBEL PRIZE

26 Central Committee Secretariat Resolution "On Measures in Connection with the Act of Provocation of Awarding the 1970 Nobel Prize for Literature to A. Solzhenitsyn"

No. St–112/gs
9 October 1970
Top Secret

To approve the proposal expressed in the communiqué from the Culture Department and Propaganda Department of the Central Committee (enclosed).

Central Committee Secretary
M. Suslov

Enclosure 1
Re: p. 1 gs, pr. No 112
9 October 1970

To the Central Committee:
On 8 October of this year, the Nobel Committee (of Stockholm, Sweden) awarded the 1970 Prize for Literature to Solzhenitsyn, with the citation: "For the ethical force with which he is developing the valuable traditions of Russian literature." As is known, Solzhenitsyn's candidacy for this prize was proposed in earlier years as well.

The works and conduct of Solzhenitsyn have been used for some time by bourgeois propaganda for anti-Soviet purposes. Awarding him the Nobel Prize is calculated to intensify this campaign further.

We consider it advisable:

1. To publish in the Soviet press (in the newspapers *Izvestia*, *Trud*, *Komsomolskaya Pravda*, and *Literaturnaya Gazeta*) a brief statement from the

Secretariat of the Board of the Soviet Writers' Union, explaining that the abovementioned action of the Nobel Committee is of a political rather than literary nature. The statement can be produced in the form of answers to questions from an *Izvestia* reporter.

2. To publish a feature in *Literaturnaya Gazeta* exposing the nature of the political manipulation of the name and works of Solzhenitsyn in the West.[1]

3. To direct the State Radio and Television Committee of the Council of Soviet Ministers (Comrade Lapin) and the Press and News Agency (Comrade Udaltsov), in view of the decision of the Nobel Prize Committee, to prepare and disseminate to foreign countries through appropriate channels the necessary propaganda materials.

4. To inform the leaders of local Party committees (in verbal form) of the provocative nature of the awarding of the Nobel Prize to Solzhenitsyn.

Culture Department and Propaganda Department of the Central Committee

Enclosure 2
Re: p. 1 gs, pr. No. 112

"A Dishonorable Game"[2]
(On the Award of the Nobel Prize to Solzhenitsyn)

According to information from foreign newspapers and radio, the Nobel Committee has awarded its prize for literature to Solzhenitsyn.

In connection with this, the Writers' Union Secretariat has made a statement to an *Izvestia* correspondent:

> As is already known to the public, the writings of this author, which were illegally sent abroad and published there, have long been used by reactionary circles in the West for anti-Soviet purposes.
>
> Soviet writers have repeatedly expressed in print their reactions to the artistic production and conduct of Solzhenitsyn, which have come, as was remarked by the RSFSR Writers' Union Board Secretariat, into conflict with the principles and problems of the independent association of Soviet writers. Soviet writers have expelled Solzhenitsyn from their Union. As we know, this decision was actively supported by all the representative leaders of the country.

We can only lament that the Nobel Committee allowed itself to be drawn into a dishonorable game, which is being played out hardly in the interest of developing spiritual values and literary traditions, but rather is dictated by speculative political views.

F. 3, op. 80, d. 644, l. 1–3. Excerpt from transcript.

Notes

1. *This article, "On the Question of Priorities," was published in* Literaturnaya Gazeta *on 14 October 1970.*

2. *Published in* Pravda *on 10 October 1970.*

27 Report of the Chief Directorate for the Preservation of Government Secrets in the Press [Glavlit] of the USSR Council of Ministers[1]

No. 988s
13 October 1970
Classified

To the Central Committee:
For information purposes we report that in connection with the award of the Nobel Prize to Solzhenitsyn, the press organizations of a number of communist parties in capitalist countries have printed articles and reports that are essentially positive in their appraisal of Solzhenitsyn's writings and conduct. From some of these publications it is possible to conclude that the decision of the Swedish Academy of Sciences is being used for daily attacks on the policies of the Communist Party of the Soviet Union.

On 9 October, the [Italian] newspaper *L'Unita* published a lengthy selection of materials, in excess of 250 lines, on the award of the prize to Solzhenitsyn, including a portrait of the writer. The selection included information from Stockholm, a report by Guerra from Moscow that attempts to prove the great authority and respect which Solzhenitsyn enjoys in the Soviet Union, citing the results of a readers' poll allegedly made by *Literaturnaya Gazeta*. The main feature is a long article by Giuseppe Boffa, "His Works and His Misfortunes." The article sets out Solzhenitsyn's biography and describes his works, paying particular attention to those not published in the USSR that have appeared in the West, which, according to the author, "have secured Solzhenitsyn's fame as a writer." Furthermore, Boffa lists the "services" of *L'Unita* in the defense of Solzhenitsyn: the newspaper published his letter to foreign editors, declared itself against his expulsion from the Writers' Union, and proclaims:

> It was precisely because of his right, upon which Solzhenitsyn insists, to disagree with the official point of view prevailing in socialist societies that he gained our attention. . . . The thoughts and works of Solzhenitsyn can be accepted or rejected, but they are an irrevocable component of that contradictory motion without which the development and affirmation of socialist society is impossible.

On 9 October, [the French] *L'Humanité* printed a long article by A. Wurmser, "Solzhenitsyn, Nobel Laureate." In his article, the author initially, and not without reason, criticizes the Swedish Academy of Sciences for the political tendency apparent in its award to Solzhenitsyn. However, having said this, Wurmser writes in reverential tones of "the great writer and his wonderful books," of how close the sufferings of the people are to him (Solzhenitsyn), and how well he understands the hopes and desires of the Soviet people. Wurmser concludes his hymn of praise thus: "The question is not whether Solzhenitsyn's understanding of the world pleases us, for it is clear that the Nobel Prize was unquestionably awarded to a valuable writer."

Wurmser's review of Solzhenitsyn and his novels satisfies the demands of bourgeois publishers. This may explain the fact that the largest bourgeois newspaper [in France], *Le Monde*, reprinted on 10 October the conclusion of Wurmser's article in its entirety without any comments whatsoever.

Volksstimme [Voice of the People], the organ of the Austrian Communist Party, in its issue for 9–10 October, published an article by Wimmer, "The Nobel Prize for Solzhenitsyn." Although the author "condemns" the political actions of the reactionary Swedish Academy, he quotes in detail from its decision, in which Solzhenitsyn is presented as "the son of Lenin's revolution, who has guarded the great democratic tradition of Russian literature," and calls Solzhenitsyn "a powerful humanist," even though his writings "may be used against socialism." Wimmer regards the reasons given for the nonpublication of Solzhenitsyn's most recent novels in the USSR as unconvincing. In this connection he cites Brecht: "The government must never fear works of art. Woe to those who take medicine for poison." On the whole the article is contradictory, although written in an objectivist spirit.

On 9 October, *Land og Folk* [Land of the People], the Dutch Communist newspaper, printed an article entitled "Solzhenitsyn Has Been Awarded the Nobel Prize," with an accompanying photograph of Solzhenitsyn. A large portion of the article is taken up by a biographical note, which is written in laudatory tones. The editors emphasize the words of the Secretary General of the Swedish Academy of Sciences that "Solzhenitsyn had never sold out his convictions." The newspaper also reports that Solzhenitsyn has gratefully accepted the decision awarding him the prize and expects to come to Stockholm to receive it.

On 9 October, *The Morning Star* (published by the Communist Party of Great Britain) printed a note, "Solzhenitsyn Receives the Nobel Prize," which describes in detail the decision of the Swedish Academy of Sciences and Solzhenitsyn's agreement to receive the prize. The note also states that "only one of Solzhenitsyn's novels has appeared in the USSR, while two other more significant works were not published."

In its 9 October issue, *Kansan Uutiset*, the newspaper of the Communist Party of Finland, likewise informed its readers of the award to Solzhenitsyn, sympathetically presenting his life and the novels he has written and declaring that "they help us to better understand human suffering." In noting Solzhenitsyn's expulsion from the Soviet Writers' Union, the newspaper stressed the fact that "membership provides the right to publish in the country."

The principal Yugoslav newspapers reacted in the same spirit to the awarding of the Nobel Prize to Solzhenitsyn. The 9 October issue of *Borba* [Struggle] printed Solzhenitsyn's portrait and a note about his award, bringing to the attention of readers the "unjust treatment" accorded him in his motherland: "even though his reputation is enormous (Yevtushenko called him 'the only Russian classic'), he is not recognized in his own country." The newspaper *Politika*, in its issue for the same date, prints the text of the decision of the Swedish Academy of Sciences and declares: "Solzhenitsyn is the product of Soviet society, its expression. His position is that of a new Dostoevsky. . . . The conservative Swedish Academy of Sciences made only a political gesture, but historians and literary critics will give him a true literary appreciation."

All these newspapers have been confiscated by the Glavlit controller and prevented from going on sale.

Head of Glavlit of the USSR Council of Ministers
P. Romanov

F. 3, op. 80, d. 644, l. 7–9. Original.

Notes

1. *Distributed to Politburo members and candidate members, and Central Committee Secretaries, on 20 October 1970 as No. P1927.*

28 Letter from A. Solzhenitsyn to M. Suslov[1]

14 October 1970
To the Secretary of the Central Committee
Comrade M.A. Suslov

Dear Mikhail Andreyevich!
I am writing to you in particular, remembering that you and I were introduced in December 1962 and that you, at the time, expressed sympathy with my work.[2]

I ask you personally to consider and to communicate to the other members of the government leadership the following proposal.

I propose that there be a reconsideration of the situation that has been created around me and my works by the unconscientious functionaries of the Writers' Union, who have provided the government with false information.

As is known to you, I have been awarded the Nobel Prize for Literature. In the period of the eight weeks preceding the awards ceremony, the government leadership has the opportunity to energetically alter the literary situation, so that the ceremony can proceed under much more auspicious circumstances than is now possible. Because the time left us is short, I will limit my proposal to its minimal dimensions:

1) To publish in the shortest possible period of time (under my personal editorship), in book form and in a significant press run, and to permit the free sale of my novel *Cancer Ward* (if Goslitizdat [State Literary Publishing House] is so ordered, the whole job can be done in two to three weeks). The banning of this book, which was approved by the Moscow prose section [of the Writers' Union] and accepted for publication by *Novy Mir*, is a plain misunderstanding.

2) To lift all sanctions (such as the expulsion of students from institutes, etc) against people accused of reading or discussing my books. To eliminate the ban against library use of the surviving editions of my previously published short stories. To announce the preparation of an edition of my collected stories (which has not yet been published).

If these measures are adopted and implemented, I can send to you for publication my new, recently completed novel, *August 1914*. This book cannot possibly present any problems for the censorship: it represents a detailed, military postmortem of the "Samsonov Catastrophe" of the year 1914, where the sacrifice and best efforts of Russian soldiers and officers were neutralized and doomed by the paralysis of the tsarist military command. The banning of *this* book in our country would be met with universal astonishment.

If a personal meeting, discussion, or reconsideration is called for, I am prepared to come.

Solzhenitsyn
Telephone: 158–66–81 (Rostopovich's dacha in Zhukovka).[3]

F. 3, *op.* 80, *d.* 644, *l.* 12. Original.

Notes

1. *Separate pages bear the resolution: "To Comrade Demichev and Comrade Shauro. Please review and discuss. M. Suslov. 16.10.70;" and the notation: "Personal. To Comrade Z.P. Tumanov. Sending you this at request of Comrade P.N. Demichev as per agreement.*

Gavrilov. 19.10.70." On the letter, there is a notation: "done in connection with a verbal request of Comrade M.B.[sic] Suslov. Shauro 07.01.71."

2. Solzhenitsyn had met Mikhail A. Suslov at the December 1962 meeting at the Kremlin between Khrushchev and members of his government and leading writers and artists. Suslov was the Politburo's specialist in ideological matters and was instrumental in later ousting Khrushchev from power. Despite this inauspicious record, Solzhenitsyn had decided to write to him as the highest-ranking leader whom he knew personally.

3. Solzhenitsyn had been invited to stay at the Moscow dacha of the celebrated cellist, Mstislav Rostropovich, as a form of protection against government harassment and surveillance.

29 Report of the Central Committee Culture Department

"On the Reaction of the Writers' Community to the Awarding of the Nobel Prize to Solzhenitsyn"[1]

15 October 1970

To the Central Committee:

On 8 October of this year, the Nobel Committee announced the award of its 1970 Prize for Literature to Solzhenitsyn, who has been nominated as a candidate every year for the past three years by certain bourgeois writers and various anti-Soviet publications.

On 9 October of this year, the Secretariat of the Writers' Union published a brief notice about this in the form of answers to the questions of a reporter from *Izvestia*. The notice stresses that the decision of the Nobel Committee was dictated by "cynical political considerations" and had nothing to do with the genuine interests of literature.

The Soviet literary community considers the award of the Nobel Prize to Solzhenitsyn as a Cold War act, directed toward the organization of a prolonged anti-Soviet propaganda campaign.

In the opinion of K. Fedin, Solzhenitsyn's prize has nothing to do with literature and is openly political in nature. N. Tikhonov said that the members of the Nobel Committee rewarded Solzhenitsyn's position, or rather his opposition to socialism. A. Surkov remarked that the Nobel Committee, in awarding the prize to Solzhenitsyn, followed the lead of anti-Soviet forces.

Appearing at a special session of the RSFSR Writers' Union Secretariat in Arkhangelsk, the writer S. Mikhalkov[2] declared: "This action pursues purely political aims and is essentially a provocation. . . . We Soviet writers view it as a routine, anti-Soviet international act."

The writers B. Kozhevnikov, N. Gribachev, B. Suchkov, S. Narovchatov, A. Rekemchuk, B. Ardamatsky, and many others view the award of the prize to Solzhenitsyn as an effort to support certain antisocialist attitudes among writers and figures in the arts in socialist countries in general and not only in the USSR.

The majority of writers view the statement of the Soviet Writers' Union Secretariat on the awarding of the Nobel Prize to Solzhenitsyn as a dignified and precise rebuff to the organizers of provocations.

Meanwhile there are some isolated statements in support of Solzhenitsyn. Thus the poet P. Antokolsky[3] said, in a conversation with Comrade Ilyin, the organizing secretary of the Moscow Writers' Organization, that he was glad that the Nobel Prize had been awarded to a "good Russian writer."

As Comrade G.M. Markov has reported, fourteen congratulatory telegrams and letters addressed to Solzhenitsyn have been received at the Soviet Writers' Union and the editorial offices of *Literaturnaya Gazeta*. Of these, eight are anonymous and six are signed by unknown persons and do not have return addresses. One letter from Minsk sharply condemns Solzhenitsyn's indecent behavior.

Reported for information purposes.

Deputy Director of the Culture Department of the Central Committee
Z. Tumanov

Director of Department Sector
A. Belyaev

F. 3, *op.* 80, *d.* 644, *l.* 18–19. Original.

Notes

1. *Sent to Politburo members and candidate members, and Central Committee Secretaries, on 15 October 1970 under No. P1895.*
2. Sergei Mikhalkov was a children's writer and well-known conformist.
3. Pavel Antokolsky was a Stalin Prize winner and a moderately talented poet of the older generation.

30 Memorandum from the Culture Department of the Central Committee "On Solzhenitsyn's Letter"[1]

27 October 1970
Classified

To the Central Committee:
In accordance with instructions, the Culture Department has already reported to the Central Committee on measures taken in connection with the award of the Nobel Prize to Solzhenitsyn and on the responses of the creative intelligentsia to reports in the Soviet press on this subject (Memorandum from the Cultural Department and Department of Propaganda of 9 October; Memorandum from the Culture Department of the Central Committee of 15 and 20 October of this year).

According to the Norwegian bourgeois newspaper *Aftenposten*, Solzhenitsyn conveyed his gratitude to the Nobel Prize Committee and expressed his intention to go and receive the prize in person, if given the chance.

The reactionary bourgeois press is exploiting the decision of the Nobel Prize Committee to step up an anti-Soviet propaganda campaign and is pointing openly to the political nature of this action.

On 14 October of this year, Solzhenitsyn wrote a letter to the Central Committee in which he demanded in unacceptable form the publication of his book *Cancer Ward*, together with his earlier published works, in the shortest possible time. Groundless charges were made against the leadership of the Soviet Writers' Union. The unduly familiar tone of Solzhenitsyn's letter differs little from that of his previous letters to the Union.

The Secretariats of the Boards of the Soviet and Russian Writers' Unions have repeatedly considered Solzhenitsyn's letters and statements and have expressed their attitude to the ideologically damaging works and indecent behavior of this writer with crystal clarity.

Thus on 22 September 1967, the Secretariat of the Soviet Writers' Union, chaired by K. Fedin, discussed in Solzhenitsyn's presence his letter addressed to the Fourth Congress of Soviet Writers containing his request to publish his novels *Cancer Ward* and *The First Circle*, previously rejected by the editorial boards of *Novy Mir*, *Zvezda*, and *Prostor*, immediately.

Comrades K. Fedin, G. Markov, A. Surkov, V. Kozhevnikov, I. Abashidze, A. Koreneichuk, P. Brovka, K. Yashen, B. Kerbabaev, V. Ozerov, G. Musrepov, L. Novichenko, and others, along with the Board Secretaries of the Soviet Writers' Union (a total of twenty-six persons), condemned Solzhenitsyn's unworthy conduct in their speeches and suggested that he should justify his attitude to the use of his name and works by bourgeois propaganda for anti-Soviet purposes. The Secretariat believes that *Cancer Ward* cannot be published.

Then M. Sholokhov suggested in writing that Solzhenitsyn be expelled from the Soviet Writers' Union as "an openly malicious anti-Soviet person."

A. Surkov remarked that *Cancer Ward* smacks of "obvious socialist revolutionary sentiments" and emphasized that a great deal of this story is reminiscent of Solzhenitsyn's play *Feast of the Victors* which was written in the same mood: "To hell with the whole lot of you!"

Solzhenitsyn has ignored the opinion of the Secretariat of the Soviet Writers' Union. His further behavior (publicizing his so-called minutes of the meeting of the Secretariat of 22 September 1967 as well as a number of other letters and materials tendentiously fabricated by him) was a gross violation of the basic provisions of the statutes of the Writers' Union.

In this connection, Solzhenitsyn was expelled from the Soviet Writers' Union by the decision of a general meeting of the Ryazan Section of the Writers' Union of 4 November 1969. The decision was endorsed by the Board Secretariat of the Russian Writers' Union.

Even after that Solzhenitsyn continued to appeal to foreign reactionary circles. He published a slanderous report in the bourgeois press about the meeting of the Ryazan Section of the Writers' Union along with his latest "open letter" to the Secretariat of the Russian Writers' Union, which provoked the profound indignation of Soviet writers and artists with its spiteful, anti-Soviet nature.

In June 1970, Solzhenitsyn's article "This Is How We Live"[2] appeared in many foreign publications. In this article, the life of Soviet society was again slandered.

Public opinion in our country viewed the award of the Nobel Prize to Solzhenitsyn as an act of political provocation that has nothing in common with the true interests of literature.

There is no point in returning to the matter of publishing Solzhenitsyn's works in the USSR.

As to Solzhenitsyn's trip abroad to receive the Nobel Prize (the award of prizes usually takes place in the city of Stockholm on 10 December), we consider it imperative to request the Department of Administrative Organs, the International Department, and the Culture Department of the Central Committee to recommend the proper course of action.

Please review.

Deputy Head of the Culture Department of the Central Committee
V. Shauro

F. 3, *op.* 80, *d.* 644, *l.* 13–15. Original.

Notes

1. *P. Demichev's signature is on the first page.*
2. This brief statement by Solzhenitsyn was a protest against the forcible incarceration in an insane asylum of the dissident biologist Zhores Medvedev. As a result of numerous protests by Solzhenitsyn and others, Medvedev was released after nineteen days. Medvedev, together with his brother Roy, later wrote a short book about his experiences, *A Question of Madness* (Knopf, 1971).

31 Memorandum from the Committee for State Security of the USSR Council of Ministers[1]

No. 2945-A29
October 1970
Top Secret

To the Central Committee:
The award of the Nobel Prize to Solzhenitsyn and his possible trip to Sweden continues to be energetically discussed among the creative intelligentsia and other representatives of the Soviet public. In particular, the following opinions have been expressed.

I. Kobzev, poet: "This time we should take the opportunity offered by the award of the prize to Solzhenitsyn to let him go abroad and then strip him of his Soviet citizenship."

Firsova, an actress at the Novosibirsk Opera and Ballet Theater: "By awarding him the prize they want to enhance interest in Solzhenitsyn. If it were in my power, I would kick him out of the country. That would be one less piece of scum to deal with. And we wouldn't have to put up with his insults."

A. Levashov, worker (Sverdlovsk): "Why do we treat this slander from Solzhenitsyn so tolerantly? He should have been deported long ago. He shouldn't be allowed to get away with slandering our people."

A. Bannikov, literary translator: "We should allow Solzhenitsyn to receive the prize so as not to start a whole new Pasternak affair."

V. Starodubova, a senior research worker at the Institute for the Theory and History of the Arts of the USSR Academy of Fine Arts: "It is not worth wasting words on Solzhenitsyn. It's a good thing that not too much of a racket has been raised about this matter in our country."

V. Arkhangelsky, prose writer: "Whatever kind of person Solzhenitsyn may be, he should be given the opportunity to receive the prize so as to demonstrate how peace-loving and tolerant we are."

A. Stein, playwright: "If we do not let Solzhenitsyn receive the Nobel Prize, we are going to lose the last of our foreign friends. First, his nomination has been supported by the leading lights of world literature. Second, they consider him a remarkable writer. And they are not far wrong."

Y. Yevtushenko:

> This is going to be a story with a tragic ending in any case:
> whether he is allowed to go and then return, or go and not
> return. There is only one way out of this situation, but nobody
> will dare choose it: recognize Solzhenitsyn, restore his mem-
> bership in the Writers' Union, and afterwards, just declare sud-
> denly that *Cancer Ward* is to be published.

A. Dementyev, literary scholar:

> The silliest thing that could be devised is to prevent him going
> to Sweden to be present at the Nobel Prize ceremony. He will
> not go for the idea of being labeled as a defector, which, on the
> whole, is not a very nice title. Will he say anything bad about
> us? He is a straightforward, uncompromising person with a
> sharp manner. He would hardly speak from an agreed script.
> He might very likely say something that will hardly be flatter-
> ing to us.

As already reported, Solzhenitsyn intends to leave for Sweden to receive
the Nobel Prize. Recently he sent a letter to Tvardovsky and stated the
following:

> You are aware of my news (8 October). I'm sorry that they are
> again attempting (through the glasses of Voronkov-Markov &
> Co.) to see in this not the glory of Russian literature, but rather
> a political game. My heart aches for those Russians who were
> worthy of this prize, but who have passed away without receiv-
> ing it.

Of interest is the opinion of Solzhenitsyn's personality given by his wife,
Natalia Alexeyevna Reshetovskaya, born 1919, a chemist, temporarily
unemployed. She said the following:

> My earlier vision of my husband has been totally destroyed.
> Previously I believed he was absolutely unique and extraordi-
> nary. He always mesmerized me. Everything was fine until he
> became famous.
> Success always spoiled him. He no longer needed other
> individuals. Whatever the company, he was always the center

of attention. And why not? He was the hub of the universe. All that interests him in other people is what he can get from them and use for his own purposes. The horrible thing is that everybody bowed down to him, and he got terribly spoiled.

It recently emerged that he has taken to philandering. When it happened the first time, I said: If she is a serious woman, you can go to her, but my life will be ended. 'No, under no circumstances are you going to ruin my career and me,' he answered. I felt incredibly miserable. He had been telling lies to me all these years. I practically abandoned all normal life for his sake, you know. Rules and regulations of incredible harshness. He gave me no latitude. If I picked up a book to read: 'Don't read it! Read my outlines or read the encyclopedia. . . . Read what I wrote in *Novy Mir*. . . . Don't watch that movie. . . . Throw that newspaper out of our home altogether. . . . Don't listen to the radio,' and so on. It was nothing less than the suppression of my personality.

Our relationship became too excruciating. He who calls on people to tell the truth, who stands up for the truth in all his works, and at home all lies! On the one hand, he's afraid I'll commit suicide, on the other, he would like us to break up.

It has been established that some time ago Solzhenitsyn started living with Natalia Dmitrievna Svetlova, born 1939, who is a postgraduate of the mechanical and mathematical department of Moscow State University and is now pregnant. On 15 October 1970, Reshetovskaya took an overdose of sleeping tablets and was hospitalized and diagnosed as "poisoned." Right now she is undergoing medical treatment at the psychoneurological department of Moscow City Clinical Hospital No. 1.

Solzhenitsyn tries to keep the true situation of his family secret. According to available evidence, Solzhenitsyn lives in the dacha of M. Rostropovich, the cellist, in the settlement of Zhukovka in the Odintsovo District of the Moscow Region. There he is putting the final touches to his manuscript entitled *August 1914* in which events are described dating from the beginning of World War I.

The KGB believes that if Solzhenitsyn officially applies for permission to visit Sweden to receive the Nobel Prize, we could comply with his request. As to the matter of his return to the Soviet Union, a decision should depend on Solzhenitsyn's behavior abroad. If Solzhenitsyn decides to stay abroad, it is hardly expedient, in our opinion, to take any measures to bring him back to the Soviet Union.

Chairman of the Committee for State Security
Andropov

F. 3, op. 80, *d.* 644, *l.* 25–28. Original.

Notes

1. *The first page bears the notation "circulate" made by M. Suslov and the signatures of M. Suslov, A. Kosygin, N. Podgorny, Al Shelepin, A. Pelshe, A. Kirilenko, D. Polyansky, and K. Mazurov. Also the notation: "Reported to Comrade L.I. Brezhnev. K. Chernenko."*

32 Report from M. Zimyanin, Editor-in-Chief of *Pravda*

No. GL–124

To the Central Committee:
General Department:
To: Comrade K.U. Chernenko
Enclosed please find a letter written by M. Rostropovich (dated 31 October) that I received on 9 November of this year.

Editor-in-Chief of *Pravda*
M. Zimyanin

Enclosure

Open Letter to the Editors-in-Chief of *Pravda, Izvestia, Literaturnaya Gazeta,* and *Sovetskaya Kultura*

Dear Comrade Editor-in-Chief:

It is no longer a secret that A.I. Solzhenitsyn lives for the most part in my house near Moscow. His expulsion from the Writers' Union took place before my eyes at the very moment when he was working hard on his novel about 1914. Now comes the Nobel Prize and the newspaper campaign around it. All of this forces me to take up my pen and write to you.

I believe this is the third Soviet writer to receive the Nobel Prize. In two cases out of three we have considered the award of the prize a dirty political game, and in one case (Sholokhov) as a proper recognition of the leading global importance of our literature. If Sholokhov had refused at the time to accept the prize from hands that had awarded it to Pasternak "out of Cold War considerations," I would understand that we continued not to trust the objectivity and honesty of the Swedish Academy members. Now it turns out that sometimes we selectively accept the Nobel Prize for Literature with gratitude, and other times we use foul language. What if Comrade Kochetov were awarded the prize next time? It would be imperative to accept it, would it not? Why, a day after the award of the prize to Solzhenitsyn, does a strange report appear in our newspapers about a conversation between a certain correspondent X and representative Y of the Secretariat of the Writers' Union recounting that *all* the prominent figures of the country (that is, obviously, all scientists, all musicians, and so on) have actively supported his expulsion from the Writers' Union? Why does *Literaturnaya Gazeta* tendentiously choose the statements of an American or Swedish communist newspaper only, out of a plethora of Western newspapers, bypassing such matchless, more popular and significant communist newspapers as *L'Humanité, Lettres Francaises,* and *L'Unita,* not to mention a host of non-communist newspapers? Even if we do not believe a certain critic Bonosky, what should we do about the opinions of such prominent writers as Böll, Aragon, and Mauriac?

I remember, and I would like to remind you of, our newspapers in 1948. How much rubbish was written about Prokofiev and Shostakovich, now the acknowledged giants of our music. For instance:

> Comrades D. Shostakovich. V. Shebalin, N. Myaskovsky, and others! Your atonal, discordant music is *organically alien* to the people . . . formalistic stunts emerge when talent is in short supply and big claims are being made for originality. The music of Shostakovich, Myaskovsky, and Prokofiev is completely unacceptable to us. There is no harmony, no order in it, no broad musicality, and no melody.

Now, when one looks at the newspapers of those years, one is unbearably ashamed of so much. Of the fact that the opera *Katerina Izmailova* has not been heard for three decades; that Prokofiev never heard the final version of his opera *War and Peace* and his Concert Symphony for cello and orchestra; that there existed official lists of forbidden works by Shostakovich, Prokofiev, Myaskovsky, and Khachaturian.

Has the past really not taught us to think carefully before we start destroying our talented individuals? Has it not taught us to refrain from speaking out against what we simply have never read or heard? I remember with pride the time I did not go to a meeting of persons engaged in cultural activities in the Central House of Artists where Pasternak was being reviled and where a speech had been planned for me in which I was ordered to criticize *Doctor Zhivago*, a book I had not yet read at the time.

Back in 1948, there were *lists* of forbidden works. Today, they prefer *verbal bans* noting that "there is an opinion" that such-and-such is not recommended. It is impossible to determine where and who *is of this opinion*. Why, for instance, was Galina Vishnevskaya prohibited from performing a brilliant song cycle by Boris Chaikovsky to Joseph Brodsky's lyrics in her concert in Moscow? Why was the performance of Shostakovich's cycle to Sasha Cherny's lyrics blocked several times although the texts have been published in our country? Why were the performances of the Thirteenth and Fourteenth Symphonies by Shostakovich accompanied by unusual difficulties? Who *"was of the opinion"* that Solzhenitsyn should be expelled from the Writers' Union? I was not able to find out, although I took a keen interest in this matter. The five Ryazan writer-musketeers would scarcely have done this by themselves without the mysterious *opinion*. It is obvious that *an opinion* prevented my compatriots from getting to know Tarkovsky's film *Andrei Rublev*[2] that we sold abroad and that I had the good fortune to see among delighted Parisians. *An opinion* obviously prevented Solzhenitsyn's *Cancer Ward* from being published, although it had already been typeset at *Novy Mir*. If it had been published in our country, it would have been openly and extensively discussed to the greater good of both author and readers.

I am not an expert in either political or economic issues affecting our country. There are people who know better about these topics than I do. But could you explain to me why so frequently the final say in literature and art rests in the hands of people who are absolutely incompetent in these fields? Why do they have the right to discredit our art and literature in the eyes of our people?

I stir up the past not so much to grumble, as to project today's newspapers into the future and not to have to hide them in embarrassment in 20 years' time.

Every person should have the right to think fearlessly and independently and to speak out on what he knows, what he has personally thought and experienced, and not to submit weakly to the *opinion* imposed on him. We are certainly able to arrive at free discussion without being constantly prompted and jerked around!

I know that an *opinion* of me is sure to be one result of my letter, but I am not afraid of it and I openly speak my mind. The talented people who will be our pride should not be beaten up in advance.

I know and like many of Solzhenitsyn's works. It is my belief that he has earned the right to write the truth as he sees it through suffering, and I do not see any reason to conceal my attitude toward him when a campaign has been launched against him.

Mstislav Rostropovich
31 October 1970

F. 3, *op.* 80, *d.* 644, *l.* 41–44. Original.

Notes

1. This letter was published in Galina Vishnevskaya's book Galina: A Russian Story (Harcourt, Brace, Jovanovich, 1964). Vishnevskaya is Rostropovich's wife.
2. The film Andrei Rublev [St. Andrew's Passions] by Andrei Tarkovsky was completed in 1966 and banned in the USSR. In 1966, the film was sold to France where it was awarded first prize at the International Film Festival in Cannes in the same year. It was released for distribution in the Soviet Union only in 1971.

33 Letter to the Central Committee from A. Chakovsky, Editor-in-Chief of *Literaturnaya Gazeta*[1]

11 November 1970

To the Central Committee:
I would like to report on a proposal to the Central Committee that *Literaturnaya Gazeta* make a statement about the "Solzhenitsyn Affair." At first, however, some preliminary considerations.

1. *Literaturnaya Gazeta* along with the leadership of the Soviet Writers' Union has repeatedly published both reports and comprehensive articles qualifying the nature of the works of Solzhenitsyn as well as his conduct. Several years ago, the newspaper expressed criticism of Solzhenitsyn's short stories that appeared in our press following *One Day in the Life of Ivan Denisovich*, in particular, the short story "Matryona's Yard."

In 1968, *Literaturnaya Gazeta* published a long editorial called "Ideological Struggle: The Responsibility of the Writers"[2] which outlined in detail the attitude of the Writers' Union to the works of Solzhenitsyn that were being widely published by bourgeois publishing houses, including *Cancer Ward*, and which contained a comprehensive review of the antisocial conduct of this writer as well.

Before the award of the Nobel Prize to Solzhenitsyn, a total of seven items appeared in our newspaper between 1968 and 1970 exposing the antiSoviet nature of several of his works and providing a political evaluation of his activities.

Since the award of the prize to Solzhenitsyn, three issues of *Literaturnaya Gazeta* have appeared, exposing the political anti-Soviet content of this action. I list the materials we have published in such detail in order to say further publication of similar articles in the *Literaturnaya Gazeta*, that is, of articles reviewing the creative work and conduct of Solzhenitsyn would be, from my point of view, only a rehash of what was done before, with no propaganda value whatsoever.

The appearance of such an article in *Pravda* would be quite another matter in light of the fact that our Party press has not yet given a detailed political critique of the "Solzhenitsyn story" throughout this whole period. It would obviously be much more advisable to publish an article on this topic in

Pravda, because someone influenced by foreign propaganda could form the impression that Solzhenitsyn is being victimized only by the "conservative part" of the leadership of the Writers' Union, whereas Party officialdom is keeping silent.

I repeat: since the matter has already gone beyond literature and has acquired a manifestly political nature, the silence of the Party press may cause puzzled rumors.

The appearance of an article in *Pravda* does not exclude one more publication in *Literaturnaya Gazeta* that would *differ*, however, from the previous ones on its methodology. On what basis should one proceed in the preparation of this article? I suppose that this publication should not be aimed at that part of the political mature intelligentsia which predominates over other readers, for whom Solzhenitsyn's story is already obvious, but should be aimed at those to whom bourgeois propaganda has succeeded in suggesting the thought that there is nothing anti-Soviet in Solzhenitsyn's works, that he is allegedly a "critical realist" who acutely reacts to the deficiencies of Soviet society and craves for its "improvement" within the framework of socialism.

For at least three years now, all bourgeois radio stations as well as the anti-Soviet press have been trying to "support" this deceitful thesis by one argument: the Writers' Union is unable "to present the facts," that is, to give readers the opportunity of seeing with their own eyes that the charges directed at Solzhenitsyn are justified. That's why "the reactionaries in the Writers' Union" are forced, they say, to use endless abusive epithets of various kinds and arbitrarily interpret the works of Solzhenitsyn, who is guilty only of "writing the truth."

In doing so, our enemies also use such cynical arguments as reminding us that some Soviet writers were at one time also declared "enemies," subsequently not only to be rehabilitated, but also ranked as part of "the gold fund" of Soviet literature.

Are there people influenced by such "argumentation" among the intelligentsia (and elsewhere)? I think that there are. This is confirmed by the letters sent to *Literaturnaya Gazeta*.

An attempt to unmask bourgeois propaganda by publishing one of Solzhenitsyn's anti-Soviet works would be not only senseless, of course, but also harmful.

However, an opportunity to prove by *facts* (and not simply by description and opinion) that Solzhenitsyn really does write anti-Soviet works should certainly not, in my opinion, be neglected.

2. From these premises flows my proposition, which comes down to the following, namely that we publish in *Literaturnaya Gazeta* a reader's letter

whose sense would be that although he, the reader, has no reason to distrust the accusations against Solzhenitsyn, as much as they have been levelled by such a respected organization as the Writers' Union, he, the reader, would like, nevertheless, to be personally certain that Solzhenitsyn really is capable of writing blatant anti-Soviet works (it wouldn't be a problem to find such a letter in *Literaturnaya Gazeta's* mail). In reply, the editorial staff would publish extensive excerpts from the play *Feast of the Victors* with appropriate comments. These quotations would be without any detriment to us, in as much as they deal with issues about which our people's opinions are unambiguous. In these writings, the Soviet Army is disgraced during the war, a Vlasovite officer and his mistress are eulogized, and so on.

To everyone who reads these excerpts it would be readily apparent that the person who wrote such material is patently anti-Soviet.

3. During the discussion of *Cancer Ward* by the Secretariat of the Writers' Union, Solzhenitsyn announced that he had written *Feast of the Victors* not as an author, but as nameless convict so-and-so. Solzhenitsyn's letter to the Congress of Writers contains a "fleeting" phrase indicating that he now supposedly "repudiates" this work. No doubt the opportunity to use such counterarguments should be taken into consideration.

It is possible to answer Solzhenitsyn's arguments that he was unfairly deprived of his freedom when writing *Feast of the Victors* as follows: real Soviet people who found themselves in a similar situation at that time differed from the anti-Soviet propagandists in that they never directed their indignation at the Soviet system, nor our Army, which led the sacred struggle against fascism, and so on. A number of published recollections are evidence of this.

4. Because of the work already done, there is no doubt that Soviet public opinion is, on the whole, well prepared to draw the correct conclusions from the entire Solzhenitsyn story. An article in *Pravda*, along with the proposed publication in *Literaturnaya Gazeta*, would dot all the i's and cross all the t's.

If the Central Committee considers this proposal acceptable in principle , the editorial staff of *Literaturnaya Gazeta* will start to prepare the relevant materials, reporting, of course, to the Central Committee. We think it scarcely appropriate to undertake this complicated work without preliminary approval in principle.

A. Chakovsky

F. 3, *op.* 80, *d.* 644, *l.* 30–34. Original.

Notes

1. *On a separate sheet are the instructions: "Brief Central Committee Secretaries as well as Comrades V.F. Shauro, A.N. Yakovlev," and the signatures of M. Solomentsev, B. Ponomarev, D. Ustinov, K. Katushev, M. Suslov, and I. Kapitonov, and a notation from A. Kirilenko: "What was the reply to Comrade Chakovsky? Comrade Mikhalkov and others have also submitted a similar proposal." The first page contains the notation: "The matter has been reported to Central Committee Secretaries. Shauro, Head of the Culture Department of the Central Committee. 4 March 1971."*

2. *The article was published on 26 June 1968.*

34 Memorandum from the Culture Department of the Central Committee "On Solzhenitsyn"[1]

11 November 1970
Classified

To the Central Committee:

Over the period of the last few years, the Soviet Writers' Union and the Culture Department of the Central Committee have repeatedly informed the Central Committee of measures undertaken in connection with the antisocial conduct of A. Solzhenitsyn and the political tendency of his creative work, which is alien to the literature of Socialist Realism and to the ideas of communism.

Following the publication of Solzhenitsyn's short stories "Matryona's Yard" and "Incident at Krechetovka Station" (*Novy Mir*, no. 1, 1963), critical articles appeared in a number of periodicals expressing serious reservations regarding the ideological and artistic content of those short stories, as well as of his previously published short novel *One Day in the Life of Ivan Denisovich*.

When the editorial staff of *Novy Mir* nominated this novel for the Lenin Prize, it led to extensive polemics in the press. On 11 April 1964, a review of readers' letters was published in *Pravda* under the heading "Lofty Demands."

The majority of those letters contained unfavorable opinions of this work. The Lenin Prize was not awarded to Solzhenitsyn.

In 1964, Solzhenitsyn submitted the manuscript of his new novel *The First Circle* to *Novy Mir*. The editorial board of the magazine considered it impossible to publish the work in its proposed form. After that, Solzhenitsyn submitted a manuscript of his *Cancer Ward* to the editorial boards of *Novy Mir*, *Zvezda*, and *Prostor*. The editorial boards of those magazines rejected it and suggested that he radically recast it. Solzhenitsyn, however, refused to make any changes in his manuscript.

On 11 September 1965, during a search of the apartment of the Moscow retiree Teush, state security confiscated typewritten copies of a number of Solzhenitsyn's works, among which were his early unknown works *Victory Celebrations*, *Candle in the Wind*, and *Republic of Labor*. The poem "A Melancholy Story," *Miniature Stories*, and others were also discovered.

Secretaries of the Writers' Union and a number of distinguished writers including K.A. Fedin, N.S. Tikhonov, G.M. Markov, V.M. Kozhevnikov, A.A. Surkov, A.B. Chakovsky, K.M. Simonov, N.M. Gribachev, L.N. Novichenko, B.S. Ryurikov, P.U. Brovka, M.N. Alexeyev, S.S. Smirnov, et al, familiarized themselves with copies of these works, as well as with *The First Circle* and *Cancer Ward*. All of them expressed a sharply negative view of the political tendency of Solzhenitsyn's creative work. The play *Feast of the Victors* caused universal indignation by virtue of its patently anti–Soviet nature.

In May 1967, Solzhenitsyn appealed to the Fourth Congress of Soviet Writers with a provocative "open letter," having duplicated and distributed hundreds of copies as a political leaflet. This letter interpreted the status of writers and literature in the USSR as perverted and was published in the foreign press and broadcast by Western radio stations during the Congress.

On the instructions of the Fourth Congress of Soviet Writers, on 12 June 1967, a conversation took place between Writers' Union Secretaries Comrades Markov, Sartakov, Tvardovsky, and Voronkov, and Solzhenitsyn concerning his "open letter" to the Congress.

On 22 September 1967, the Secretariat, consisting of 26 persons and presided over by K. Fedin, discussed the creative work, letters, and statements of Solzhenitsyn in the presence of the writer for several hours. Secretaries M. Sholokhov, B. Polevoy, and S. Mikhalkov, who were unable to be at the meeting, sent letters outlining their point of view on the issues being discussed. In reviewing the play *Feast of the Victors* Sholokhov proposed expelling Solzhenitsyn from the Soviet Writers' Union "as an openly and maliciously anti-Soviet person."

K. Simonov had earlier put in writing his opinion concerning the novel *The First Circle*: "I do not accept the novel at its most essential starting point, in its lack of confidence in the sound basis of our society."

Comrades K. Fedin, G. Markov, A. Surkov, V. Kozhevnikov, I.A. Abashidze,[3] A. Korneichuk, P. Brovka, K. Yashen, B. Kerbabaev, V. Ozerov, G. Musrepov, L. Novichenko, and others condemned Solzhenitsyn's unworthy conduct in their speeches and explained their attitude by citing bourgeois propaganda's uses of his name and works for anti-Soviet purposes. Every person who spoke at the meeting mentioned the resentfulness, the lack of faith in the vital forces of the Soviet system, and the vindictiveness that ran through all of Solzhenitsyn's works and are especially prevalent in the play *Feast of the Victors*, and the Secretariat noted the impossibility of publishing *Cancer Ward*. A. Surkov, L. Novichenko, and others pointed out that, in this work, Solzhenitsyn essentially propagates the idealistic views of Solovyov, Mikhalovsky, and Kropotkin; that his manuscript "smacks of manifest Socialist Revolutionary tendencies" (A. Surkov).

G. Markov and K. Yashen spoke in favor of expelling Solzhenitsyn from the Soviet Writers' Union, in the event that he would not implement the recommendations of the Secretariat.

Solzhenitsyn's entire subsequent behavior demonstrated that he was arrogantly ignoring the criticism of the literary public and scorning the recommendations and advice of the Secretariat. Furthermore, Solzhenitsyn actually took the path of struggle against the Soviet Writers' Union, appealing more and more openly to the bourgeois press. For example, the so-called "minutes" of the meeting of the Secretariat compiled by Solzhenitsyn were published abroad on 22 September 1967. His letters to the Soviet Writers' Union and other materials were published abroad as well. These actions were the most gross violation of the statutes of the Soviet Writers' Union.

On 13 July 1967, the Culture Department reported to the Central Committee with a special memorandum "On the Conduct and Views of Solzhenitsyn." With permission of the Central Committee, the content of the memo was verbally brought to the attention of Party activists in the republics, territories, and regions of the country (in speeches by senior officials of the Culture Department; at conferences of Central Committee Secretaries of the Union Republics; at a number of Party territorial and regional committee meetings held in the Culture Department of the Central Committee, as well as at a seminar of Central Committee Second Secretaries of the republics, territories, and regions of the country; at regional conferences and various seminars organized by Party Committees).

Even before Solzhenitsyn's appeal with his "open letter," some of his works which (in the words of Solzhenitsyn himself) were not intended for print, were already being published abroad. For example, his *Miniature Stories* appeared in Russian in the emigré literary magazine *Grani*, and *Possev*[3] published a collection of his works, including one not published in the USSR.

119

In the spring of 1968, the widespread publication and publicization of *The First Circle* and of *Cancer Ward* started as well.

Solzhenitsyn confined himself on this occasion to a formal letter to *Literaturnaya Gazeta*. In this letter, he essentially expressed his concern for the fact that foreign publishing houses, in their haste to publish *Cancer Ward*, ran the risk of corrupting the text of the novel. Solzhenitsyn's letter did not contain any protest over the use of his name and his works for anti-Soviet purposes.

To inform the general Soviet public, the Secretariat of the Writers' Union prepared an article containing a principled critique of Solzhenitsyn's anti-social conduct and cited evidence of his gross violation of the statutes of the Writers' Union. The article appeared in *Literaturnaya Gazeta* on 26 June 1968 and was called "The Ideological Struggle: The Responsibility of the Writer."

In the article, Solzhenitsyn's ideological retreat from the principles and tasks bound up with the voluntary unity of Soviet writers was clearly set forth. "He preferred to take a different path—that of attacking the basic principles by which Soviet literature is guided," stated the *Literaturnaya Gazeta*. The article emphasized that Solzhenitsyn's name itself and just about all his works, along with his letter to the Fourth Writers' Congress, are used by Western propaganda in the ideological struggle against the Soviet Union. In exposing the demagogic, hypocritical behavior of Solzhenitsyn at the meeting of the Secretariat on 22 September 1967 and in succeeding months, *Literaturnaya Gazeta* stated: "It has become crystal clear that the role assigned to Solzhenitsyn by our ideological enemies suits him perfectly."

Showing both restraint and patience, the Writers' Union gave Solzhenitsyn both the opportunity and time to realize the erroneous nature of his views. The article in *Literaturnaya Gazeta* stated: "The writer Solzhenitsyn could devote his literary abilities completely to his homeland and not to its ill-wishers. He could, but doesn't want to. Such is the bitter truth. Whether Solzhenitsyn wishes to find a way out of this deadlock depends primarily on himself."

Even after that, however, Solzhenitsyn drew no conclusions for himself. He kept categorically demanding the publication of *Cancer Ward* in the USSR, in the course of which all his statements and letters to the Writers' Union were also published abroad.

Party activists and the Soviet writers' community repeatedly exposed the antisocial conduct of Solzhenitsyn and subjected it to scathing criticism. In October 1969, a meeting of Moscow communist writers expressed the opinion that it was becoming urgent to consider the question of whether Solzhenitsyn could be allowed to remain in the ranks of the Writers' Union.

On 4 November 1969, by decision of a general meeting of the local Ryazan Writers' Organization, where he was a member, Solzhenitsyn was removed from membership of the Writers' Union. Solzhenitsyn was present at this meeting.

The Secretariat of the RSFSR Writers' Union chaired by L. Sobolev endorsed this decision on 5 November 1969. Comrades G. Markov, L. Tatyanicheva, F. Taurin, A. Keshokov, V. Fedorov, A. Barto, D. Granin, V. Pankov, V. Zakrutkin, S. Khakimov, and the Secretaries of the Union took part in the discussion of this issue. The Secretariat emphasized that Solzhenitsyn himself had for a long time been opposed to the Soviet Writers' Union and had in practice represented positions hostile to the cause of socialism.

Solzhenitsyn was invited by official telegram to come to the meeting of the Secretariat of the RSFSR Writers' Union, but did not appear.

Literaturnaya Gazeta carried a notice on 12 November 1969 about Solzhenitsyn's expulsion from the Soviet Writers' Union. On 17 November 1969, the RSFSR Writers' Union received the next "open letter" from Solzhenitsyn that had already been published on 15 November in *The New York Times*. In his letter, Solzhenitsyn described our society as "seriously sick" and said that "hate, hate no less evil than racism" has become its "sterile atmosphere." Solzhenitsyn slanderously called the leaders of the Soviet Writers' Union "the blind leading the blind."

On 26 November 1969, a communiqué from the Secretariat of the Soviet Writers' Union was published in *Literaturnaya Gazeta*. In this communiqué, it was pointed out that Solzhenitsyn "proved" with his "open letter that he takes positions that are alien to our people and confirmed thereby the necessity, the justice, and the inevitability of his expulsion from the Soviet Writers' Union."

The Secretariat of the RSFSR Writers' Union pointed out that in his actions and statements, Solzhenitsyn had essentially "joined with those who oppose the Soviet social system." It was emphasized in the communiqué that the writers of our country would not stand in Solzhenitsyn's way if he "chose to go where his anti-Soviet works and letters are always greeted with such rapture."

The decision on the expulsion of Solzhenitsyn from the Soviet Writers' Union has been energetically supported by the literary public of the country. The Culture Department has informed the Central Committee of this (memos from the Department of 13 and 18 November 1969).

In December 1969, at the joint plenum of Soviet creative associations, an extensive critique of the antisocial actions and creative works of Solzhenitsyn was again given in a report by G.M. Markov, Board Secretary of the Soviet Writers' Union. In their speeches, the plenum participants supported the decision to expel Solzhenitsyn from the Writers' Union. Details of the plenum were published in the literary press and issued as a separate report as well.

In June 1970, Solzhenitsyn's unbridled and slanderous article "This Is the Way We Live" appeared in many foreign publications. In this article, the author portrays life in the USSR as a system of violence, violations of the law, and evil deeds, as a variant of living in a gas chamber. According to Solzhenitsyn, "this devious suppression of people without searching for any guilt" is applied to "anyone who shows an interest in social problems."

Whipping up anti-Soviet propaganda around Solzhenitsyn, circles hostile to our country have made attempts to elect him an honorary member of the International PEN Club. These attempts were a complete failure due to the concerted efforts of Soviet writers and of representatives of socialist countries in the PEN Club.

In the course of the past three years, Solzhenitsyn has been systematically nominated for the Nobel Prize. In July 1970, a group of French literary as well as cultural figures nominated him again. On 8 October, the Nobel Prize was awarded to Solzhenitsyn.

In a memo on 9 October of this year, the Culture and Propaganda Departments of the Central Committee informed the Central Committee "On Measures Taken in Connection with the Provocative Act of the Award of the 1970 Nobel Prize for Literature to A. Solzhenitsyn."

On 9–10 October, a report of the Soviet Writers' Union entitled "Foul Play" appeared in *Pravda, Izvestia, Komsomolskaya Pravda*, and in the literary press. In this report, the awarding of the prize to this writer was qualified as an action dictated by cynical political calculations.

On 14 October, a feature article "On Priorities" was printed in *Literaturnaya Gazeta*, describing the unsavory circumstances surrounding the nomination of Solzhenitsyn for the Nobel Prize by a spiteful, right-wing White Guard newspaper in Belgium called *Chasovoi* [The Sentry]. The article emphasized that the hypocritical concern of the Nobel Prize Committee for the "ethical force" of literature had, in Solzhenitsyn's case, a strikingly obvious political motivation.

On 17 October of this year, *Komsomolskaya Pravda* carried an article from the Novosti Press Agency called "Where Does the Nobel Prize Committee Look for Writers' Talent and Fame?" It was pointed out in the article that Solzhenitsyn easily yielded to flattery by people who were not choosy about their means when it came to struggling against the Soviet system, and that "the further [he goes], the more literature in his works gives way to political lampoons."

In its memos of 15 and 21 October of this year, the Culture Department reported to the Central Committee on the responses of creative workers to the award of the prize to Solzhenitsyn and to the publication of materials on this subject.

At the present time, the Soviet Writers' Union is preparing articles that will return once again to a critique of Solzhenitsyn's views and conduct.

We regard it as essential to instruct the Department of Administrative Organs, the Propaganda Department, the International Department, and the Culture Department of the Central Committee to prepare proposals in connection with Solzhenitsyn's possible travel abroad.

Deputy Head of the Culture Department of the Central Committee
V. Shauro

F. 3, *op.* 80, *d.* 644, *l.* 74–81. Copy.

Notes

1. *Distributed to Politburo members and candidate members, and Central Committee Secretaries, on 12 November 1970 under No. P2198.*

2. *Mistake: I.V. Abashidze is correct.*

3. Possev *was the name of the book publishing division of the NTS (see Document 12, Note 1).*

35 Memorandum from the Committee for State Security of the USSR Council of Ministers[1]

No. 3125–Ts
14 November 1970
Classified

To the Central Committee:
According to information received by the KGB, some writers have expressed the opinion that Solzhenitsyn may donate the monetary award from his Nobel Prize to the Vietnamese Children's Aid Foundation.

Taking into account the provocative nature of this action, we would consider it advisable, using the proper channels, to inform our Vietnamese friends and express our wish that they "refuse to receive any monetary donations from Solzhenitsyn who has compromised himself through his anti-socialist activities" (if Solzhenitsyn in fact makes such a decision).

Deputy Chairman of the Committee for State Security
Tsvigun

F. 3, *op.* 80, *d.* 644, *l.* 47. Original.

Notes

1. *Distributed to Politburo members and candidate members, and Central Committee Secre-taries, on 14 November under No. P2218.*

36 Telegram from the USSR Embassy in Sweden

Special No. 694
15 November 1970
From Stockholm
Top Secret
Urgent

An unfriendly campaign against the Soviet Union is in progress in Sweden in connection with the award of the Nobel Prize to Solzhenitsyn, although its scope is somewhat less than before.

Certain international reactionaries whose goals in the ideological struggle against us coincide with those of Sweden's reactionaries are primarily behind the decision of the Swedish Academy. This action should also be regarded as an attempt to balance anti-American sentiments and criticism of the United States in Sweden by increasing anti-Soviet statements as well.

The orientation of the campaign remains the same: Solzhenitsyn's work is praised and the prevailing situation in Soviet literature and art distorted. Rostropovich's statement supporting Solzhenitsyn is being used in particular for these purposes. It is characteristic that the social democratic press is no less active in these anti-Soviet statements than that of the bourgeois parties.

Preparations are being made for the period around the date of the awards ceremony (10 December); a movie premiere based on the book *One Day in the Life of Ivan Denisovich*, a radio play, and a number of television broadcasts are being planned. Solzhenitsyn's books are being widely advertised; his possible public appearances in Sweden are also being planned.

Thus, it can be expected that the level of anti-Soviet activities will be stepped up, no matter what decision is taken on Solzhenitsyn. In our estimate, the orientation of this campaign will remain the same either way—only its forms will differ. In particular, a trip by Solzhenitsyn to the awards ceremony would be trumpeted as a concession on our part to pressure from anti-Soviet forces.

In view of the above, with questions of principle in mind and taking into account our foreign and domestic interests, it seems preferable to us to answer the question of Solzhenitsyn's trip to Sweden in the negative.

For tactical reasons, we should not make any official statements on Solzhenitsyn to avoid feeding anti-Soviet propaganda. In this connection, it would also be expedient not to announce the nature of our decision until the very last moment and, in any case, not before the conclusion of Defense Minister Comrade A.A. Grechko's visit to Sweden.[1]

Maltsev

F. 3, *op.* 80, *d.* 644, *l.* 55–57. Copy.

Notes

1. *Grechko's visit to Sweden took place from 2–6 December 1970.*

37 Memorandum from the Central Committee Department of Relations with Communist and Workers' Parties of Socialist Nations and the Culture Department

"On Instructions to the USSR Ambassador to the Democratic Republic of Vietnam"[1]

17 November 1970
Classified

To the Central Committee:
According to a KGB report (No. P2218), some Soviet writers have said that Solzhenitsyn may transfer the monetary award that Nobel Prize winners are supposed to receive to the Vietnamese Children's Aid Foundation.

Taking into account the provocative nature of such an action, we consider it advisable via the USSR Embassy in Hanoi to inform our Vietnamese friends verbally about our attitude toward Solzhenitsyn and to express our wish that they should react to this action accordingly (if Solzhenitsyn in fact makes such a decision).

A draft Central Committee resolution is enclosed.

K. Rusakov
V. Shauro

F. 3, *op.* 68, *d.* 1397, *l.* 78. Original.

Notes

1. *Distributed for a vote to Politburo members on 17 November 1970 under No. 183–101.*

38 Politburo Resolution

"On Instructions to the USSR Ambassador to the Democratic Republic of Vietnam"

No. P183/134
18 November 1970
Top Secret

The instructions to the USSR Ambassador to the Democratic Republic of Vietnam (enclosed) are approved.

Central Committee Secretary

Enclosure
Re: point 134 of minutes no. 183
Classified

Hanoi
To the USSR Ambassador:
Visit the Central Committee of the Vietnam Workers' Party and the Mission of the Central Committee of the National Liberation Front of South Vietnam and inform our Vietnamese friends verbally of the following:

As is well known, anticommunist circles in the West have been fueling an ongoing campaign for speculative political reasons in connection with the award of the Nobel Prize to Solzhenitsyn for his works of an anti-Soviet, antisocialist nature published in capitalist countries. Lately, they have been spreading information that Solzhenitsyn supposedly intends to transfer the monetary award that is due to the winners of this prize to the Vietnamese Children's Aid Foundation.

Soviet organizations conclude that both the award of the prize itself to Solzhenitsyn and his possible demagogic intention to render assistance to Vietnam are part and parcel of the same provocative plot by imperialist and other anticommunist circles.

Officials in Moscow request that our Vietnamese friends take the foregoing into account and react accordingly, if this issue confronts them.

Telegraph your implementation.

F. 3, *op.* 80, *d.* 644, *l.* 48–49. Excerpt from minutes.

39 Memorandum from the Culture Department of the Central Committee

"On the Publication of Materials on Solzhenitsyn"[1]

20 November 1970
Classified

To the Central Committee:
The Culture Department of the Central Committee reported to the Central Committee in its memo of 11 November of this year that the Secretariat of the Writers' Union was preparing material for publication on the Nobel Prize awarded to Solzhenitsyn.

It was supposed that articles would appear in the form of a statement from a group of well-known Soviet writers and an editorial in *Literaturnaya Gazeta* in which it would be possible to clarify further some of the issues involved in evaluating Solzhenitsyn's views and work.

During the preparation of these materials, a number of prominent Soviet writers expressed their readiness to sign a statement. At the same time, Comrade Fedin, First Secretary of the Soviet Writers' Union, and Comrade Tikhonov, Secretary of the Soviet Writers' Union, who largely agreed with the prepared text of the statement, insistently object to publishing a statement over the signatures of well-known Soviet writers.

Comrade Fedin considers that such a statement may create a false idea of Solzhenitsyn's real place in literature. In addition, some prominent figures will be unable to sign the statement for various reasons (illness, long assignments, foreign tours). The absence of a number of signatures might create the wrong impression in the literary community.

Taking into account the fact that previous statements and reports on Solzhenitsyn were published by the Secretariat of the Soviet Writers' Union or the RSFSR Writers' Union, Comrades Fedin and Tikhonov feel that if the publication of the prepared materials is indeed deemed advisable, the previously accepted form should be maintained in this case as well.

The leaders of the Soviet Writers' Union (Comrades Fedin and Markov) request that the statement be published not only in the literary, but also in the central political press. (Texts of the materials are enclosed.)

The Culture Department of the Central Committee supposes it possible to agree with the opinion of Comrades Fedin and Tikhonov regarding the publication of the aforementioned materials.

Please review.

Head of the Culture Department of the Central Committee
V. Shauro

Enclosure

"A Necessary Explanation"

In answer to the article "On Priorities" published in the *Literaturnaya Gazeta* on 14 October 1970, Karl Ragnar Gierow, Permanent Secretary of the Swedish Academy, sent to our editorial office a letter explaining that Nobel Prizes in various fields "are awarded for the contribution to each of these fields, and not for their views or their contribution to other fields." He reports that first, "the Nobel Prize for Literature is awarded by a vote and, secondly, no pressure is accepted from any quarter."

Essentially, that is the whole letter. Mr. Gierow acted very courteously in explaining to us the principles behind the award of the Nobel Prize. We thank him. And, as the saying goes, you scratch my back, and I'll scratch yours. We, in our turn, would like to explain some things and, by the way, not only to him, but to all those gentlemen abroad who, like our addressee, are not averse to arguing over the objectivity of the Nobel Prize Committee.

Mr. Permanent Secretary tried to convince us that in his letter to *Literaturnaya Gazeta* he refuted the allegation that the Nobel Prize for Literature was awarded this year for political reasons. He announced the exact same thing, not without aplomb, in his interview with Swedish and other journalists.

Thrice blessed is he who believes; believing warms the heart!

The only thing we do not understand is why Mr. Gierow decided to polemicize on this issue with the *Literaturnaya Gazeta* in particular. Wouldn't it be simpler or more natural for him to argue with those organs of the press that are located closer to him—if not territorially in all cases, then certainly politically?

For instance, all he would have to do would be to turn to those organs of the bourgeois press from different countries that have expressed their opinion of the true reasons for the award of the prize to Solzhenitsyn (numerous quotations of this sort are cited in the letter of the Secretariat of the Soviet Writers' Union we are publishing today).

We could help Mr. Gierow by quoting several other analogous opinions. On 6 November, for instance, the West German *Die Zeit* [Time] published an article characterizing the decision of the Nobel Prize Committee as a new chess move in the Cold War, an obvious put-up job. The article stressed "the whole fuss surrounding Solzhenitsyn is a nasty business."

And here is a voice from another part of the world. The Sinhalese weekly *Mavbima* writes in an editorial: "What is the merit of this prize when the Nobel Prize Committee's decision proceeded not from Solzhenitsyn's contribution to world literature, but from his political activities, which, as his works have shown, have been blatantly anti-Soviet for a long time now. In any event, he has acted against the fundamental principles of socialism.

The award of the Nobel Prize to Solzhenitsyn is "an open political demonstration, in the first instance, against the Soviet Union," asserts an obscure Swedish newspaper called *Norrskenflamman* in its editorial. (This is already much closer to you, Mr. Gierow.) Mr. Fredrikson, Editor-in-Chief of the newspaper *Aftonbladet* (also Swedish) points out that the United States and all anti-Soviet forces are going to be happy with the selection of Solzhenitsyn's candidacy, especially "certain circles and organizations active outside the USSR and spreading, in particular, anti-Soviet leaflets that turn out to be essentially fascist when studied more closely."

Do you see how it turns out, Mr. Gierow?

It would be interesting to know if you would send letters "of protest and explanation" to all these organs of the press that have shown striking unanimity with *Literaturnaya Gazeta* in determining the real reason for the award of the prize to Solzhenitsyn.

Maybe you would be interested in how we ourselves explain such unanimity. Well, the explanation is very simple. There are facts so evident it is impossible to distort them.

Obviously, far from all newspapers and magazines are condemning the Swedish Academy for, as *Neue Züricher Zeitung* put it, "[sticking] its hands into a political fire." Many of them rejoice over the award openly. The main thing, however, remains irrefutable: even the bourgeois newspapers, which cannot be accused of attraction to our social system and Soviet literature, do not dispute the political motivation behind the award of the prize to Solzhenitsyn; in fact, they admit it frankly.

Trust us, Mr. Gierow: if these newspapers had only the slightest opportunity to subscribe to your hastily written clarification, they would have certainly done so. But it is, as the saying goes, physically impossible to overlook the antisocialist tendency of many of Solzhenitsyn's works. Solzhenitsyn unequivocally expressed his attitude to our Soviet society and to our entire social system in his play *Feast of the Victors*, written in verse many years ago. The play is set during the final stages of World War II, when our army dealt the final blow to fascism and brought long-awaited liberation to Europe's nations. And this great army, in Solzhenitsyn's depictions, seems like a throng of pillagers, dolts, and rapists. Incredible, but true! The only person to whom the author gives full support and admiration without reservation—Captain Nerzhin— "is inspired" by a special aim to help a female fellow traitor to escape to the Vlasovites.

Is it possible even to imagine a Soviet man who could write: "Contrived Matrosovs, silly Zoyas?"[2] But Solzhenitsyn did, in fact, write this. He has dared to defame what is most sacred to our people, their pride and their glory. Were those Soviet soldiers who threw themselves at Hitler's machine guns on different fronts at different times to pave the way to victory for their comrades in arms, merely "invented?" Were thousands and thousands of heroes who deliberately met their death in the name of their motherland's victory, merely "invented?" And what about the desecration of Zoya Kosmodemyanskaya, who mounted the scaffold in the name of victory over fascism?

We bow our heads to the blessed memory of those heroes and beg our readers' pardon for citing statements generated by vehement hate. But we are forced to cite these words—rare of their kind—just to let the people know what Solzhenitsyn's prize is based on.

In this connection, I would like to focus on a circumstance of no small importance. During the discussion at the Secretariat of the Soviet Writers' Union in September 1967, a number of his works, including the play *Feast of the Victors*, were discussed. Solzhenitsyn announced at that time that he wrote his play when he had been unjustly convicted and imprisoned and that he supposedly repudiated it now.

One might believe this if *Cancer Ward* and *The First Circle*, published in the West, had not appeared following this repudiation. It became absolutely clear that the sum of the conceptions making up Solzhenitsyn's entire nature was in the play *Feast of the Victors*. The true value of his hypocritical repudiations has now more clearly come to light.

Cancer Ward and *The First Circle* like *Feast of the Victors* embody a distorted view of Soviet society and a denial of socialism and its great achievements.

Solzhenitsyn terms the elevated sense of collectivism, this inherent characteristic of our people, a "glorified herd instinct." Following the line of his play, Solzhenitsyn again scoffs at Matrosov's feat of arms, at a true patriot's most cherished love for his homeland. The Soviet people are portrayed in his book as downtrodden and benighted. And it looks as if there were nothing before: no five-year plans, no Komsomolsk-on-Amur, no

Dnieper Hydroelectric Power Station, no Magnitogorsk, no heroic conquest of the Arctic and space, nor the great victory over fascism—nothing for which we have lived and in which we take pride.

But what are we talking about? What does Solzhenitsyn care about all this, about heroism or patriotism, or an elevated sense of civic responsibility? He is thoroughly imbued with malice and hate. For example, the characters in his *Cancer Ward* question and philosophize about whether to love their homeland or not; to consider Pavka Korchagin and his kindred spirits and comrades in arms as heroes or not, and so on. To a normal Soviet person, even to pose such questions is simply blasphemous.

Or take the way he portrays Soviet spacemen. "Before blast-off, of course, they'll hold a meeting by the rocket launcher. The crew will make a solemn vow to conserve fuel, to beat all speed records in space, not to stop the spaceship for repairs en route. . . ."

How disgusting to write like this about people ready to perform heroic deeds in the name of the homeland! Mankind will never forget the creative enthusiasm of Korolev, nor the radiant smile of Gagarin, nor the courage of his glorious colleagues bravely storming fathomless space. And Solzhenitsyn drones on, smirking disgustingly: ". . . not to stop the spaceship for repairs en route."

But what *does* he like, after all? Maybe Soviet literature? Nothing of the sort! "Gorky is very correct, but rather unattractive;" "Mayakovsky is very correct, but inflexible;" "*Vassa Zheleznova*[3] makes a painful impression;" "Mayakovsky considered it an honor to rise above the newspaper," and so on.

As if anticipating accusations of political and also personal immorality, Solzhenitsyn haughtily declares that he practices so-called "moral socialism." He does not explain what that is supposed to mean. We also never hear an answer to the question of what specific social system this "moral socialism" presupposes; does it exclude the ability to desecrate the Soviet way of life and the army that rescued mankind from Hitlerism? Does it presuppose ultimately fraternizing with the fatherland's enemies, even NTS renegades?

Once the notorious Boris Savinkov[4] gave his answers to questions that were similar in spirit. Long before Solzhenitsyn, he declared solemnly: "For Russia there is only one possible form of socialism—the moral one." But in doing so, Savinkov openly dotted all the i's and crossed the t's, adding "without the Bolsheviks."

The reactionary newspapers are filled with Solzhenitsyn's epistles. They can be heard over various foreign radio stations established especially to fight us.

Solzhenitsyn has repeatedly claimed that he was not the one to send them to our enemies' camp. Oh, really? But his letters to the Writers' Union, the "minutes" of meetings that he made himself only a day or two afterwards were published in *The New York Times* or in other publications "just as

133

sympathetic" to our country before they even reached their Soviet addresses. How can that be? And who is Solzhenitsyn's real addressee? Wouldn't it be simpler and more honest not to go through these contortions but to mail his letters directly to those for whom they are intended, to his foreign sponsors?

Appeals to our country's writers and other organizations are for Solzhenitsyn no more than camouflage. The true nature of this "moral socialist" manifests itself in the news pages of those Western European and American organs of propaganda that now make no secret that Solzhenitsyn dreams of a system where all existing social and civic principles will be reviewed and rejected.

In his speech at the meeting of the Secretariat of the Soviet Writers' Union and in his "open letter" to the RSFSR Writers' Union, Solzhenitsyn spoke his mind, saying that a writer is ostensibly *free* from social and class interests. Donning the cloak of "a boundless humanist," Solzhenitsyn has for many years now been carrying on a very real class struggle against his motherland and socialism.

Solzhenitsyn has repeatedly declared that he stands "above the fray" and is concerned only about "eternal" categories of existence. In reality, in all of his works, including the epistolary ones, he is obsessed with strictly specific goals: to denigrate everything achieved by our people in the years of Soviet rule and to misinterpret and traduce the concept of socialism.

It is extremely logical that the counterrevolutionary rabble, the emigré and White Guard dens like the NTS, are the most vehement propagandists of Solzhenitsyn's concoctions. This is the logic of the same class struggle that Solzhenitsyn purports to deny.

In making its decision on the literary prize, the Nobel Prize Committee spoke about "ethical force," and about the traditions of Russian literature that are supposedly present in the works of Solzhenitsyn. But lies and duplicity are as far from morality as from the traditions of Russian literature. This means the prize has not been awarded for these reasons. Perhaps it has been awarded for the rich and figurative language that is an integral part of an art work?

Even such a fervent anti-Soviet propagandist as G. Adamovich, a specialist in the study of literature and well known in bourgeois circles,[5] was forced to admit that the novel *The First Circle*, for instance, was rather a kind of rough copy or draft of a novel from the literary point of view. But then Adamovich supposedly just in time recollected something (not to blurt out too much!) and exclaimed: "How trivial, how irrelevant is this or that awkward phrase, or not quite finished page, in this powerful stream (ie, of anti-Sovietism—Eds.)!

That's the way it is, Mr. Gierow. We would like to thank you again for the "explanation" you sent. In exchange, we offer you our own. We do not blame you at all for the fact that you failed to give any coherent reason for the award of the prize to Solzhenitsyn for his "literary merits," since we understand that one cannot prove the unprovable. Nor can your letter be regarded as a model of the epistolary genre. You must have known better days when your writing was easier, simpler and most importantly more honest.

"Our Opinion"

On the second day after the award of the Nobel Prize to A. Solzhenitsyn, the Soviet Writers' Union made a statement to the press characterizing this action as provocative, having nothing to do with the interests of literature, and made for purely political anti-Soviet purposes.

The weeks since that time have produced much new evidence to prove the correctness of this description. The voices of bourgeois propagandists have blended in a frenzied chorus of praise for Solzhenitsyn and cries against our country and the entire socialist culture. Radio and television stations and newspapers, beginning with the "respectable" organs of capitalism monopolies and ending with openly pogromist, anticommunist, neo-Nazi and White emigré rags not only glorify Solzhenitsyn in every possible way, but also speak openly about the political objectives of this glorification.

The American weekly *Newsweek* points out that the "political winds around the award of the prize to Solzhenitsyn have begun to blow with new strength." The British magazine *The Economist* admits that "the Nobel Prize Committee has acted for political reasons," that "Solzhenitsyn's novels are of an unconcealed political nature, and it is quite possible that some people defending him are acting for political reasons as well." The Swiss *Neue Züricher Zeitung* points out that by its decision, the Swedish Academy has "stuck its hands into the political fire."

The absolutely reactionary *Figaro Littéraire*, that dedicated five columns to the award of the prize to Solzhenitsyn, worded the headline of one of its articles in the following manner: "His Goal—Man's Struggle Against the System." The weekly *Express* characterizes the award of the prize to Solzhenitsyn as "a political gesture" and notes that this man "does not give a damn about socialism."

Finally, *Russkaya Mysl* [Russian Thought], an openly White Guard newspaper that has been dreaming for decades of a tsarist general riding into Moscow on a white horse to "the mellow chimes of the Kremlin bells," but is still waiting in vain for this "triumph," carried an editorial about another "bright holiday" in the following manner:

"Thursday, 8 October, noon. A phone call, an agitated voice:

—Solzhenitsyn got the Nobel Prize!

The first feeling was not simply of joy, no, but rather a deep, unexpected satisfaction. . . ."

Do we need more persuasive confirmation of the correctness of the Writers' Union's evaluation when defining its attitude to this disgraceful decision by the Nobel Prize Committee?

There is no need to rehearse the events leading up to Solzhenitsyn's fall. Our press provided detailed information on it at the time.

After a number of attempts to explain to Solzhenitsyn that his antisocial conduct and his works play into the hands of the most malicious enemies of the Soviet Union and the whole socialist camp, it became clear that he was deliberately striving for "laurels" that would shame an honest Soviet person; Solzhenitsyn wanted to gain the dubious glory in the bourgeois world of an anti-Soviet propagandist. Well, he has gotten what he wanted.

All those outside our country who rapturously praise Solzhenitsyn to the skies declare that he should immediately be numbered among "the greatest" and "the most eminent." We know, however, how easy it is to become "eminent" with bourgeois propagandists. All anyone, even a third-rate writer, has to do, is become active in the field of anti-Sovietism. The enthusiastic appreciation of his creative work will inevitably be secured.

No one forced Solzhenitsyn to join our Union. He himself once asked for admittance and submitted the appropriate application.

The Soviet Writers' Union is not only an association of writers, but also a union of persons who hold the same viewpoints, who advocate Soviet rule and actively participate in the construction of socialism. It was natural that Solzhenitsyn, who has taken a path incompatible with this stipulation, has found himself outside the Soviet Writers' Union.

As a compensation, he has now been awarded the Nobel Prize, which with good reason could be called a prize for antisocialist activities.

We are firmly convinced that the anti-Soviet uproar raised in this connection by bourgeois propagandists will not only confirm once again that Solzhenitsyn is on a track incompatible with the civic responsibilities of a Soviet person, but will also open the eyes of those foreign writers who until now have not noticed the real, political, anti-Soviet reason behind the "Solzhenitsyn Story."

It is these spiteful attacks on our country and our socialist culture, which have worsened in the bourgeois press in the last few weeks, that have forced us to take up our pens to say the following:

No matter how much the anticommunists rage in anger, no matter what prizes they bestow on those who assist them in trying to undermine the moral and political fabric of our society and our Soviet literature, the Soviet writer will go his own way. Together with the Party. Together with the people.

F. 3, op. 80, *d.* 644, *l.* 82–83. Copy.

Notes

1. *Distributed to Politburo members and candidate members, and Central Committee Secretaries, on 20 November 1970 under No. P2276.*

2. Alexander Matrosov was a soldier in World War II who sacrificed himself with an act of heroism by throwing himself onto a German machine gun nest and allowing his comrades to attack. Zoya Kosmodemyanskaya was a partisan who blew up a German ammunition dump and was caught and hanged. Both were made the subject of countless poems, stories, and plays after the war, and their exploits were rammed down the throats of Soviet youth as examples of how to behave.

3. A long novel by Gorky in the style of Socialist Realism, published in 1935.

4. Boris Savinkov (1879–1925) was a leader of the Socialist Revolutionary Party who participated in Kerensky's Provisional Government after the collapse of tsarism and then led the right wing of his party against the Bolsheviks (he was implicated in, among other things, the attempted assassination of Lenin). Having emigrated, he was caught by the Soviet security service while trying to enter the country secretly and sentenced to ten years in jail, where he died in 1925.

5. Georgi Adamovich was a minor poet who had emigrated from the Soviet Union in 1922 and became an influential critic for a number of emigré journals in Paris. He generally advocated a closer relationship between emigré and Soviet literature than most of his peers.

40 Memorandum from the Committee for State Security of the USSR Council of Ministers and the Public Prosecutor's Office[1]

No. 3181–A
20 November 1970
Top Secret
Special File

To the Central Committee:

When analyzing the materials on Solzhenitsyn and his works, one cannot fail to arrive at the conclusion that we are dealing with a political opponent of the Soviet social and state system. His anti-Soviet position has already been precisely defined in his novel *The First Circle* and, in the opinion of those who have read his unpublished work, in *The Gulag Archipelago*. Without considering Solzhenitsyn's other works (stories, plays) which he speaks of as not intended for publication, Solzhenitsyn's political credo can be precisely traced in his two letters: "The Fourth Congress of Soviet Writers" and in "defense" of Zhores Medvedev. The letter to the Fourth Congress actually served as a signal to right-wing Czechoslovak writers to attack openly the Communist Party of Czechoslovakia and the existing system there.[2] The letter in "defense" of Zhores Medvedev was a signal for the moral use of Solzhenitsyn's name in the anti-Soviet campaign abroad. In addition, Solzhenitsyn fabricated material on his expulsion from the Writers' Union that was then published in the West in the so-called book *Solzhenitsyn, A Documentary Record*.[2] Since all this preceded the award of the Nobel Prize to him, it confirms *per se* that the West has paid for Solzhenitsyn's "political services."

At the same time, a certain duplicity has arisen in the social "faces" of Solzhenitsyn. On the one hand, his name is used in foreign anti-Soviet campaigns and even serves as a rallying cry for the consolidation of persons and organizations with hostile attitudes toward our country; on the other hand, some of our intellectuals, encouraged by revisionism in the communist movement, aspire to see in him a talented writer who needs their support. These intellectuals close their eyes to his anti-Sovietism.

But Solzhenitsyn himself behaves defiantly, does not reckon with the opinion of Party officialdom, willingly takes the part of "leader" of anti-Soviet elements at the West's dictation, and tries to instigate openly antisocial actions against our country. With all his conduct and activities, he directs public opinion against the leading role of the Party, ever trying to deceive the public. In this way, he attempts to gain authority with Soviet intellectuals. This became particularly evident in connection with the award of the Nobel Prize to him. Whereas Solzhenitsyn openly declares that he accepts the prize and is ready to leave for Sweden to receive it, he nevertheless takes no practical steps to file the necessary visa papers. The impression is growing that he is inspiring the usual scandal around his name.

Under such conditions, it is appropriate to raise the question: in what case will Solzhenitsyn's activity do less harm—if he stays in the country or if he is deported from the country?

If Solzhenitsyn continues to reside in the country after receiving the Nobel Prize, it will strengthen his position, and allow him to propagandize his views more actively. Given that Solzhenitsyn has not responded to the writers' community, the public will view the award of the prize as weakness on the part of the government and as an opportunity to wage hostile activities against the land of socialism with impunity. He will continue to play the part of an internal emigré publishing his works abroad. His name will be used by hostile circles as a rallying cry for anti-Sovietism.

The deportation of Solzhenitsyn from the Soviet Union would deprive him of his position as an internal emigré and of all the advantages pertaining to that status.

Solzhenitsyn will undoubtedly use his stay abroad to promote his anti-Soviet activities. The act of deportation will nevertheless cause a short-term, anti-Soviet campaign abroad involving also some part of the communist press.

At the same time, in the eyes of the Soviet people, Solzhenitsyn will no longer be an ambiguous figure because the attitude of the Soviet state toward him will be expressed directly and openly. This will have a positive influence on the correct orientation of public opinion regarding Solzhenitsyn.

Having weighed all these circumstances, we consider it advisable to settle the matter of Solzhenitsyn's deportation from the Soviet state.

There are three possible options:

—to cancel Solzhenitsyn's visa after his departure for Sweden to collect the Nobel Prize and to forbid his return to the Soviet Union;

—not to interfere with Solzhenitsyn's possible decision to go abroad himself;

—to issue a Decree of the Presidium of the Supreme Soviet of the USSR on the revocation of Solzhenitsyn's Soviet citizenship and his compulsory deportation from the USSR.

Meanwhile, we must not overlook the fact that doctors have concealed a suicide attempt by Reshetovskaya, Solzhenitsyn's wife, and criminal proceedings should be instituted concerning this matter.

Please review.

Andropov
Rudenko

Enclosure
Draft

Decree of the Presidium of the USSR Supreme Soviet "On the Revocation of A.I. Solzhenitsyn's Soviet Citizenship and Deportation from the USSR"

On the basis of Article 7 of the Law on Citizenship of the Union of Soviet Socialist Republics of 19 August 1938, the Presidium of the Supreme Soviet of the USSR decrees the following:

1. For attempts to denigrate Soviet society incompatible with the lofty title of a citizen of the USSR and for literary activities that have become a tool of the most reactionary anticommunist forces in their struggle against the principles of socialism and socialist culture, to revoke the USSR citizenship of Alexander Isaevich Solzhenitsyn, born 1918, native of the city of Kislovodsk.

2. To deport A.I. Solzhenitsyn from the Soviet Union.

Chairman of the Presidium of the USSR Supreme Soviet
N. Podgorny

Secretary of the Presidium of the USSR Supreme Soviet
M. Georgadze

Moscow, The Kremlin

F. 3, *op.* 80, *d.* 644, *l.* 70–73. Copy.

140

Notes

1. *Distributed to Politburo members and candidate members, and Central Committee Secretaries, on 20 November 1970 under No. P2277.*
2. Edited and with an introduction by Leopold Labedz (Penguin, 1970).
3. In July 1967 the Czech writer Pavel Kohout had caused a sensation by reading Solzhenitsyn's "Letter to the Fourth Congress of Soviet Writers" aloud to a congress of Czech writers. The letter subsequently became a rallying point for the Czech reform movement (which was crushed by the Soviet invasion in August 1968).

41 Memorandum from the International Department of the Central Committee and the USSR Ministry of Foreign Affairs[1]

No. 2147/GS
No. 25–S–1993
23 November 1970
Classified

To the Central Committee:
According to a report from the USSR Embassy in Stockholm (Special no. 694), in connection with the award of the Nobel Prize to Solzhenitsyn, anti-Soviet attacks in the press, on the radio and on television are being prepared and special movies are being released, etc. These attacks could conceivably become stronger as the date of the award—10 December—approaches. No counteraction to this propaganda on the part of the Swedish government has been observed. Furthermore, the Swedes have made attempts to use diplomatic channels to send Solzhenitsyn a notification of the prize.

It appears advisable to instruct the Soviet Ambassador in Sweden to meet with the Swedish Minister of Foreign Affairs to make our feelings known to him concerning this anti-Soviet campaign, and to stress as well that proper measures taken by the Swedish government to stop the anti-Soviet propaganda would be in the interests of both Sweden and the Soviet Union.

A draft resolution is enclosed.

Please review.

V. Ponomarev
V. Kuznetsov

F. 3, *op.* 68, *d.* 1401, *l.* 154. Original.

Notes

1. *Distributed to Politburo members and candidate members, and Central Committee Secretaries, for voting on 24 November 1970 under No. 184–42.*

42 Politburo Resolution

"On Instructions to the Soviet Ambassador in Stockholm in Connection with Awarding the Nobel Prize to Solzhenitsyn"

No. P 184/159
27 November 1970
Top Secret

Draft instructions to the Soviet Ambassador in Stockholm with the amendment approved (enclosed).[1]

Central Committee Secretary

Enclosure
Re: point 59 of Minutes No. 184

Stockholm
To the Soviet Ambassador:
Visit Mr. T. Nilsson, Minister of Foreign Affairs of Sweden, and announce to him the following:

Both Soviet literary circles and the Soviet public at large consider the decision of the Swedish Academy to award the Nobel Prize to Solzhenitsyn as an unfriendly act with respect to the Soviet Union and are filled with indignation.

A widespread campaign hostile to the Soviet Union and developed recently in Sweden by certain circles is seen as a detriment to Soviet-Swedish relations. The fact that no counteraction is being taken against this campaign causes perplexity on the part of the Soviet Union.

Meanwhile, an effort to stop this anti-Soviet propaganda would undoubtedly be in the interests of Soviet-Swedish relations.

We express the hope that the Swedish government will take our concerns into careful consideration and will take possible steps on its own to ensure that the said campaign will not be allowed to cause relations between Sweden and the Soviet Union to deteriorate. It is expected, in particular, that foreign Swedish missions will abstain from participating in events bearing any relation to Solzhenitsyn.

Telegram your implementation.

F. 3, *op.* 80, *d.* 644, *l.* 52–53. Excerpt from minutes.

Notes

1. *A. Kosygin's amendment related to a change in the last sentence in the penultimate paragraph of the draft instructions (see enclosure). The original stated: "It is to be expected, in particular, that foreign Swedish missions will abstain from participating in events associated with the implementation of the Academy's decision to award the literary prize to Solzhenitsyn."*

43 Report from the Committee for State Security of the USSR Council of Ministers[1]

No. 3249–Ts
28 November 1970
Top Secret
Special File

To the Central Committee:
The KGB has obtained information that Solzhenitsyn has recently intensified his contacts with foreign representatives stationed in Moscow. On 24 and 26 November he met [Per] Hegge, a correspondent of the Norwegian newspaper *Aftonposten*. Z. Medvedev, who is well known for his antisocial activity, was present at one of these meetings. On 27 November, Solzhenitsyn called on the Embassy of Sweden.

On 27 November, Solzhenitsyn sent a letter to Switzerland addressed to F. Heeb[2] who, according to reports in the foreign press and radio, is his agent abroad responsible for literary royalties. The content of the letter was as follows:

> I have already written to the Nobel Foundation that I am cancelling the trip to Stockholm, because I am afraid I'll not be allowed back home again. I suggested that the gentlemen from the Nobel Foundation should deliver the certificate and the medal to me in Moscow. After talks with you, however, I asked to transfer a part of the Nobel Prize money to my account in a Swedish or Swiss bank so that you could use the money. (Moreover, according to the Nobel regulations the whole sum must be withdrawn from the account no later than 1 November 1971.)
>
> I hope that the money will be available to you by the end of December or early January. I would like to ask you to transfer to me personally $3,000 via the Foreign Trade Bank. In doing so, please indicate that this is only part of the Nobel Prize.[3]
>
> To the best of my knowledge, such prizes are not taxable according to international law. Depending on what kind of obstacles arise and whether I will receive the full sum or not, I may or may not ask you for further remittances.

I will be very much obliged if you could respond immediately upon receiving this letter. My mailing address as of today is as follows: Moscow, K–9, ul. Gorkogo, 12, kv. 169. Svetlova, Natalia Dmitrievna (you may or may not add: for A.I. Solzhenitsyn).

For remittances made via the Foreign Trade Bank please indicate my previous address: Ryazan, 12, ul. Yunnatov, 8/1, kv. 11, Solzhenitsyn, Alexander Isaevich.

I hope that you are well and that worries over my case have not troubled you too much.

My best regards to you and your family.

If the Nobel Foundation consents to holding the ceremony and bestowing the prize insignia in Moscow, I certainly will ask them, it goes without saying, to invite you to the ceremony.

Deputy Chairman of the Committee for State Security of the USSR Council of Ministers
S. Tsvigun

F. 3, *op.* 80, *d.* 644, *l.* 94–95. Copy.

Notes

1. *Distributed to Politburo members and candidate members, and Central Committee Secretaries, under No. P2319.*
2. Dr. Fritz Heeb was a prominent Zurich lawyer and member of the Swiss Social Democratic party. His services had been obtained with the help of Solzhenitsyn's friend Lev Kopelev, who had extensive contacts in the German-speaking world.
3. *The Nobel Prize was worth 2,000,000 Swedish crowns (about $225,000) at the time.*

44 Telegram from the USSR Embassy in Sweden

Special no. 742
1 December 1970
From Stockholm
Classified

I visited Mr. Nilsson, Minister of Foreign Affairs, and, according to your instructions, made a statement to him in connection with the award of the Nobel Prize to Solzhenitsyn.

Nilsson said that the Swedish Academy makes its decisions on the award of the prize and publishes them in the press absolutely independently of the government of Sweden. In his words, the Swedish government has no influence either on these decisions or how they are covered in the press. At the same time, he admitted that the creative works of writers to whom the prize has been awarded are quite often appreciated in a different way in their motherland than by the Swedish Academy.

The Minister pointed out that there are no contradictions whatsoever between the USSR and Sweden in any sphere of activity under the control and direction of the Swedish government. He said that, according to their estimate, the Soviet-Swedish relations are developing well.

For his part, he also noted that the decision to award the Nobel Prize to Solzhenitsyn was indeed of a political nature and was directed against the Soviet Union. He expressed the hope that the Swedish government would find an opportunity to prevent a campaign to worsen relations between the USSR and Sweden from developing in this connection. He stressed that it was to be expected that foreign Swedish missions would abstain from participating in events related to Solzhenitsyn.

Nilsson declared that any intervention by the Swedish government in matters related to the award of the prize was out of the question.

This formulation allows us to assume that Swedish officials abroad will not participate in events relating to Solzhenitsyn.

A letter from Solzhenitsyn sent to the Swedish Academy (we are sending the translated text via TASS) was published in the Swedish press. The letter is accompanied by various speculations.

Mr. Stole, a representative of the Nobel Foundation, has announced that further talks will be conducted with Solzhenitsyn about the place and form of the prize award, as well as about the use of the prize money. Both in his statement and in the press there are indications of a wish not to exclude the possibility of Solzhenitsyn's coming to Sweden to deliver a "Nobel lecture."

An article by a *Svenska Dagladet* correspondent notes that, according to diplomatic circles in Moscow, it would be difficult to involve the Swedish Embassy in Moscow in an official ceremony to award the prize, because this might damage relations between the Soviet Union and Sweden.

Maltsev

(In outgoing report No. 42888 of 27 November 1970, Comrade Gromyko gave instructions to visit Mr. Nilsson, Minister of Foreign Affairs of Sweden, and make a statement in connection with the award of the Nobel Prize to Solzhenitsyn.)

F. 3, op. 80, d. 644, l. 62–64. Copy.

45 Memorandum from the USSR Minister of Foreign Affairs[1]

No. 2235/GS
3 December 1970

To the Central Committee:
In accordance with Resolution No. P184/59 of 27 November 1970, the Soviet Ambassador to Sweden made a statement to Mr. Nilsson, Minister of Foreign Affairs of Sweden, in connection with the award of the Nobel Prize to Solzhenitsyn (special No. 742 from Stockholm).

In his response, Nilsson told the Soviet Ambassador that any intervention by the Swedish government in matters related to the award of the Nobel Prize was out of the question. Nevertheless, it is known that Solzhenitsyn met in Moscow with Ambassador Jarring of Sweden.

In his letter of 27 November to the Swedish Academy and to the Nobel Foundation, Solzhenitsyn reported that he would like to receive the Nobel certificate and medal in Moscow.

Attempts could conceivably be made to use the Swedish Embassy in Moscow to award the certificate and medal to Solzhenitsyn. The Minister of Foreign Affairs considers it advisable to issue an appropriate warning to the Swedish Ambassador in addition to the measures already taken.

A draft resolution is enclosed.

Please review.

V. Kuznetsov

F. 3, op. 68, d. 1406, l. 78

Note

1. *Distributed to Politburo members and candidate members, and Central Committee Secretaries, for voting on 3 December 1970 under No. 184/131.*

46 Report from the Committee for State Security of the USSR Council of Ministers[1]

No. 3271–A
3 December 1970
Top Secret

To the Central Committee:

The KGB has obtained information that the following telegram from the Nobel Prize Committee was sent to Solzhenitsyn (at the address of Svetlova, his mistress):

We thank you for your open letter and the rest of your material. We regret, but do understand, your motives for not coming. As a convenient form of publication we will read out the letter as an acceptance greeting from the prize winners not present at the banquet on 10 December. At the same time, the text will be passed on to the press. However, the full contents of this letter have not yet been passed to the press. We will return to the matter of the certificate and award of the medal. We thank you for the Nobel text. We would appreciate receiving the manuscript no later than 1 April 1970. The prize will be disposed of according to your wishes.

Chairman of the Committee for State Security
Andropov

F. 3, *op.* 80, *d.* 644, *l.* 58. Original.

Note

1. *Signed by M. Suslov, A. Kirilenko, L. Brezhnev, A. Kosygin, G. Voronov, K. Mazurov, A. Pelshe, N. Podgorny, D. Polansky, P. Shelest, and A. Shelepin.*

47 Politburo Resolution

"On the Statement Made to Sweden's Ambassador to the USSR in Connection with Awarding the Nobel Prize to Solzhenitsyn"

No. P185/7
4 December 1970
Top Secret

The draft statement to the Ambassador of Sweden in the Soviet Union is approved (enclosed).

Central Committee Secretary

Enclosure
Re: point 7 of minutes No. 185
Classified

Text of the Verbal Statement to be Made to the Ambassador of Sweden in the USSR

The decision of the Swedish Academy to award the Nobel Prize to Solzhenitsyn has aroused indignation both in Soviet literary circles and in the Soviet public at large.

The campaign instigated by certain circles in Sweden in connection with the decision of the Swedish Academy is intended to damage Soviet-Swedish relations. This is not in the interests of either the Soviet Union or Sweden.

In a conversation with the Soviet Ambassador on 1 December, Swedish Foreign Minister T. Nilsson declared that any intervention by the Swedish government in matters connected with the award of the Nobel Prize was out of the question.

Therefore the Soviet government expects the Swedish Embassy in Moscow to adhere to the line laid down by Minister Nilsson and abstain from participating in events associated with the award of the Nobel Prize to Solzhenitsyn.

F. 3, op. 80, d. 644, l. 59–60. Excerpt from minutes.

48 Report from the Committee for State Security of the USSR Council of Ministers[1]

No. 3511–A
28 December 1970
Classified

To the Central Committee:
As was previously announced (No. 3249–Ts of 28 November 1970), Solzhenitsyn is showing interest in having part of the monetary award from the Nobel Prize Foundation sent to him from abroad.

On 2 December 1970, the sum of $3,000 was transferred from Stockholm to the Foreign Trade Bank of the USSR addressed to Solzhenitsyn (indicating the address of his mistress Svetlova, research officer at the Institute of the International Working Class Movement), as a part of his Nobel Prize. In accordance with the established procedure, transfers received at the Foreign Trade Bank from foreign banks are subject to remittance.

Chairman of the Committee for State Security
Andropov

F. 3, *op.* 80, *d.* 644, *l.* 68. Original.

Note

1. *A notation on the document reads: "On 29 December, Comrades Brezhnev, Kosygin, Podgorny, and Kirilenko were briefed. M. Suslov."*

49 Politburo Resolution

A Question from the Committee for State Security and the USSR Public Prosecutor's Office (On Solzhenitsyn)[1]

No. P187/XI
7 January 1971
Top Secret

To charge a committee consisting of Comrades M.A. Suslov, A.P. Kirilenko, Y.V. Andropov, V.V. Grishin, P.N. Demichev, V.F. Shauro, and G.M. Markov with additional study of this matter, taking into consideration the exchange of opinions at the Politburo session and to present appropriate proposals to the Central Committee if necessary.

Central Committee Secretary

F. 3, op. 80, d. 644, l. 69. Excerpt from minutes.

Note

1. *No minutes of this matter were kept at the Politburo session.*

50 Letter from Solzhenitsyn to the Chairman of the Council of Ministers of the USSR[1]

18 February 1971
To Comrade Kosygin, Chairman of the Council of Ministers of the USSR

Statement:

I am forced to appeal directly to you, the head of the government of the USSR, due to the fact that lower-level and mid-level agencies (*Vneshposyltorg*[2] and the Ministry of Foreign Trade) are avoiding a resolution of this issue.

As you know, I have received the Nobel Prize. Intending to use it in the USSR, I requested an initial sum. However, Vneshposyltorg (in addition to the artificial obstacle of "confirmation from the Writers' Union of receipt of the Nobel Prize") agrees to issue only 65 percent of my sum, taking away 35 percent, as has been done with authors' fees since June 1969.[3] The relevant order concerning deductions from payments is kept in strict confidence, which testifies to the *illegality* of the decision, since if it were a *law*, there would be no need to keep it secret. But even this secret order cannot contain instructions regarding the Nobel Prize for Literature:

—in view of the fact that this case was unforeseeable and exceptional;

—in view of the fact that under international law, as well as under the laws of the USSR, prizes (including Nobel Prizes) are not subject to any taxes or levies.

I request you to issue the following instructions to the Ministry of Foreign Trade stating the following:

1) That Vneshposyltorg allow me unimpeded to convert into cash in the full amount the sums coming to me as a result of receipt of the Nobel Prize;

2) That I be allowed also to acquire an *apartment* in Moscow for hard currency. (As a general rule, this also requires a Moscow residence permit, which I do not have. But I think that it is time to admit that the effort to exclude me from Moscow by using my Ryazan residence permit is unrealistic and useless: I am not going to live in Ryazan *even under a court order*).

However I would like to pose the question more broadly: does the state really desire to attract additional hard currency into our country? If the answer is yes, then it does not make sense to make the receipt of, for example, literary payments, *pointless* for authors, due to numerous deductions. As regards myself, I could attract to our homeland amounts significantly exceeding my personal requirements, and thus use them for the general good—if the incoming funds were not reduced in value and rendered virtually worthless by the practices of the Finance Ministry and the Foreign Trade Ministry.

Solzhenitsyn

*F.*3, *op.* 80, *d.* 644, *l.* 161. Original.

Notes

1. *A separate sheet bears the instruction: "General Department of the Central Committee. I request that this be circulated to Politburo members and candidate members, and Central Committee Secretaries (Instruction of Comrade Kosygin) A. Gorchakov. 25 February 1971."*
2. *Vneshposyltorg* —an acronym for the All-Russian Association for Trade in Foreign Packages, a department of the Ministry of Foreign Trade of the USSR.
3. *Before the USSR joined the Universal (Geneva) Copyright Convention in 1973, an author receiving payment in convertible hard currency could make use of the payment in the following ways:*
   a) *Put it in a type B account in the USSR Foreign Trade Bank and use it only in part for trips abroad with the permission of the hard currency administration of the USSR Finance Ministry;*
   b) *Buy Vneshposyltorg USSR certificates, which withheld 35 per cent from the author;*
   c) *Receive the entire sum in rubles.*

51 Report from the Committee on State Security of the USSR Council of Ministers[1]

No. 1630–A
25 June 1971
Top Secret

To the Central Committee:
Enclosed is Solzhenitsyn's book *August 1914*, "Knot 1,"[2] published in Paris (YMCA Press) and a short summary of its contents.

In the afterward "For the Russian-Language Edition Published Abroad in 1971," Solzhenitsyn writes:

> This book cannot now be published in our homeland in any
> form except samizdat, due to censored expressions, something
> incomprehensible to normal human common sense, and even
> for one reason alone, that I would no doubt have had to write
> the word God with a lower case letter. I could not stoop to this
> degradation. The directive to write God with a lower case let-
> ter is cheap atheistic pettiness . . . for the concept which signi-
> fies the highest creative powers of the Universe, one capital let-
> ter could be allowed.

From surveillance information we know that Rostropovich, Chukovskaya and her daughter, Tvardovsky, Kopelev, Zhores Medvedev, and certain other persons close to the author are familiar with the manuscript of this book.

We also know that Chukovskaya; Dr. E.Y. Kolman, who has been investigated by the KGB in connection with his hostile statements; Svetlova, the woman whom Solzhenitsyn lives with; and others have expressed negative opinions about the literary qualities of this work.

At the present time Solzhenitsyn is working on the second part of the book, *October 1916*.

Chairman of the KGB
Andropov

Enclosure

[The full summary of *August 1914* has been omitted from the American edition. However, the concluding remarks are of interest.]

. . . The excerpts cited above and the book as a whole lead one to the conclusion that the author is not at all indifferent to the possibility that Russia might have developed along capitalist lines during that period. His sympathies are entirely on the side of well-educated and nationalistically minded officers like Vorotyntsev, Martov, and others; of highly qualified engineers like Arkhangorodsky and Obodovsky; and of landowners and industrialists who managed their businesses in a rational and flexible manner. His criticism of the tsarist regime goes no further than that of the mildest form of Menshevism, that is, it is based on reformist, nationalist, and chauvinist positions.

The novel contains no clear analysis of the social and political situation at the time, and if it is possible to speak of the author's philosophical views, they are nothing more than a distorted reflection of the philosophical and religious views of L.N. Tolstoy. This emerges to a certain extent in his assessments of military campaigns, in his preaching of abstract, non-class-oriented virtues, and of self-perfection in his discussions of the meaning of history.

In general the tendencies embodied in a whole series of political problems that are only touched upon in this novel indicate the likelihood that any interpretation of them in later volumes planned by the author will be conducted from positions alien to our ideology.

Correct.

Deputy Head of the KGB
Directorate of the USSR Council of Ministers
Nikashkin

F. 3, op. 80, *d.* 656, *l.* 3–13. Original.

Notes

1. *Sent to Politburo members and candidate members, Central Committee Secretaries, and V. Shauro, 1 July 1971.*
2. "Knot" or "fascicle" (*uzel* in Russian) was the term Solzhenitsyn used to define each volume of his multi-volume series of novels known collectively as *The Red Wheel. August 1914* was the first in the series.

52 Memorandum from the Committee of State Security of the USSR Council of Ministers[1]

No. 2067–A
16 August 1971
Special File
Top Secret

On 12 August of this year in connection with information received about a meeting scheduled between an NTS emissary and Solzhenitsyn, government security agents took measures to detain the foreigner.

However, during one of the stakeouts organized for this purpose at Solzhenitsyn's dacha in the Naro-Fominsk district, Gorlov, an employee of the USSR State Institute of Standardized and Experimental Design and Engineering Research of the USSR State Construction Agency, was detained and brought to the police. After his identity was established he was released. For purposes of confidentiality he was told that the stakeout at the dacha was organized in response to a warning about a planned robbery.

Solzhenitsyn, who at the present time is in a state of anxiety due to fears that his social origins are going to be exposed in the press, used this event as an opportunity to prepare and distribute another in a series of letters to the West. (Text is enclosed).

The situation described by Solzhenitsyn in the letter is, with the exception of Gorlov's detention, sheer fantasy. Gorlov indicates in an explanation submitted to the KGB that he in no way links the incident at the dacha with the agencies of state security and that he had no basis whatsoever for such a conclusion. In his opinion, all of this is now "being used for purely political purposes."

In connection with this, Solzhenitsyn will be informed that the participation of the KGB in this incident is a figment of his imagination, and that the whole episode was purely of a law-enforcement nature. Therefore he should have contacted the police in the first instance.

In order to neutralize the negative consequence we consider it advisable to have the USSR Ministry of Internal Affairs contact the police to confirm the "robbery" version of events.

Please review.

Chairman of the Committee of State Security
Andropov

Enclosure

An Open Letter to Minister of State Security Andropov[2]

For many years, I have borne in silence the lawlessness of your employees: the inspection of all my correspondence, the confiscation of half of it, the tracking down of my correspondents, their persecution at work and by state agencies, the spying around my house, the shadowing of visitors, the tapping of telephone conversations, the drilling of holes in ceilings, the placing of recording apparatus in my city apartment and at my cottage, and a persistent slander campaign against me from the platforms of lecture halls when they are put at the disposal of officials from your ministry.

But after the raid yesterday, I will no longer be silent. My cottage at Rozhdestvo, in the Naro-Fominsk region, was unoccupied, and the eavesdroppers were counting on my absence. I, however, had come back to Moscow after being taken ill suddenly, and had asked my friend Alexander Gorlov to get a spare part for the car from my cottage. But it turned out the house was unlocked, and voices could be heard from within. Gorlov stepped inside and demanded the intruders' documents. In that small structure, where three or four can barely turn around, there were about ten of them in plain clothes. At a command from the senior officer—"Take him into the wood and silence him!"—Gorlov was grabbed, knocked to the floor, dragged face down into the woods, and beaten viciously. While this was going on, others took a roundabout route through the bushes, carrying parcels, documents, and other objects (including perhaps some of the apparatus they had brought before) to their cars. However, Gorlov fought back vigorously and yelled, summoning witnesses. Neighbors from other lots came running in response to his shouts, barred the intruders' way to the highway and demanded their identification documents. Then one of the intruders presented a red identification card and the neighbors let them pass. Gorlov, with a battered face and his suit in ribbons, was taken to a car. "Fine methods you have," he said to his escorts. "We are *on an operation*, and on an operation we can do anything," they replied.

The one who, according to papers he had shown the neighbors, was a captain, and according to his own statement was called Ivanov, drove Gorlov first to the Naro-Fominsk police station. The local officers greeted "Ivanov" with deference. "Ivanov" then demanded from Gorlov (!) a written explanation of what had happened. Although he had been severely beaten, Gorlov put in writing the purpose of his trip and all the circumstances. After that the senior intruder demanded that Gorlov should sign an undertaking *not to give the matter any publicity*. Gorlov flatly refused. Then they set off for

Moscow, and, on the road, the senior intruder gave Gorlov, word for word, the following warning: "If Solzhenitsyn finds out what took place at the dacha, you're finished. Your career [Gorlov is a candidate of technical sciences, has presented his doctoral dissertation, and works in the Design and Technical Research Institute of the State Construction Administration] will go no further; you will not be able to defend any dissertation. This will affect your family, your children, and, if necessary, we will put you *inside*."

Those who know how we live know the full feasibility of these threats. But Gorlov did not give in to them, refused to sign the pledge, and is now threatened with reprisals.[3]

I demand from you, Citizen Minister, the public identification of all the intruders, their punishment as criminals, and a public explanation of this incident. Otherwise I can only conclude that they were sent by *you*.

A. Solzhenitsyn
13 August 1971

Correct: Head of the KGB Directorate of the USSR Council of Ministers Bobkov

F. 3, *op*. 80, *d*. 645, *l*. 2–6. Original.

Notes

1. *The first page bears the resolution: "Agreed. M. Suslov 18/8" and the signatures of D. Polyansky, K. Mazurov, A. Pelshe, F. Kulakov, and G. Voronov; on the last page is the note: "Comrades L.I. Brezhnev, V.V. Grishin, A.P. Kirilenko, A.N. Kosygin, N.V. Podgorny, and A.N. Shelepin not present. Secretariat of Comrade Y.V. Andropov informed. N. Solovyev."*

2. See *The Oak and the Calf,* Appendix 17.

3. Alexander Gorlov was subsequently dismissed from his institute and prevented from defending his doctoral dissertation. He emigrated to the USA in August 1975 and two years later published a short book recounting his experiences: *Sluchai na dache* [An Incident at the Dacha], YMCA Press, Paris, 1977.

53 Memorandum from N. Shchelokov[1] "On the Solzhenitsyn Question"[2]

No later than 7 October 1971

In resolving the Solzhenitsyn question the following circumstance must be kept in mind.

1. Solzhenitsyn has become a major figure in the ideological struggle. This is a reality which cannot be ignored. To be silent on this point or to avoid it is out of the question. The anti-Soviet forces have made him their reactionary banner.

2. Objectively, Solzhenitsyn has talent. He is a literary phenomenon. In this respect, there is no doubt that he is of interest to the Soviet government. It would be extremely useful to have his pen serving the interests of the people. Given a proper resolution of the "Solzhenitsyn Problem," it would be completely feasible to attempt to steer his creative interests toward ideologically irreproachable themes.

3. *In resolving the Solzhenitsyn question we must analyze past mistakes made in dealing with people in the arts.*[3] Above all, we must take into account the mistakes made in dealing with Solzhenitsyn himself. Khruschev raised Solzhenitsyn to unheard-of heights as his supporter in the struggle against the personality cult. Prominent men of letters praised him to the skies, comparing his talents with those of Lev Tolstoy. On the basis of his very first short novel, *One Day in the Life of Ivan Denisovich*, he became a member of the Writers' Union at a time when many writers were not granted this honor even after five or six books. It is not clear why Solzhenitsyn was removed from the Writers' Union for his book *Cancer Ward*, which was written from the very same ideological position as *One Day in the Life of Ivan Denisovich*. In the first instance, he was received into the Writers' Union. In the second instance, he was removed from the Writers Union. This kind of inconsistency weakens our position in the struggle for ideological purity in our literature. It makes our treatment of Solzhenitsyn himself incomprehensible and inconsistent.

The "Solzhenitsyn Problem" was created by literary administrators who should have known better.

4. Writers who hold shaky ideological positions and demonstrate ideological instability in their literary works should be constantly watched and monitored. They need training and guidance. In this case, yelling at them, giving orders, and hounding them are ineffective methods. Here a

161

more intellectual approach is required. Solzhenitsyn's works could have been published in the Soviet Union after painstaking editing. One way or another, even without the author's consent, works such as these can be edited down and published so that subsequently they can be hushed up. The author must not be forced to seek publication abroad. It is already well known that there is no interest abroad in those authors whom we ourselves elevate. Thus we should "elevate" those authors whose works could damage the Soviet government, but we should "elevate" them in such a way that the anti-Soviet tone of their work completely disappears. This is possible, it has been proven by history. *In this case, what needs to be done is not to execute our enemies publicly, but to smother them in embraces. This is a basic truth, of which those comrades who manage literature should be aware.*

5. In the Solzhenitsyn business we are repeating the same glaring errors that we committed with regard to Boris Pasternak. Pasternak is definitely a major Russian writer. He is more significant than even Solzhenitsyn, and the fact that his novel *Dr Zhevago* [sic] was awarded the Nobel Prize contrary to our wishes was definitely a glaring error on our part, and was aggravated a hundred times by our incorrect position after the prize was awarded to him. *Dr Zhevago* should have been "edited down" and published here in this country. In that case, there would certainly have been no interest in the book in the West, especially because the ideological content could have been brought to the necessary level. Be that as it may, *Dr Zhevago* attracted the burning interest of readers here since there was such a hue and cry surrounding it. *Dr Zhevago* made the rounds in manuscript form. Foreign editions of it reached our country and it received wide attention on the radio. Concealing a literary work in this way is impossible in this day and age, when there are such widespread contacts with foreign countries and such easy access to Western broadcasts. We must take these facts into account. Unfortunately, no one is taking them into account.

It is time for our publishing houses to understand that today they must not reject literary works, but transform them.

Today once again the spotlight is on Pasternak. A series of articles has been printed which accord him the status of a great Russian writer. Now people are asking why we adopted such a strange attitude toward Pasternak when now we are singing his praise. The same thing could happen with Solzhenitsyn.

6. In the past, as a result of insufficiently flexible policies toward major Russian writers, some of them have ended up abroad. A list of such writers would include Bunin, Andreyev, Kuprin, and others.[4] Konenkov was another one who ended up abroad. *History shows that our treatment of these writers was wrong. We demanded of them things which they could not deliver by virtue of their class affiliation and their class upbringing.* Now our attitudes toward these people have become clearer. But we should draw certain conclusions on the basis of what happened. *These conclusions consist of the following: that our attitude toward the creative intelligentsia should be more flexible, more tolerant, and more judicious.*

7. Fairly soon Daniel and Sinyavsky will be released from their places of confinement. With their release there is no doubt that interest in them among all anti-Soviet elements will increase. These scum will become martyrs for an idea, and we are the ones who have made them into martyrs. And here, too, there were a goodly number of methods we could have used to render them harmless, without resorting to extreme measures. *The problem of Sinyavsky and Daniel has not been removed, but rather aggravated.* We don't need to aggravate the "Solzhenitsyn Problem" in the same way.

8. How should we resolve the "Solzhenitsyn Problem" now?

First of all, there is no point in creating obstacles to him going abroad to receive the Nobel Prize.

Secondly, under no circumstances should the issue of depriving him of his citizenship be raised. We need to do our work with the goal of having Solzhenitsyn conduct himself with dignity while he is abroad. We need to work things out so that Solzhenitsyn speaks the following phrases: "I have no differences with the Soviet authorities. I have no differences with the Party. I am a Soviet writer. I am proud of what is happening in the country. I have differences with my literary colleagues. These are professional differences. They have always existed and always will, as long as there is literature." The emphasis needs to be on the professional nature of the differences. Solzhenitsyn should be given an apartment without delay. He needs to receive a residence permit and have his needs catered to. One of the higher-ups needs to sit down and talk with him, to remove the bitter taste that his persecution has, no doubt, left in his mouth. In a word, we need to fight for Solzhenitsyn, not toss him out. We need to fight for Solzhenitsyn and not against Solzhenitsyn.

F. 80. Original.

Notes

1. Then the Minister of Internal Affairs.

2. *A separate page has the order: "To Comrade G.E. Tsukanov: Keep this note temporarily. L. Brezhnev." On the first page is a notation by Brezhnev: "Memo from Comrade N.A. Shchelokov."*

3. *Here and following the text was underlined by L. Brezhnev.*

4. Writers who emigrated in the years following the October Revolution.

54 From the Minutes of a Meeting of the Secretariat of the Central Committee of the Communist Party

7 October 1971
Meeting chaired by: Comrade M.A. Suslov
Present: Comrades Demichev, Kapitonov, Kulakov, Solomentsev, Ustinov
Off the Record

Suslov: There is a memo from Comrade Shchelokov regarding Solzhenitsyn. You have familiarized yourselves with it. The main point is to decide the question of where Solzhenitsyn's residence is to be. The musician Rostropovich, at whose dacha in Zhukovka he is now living, has raised the question of having Solzhenitsyn evicted from his dacha.[1] But in order for him to move, he needs to be allowed to live somewhere. Now he does not have a Moscow residence permit. His apartment is in the city of Ryazan, but that apartment is now occupied by his wife, from whom he is divorced.[2] Now Solzhenitsyn is married to another woman[3] who lives in Moscow and has a two-room apartment, and in fact Solzhenitsyn is spending all of his time there.

Ponomarev: Maybe it would be better to send him back to Ryazan?

Demichev: But he doesn't have an apartment in Ryazan.

Katushev: To allow him to build a dacha on his garden plot near Maly Yaroslavl where he has a summer house would hardly be advisable, since many workers from Moscow and other cities live there.

Suslov: For the time being we could do the following: not decide this question now, consult with the KGB as to whether it would be better to send Solzhenitsyn away from Moscow, or let him live with his new wife in her apartment in Moscow, which would make it possible to watch him more effectively. Then we can discuss this question again.

Resolved: To limit the discussion to an exchange of opinion.

Minutes from a meeting of the Secretariat of the Central Committee in 1971. Original.

Notes

1. It is difficult to know what prompted this statement. Neither Rostropovich nor Solzhenitsyn have ever given the slightest indication that Rostropovich wanted to evict the latter from his dacha.
2. This was not true. Natalia Reshetovskaya, Solzhenitsyn's first wife, did not agree to a divorce until two years later, in March 1973, despite the fact that Solzhenitsyn was living with Natalia Svetlova and had already had a child by her.
3. Solzhenitsyn did not marry Natalia Svetlova until April 1973.

55 Report from the Committee for State Security of the USSR Council of Ministers[1]

No. 3720–A/OV
27 October 1971
Special File
Top Priority

To the Central Committee:
As a result of surveillance activities, working notes and drafts have been discovered in Solzhenitsyn's possession, tracing his possible plan to write a new work (as a sequel to *August 1914*) which would misrepresent certain events of World War II.

Describing the circumstances of the capture of the traitor Vlasov and the siege of the army which he commanded, Solzhenitsyn observes that Vlasov was

> . . . one of the most successful generals at the beginning of the war and as the commander of the 99th Rifle Division he captured Peremyshl and for six days held the city. On June 22 his division was not taken by surprise; later, as commander of the 37th Army near Kiev, he escaped from encirclement and then became the commander of the 20th Army near Moscow, which struck the first blow there.

Attempts to break the blockade during encirclement were in vain, as the allied armies, according to Solzhenitsyn's notes, "received no reinforcements, military supplies, or food, and the soldiers were sacrificed to expediency, and it was not Vlasov who destroyed the army." Solzhenitsyn draws an analogy between the events described and the routing of the 2nd Army under the command of General Samsonov in Prussia in August 1914.

"At the time Vlasov was taken captive," Solzhenitsyn writes further, "some captured generals had already declared their disagreement with the way domestic and foreign policy were being conducted," and he cites Major Generals F. Trukhin, I. Blagoveschensky, V. Malyshkin, and others.

In his notes Solzhenitsyn also gives details of how the Germans created units consisting of former members of the Soviet Army who had surrendered and been taken captive, emphasizing that "almost until the very end of the war, Vlasov had nothing to do with the voluntary units."

During the last days of the war, Vlasov gave his troops an order, Solzhenitsyn claims, to switch to the side of the insurgent Czechoslovaks [sic] in Prague, and he was the one who allegedly had a decisive role in saving that city. "This was how they cleaned out Prague."

Solzhenitsyn's descriptions of the political program of the treasonous fascist collaborators is worth special attention, as it includes the following points: "Approval of February [Revolution]. October [Revolution]—a crisis. Demagoguery and terror. Where is the land? Where is freedom for the workers? Restore freedoms. The Communist Party should be disbanded, the machinery of oppression destroyed. But that is not within our power and here is where help from Great Germany comes in! Economy: land—state property, small and medium private commerce, transport and heavy industry—nationalized, collective farms—on a voluntary basis, land—leased from the state. Preserve: public education, health care, social security. Do not indiscriminately get rid of everything connected with the word 'Soviet.'

Also among the contents of Solzhenitsyn's notes are the theses of the so-called Grigorenko letter (he is receiving compulsory treatment in a psychiatric hospital) on the magazine *Voprosy Istorii KPCC* [Problems of the History of the Communist Party] in which the author slanderously describes events on the eve of and during the first days of World War II.[2] Solzhenitsyn has marked off the following passages from the letter:

"—After 1937 in the army—the psychosis of 'sabotage by the commanders,' and the commanders were paralyzed;"

"—So as not to anger Hitler—they built no new air fields. Aviation services were crowded into the old ones, known to Germany;"

"—They destroyed the old defensive frontier, and built no new one;"

"—In three days, 90 percent of the air force was wiped out;"

"—Only six hours later did Moscow allow them to open fire in response;"

"—The troops of the second echelon greeted the retreating heroes with bursts of fire ('Traitors, you opened the front!')"

"—There wasn't even a mobilization plan for restructuring industry;"

"—They made supply deliveries to Germany from 1939–1941, although Germany did not fulfill its obligations according to the pact;"

"—It was the people who paid for all the mistakes of the government;"

"—The Hitlerites lost four million (on all fronts) and we lost thirteen and a half million (on one front);"

"—The greatest unprecedented betrayal in history!"

On the basis of this letter, Solzhenitsyn concludes: "Baklanov's work *July 1941* is mere window dressing."[3]

Chairman of the Committee for State Security
Andropov

F. 3 op. 80, *d.* 645, *l.* 8–10. Original.

Notes

1. *The first page bears the signatures of M. Suslov, A. Kirilenko, D. Polyansky, A. Kosygin, N. Podgorny, A. Shelepin, V. Grishin, A. Pelshe, F. Kulakov, and L. Brezhnev.*

2. General Pyotr Grigorenko was a retired major-general who had served with distinction in World War II. In 1964 he had been arrested and confined for a while to an insane asylum for his dissident activities, and in 1969 was confined again, this time for five years. Shortly before his arrest he had written his critical "theses" on an article in *Voprosy Iistorii KPCC* about the start of World War II, leading Solzhenitsyn to invite him for a visit to discuss Soviet military incompetence at the outbreak of the war.

3. Grigory Baklanov, a moderately liberal novelist and short story writer, had made a name for himself during the Khrushchev "Thaw" as the author of several works about World War II that were more truthful about Soviet weaknesses than most earlier works. *July 1941* appeared in 1965.

56 Memorandum from the Committee for State Security of the USSR Council of Ministers and the USSR Ministry of Foreign Affairs

No. 1924/gs
16 November 1971
Classified

To the Central Committee:
Last year the Swedish Academy awarded Solzhenitsyn the Nobel Prize. In accordance with the provisions of Executive Order P184/59 of 27 November[1] and P185/7 of 4 December 1970, Foreign Minister Nilsson of Sweden and Ambassador Jarring, the Swedish Ambassador in Moscow, were informed that the Swedish Academy's decision was characterized as an unfriendly action toward the USSR. The statement said that the Soviet Union expects that Swedish representatives abroad will refrain from participating in events having to do with Solzhenitsyn.

The Swedish government acknowledged our communications and the Nobel Medal and Diploma were not presented to Solzhenitsyn.

According to a report from the Soviet Embassy in Stockholm, recently, reactionary circles in Sweden and a number of other Western countries have again been trying to use Solzhenitsyn to damage the interests of the Soviet Union. In light of this, it is of particular interest that according to reports in the Swedish press, the Swedish Foreign Ministry recently informed the Nobel Foundation that it has agreed to convey the Nobel Prize to Solzhenitsyn through the Swedish Embassy in Moscow.

We deem it advisable to instruct the Soviet Ambassador to Sweden to reaffirm to Foreign Minister Wickman our previous position on this issue and to state that the Soviet Union expects the Swedish Embassy in Moscow to refrain from any participation in events related to the awarding of the prize to Solzhenitsyn.

A draft of the resolution is enclosed.[2]
Please review.

Y. Andropov
A. Gromyko

F. 3, *op.* 69, *d.* 221, *l.* 52. Original.

Notes

1. *Distributed to Politburo members for a vote under 26–11 for 1971 .*
2. *19 November 1971 resolution No. P26/44 (see Document 57) was adopted by the Politburo.*

57 Politburo Resolution

"On the Instructions to be Given to the Soviet Ambassador in Stockholm Regarding Solzhenitsyn's Nobel Prize"

No. P26/44
19 November 1971
Top Secret

Approve the draft instructions to the Soviet Ambassador in Stockholm (enclosed).

Secretary of the Central Committee

Enclosure
Re: point 44 of transcript No. 26
Top Secret

Stockholm
To the Soviet Ambassador:
Visit Foreign Minister Wickman and make the following statement to him:

As is well known, certain circles in Sweden and outside Sweden have again been trying to use the award of the Nobel Prize to Solzhenitsyn to damage Soviet-Swedish relations. Specifically, attempts are being made to present the prize to Solzhenitsyn through the Swedish Embassy in Moscow. In connection with this, much attention has been attracted in the Soviet Union to the report in the Swedish press that the Swedish Foreign Ministry informed the Nobel Foundation of the Moscow Swedish Embassy's intent to convey the prize to Solzhenitsyn.

In connection with this, I have been instructed to reaffirm the position of the Soviet Union in regard to the awarding of the Nobel Prize to Solzhenitsyn as outlined in December of last year to Foreign Minister Nilsson and to the Swedish Ambassador to the USSR, Ambassador Jarring. In the Soviet Union now as before, the awarding of the prize and also the intention to present it to Solzhenitsyn through the Swedish Embassy in Moscow is perceived as an unfriendly act toward the Soviet Union, which could damage relations between our countries.

On 1 December 1970 Foreign Minister Nilsson informed the Soviet Ambassador that intervention by the Swedish government in matters connected with the award of the Nobel Prize is out of the question. For that reason, the Soviet Union expects the Swedish Embassy in Moscow to refrain from participating in any activities connected with the presentation of the prize to Solzhenitsyn.

Telegraph your implementation.

F. 3, *op.* 80, *d.* 645, *l.* 11–12. Excerpt from the minutes.

58 Report from the Committee for State Security of the USSR Council of Ministers[1]

No. 2953–A
23 November 1971
Top Secret

To Comrade L.I. Brezhnev:
Enclosed is a translation of an article about Solzhenitsyn from the [German] magazine *Stern*.

Chairman of the KGB
Andropov

Enclosure
Stern **No. 48 of 21.11**
Translated from German

A Boorish Family

This is how Irina, aunt of the Nobel Prize Laureate Solzhenitsyn, speaks of her relatives, formerly large landowners. In his new book, over which Western publishers are arguing, he described the exotic lifestyle of his family members on the eve of World War I. Aunt Irina also has a place in the book. *Stern* sought out this 82-year-old woman in Southern Russia.

"Russia has to be run by fools. Russia cannot manage any other way." Soviet writer and Nobel Laureate Solzhenitsyn puts this bitter truth in the mouth of an officer of the Russian general staff, an intelligent and sympathetic, if unimportant character, who appears on page 740 of his new novel. The book has just been issued by the Langen Muller publishing house. But it caused a sensation even before that. And not only because the right to publish it is in dispute, and not only because another publisher, Luchterhand, has mobilized the laws and is accusing Langen Muller of "publication theft." The novel has become very popular owing both to its literary qualities and contents.

Heedless of the dimwitted bureaucrats of the Soviet censorship, Solzhenitsyn has poured into this latest work his heartfelt hatred of the Establishment that torments long-suffering Mother Russia. While doing this, he cleverly uses proven methods to evade imprisonment for hostility toward the state: he shifts the action of his novel to prerevolutionary times. However, it is immediately clear to anyone reading the novel that in portraying historical events, the writer is raising current issues. The historical event is the battle near Tannenberg which took place in August 1914, in the course of which the Russian Army was surrounded and destroyed.

With irony and despair Solzhenitsyn describes the arrogant generals, their intrigues, their fear of the enemy and of the tsar. Of General Artamonov he writes: "A martinet dressed in general's uniform, who initially was to begin with a bright non-commissioned officer who might have made a model soldier. Or a true servant of the church: a strapping fellow with a booming voice, with just the right degree of laziness to swing the censer like a true performer . . . and why had he become an infantry general? Why had 60,000 Russian soldiers been placed under his inept command?"

Red tape at headquarters, idiotic commands, grueling movements by military units that march senselessly until chaos leads to disaster.

171

Solzhenitsyn describes all this with an amazing grasp of detail and makes his criticisms with the knowledge of a general staff officer.

The reader observes the ruin of the 2nd Russian Army through the eyes of the young officer Vorotyntsev, who from the lounge car at the headquarters of Commander-in-Chief Archduke Nikolai Nikolaevich embarks on a long journey to the front, in order to determine what has happened. Here staff officers arrange a sumptuous dinner at the height of battle. Here members of the general staff spend hours each morning grooming and dressing themselves, like women, rather than thinking of battle. Orders are given to the soldiers by radio in uncoded form and within an hour they are known to Hindenburg and Ludendorff. No one knows a thing about the enemy.

Full of disgust, Vorotyntsev gallops day and night from one division to another, organizing counterstrikes and forcing fleeing regiments to halt. He is wounded and then surrounded, and, with several Cossacks, breaks through the encircling forces. He returns to the Grand Prince's headquarters, and in a salon decorated with Persian rugs, reports to the Commander-in-Chief on what he has seen, hiding nothing.

Outwardly, life at headquarters continues to flow tranquilly along its course, writes Solzhenitsyn. Count Mengden, an aide-de-camp and member of the cavalry guard continues, as before, to busy himself with the pigeons between the cars of the grand duke and the quartermaster. He lures the pigeons by whistling, lets them go, and adjusts his sword belt.

The reader does not sense the autobiographical element in the novel. At first glance, it seems that Solzhenitsyn is describing himself in the figure of Vorotyntsev. But can that be the case, when the writer was only born in 1918?

And yet there is an answer to the question of where Solzhenitsyn got his specialist's point of view, his detailed knowledge of the East Prussian landscape, and his deep understanding of the psychology of the military leader and the soldier. During World War II, he was the commander of a battalion and fought in Eastern Prussia. There, in 1945, wearing the medals of a captain, he was arrested and sentenced to eight years in corrective labor camps to be followed by exile, for criticizing Stalinist policy and the conduct of the war in letters he wrote and sent by courier.

All the actors in Solzhenitsyn's novel who bear their own names are long dead. All except for one person. Her name is Irina. She is presented at the very beginning of the novel as an attractive, young, and very rich woman. She is married to Roman, who is always dressed in the English style as a landowner. Who is Irina? *Stern* correspondent Dieter Steiner learned that her name is Irina Ivanovna Shcherbak and that she is Alexander Solzhenityn's aunt, the sister-in-law of Solzhenityn's mother, who died in 1944 of tuberculosis.

Irina Shcherbak is now 82 years old. She lives in Georgievsk, a small town near the Caucasus resort of Kislovodsk. That was where Dieter Steiner visited her recently.[2] He describes her as

> . . . an old woman, stooped over and almost blind, but still energetic and with a lively mind, dwelling in the annex of an old peasant home. Her room is about six feet by nine, with a sloping clay floor and whitewashed walls. She sits on an iron bed, above which hang an icon under glass and a wooden cross. Her dog Druzhok [Little Friend], a decrepit shaggy mutt, sleeps under the bed. A quarter of the room is taken up by the brick stove, on which there is a pot, two metal plates, and a bag of flour. I sit on a squeaky stool. 'So you see how I live now,' says Irina. 'This is after 53 years living under the commissars! I get ten rubles a month from the state and fifteen rubles from Sanya [Alexander Solzhenitsyn]. I'm the only one of all his relatives still alive.'

Until now, little has been known about the history of the Solzhenitsyn family. What is there to be found in the archives? "Alexander Isaevich Solzhenitsyn was born 11 December 1918 in Kislovodsk in the North Caucasus into the family of a teacher." It's true that even from this you can deduce his petty-bourgeois origin. Irina Shcherbak knows the history of the family in significantly more detail. Solzhenitsyn's father, Isai,[3] was the son of a large landowner. In his marriage in 1917 "money attracted money;" he married Taisia, the daughter of a large landowner, Zakhar Shcherbak.

Solzhenitsyn's mother grew up in a home furnished like a palace. Her brother Roman also made a good match. His wife Irina, who is impoverished today, inherited a fortune of millions from her father. She was the richest member of the family and since she passed all her money to her husband, he lived like a feudal lord.

Sadly, Irina remembers the times before the First World War, when she and her husband made a long trip abroad. In Stuttgart, they visited the Daimler factory and bought a cigar-shaped sports car. Roman planned to use it to take part in the Moscow–St. Petersburg auto race. He already had one car, a Rolls Royce. In all of Russia then there were only nine such cars. When the war started, Commander-in-Chief Grand Duke Nikolai Nikolaevich requisitioned this luxurious car for himself.

Returning from exile in 1956, Solzhenitsyn visited his Aunt Irina in Georgievsk and sat with her for days, questioning her about the family's history. Her stories were partially included in *August 1914*. Here is how he describes Uncle Roman: "He especially liked to travel and to shock Europeans with his Russian rowdiness and peculiarity. At the Louvre, in the round crimson room where the Venus de Milo stands, and where there is not a single chair, he was capable of offering a ten-franc note to an observer with a sweeping gesture and the words, 'Get a chair.' And while Irina looked at the displays, he placed a cigarette in his mouth and played with his lighter. In the next room, it was the same story: 'A chair. Here. Over here.' "

Roman and Irina lived in the house of Solzhenitsyn's grandfather, whom the writer in his book calls not Shcherbak, but Tomchak. Here he describes a scene when his uncouth grandfather, "that picturesque Russian . . . in a deliberately exaggerated suit which was not simply citified, but looked like something one might wear at a carnival," is searching for the owner of a boarding school for the children of noble families in order to register his daughter there. "Tomchak did not know how to speak *sotto voce*, as one ought. Even when he was in the classroom, he yelled loudly, as if he were standing next to a wagon with a donkey harnessed to it and urging on a stubborn ox."

Solzhenitsyn portrays his mother Taisia in the figure of Ksenya. Solzhenitsyn writes of her: "When Ksenya went home on vacation, she was frightened by the crudeness of her family members. Once she invited her friend Sonya (a Jewish girl), and seeing her family's Neanderthal crudeness through her friend's eyes, she burned with shame. Old man Tomchak beat his wife, and at times when he argued with his son, he would reach for his knife."

Irina did not like the family she had entered into when she married according to her father's will. "It was a family of boors," she writes in her memoirs. She made these notes for her famous nephew, since she couldn't tell him everything during his brief visit. She gave her memoirs to *Stern*.[4] "Our landowners," she writes, "lived like pigs: wine, cards, debauchery." On Solzhenityn's mother, she said: "She graduated from school with a gold medal and therefore considered herself smarter than others. In fact she was conservative, arrogant, and ridiculous."

Solzhenitsyn's parents married in 1917 at the front, where his father, an officer, was fighting. In 1918, he returned to the village of Sablya, where he had land holdings. Soon the Civil War began. The Red Army began persecuting landowners. Many of them were shot. One day Irina got a telegram from Taisia, Solzhenitsyn's mother: "Isai [sic] is severely ill." She and her husband immediately went to see Solzhenitsyn's father and found him in the hospital, mortally wounded. A hunting accident—that was the official version. But it's possible that it was suicide. Several minutes before he died, he said to Irina: "Take care of my son. I know that I will have a son." Taisia was three months pregnant at the time.

Alexander Solzhenitsyn was born in his Aunt Irina's house. The family's property was confiscated by the Reds. Taisia got work as a stenographer in the Rostov police station. Alexander remained with his Aunt Irina for a time. Uncle Roman worked as a bus driver at that time. After his death in 1944, Irina was left without means of survival. Seventeen days later Taisia died of tuberculosis. Irina buried her in her husband's grave, since she could not get enough money together for a burial.

At that time Officer Alexander Solzhenitsyn was fighting at the front. He had studied mathematics and physics in Rostov, passing his examinations with excellent marks. During the war, he married Natasha, the daughter of a Jewish merchant.[5] When he was released from prison in 1953, his wife did not go into exile with him. Irina Shcherbak recalls:

> In 1956, Sanya returned. He went to his wife in Rostov. She was living with another man. He was crushed by this. He settled in Ryazan, approximately 180 kilometers from Moscow. After he got a decent position there as a teacher of mathematics, Natasha decided to go back to him.[6] Sanya came to me for advice. I told him frankly that I respect only those wives who are prepared to follow their husbands into exile. In my view, anyone else is just a kept woman. However, Natasha was stubborn, she had Sanya wrapped around her little finger, and she moved in with him and even brought her mother and sister with her. And Sanya lived with those three women until he left them last year and became involved with another, younger woman.

Irina Shcherbak remembers her last meeting with her famous nephew with some bitterness. It was in 1970. Solzhenitsyn invited his aunt to Ryazan and sent her money for the trip. "When I got off the train," recounts the old women, "I suddenly saw that Sanya and Natasha were hiding in the station building. I looked poor in my old clothes, and they were ashamed of me. If I had had money, I would have returned home immediately. But I had only twenty kopecks."

Irina Shcherbak did not confirm rumors that the writer, who was expelled from the Writers' Union in 1969 and who has not published a line since then, is living in great poverty. "They live like members of the bourgeoisie," she says. "In the West, Solzhenitsyn has become a multimillionaire, thanks to his books. They often go to Moscow and to the theatre and concerts."

Irina intended to stay in Ryazan for three months. She left after 17 days. In her last letter she wrote to her famous nephew: "Sanya, you are not treating me well. And even now I see in you the little boy who I so often carried in my arms."

A true copy: Chief of the Directorate of the Committee for State Security of the USSR Council of Ministers
Bobkov

F. 3, *op.* 80, *d.* 645, *l.* 14–22. Original.

Notes

1. *The document has the following note: "Reported to Comrades Brezhnev, Suslov, Kirilenko. To Politburo archive. K. Chernenko."*

2. It was not possible for the *Stern* correspondent, Dieter Steiner, to visit Irina Shcherbak without the express permission and assistance of the KGB, since Georgievsk was closed to foreigners and Steiner spoke almost no Russian. The complicity of the KGB appears to have been concealed not only from Soviet readers (when the *Stern* article was reprinted in the Soviet press) but also from Brezhnev and other members of the Politburo.

3. An example of the limited extent of the KGB's knowledge at this juncture. Solzhenitsyn's father's first name was Isaaky. His mother had shortened the son's patronymic to Isaevich to avoid both the awkwardness of "Isakiyevich," and the latter's associations with the Jewish name "Isaak."

4. Irina was browbeaten by officials into handing over her notes about the family and they remained in the possession of the KGB. When the author of these notes visited *Stern's* editorial offices and spoke with Steiner in 1977, the photographs from his visit were still in the files, but Irina's notes had "vanished."

5. Natalia Reshetovskaya was the daughter of a Cossack, not a Jew (see Document 11).

6. Irina's version of these events is tendentious. It is true that while Solzhenitsyn was in the labor camps, Natalia divorced him (with his approval) to avert sanctions against her as the "wife of an enemy of the people." While working as a chemist in Ryazan, she lived with a fellow scientist, Vsevolod Somov, for a while, and looked after his two orphaned children. When Solzhenitsyn returned to Central Russia from his exile in Kazakhstan in 1956, he got a job as a teacher in Vladimir Province, a hundred miles east of Moscow. It was then that he and Natalia met again and decided to restore their marriage, and only after that that Solzhenitsyn moved to Ryazan.

59 Report from the Committee for State Security of the USSR Council of Ministers[1]

No. 3256–Ts
25 December 1971
Special File
Top Priority

To the Central Committee:
The KGB is receiving reports indicating that a new anti-Soviet campaign is under way in the West, connected with the name of Solzhenitsyn. In this round of the campaign, letters sent by Solzhenitsyn to the Nobel Foundation and the Swedish Academy are being used, letters in which he informed them of his refusal to go to Stockholm to receive the laureate's diploma and medal in view of the fact that he allegedly would not be permitted to return to the USSR. The bourgeois press is attempting to pass off these statements as official statements forbidding Solzhenitsyn to go abroad.

In these same letters, Solzhenitsyn continues to insist on being presented with the laureate symbols in the Swedish Embassy in Moscow, in an official setting with the participation of all those who desire to be present and with the traditional speech given by the Nobel laureate. For this occasion Solzhenitsyn has prepared and given to a small number of people the new version of a speech in which he intends not only to address literary issues but also to deal tendentiously with a series of social problems.

The surveillance information received by the KGB indicates that Solzhenitsyn is presently working intensively on *October 1916*, which will be a sequel to the novel *August 1914*, published in the West. It is believed that the new novel will contain a description of the actions of Russian soldiers on the southern part of the front and specifically the Brusilov salient. In this work the author intends to portray Rasputin.

According to Solzhenitsyn, work on *October 1916* has turned out to be much harder than he expected. This is because the author aims to construct the novel on the basis of documentary evidence; however, as he himself writes in the afterward to *August 1914*, "any gathering of materials available to others is barred to me." At the same time he states that *1917* "will go easily for me."

In addition, materials received indicate that even close friends of Solzhenitsyn who fully share his political views give *August 1914* low marks

177

on various points.

The literary critic Lakshin has written, "Sympathizing most of all with the patriotic officer class, engineers, and the enlightened bourgeoisie, Solzhenitsyn does not provide them with any contrasting intelligent people to talk to from among the soldiers or the working class. . . . The working class is not shown in Solzhenitsyn's novel."

The figure of Lieutenant Lenartovich, who is discovered to be a Bolshevik and is the only Bolshevik in the novel, does not fit the true image of a Bolshevik of that time, writes writer [Lev] Kopelev. "Lenartovich," says Kopelev, "is completely irrational. He should have helped the head doctor tend to the wounded, and should not have behaved disdainfully toward him, and should not have let himself be taken captive. Even the fact that he gives Lenartovich German ancestry is all wrong. It means that he does not care about Russia's fate."

However, some of Solzhenitsyn's friends believe that this generalized presentation of the image of a Bolshevik is deliberate and will help the author in *October 1916* and subsequent novels to show that only such people can rise in the Party. "For this reason," says [Roy] Medvedev, "Lenartovich will, in the future, probably rise into the nomenklatura of the Bolshevik organization. Later he will rise to the level of a member of the Central Committee."

Through Heeb, his agent abroad, Solzhenitsyn regularly receives from his Swiss bank account substantial sums in foreign currency, deposited there by bourgeois publishers for his work published in the West. With these sums, he obtained cars without waiting in line, one for the mother-in-law of the woman he lives with, E.F. Svetlova, a Party member and department head at the State Institute of Standardized Design and Engineering Research of the USSR State Building Commission, and for his former wife Reshetovskaya. From these same funds Solzhenitsyn intends to buy himself a cooperative apartment in the city of Moscow, another car, and he regularly buys groceries and other things in hard-currency stores.

According to our surveillance information, Solzhenitsyn intends to bequeath 85 percent of the money which he has abroad for the construction of a church in the West.[2]

We have learned from our operatives that many members of the Soviet creative intelligentsia regard Solzhenitsyn's activities as anti-Soviet. "The aura of genius and martyrdom, the reputation of Solzhenitsyn as a fighter for truth, which certain elements tried to attach to Solzhenitsyn, is conspicuously and tangibly disappearing and evaporating." (According to poet T. Solodar.)

According to the writer B. Polevoy,

> Solzhenitsyn is a typical example of literary carpetbagging. He
> does everything he can to make it look as if our government
> has crowned him with a wreath of thorns. He wants to appear
> miserable and suffering in the eyes of Europe, America, and
> most of all, the Zionists. Although he is Russian, he plays effec-
> tively on our enemies' hatred for our country.

Poet I. Abashidze: "I have seen few people as insolent as Solzhenitsyn. Our
government is very tolerant of such a scoundrel! After I saw him several times
at the Secretariat, I became convinced that he is a bastard."

Literary critic D. Starikov: "Solzhenitsyn plays on his own and others'
hatred of us. And he gets away with it all, and that is why recently he has
gotten thoroughly insolent."

Writer L. Leonov: "With the aid of the West, Solzhenitsyn has received a
martyr's halo and we are asked about this at practically every meeting with
readers. Hasn't the time come to tell our people everything honestly and
directly—what kind of writer and person this is? It would not be so hard to
find a forum and an occasion to speak out about this."

Composer D. Kabalevsky: "We talk and talk, and Solzhenitsyn goes on
unrestrained; he understands perfectly well that he has become a weapon in
the hands of our fiercest enemies, but not only does he reconcile himself to
this role, he tries to exalt it and strengthen it."

Playwright I. Shtok: "Solzhenitsyn has become a banner of anti-
Sovietism . . . he strolls around Moscow without a care in the world,
supplying our enemies abroad with ideological anti-Soviet weaponry, and we
forgive him everything. How long will this go on?!"

Screenwriter K. Mints: "In England they didn't hesitate to deport one
hundred of our people for some imaginary espionage and here we are
pussyfooting just over Solzhenitsyn—an obvious supplier of anti-Soviet filth
abroad."

USSR Writers' Union member V. Kreps:

> Psychologically, Solzhenitsyn is a very effective figure for their
> propaganda: after all he lives in the USSR, so he sees every-
> thing with his own eyes, and he endures everything personally!
> Aren't there any decisive measures that could be taken to
> deprive our enemies of this trump card, Solzhenitsyn? If some
> fear that that would occasion a new wave of slander, well, those
> waves are not abating as it is, but only growing."

Taking the above into account, we are taking steps to limit the impact of Solzhenitsyn's antisocial actions.

Deputy Chairman of the KGB
Tsvigun

F. 3, op. 80, d. 645, l. 25–29. Original.

Notes

1. *The first page has the following note by M. Suslov: "Circulate" and the signatures of D. Polyansky, K. Mazurov, A. Kosygin, V. Grishin, N. Podgorny, A. Shelepin, (twice—Eds.), P. Demichev, A. Pelshe, and F. Kulakov.*
2. This appears to be a garbled version of Solzhenitsyn's plan, later abandoned, to finance the building of a church in Russia, to be designed by the dissident architect Yuri Titov.

60 Report of the Committee for State Security of the USSR Council of Ministers[1]

No. 3318–A
31 December 1971
Special File
Top Secret

To the Central Committee:
According to surveillance information obtained by the Committee for State Security, Yakir[2] has transmitted to U. Fromm, a reporter from the West German newspaper *Die Welt*, the following text of a letter by Solzhenitsyn:[3]

There are many ways of killing a poet.

The method chosen for Tvardovsky was to take away his beloved child—his passion—his journal.

They were not satisfied with sixteen years of insults, meekly endured by this hero so long as his journal survived, so long as literature went on without interruption, so long as people could be printed in it, so long as people could go on reading it. They were not satisfied! So they lit fires around him: scattered his forces, destroyed his journal, dealt with him unjustly. And within six months these fires had consumed him. Within six months he was mortally sick; and only his characteristic fortitude sustained him till now, conscious to the last. Suffering to the last.

Third day. The portrait over the coffin shows the dead man about age forty, his brow unfurrowed by the galling yet cherished burden of his journal, radiant with that childlike bright trustfulness which he carried with him throughout his mortal life and which returned to him even when he was doomed.

To the most beautiful music, wreath after wreath is borne. . . . Here is one 'From Soviet soldiers. . . .' With good reason. I remember how soldiers at the front knew to a man the difference between *Tyorkin*,[4] which rang so miraculously true, and all other wartime books. And let us remember, too, how army libraries were forbidden to subscribe to *Novy Mir*, and how not so long ago men in barracks were hauled in for questioning if they read the light blue journal.

And now the whole awkward squad from the Writers' Union has tumbled onto the stage. In the guard of honor we see the very same seedy deadbeats who once hunted and harassed him with unholy cries. Yes, it's an old, old custom, ours, dating from the time of Pushkin: dead poets must fall into the hands of their enemies. The body is speedily disposed of, and the situation saved with a few glib speeches.

They plant themselves around the coffin like a circle of stones, and think that they have isolated it. They break up our one and only journal, and think that they have conquered.

But you know and understand nothing of the last century of Russia's history if you see in this a victory rather than an irreparable blunder.

Madmen! When the voices of the young ring out, harsh and peremptory, how you will miss this patient critic, whose gentle admonitory voice was needed by all. That is when you will be ready to dig up the earth with your hands to bring back Trifonich. But by then it will be too late.

On the Ninth Day.

Together with the report of the foregoing text, we are sending photographs which were taken of Solzhenitsyn while attending Tvardovsky's funeral.[5]

Andropov
Chairman of the Committee for State Security of the USSR Council of Ministers

F. 3, *op.* 80, *d.* 645, *l.* 30–31. Original.

Notes

1. *The signatures of P. Demichev, M. Suslov, N. Podgorny, K. Mazurov, A. Pelshe, A. Shelepin, V. Grishin, F. Kulakov, G. Voronov, and D. Polyansky are on the first sheet; on the last sheet there is the note: "Comrades A.N. Kosygin, D.S. Polyansky are on vacation; Comrade A.P. Kirilenko is in Chile. N. Solovyov."*

2. Pyotr Yakir was the son of a celebrated Soviet army commander, Iona Yakir, who was executed in Stalin's purge of the Red Army in 1937. Having spent his entire childhood in a variety of prisons—see his *A Childhood in Prison* (Macmillan, 1972)—he became a historian, and joined the dissident movement in the late sixties.

3. It was not a letter, but an elegy in prose, which Solzhenitsyn distributed in samizdat. See *The Oak and the Calf*, Appendix 19.

4. Tvardovsky's humorous mock epic poem, *Vasily Tyorkin*, about a peasant soldier caught up in World War II, was immensely popular with the Soviet public and also one of Solzhenitsyn's favorite works.

5. *Tvardovsky died on 18 December 1971. A service was held at the Central Writer's Club and the funeral took place on 21 December 1971 at Novodevichy Cemetery in Moscow.*

PART III
1972–1973
APPROACHING CRISIS

First Lieutenant Solzhenitsyn (r.) and a fellow officer on the Red Army's western front some time in 1943. Solzhenitsyn was twenty four years old at the time.

Solzhenitsyn shortly after the capture of Orel in August 1943. The medal on his chest is the Order of the Patriotic War, which he was awarded for gallantry in battle.

Seuil

A sketch of Solzhenitsyn made by a fellow inmate soon after their arrival at Solzhenitsyn's first labor camp in Moscow in 1945.

Seuil

Solzhenitsyn as he appeared at his last and most severe labor camp, Ekibastuz (the camp described in One Day in the Life of Ivan Denisovich*). Having succeeded in smuggling out his number patches, Solzhenitsyn took this photograph of himself shortly after his discharge and arrival in southern Kazakhstan to start a period of indefinite internal exile.*

Seuil

Solzhenitsyn in his officer's pea-jacket shortly after his arrival in southern Kazakhstan.

Solzhenitsyn at Ryazan station in 1957, one year after his release from internal exile. The hole in his suitcase had been made by a camp guard while he was still a prisoner.

Solzhenitsyn examining a photo album in the Kremlin office of Khrushchev's private secretary, Vladimir Lebedev, around the time of the publication of One Day in the Life of Ivan Denisovich, *1953.*

A. Popova

Solzhenitsyn with his first wife, Natalia Reshetovskaya, in the spring of 1953.

Z. Medvedev

The "dacha" in Naro-Fominsk that Solzhenitsyn purchased with some of his royalties from One Day in the Life of Ivan Denisovich, *in 1953.*

Solzhenitsyn in September 1965 in the days following the KGB's confiscation of his archive from Veniamin Teush during a police raid.

Solzhenitsyn at Kornei Chukovsky's dacha in Peredelkino in May 1967 on the day when his "Open Letter to the Fourth All-Union Congress of Soviet Writers" was broadcast back to the Soviet Union by the BBC.

Ullstein

Solzhenitsyn with Heinrich Böll in Frankfurt immediately after his expulsion from the Soviet Union on February 14, 1974.

W. Spiller/Magnum

Solzhenitsyn brought his family to his home in Zurich after their departure from the Soviet Union on March 29, 1974.

Solzhenitsyn receiving his Nobel Prize for Literature in Stockholm in December 1974, four years after it had been awarded to him.

Solzhenitsyn giving the Commencement Address at Harvard, June 9, 1978. The text of his address was later published under the title "A World Split Apart."

Solzhenitsyn and Natalia Svetlova in Vladivostok on the day after their return to Russia, May 28, 1994.

61 From the Minutes of a Politburo Session

7 January 1972
Top Secret

Presiding: Comrade L.I. Brezhnev
Present: Comrades Voronov, Kulakov, Mazurov, Pelshe, Podgorny, Polyansky, Suslov, Shelepin, Andropov, Demichev, Katushev

Comrade Andropov's report on the presentation of the Nobel Prize to Solzhenitsyn
    After an exchange of opinions, it was considered inadvisable for the time being to allow the presentation of the Nobel Prize to Solzhenitsyn.

From minutes of Politburo sessions for 1972. Original.

62 From Minutes of a Meeting of the Central Committee Secretariat

16 February 1972
Presiding: Comrade A.P. Kirilenko
Present: Comrades F.D. Kulakov, P.N. Demichev, M.S. Solomentsev, I.V. Kapitonov, K.F. Katushev, B.N. Ponomarev

On Solzhenitsyn
Demichev reported to the Secretariat that articles opposed to Solzhenitsyn published in our press as well as in the foreign press have dramatically undermined his authority and are of major importance. However, in spite of this, Solzhenitsyn persists in pursuing his anti-Soviet propaganda.

The Central Committee Secretariat has favored taking measures to suppress Solzhenitsyn's hostile activity.

From minutes of the Central Committee Secretariat meetings for 1972. Original.

63 E. Furtseva's Letter to the Politburo[1]

17 February 1972
Special File

On February 17 of this year I received a letter from A. Solzhenitsyn, which I am enclosing.

In this connection, I would like to state my views on Solzhenitsyn and his political and literary positions.

Having worked among the intelligentsia for many years, and communicating daily with people in the arts and culture, I am well acquainted with their opinions and attitudes toward Solzhenitsyn, who has consistently spoken out as an open enemy of our system and the Soviet people.

Their opinion is unanimous. As is known, writers at their meetings, workers at large factories, and theater artists, including the Bolshoi soloists, A. Maslennikov, G. Andryushchenko, and others, have sharply condemned Solzhenitsyn. Their indignation rose again after the reprinting of the article from the West German magazine *Stern* in *Literaturnaya Gazeta*, exposing the social roots of Solzhenitsyn's "oeuvre" and his moral character.

However, honest Soviet artists are profoundly concerned that Solzhenitsyn's hostile positions are not getting the public evaluation they should in the press. With the exception of a few, brief, and rather unconvincing notes on Solzhenitsyn (for example regarding the award of the Nobel Prize to him), *Literaturnaya Gazeta* has published over the years only two items worthy of attention—a politically astute letter from the American Communist singer Dean Reed and the reprint of the abovementioned article from *Stern*.

Such a state of affairs has, in my view, had serious negative consequences. Solzhenitsyn himself, it seems, confident of his impunity, is growing ever more impudent as witnessed by his recent statement about the alleged harassment in our country over many years of the poet Tvardovsky, which was printed by many bourgeois newspapers and repeatedly broadcast by Western radio stations. Certain representatives of the artistic intelligentsia in turn suppose that Solzhenitsyn is getting away with everything, and are themselves beginning to lose a sense of responsibility for their work and their public conduct.

Solzhenitsyn is a powerful and intelligent person, capable of having the most harmful influence on unreliable and unstable people. I would like to cite my conversation with the singer Dean Reed, which took place at his request at the end of last year. Reed recounted how people came up to him in the restaurant of the Hotel Rossiya and at concerts and tried to convince him that his letter on Solzhenitsyn was perceived negatively by the intelligentsia and the youth of our country. "The thing that shocked me most of all," said Reed, "was that Soviet people called my article incorrect; as before, I am deeply convinced of my correctness." I assured Reed that his indignation over Solzhenitsyn is shared by all Soviet people.

I am convinced that many questions regarding relations with the intelligentsia would be solved and we would consolidate it better if strict measures were taken to deal with Solzhenitsyn. All his life he has hated Soviet rule and cannot live among a people and in a society that is hateful to him.

Therefore I ask you to review the question of deporting Solzhenitsyn abroad. Such a measure, I am certain, would cause much less damage than Solzhenitsyn's continued residence and disruptive anti-Soviet activities in our country.

A way could be prepared for this decision by the publication of articles and letters from major figures in literature, art, and science, and the conducting of meetings of workers at the country's leading factories. I am convinced that the Soviet public will demand that Solzhenitsyn should be removed from our country.

Communist Party member
E. Furtseva
17/II-1972

P.S. As for Solzhenitsyn's reference to my interview in the US, that is his usual crude fabrication.

Enclosure
To the USSR Minister of Culture
E.A. Furtseva

Dear Ekaterina Alexeyevna:

I heard that in one of your interviews you made the statement that the Soviet government does not object to the presentation of the Nobel Prize to me in Moscow, which the Swedish Academy has entrusted to their Permanent Secretary K. Gierow. That is natural: in any country the award of the Nobel Prize to one of its citizens is considered a national honor—far greater, for example, than an Olympic gold medal.

However, the time of the award is approaching (the Secretary of the Academy is intending to come this spring) and the question remains: where will the presentation take place? The Swedish Embassy prefers to keep its distance from this ceremony, apparently supposing that the Soviet government has an unfavorable attitude to it. However, if the Embassy officially learns that the ministry which you head has no objections, I think that it would be glad to change its decision and provide its premises. But even if that is not the case, you have at your disposal numerous other buildings in Moscow.

Of course, the award could also take place in the cramped conditions of a home. But I think that you, as Minister of Culture, and your experts understand: if not now, then ten to fifteen years from now, the fact that premises could not be found in Moscow for the award of the Nobel Prize to a Russian writer will be perceived in the history of our culture as a national shame.

Whatever the circumstances, I personally invite you to attend this ceremony.

A. Solzhenitsyn
12 February 1972
Moscow, K–9
ul. Gorkogo, 12, kv. 169

F. 3, *op.* 80, *d.* 645, *l.* 39–43. Signed.

Note

1. *The first page bears the resolution: "Brief through circulation. A. Kirilenko" and the sig-natures A. Kosygin, N. Podgorny, A. Pelshe, P. Demichev, G. Voronov, D. Polyansky, A. Shelepin, V. Grishin, F. Kulakov; the last page bears the notation: "A report has been made to Comrade A. P. Kirilenko on the proposal of Comrade Furtseva contained in this memorandum (see memorandum to Comrade Y. Andropov of 20.11.72, No. 421–A, V. Galkin, 23.11.72)."*

64 Memorandum of the Committee for State Security of the USSR Council of Ministers[1]

No. 421–A
20 February 1972
Special File
Top Secret

To the Central Committee:
The Committee for State Security has obtained surveillance information that Solzhenitsyn is intensively preparing a ceremony for the award of the Nobel Prize insignia which is due to take place in Moscow in the apartment of his mistress N.D. Svetlova.

At the present time Solzhenitsyn has prepared the final version of the Laureate's traditional speech, and says the following about its contents:

> I have now put it into the following shape. First I deductively infer the divine origin of art. Accept this or not as you like. Then Dostoevsky is turned upside down, with the stairs leading downward. The third chapter descends even further into the nether world. In the fourth chapter I crawl to the surface for a calm review, and I link what earthly affairs I can with this.

Solzhenitsyn intends to invite thirty to forty Soviet citizens to the awards ceremony, including Andrei Sakharov, Roy Medvedev and his wife, Lev Kopelev, Raissa Orlova,[2] Lidia Chukovskaya, [Anna] Berzer,[3] and a number of other persons known for their antisocial activities, and also up to ten foreign correspondents. In addition, he intends to publish a list of the participants in this ceremony and their photographs in the West.

Recently he and his circle have intensively circulated rumors to the effect that PEN Club President Heinrich Böll will also take part in the awards ceremony of the Nobel medals.

Böll came to Moscow on 15 February, where he was met by, in addition to official representatives of the foreign commission of the Writers' Union, the writer Kopelev,[4] a close friend of Solzhenitsyn. After the meeting, Kopelev had a lengthy conversation with Böll in a restaurant, and then showed him the home where Solzhenitsyn's mistress Svetlova lives.

Taking these circumstances into account, it would seem advisable to assign the Secretariat of the USSR Writers' Union to conduct a conversation with Böll, in the course of which he should be told about the rumors spread by Solzhenitsyn, informed about the negative attitude of the Soviet public to Solzhenitsyn's activities, and advised that he not link his name to actions that could harm his relations with Soviet writers.

Chairman of the Committee for State Security
Andropov

F. 3, op. 80, *d.* 645, *l.* 48–49. Original.

Notes

1. *A separate sheet bears the resolution: "Comrade P.N. Demichev. Please note that the last paragraph of this memo was implemented. A. Kirilenko 22.02.72," and the notation: "Comrade P.N. Demichev reported that he gave instructions for the proposal contained in this memorandum to be implemented. V. Galkin" and the signature of P. Demichev. The first page of the document bears the following resolution: "Brief via circulation. A. Kirilenko" and the signatures of A. Kosygin, N. Podgorny, A. Pelshe, P. Demichev, G. Voronov, D. Plyansky, A. Shelepin, V. Grishin, and F. Kulakova. The last page has the notation: "Comrade P.P. Laptev (KGB) has been informed. V. Galkin 22.02.72."*
2. A literary critic and Kopelev's wife.
3. The copy editor at *Novy Mir* who had worked most closely on *One Day in the Life of Ivan Denisovich* and became friends with Solzhenitsyn.
4. Kopelev had become a personal friend of Böll through his German studies.

65 Report from the Committee for State Security of the USSR Council of Ministers[1]

No. 438–A
22 February 1972
Special File
Top Secret

To the Central Committee:
According to surveillance information, the President of the [International] PEN Club,[2] the West German writer H. Böll, had a lengthy talk (around three hours) on 20 February 1972 in Moscow with Solzhenitsyn at the apartment of the woman he lives with, Svetlova. Writers' Union member Kopelev, expelled from the Party for antisocial activities, also took part in the conversation.

During the talk, Solzhenitsyn alleged that he is "constantly followed like an evil criminal," that he is deprived of access to archival materials and that he is prevented from visiting places connected with the work on his new book (such as the former Tauride Palace in Leningrad). Later he emphasized: "I live in Russia, but apart from these four walls I don't see anything. People who meet with me and help me to gather material are also subjected to persecution."

Böll answered that even in his country "a person striving for freedom can be treated like a leper."

At the same time, Solzhenitsyn showed Böll a list of people whom he intends to invite on the occasion of the award of the Nobel Prize.

Regarding possible meetings between Böll and Soviet writers, Solzhenitsyn requested that through them, and specifically with the help of K. Simonov, he try to further the effort for writers in the Soviet Union to get official permission to have access to archival materials.

Concluding their talk, Solzhenitsyn and Böll arranged to meet in the near future.

Chairman of the Committee for State Security
Andropov

F. 3, *op.* 80, *d.* 645, *l.* 51. Original.

Notes

1. On the first page is the instruction: *"Circulate to Politburo. Kirilenko"* and the signatures of D. Polyansky, G. Voronov, A. Shelepin, V. Grishin, A. Pelshe, N. Podgorny, F. Kulakov, A. Kosygin, P. Demichev.
2. There were no centers of International PEN in the Soviet Union at this time, despite Soviet efforts to join during the period of "the Thaw" in the early sixties. Soviet official and literary circles were extremely sensitive to PEN's influence, however, and were anxious to have good relations with its leadership (see Document 34).

66 Report from the Committee for State Security of the USSR Council of Ministers[1]

No. 601–A
11 March 1972
Special File
Top Secret

To the Central Committee:
In addition to our memo no. 438–A of 22 February 1972 on meetings between the PEN Club President and West German writer H. Böll and Soviet literary figures, we report that in Leningrad, Böll refused official contacts with representatives of the writers' organization and had private conversations with Writers' Union member E. Etkind,[2] who made politically damaging statements.

During the meetings, Böll and Etkind discussed the work of certain Jewish writers. Böll also displayed an interest in problems related to the study of Hebrew.

Upon his return to Moscow from a trip around the Soviet Union, Böll had meetings on 8 March 1972 with L. Kopelev and B. Okudzhava,[3] writers known for their antisocial behavior. He also intends to visit writer A. Galich,[4] who was recently expelled from the Writers' Union.

On 9 March, Böll again met with Solzhenitsyn and Kopelev in a private apartment.

Chairman of the Committee for State Security
Andropov

F. 3, op. 80, d. 645, l. 53. Original.

Notes

1. *The document bears the signatures of M. Suslov, F. Kulakov, A. Shelepin, A. Pelshe, A. Kosygin, and D. Polyansky; on the reverse side is the notation: "Comrade Voronov on vacation, V.V. Grishin travelling on business, A.P. Kirilenko on vacation, K.T. Mazurov ill, A.Y. Pelshe on vacation, N.V. Podgorny on vacation, P.N. Demichev on vacation. V. Galkin 14.03.72."*

2. Efim Etkind was a leading Leningrad literary critic and translator who had become friends with Solzhenitsyn soon after the publication of *One Day in the Life of Ivan Denisovich*. He was also an early and enthusiastic supporter of the then young and unknown poet Joseph Brodsky. In 1975 he emigrated to Paris.

3. Bulat Okudzhava is a poet and ballad singer of Georgian nationality, although he writes in Russian. His satirical ballads circulated, for the most part, unofficially on homemade tape recordings.

4. Alexander Galich, a prominent Jewish playwright, poet, and ballad singer, was expelled from the Writers' Union in 1971 and was pressured into emigration in 1974. He died in Paris in 1978.

67 Memorandum from the Committee for State Security of the USSR Council of Ministers and the USSR Public Prosecutor's Office[1]

No. 778–A
27 March 1972
Special File
Top Secret

To the Central Committee:
In analyzing materials related to Solzhenitsyn, as well as his writings, it is impossible not to conclude that we are dealing with a political opponent of the Soviet state and social structure. Solzhenitsyn's hatred of the Soviet authorities and his attempts to combat them can be traced throughout his entire conscious life, at various times varying only as to methods, the degree of his activity, and the resources available for disseminating his views, which are alien to socialism.

As a student he wrote anti-Soviet essays and read them to a small circle of friends. During World War II, lacking a sympathetic audience in the army, he outlined his views in letters and diaries, drawing up a program for the reorganization of socialist society. At the first opportunity he attempted to put together an anti-Soviet group, for which he was sentenced in 1945 to seven years of imprisonment. (He was rehabilitated in 1956.) After the publication of *One Day in the Life of Ivan Denisovich*, Solzhenitsyn disguised himself as an opponent of the consequences of the personality cult, and began not only to spread anticommunism, but also to provoke people to violate socialist law and order.

Solzhenitsyn's political credo constitutes a denial that socialist revolution is a historical law of social development, and a confirmation of the superiority of the capitalist means of production and forms of statehood. ". . . rule by the soviets ceased to exist on 6 July 1918," stated Solzhenitsyn in one of his conversations.

> In a totally brazen fashion all the elections at the Third, Fourth, and Fifth Congresses of the soviets were falsified. . . . Starting in January of 1918, the Bolsheviks, along with the 'left' socialist

revolutionaries forced the 'right-wing' socialist revolutionaries out of the soviets. . . . And the 'left' social revolutionaries remained. Then the elections at the Fifth Congress were fabricated. . . . The peasantry was for the 'left' socialist revolutionaries. The peasantry was boiling with indignation. The people possessed the truth, not the Bolsheviks.

Aligning himself with the restorationists, Solzhenitsyn in his work *The First Circle* states that the Russian peasant had a tranquil time of it twice in his life: during the period "of the wonderful seven-year NEP in Russia," when there were no collective farms, and under the Germans, when the latter returned to the peasant a patch of his own land.

The building of socialism, according to Solzhenitsyn, involves the unrestrained exploitation of people. Camps, the labor of prisoners who lack all rights—these are not chance phenomena, but rather a system planned by the state for the use of labor. ". . . The wealth of the country was created by prisoners' labor, they were the ones who achieved new heights in science, and erected the Dnieper Hydroelectric Stations, built new cities, and dug canals" (*The First Circle*).

In his play *The Republic of Labor*, a joyous march with banners, flowers, and children is portrayed; a loudspeaker thunders on stage; and a powerful chorus enthusiastically sings:

> We shall raise the banner!
> Comrades! Over here!
> Come join us in constructing
> A republic of labor!

When the curtain parts, the audience sees a prison camp, which serves as the background for the whole play.

In the unpublished play *Feast of the Victors* Solzhenitsyn writes: "The USSR! It is as civilized as an uncleared forest! A forest! There are no laws! There is only power—they just grab you and torture you, finding justification in the constitution where they can, and ignoring it when they can't!"

Speaking out against communist ideology and the practice of building socialism, Solzhenitsyn strives to create a circle of people sharing his opinions in order to involve more and more people in antisocial acts and provocations. His method involves writing and distributing "open letters." His letter to the Fourth Congress of the Union of Soviet Writers in 1967, for all practical purposes, served as a summons to the right-wing Czechoslovak writers to speak out openly against the Communist Party of Czechoslovakia. Other lampoons followed. In one of them, the so-called, "Open Letter to the

Secretariat of the Writers Union of the Russian Federation,"[2] Solzhenitsyn wrote, ". . . The blind leading the blind! You don't even notice that you are dragging yourselves in the direction opposite to the one you proclaim. In this time of crisis for our ill and suffering society, you are incapable of proposing anything constructive, anything good, all you have to offer are your hatred and vigilance. . . ."

Right now he is looking for ways to stir up church officials against the state. In this connection, his letter sent 16 March of this year to Patriarch Pimen is worthy of attention.[3] In particular, it says,

> . . . We have to give our children over, defenseless, not into neutral hands, but to the domain of atheistic propaganda of the most primitive and unscrupulous sort . . . to an adolescence, cut off from Christianity . . . the only opportunity for moral upbringing is a narrow chink between the clipboard of the political agitator and the criminal code.
>
> A half-century of our past is already beyond reclaiming, and I don't speak of remedying the present, but how can we save the future of our country?

In conclusion he calls upon the Patriarch to sacrifice himself in protest against the actions of the atheist state.

Similar writings by Solzhenitsyn which he has passed on to the West are eagerly picked up and used by bourgeois propaganda outlets and revisionist circles and widely employed in the struggle with communism.

An analysis of Solzhenitsyn's behavior throughout his entire conscious life indisputably proves he has deliberately and irrevocably embarked on the path of struggle with the Soviet government and will wage this struggle regardless of everything.

Solzhenitsyn's antisocial activity before he was expelled from the USSR Writers' Union has repeatedly been the topic of public discussion and attention in the Soviet press. He received offers of aid and assistance in his literary work, and his actions besmirching the title of Soviet writer were also pointed out to him. However Solzhenitsyn ignored all of this.

His provocative behavior, especially after he was awarded the Nobel Prize, has been encouraged by material support in the form of funds from abroad and deposits in foreign banks. In a short time he has used this money to buy two cars, has paid his former wife ten thousand hard-currency rubles in alimony, and is constantly converting foreign currency into certificates.[4]

Under these circumstances, some citizens perceive the fact that Solzhenitsyn is acting with impunity as an indication that we are afraid to touch a person known in the West, who is moreover an imaginary victim of the "personality cult." Solzhenitsyn's behavior serves as an example of how it is possible to live on money received from the West for the publication of anti-Soviet works.

Naturally, in this situation the issue arises either of criminally prosecuting Solzhenitsyn or expelling him from Soviet territory. It would appear expedient to select the latter course of action.

This having been said, it should be understood that Solzhenitsyn's expulsion and his presence abroad will be used by our enemies to fuel their anti-Soviet activities. At the same time, though, in the eyes of the Soviet people, Solzhenitsyn will cease to be an ambiguous figure, as the attitude of the Soviet state toward him is made clear.

Based on the above, we propose the option of adopting a Decree of the Presidium of the USSR Supreme Soviet to strip Solzhenitsyn of his Soviet citizenship and expel him from the territory of the Union of Soviet Socialist Republics (a draft of the decree is attached) and to provide TASS with a relevant press release.

The expulsion of Solzhenitsyn should be handled by the KGB.

Please review.

Chairman
Committee for State Security
Andropov

USSR Public Prosecutor
Rudenko

Enclosure
Draft

Resolution of the Central Committee
"A Question from the Committee for State Security and the USSR Public Prosecutor's Office"

To adopt the proposal of the KGB and the Public Prosecutor's Office.

To approve the draft Decree of the Presidium of the USSR Supreme Soviet on revoking the Soviet citizenship of A.I. Solzhenitsyn.
Secretary of the Central Committee

Draft

Decree of the Presidium of the USSR Supreme Soviet "On the Revocation of Solzhenitsyn's Soviet Citizenship and His Deportation from the USSR"

On the basis of Article 7 of the "Law on Citizenship of the Union of Soviet Socialist Republics" of 19 August 1938, the Presidium of the USSR Supreme Soviet resolves:

1. For attempts to defame Soviet society incompatible with the high title of citizen of the USSR, for the use of subject matter in literary work that has became a weapon in the hands of the most reactionary anticommunist forces in the fight against the principles of socialism and socialist culture, to revoke USSR citizenship from Alexander Isaevich Solzhenitsyn, born 1918.

2. To deport Solzhenitsyn from the territory of the Soviet Union.

Chairman of the Presidium of the USSR Supreme Soviet
Secretary of the Presidium of the USSR Supreme Soviet

F. 3, op. 80, d. 645, l. 59–65. Original.

Notes

1. *Page one has a note by M. Suslov: "1. Circulate and study. 2. Politburo," and the signatures of M. Suslov, N. Podgorny, F. Kulakov, A. Kosygin, D. Polyansky, G. Voronov, V. Grishin, and A. Shelepin.*

2. Solzhenitsyn's open letter was in response to his expulsion from the Writers' Union, see *The Oak and the Calf*, Appendix 12.

3. Solzhenitsyn's "Lenten Letter to the Patriarch" was released by him into samizdat in April 1972.

4. Such certificates were purchased through Vneshposyltorg and could be used to buy otherwise scarce or unavailable goods in special stores.

68 From the Minutes of a Politburo Session

30 March 1972
Top Secret

Meeting chaired by Comrade L.I. Brezhnev
Present: Comrades Voronov, Grishin, Kirilenko, Kosygin, Kulakov, Kunaev,
Podgorny, Polyansky, Suslov, Shelepin, Shelest, Shcherbitsky, Andropov,
Demichev, Masherov, Mzhavandze, Rashidov, Solomentsev, Ustinov,
Kapitonov, Katushev, Ponomarev

1. Report from Comrade Andropov.
(Comrade Andropov's report was not recorded.)
Brezhnev: It was good to hear Comrade Andropov's report. At various times
we have been informed on this issue in one way or another, but this
information was sporadic and now we have been given concentrated and
systematized material, which creates a full impression of the state of affairs in
this area and specifically, of the work of the KGB and its employees and
reveals activity which has as it were, been obscured from view, and been
carried out behind the backs of the working class, of the laboring peasantry,
and of our intelligentsia, and is being carried out against their interests and
against the interests of our socialist state and our Party.

It seems to me that it would be wrong to reduce the affair to some isolated
facts. Taken together they represent a large and comprehensive issue. All of
these dark deeds, if I may call them that, are being carried out by a small
circle of people, as we see from the reports, and we sense that from other
sources as well, specifically from letters coming to the Central Committee
and so on.

We know very well that the people are dedicated to the Party, and that our
people are hard working and honest. They have absorbed the ideas of Lenin
and the ideas of the Party, and with these ideas, and with this great banner of
the October Revolution they have travelled a difficult but glorious path. All
sorts of obstacles were encountered on this path, including World War II,
the most difficult war ever fought. And our people endured this war, and not
only withstood it, but routed the enemy. Only a people of strong moral fiber,
with clear goals in their lives and activities, and with sacred ideals could have
come through such a trial.

199

Recent years have shown that the Soviet people fulfill and overfulfill plans set forth by our Party, and that the people are devoted to the party selflessly no matter what. One five-year plan after another has been fulfilled successfully, owing to the industriousness, wisdom, and ideological stability of our Soviet people, and the Party's systematic and correct education of the people. We would not have such successes if the people did not perceive the ideas and tasks of our Party as a matter of vital and immediate importance to them. It is thanks only to that, thanks to socialist ideology, that we have such colossal successes, which have allowed us to become a great power in a very real way, without whom no serious international issues can be resolved. The international authority of our country gets stronger everyday.

With this as the general background, if I may say so, the moral and political condition of our society is good and healthy. Our people are dynamically moving forward toward the cherished goal of communism; the people are marching, and everything we have just heard comes not from the people, not from those people who achieved victory in the war and who achieve victories in labor today, not from the real workers in the factories, plants, and collective and state farms, not from the laboring intelligentsia, but from a handful of renegades.

We know that the people welcomed the decisions of the Twenty-Fourth Party Congress and our plans, and now the people are reporting on the fulfillment of the first year of the five-year plan.

But listening to this report today, we have to ask ourselves why the generally healthy organism of our society suffers from such growths, and why they are eating away at a healthy organism, why they are surviving in our country. I think that there are several reasons. We must not oversimplify in answering this question.

First of all, it is clear that this is the result of shortcomings in our work, and the fact that our vigilance has grown slack, that somewhere we have ceased to carry on a truly Bolshevik-style struggle with such phenomena, and nip them in the bud when they are in an embryonic state, rather than letting them exist and spread, even on a small scale. We must look on this as part of the class struggle. This struggle remains international as well as domestic, thanks to actions aimed at a certain backward segment of our population.

While we should not imagine that we will not have enemies or that we will liquidate them in the course of a single five-year-plan or a set time period, we nonetheless must not let such shortcomings exist for a long period and spread, bringing harm to our common cause, the building of communism. We must see those shortcomings and draw practical conclusions from them, especially because some of these renegades are now engaged in open warfare; for example Yakir, Dzyuba,[1] and their henchmen. We need to make it clear in a tangible way that we will not allow these people, the scum of human society, to poison our healthy atmosphere.

The second and even more weighty reason, it seems to me, for these shortcomings is the absence of a struggle with the symptoms of nationalism. The problem is that nationalism in particular is the most favorable breeding ground for anti-Sovietism and anticommunism. This is where various dubious ideas arise and where primitive people gather. Nationalism, as Lenin said, is an evil phenomenon that undermines our unity and is especially dangerous when we cease to wage a genuine, consistent, Bolshevik-style struggle against it.

And finally, I think that a not-insignificant reason is that our ideological work is weak in some areas. Not everywhere do we have strong personnel in the field doing ideological work; there is little aggressive ideological work being carried out; facts indicate that at times we are more engaged in defensive work than in going onto the offensive; and we forget that the whole imperialist machine is geared up to battle us. If we assume a defensive posture, we will definitely lose and we will reduce the effectiveness of our struggle. Meanwhile, our powerful trump cards, such as internationalism and friendship among peoples—these are a great source of wealth which Lenin bequeathed us and cautioned us to cherish like the apple of our eye. We do not always use them to our advantage with sufficient skill, although it would seem that with such strong motivations at our disposal we could wage well-argued, offensive ideological work literally on all fronts.

Take a phenomenon like the Dzyuba group and the program written by that group and so on. The Ukrainian Central Committee knew about this phenomenon long ago, way back in 1966. And we are examining it only now. If the Ukrainian Central Committee had taken measures in a timely fashion, we would not be hearing about such facts today, but the Ukrainian Central Committee began to react only five years later, when this material had been published abroad. By the way, a wide variety of press reports has appeared here about this or that republic being independent. For example, there was something recently in basically positive tones in one of our magazines about Tuva, about its successes, and people started immediately writing about how Tuva has become an independent state. Why and when did Tuva become an independent state?

All these phenomena only damage us. We are all preparing to mark the fiftieth anniversary of the Union of Soviet Socialist Republics, formed by Lenin and strengthened by the Party. That is why I think that this is the right time for us to discuss this question in greater detail, with more care, to take a look around and come to an agreement about which measures to take. This question is thus a timely one, and Comrade Andropov's report is in all respects useful and correct.

I would ask comrades to speak their thoughts on this issue.

Kunaev: I believe that Comrade Andropov's report deserves very serious attention. The facts cited in his report provide an understanding of these people's activities. Comrade Brezhnev's introduction to the discussion of this issue has put before us a very important task which we must reflect upon and we must organize the practical means to carry it out.

In my view, the most important thing is personnel. We need to organize the work with our personnel in such a way that (especially in the national republics) not only will no one be offended, but on the contrary, the sacred phrase "friendship among peoples" will be an integral part of our work with our personnel. In our republic, Kazakhstan, for example, we have more than one hundred nationalities and ethnic groups working. I should say that in our republic there are no hard feelings, but still sometimes we apparently commit certain errors in our work or are inattentive to certain nationalities. We need to keep this in mind. Moreover we also need to remember that at one time Kazakhstan was a place of exile and that some of these exiles are still around. They live there and many of them are active; for example, Rukhimovich, who is in Karaganda, engages in activities that are flagrantly Trotskyite in nature. In Kazakhstan there are eight hundred thousand [ethnic] Germans. We publish a special German-language newspaper for this group called *Friendship*. There have been no serious problems with these groups of people. Also it needs to be remembered that Kazakhstan is on the border with China and our people are exposed to intense Chinese propaganda from radio and other media. For example, the Uigurs, of whom we have more than one hundred and twenty thousand, have raised the issue of liberating Sintzyan, because there are more than six million Uigurs there. In Kazakhstan there are forty thousand Koreans. Among them there are certain groups that evidently require more work on our part, because they receive visitors from the embassy in Moscow and this needs to be kept in mind. Of course, various statements made by Yakir, Sakharov, and Solzhenitsyn reach us, too, one way or another, but what I want to say in connection with that is that we really need, as Comrade Brezhnev said, to nip phenomena of this type in the bud. We had a case where a small group of intellectuals got together for discussion and even decided that it was time to rehabilitate certain people and reestablish the "good name" of the previous anti-Soviet leadership of Kazakhstan. We found out about it and immediately, without delay, sorted these comrades out. Some of them were excluded from the Party. The intelligentsia in general was told about what had happened, and they not only ceased their activities, but even came to us and apologized, and said that they had been deluded, that this was a temporary delusion, and please forgive us, and so on. And they not only came to us, but apologized to their comrades. This is how the struggle needs to be waged. I think this is the right way.

Grishin: I agree with all of today's speakers and will act on Comrade Brezhnev's instructions. It is really true, comrades, that on the whole our situation is a good one. This is clear judgment from Moscow, our capital city. All the facts set forth in the report concern a small group of people and they (these phenomena) have no support among the people nor do they have support among significant numbers of the intelligentsia. But Leonid Ilyich was correct in saying that we must keep in mind that there is an intense class war going on and that our enemies are doing everything they can to harm us. They recruit various resentful renegades such as Dzyuba, Yakir, Solzhenitsyn, and others. In Moscow we need to pay particular attention to ideological work, and weed out the kinds of phenomena mentioned in the report, because Moscow is where we have the largest numbers of tourists, various delegations, and conferences. In a word, people come from all over the world (not to mention, from all over the country) with various purposes, for various reasons, and maybe even with various specific goals. And we must keep this in mind in our work. This is why we have tremendous tasks before us as we educate our people in the spirit of the Party.

Leonid Ilyich was correct in saying that among these renegades there is not (and indeed there is no way there could be) a single working person, not a single member of the intelligentsia who is distinguished or significant in any way. These people are simply no-names. Who are Yakir and his group, really?[2] I think that this group, and Yakir himself in particular, flaunt their impunity. Yakir says, without mincing words, that there are people in prison who have done no more than he has, and yet he is free, although he has done more.

And who is Solzhenitsyn? Solzhenitsyn is a true degenerate. I think we need to put an end to the Yakir and Solzhenitsyn issues. How to do so is another matter. We need to make some specific proposals, but they definitely need to be removed from Moscow. The same thing with Sakharov. Maybe somebody needs to have a talk with him—I don't know, but the situation with him also needs to be brought to an end, because he is gathering people around him. And although this group is a small one, it is harmful.

We know little about what this samizdat thing is all about, where and how it is done, where the literature is published, and how it is gotten out of the country.

I think that Leonid Ilyich was correct in saying that in manifestations of nationalism, we should see anti-Sovietism and anticommunism, and that we need to do our practical work accordingly. Nationalism has become a weapon in the hands of all the foreign intelligence services and imperialist forces in the struggle with us. It is one of the phenomena that could cause us serious harm. We need to factor this in. Nationalism has manifested itself in certain of the Baltic republics, and recently, as we have seen, in the Ukraine. This is why we must draw very serious conclusions from this and implement practical measures.

We must not discount Zionism either. We have several of these groups. I think that we need to limit the departure of Jews for Israel, or if we do send them, we should not do it through Moscow for Jews from all over the country, because they come here with their pianos and their cars and have big send-offs at the airport. And this is done on a grand scale. I think this should stop.

Recently there has been a tendency to turn a blind eye to these anti-Soviet groups (and to Sakharov, and Solzhenitsyn, and Dzyuba, and Yakir) which exist for the purpose of engaging in anti-Soviet actions. And they take refuge in the fact that they are going unpunished. And, as Comrade Brezhnev said, we really are on the defensive.

I want to say that we will draw all the necessary conclusions from what has been said at this session and will take practical measures. Perhaps we should make a decision on this issue? Maybe we should make a note to conduct practical work in accordance with the exchange of opinions at this Politburo session.

Solomentsev: Nationalism is itself dangerous, and it is all the more dangerous when it is interwoven with anti-Sovietism and anticommunism. There really is unity among our people and we are proud of that. For that reason the facts indicated in Comrade Andropov's report should concern us all the more. They are causing tremendous harm, although they are individual cases, and they are particularly harmful to our young people.

This can be traced, first of all, to shortcomings in our ideological work. We need to conduct our work so as to instill the whole people with intolerance toward such phenomena. Then they will not spread.

I think that one of the serious reasons for the facts we have heard is the harm that Khrushchev did in his time. I should point out that it was he, Khrushchev, who discovered Yakir, who made overtures to him and encouraged him. He discovered Solzhenitsyn and raised him up, that scum of society. And look at the implications of his rather free interpretation of the situation, that we have no political enemies and so on. I think that all this in its time caused serious harm, and we need to see this harm.

Nationalism reveals itself in our country in a variety of ways, and I think that this is where our enemies catch us—they place their bets, namely, on the nationalist mood. For example, what does it mean when there is talk about whether or not to study Russian? Or signs on the streets and in shops only in the local native language? At public meetings, someone raises the issue that everyone should speak only in the native language although half or sometimes more of the people, don't speak this "native language."

We really are getting a little too carried away with all sorts of old historical symbols, which can sometimes lead to Russification. In the oblasts and republics there is a trend toward resurrecting the old coats of arms. And take sports. Aren't passions getting stirred up around various sporting events? It's been correctly pointed out here that it is the work force that decides everything. The hiring and placement of personnel need to be taken seriously. We have a whole series of shortcomings in this area. Sometimes the people at the top managerial levels are taken completely from the local ethnic groups. And there are republics such as Hakasia [sic][3] where the indigenous peoples make up only 6 or 7 percent of the population.

I think that Solzhenitsyn and Yakir should be exiled from the Soviet Union as enemies of the people.

Brezhnev: The problem is, as Comrade Andropov said, that there is no law that makes political indiscretions a punishable offense.

Andropov: Yes, it's true, there is no such statute on political espionage.

Ponomarev: It is right that the question has been raised for discussion in the Politburo and it has been done at the right time. It is true that if we look at the way our people live, the foundations of our society have become so strong that just a few years ago it would have been hard to imagine. People live significantly better. Their standard of living grows every day, and every working person understands that. The culture of our people is growing.

. . . We are now making preparations for the fiftieth anniversary of the formation of the USSR. Ethnic groups in our country are drawing closer and closer in every way, which is all the more reason why we cannot tolerate such developments, such facts. Every day we win new positions in the world. The authority of the Soviet Union is growing. There are now seventy states in the world that have been liberated from colonialism. This is a great victory for us, too, and yet here inside the country we cannot handle this Solzhenitsyn character, and this Yakir and Sakharov.

Our main task, in my view, is to improve ideological work.

There is also the phenomenon of Russism.[4] In our ideology we need to be intolerant of all sorts of nationalism. The essence of our approach is a genuine Leninist, internationalist education of the people. That is the main task we face in public education.

Suslov: I feel that today in the Politburo we are discussing a very important question of principle. And it is a question of principle largely because its time has come. This is apparent from Comrade Andropov's report. The situation in the country truly is quite good as Comrade Brezhnev has said, but against the background of that good situation we must remark and not underestimate such facts as have been mentioned here. They are few in number. And the people responsible for them are also few in number, but nonetheless it would be wrong to underestimate them. After all, it takes thousands of people to construct a building which can be demolished by just one person. We have various renegades here—like Ilyin[5] and others. And if we don't take the necessary measures in response to these phenomena (and I don't mean any measures but effective and timely ones) then our cause could suffer great harm.

Our line was and is the correct line. In the last few years we have done a lot for the ideological, economic and cultural activity of our Party and our people, but, unfortunately, we have not yet done everything. We have not liquidated all of the results of Khrushchev's period. He really was the one who said that we have no political opponents, no political enemies. Didn't this harm the people? Of course it did. I would say that it was not only Khrushchev who raised up Solzhenitsyn and praised him to the skies, but Mikoyan was guilty, too. In spite of the fact that the Central Committee Secretariat categorically objected at the time, Khrushchev and Mikoyan insisted on publishing Solzhenitsyn, praising him to the skies, and after that you all know what happened with him. I think that it is not quite right to talk about shortcomings in the law. We have enough laws. We just have to make use of them confidently and without hesitation. Take that Yakir for example. He betrayed his father's cause. His father was a wonderful fighter, and a real revolutionary.[6] But he is a scoundrel. And we should not be afraid to deal with a renegade like him. I feel that we cannot let Solzhenitsyn remain any longer. We need to bring his case to a close. He needs to be removed from Moscow. Whether he is removed to somewhere within the country or abroad is another matter. That is something we need to consider.

About Sakharov. I agree with my comrades that we need to consider Sakharov. However, I feel that the time has passed when we can try to persuade Sakharov or make any requests of him. This will do absolutely nothing for us. And we need to resolve the Sakharov issue once and for all as well.

Our main task is to improve our ideological work. Comrade Brezhnev was right in saying that bourgeois nationalism is the main form of anti-Sovietism, and recently our enemies have made it into a strong weapon against us. We must not forget this.

Kirilenko: Today, comrades, we are discussing an issue of great political importance. I completely share my comrades' opinion that the general political situation in our country is very good. The state of mind of the people is excellent. In labor and politics, the people are becoming more and more active. The Soviet people are heading toward the fiftieth anniversary of the formation of the USSR on the basis of the decisions of the Twenty-Fourth Party Congress and in doing so they have assumed great labor commitments. With this excellent situation as the context, the manifestations of nationalism about which we are talking here cannot but worry us. The facts about which Comrade Andropov and the other comrades have talked must not be underestimated. There are still scum in our society, fierce enemies of the motherland, and we cannot forget this. . . .

There was mention of Yakir and Solzhenitsyn. In my view, administrative measures should be taken against these people. As regards Yakir, he should simply be isolated. The fact that Yakir is the son of a hero should not blind us to what he really is. His father really is respected, and deservedly so, but [Yakir] deserves the strictest punishment. In any case, he needs to be isolated from Moscow as quickly as possible.

Solzhenitsyn is a vivid example of anti-Sovietism. He is an anti-Soviet slanderer of the first order. Why do we put up with him here in Moscow? He needs to be removed from the territory of this country. Of course, there will be expenses associated with this, but better to bear those expenses than to put up with him here.

They say that a general decision needs to be taken on this issue. It seems to me that we need to give our evaluation and instruct the Party organizations to intensify their ideological work, using the available rights of administrative action to the fullest.

Demichev: I completely agree with the comrades who have spoken. On the ideological front the situation is complicated. Imperialist propaganda, armed to the teeth, is having an impact on Soviet society. The Maoist leadership is working against us, as are various organizations in the capitalist states. But in spite of that, we are counteracting bourgeois propaganda and rebuffing ideologically harmful activities. Things are going significantly better for us than before. In the past, imperialism attempted to act by means of economic sanctions. Now the bourgeois countries understand that they cannot hurt us with economic sanctions. For that reason capitalist propaganda now pays particular attention to the organization of ideological subversion against our country. All subversive acts organized within our country and abroad are directed against us, and find fertile soil abroad in the activities of bourgeois ideological organizations.

Our artists' and writers' associations are ideologically strong. The recent congresses of writers and filmmakers demonstrated a high ideological unity and were proof of this. Such venerable writers as, for example, Simonov, are strong spokesmen for high ideological cohesion. Even Simonov stated that Solzhenitsyn is his main ideological opponent, and, as we know, in the past Simonov has not always spoken from a correct position.

Solzhenitsyn does not want to leave the Soviet Union. He lays claim to the role of ideological mentor to our writers. Bourgeois propaganda places emphasis specifically on Solzhenitsyn and wants to have him not abroad, but in our country. As for artistry and literary skill, Solzhenitsyn is not what he passes himself off to be. He uses Stalin's personality cult and various individual shortcomings in our development, emphasizes Zionism and religious believers and so on, and wants to win authority using these things as props. Our ideological enemies count on nationalism as the primary weapon in the struggle against the Soviet system. This is why the struggle against nationalism is now taking on an exceedingly great significance.

Mzhavanadze: The Politburo has acted correctly in placing such an important issue before the session. We have a situation where people are moving back and forth among the republics and there is a constant redistribution of people. In our republic there are a large number of Jews, and among them are many who are degraded and corrupted. So it is no accident that among those desiring to emigrate to Israel there are many people from Georgia.

There are very many shortcomings in our ideological work. I think that Solzhenitsyn would not have made it as far as receiving the Nobel Prize if at times we had not encouraged him. You recall that Khrushchev gave instructions to publish his short novel *One Day In the Life of Ivan Denisovich*.

Recently we in Georgia conducted a plenum of the Party City Committee, to discuss the decisions of the Central Committee, and yesterday we had a plenum of the republic's Central Committee to discuss the decisions of the USSR Central Committee on the preparations for the fiftieth anniversary of the formation of the USSR. The plenum of Georgia's Central Committee, as well as the plenum of Tbilisi's City Committee warmly and unanimously approved and supported the decisions of the USSR Central Committee. These decisions will help us to eliminate shortcomings in our work and fulfill the tasks of the ninth five-year-plan and the decisions of the Twenty-Fourth Party Congress.

Podgorny: The nationalities issue is one of the more complicated and difficult issues in our experience. And the fact that this issue has been resolved in the Soviet Union correctly is a victory for our Party and it is a source of pride to us. As a result of the correct resolution of the nationalities issue, friendship among our peoples grows stronger from year to year, and the ideological and political unity of the Soviet people also increases and grows stronger. And of course, all of us, when we hear about such nationalist manifestations as have been reported on here, respond with disappointment. What causes this, and what do we need to do to ensure that such things don't happen in the country, in order to provide for the proper ideological and political education of our people?

The Soviet Union gets stronger and stronger from year to year in all respects. Economically, it is now impossible to shake us. Our enemies know that friendship among the peoples of the Soviet Union is our bastion of strength, it is our fortress, and so that is why they want to drive wedges between our nationalities. Even our "friend" China speaks out in favor of independence for the Soviet Ukraine. Of course, when bourgeois figures speak this way, it is no surprise, but when Chinese Communists do this, that should give us pause. Are there grounds for nationalism? I believe that there are no such grounds. There have been enormous achievements made in all the republics in economics and culture. We have good writers' groups operating in all the republics and even in many regions. Ideological and political life in each of the republics is in full flower. And this, of course, is not to the taste of hostile elements such as Yakir, Solzhenitsyn, and Dzyuba.

Yakir, of course, harbors a grudge against the Soviet leadership and, under the influence of bourgeois ideology coming from the West, pours out his anger through various actions against our way of life and our reality.

Take Solzhenitsyn. He is not an ordinary person but has roots in the propertied classes, and naturally he cannot forgive the Soviet authorities that. Information on Solzhenitsyn published in a West German magazine shed light on him. Of course there is no way that such activist nationalists as Shukhevich, who commanded the armed forces of the OUN,[7] could be loyal.

. . . In spite of the fact that we have strengthened our radio and television programs, there are still many shortcomings in our work. Not infrequently there are songs on the radio that praise the old days or mention not Soviet Russia, but just Russia, which the singer supposedly cannot live without. And Ukrainians say that they cannot live without the Ukraine, etc.

All this leads to nationalist distortions. Solzhenitsyn carries on hostile activities. He is a hostile person, and should not be in Moscow. But I think that he should not be sent out of the country. He himself did not express a desire to go to Sweden for the prize. I do not think that he should be expelled. There are places in the Soviet Union where he will not be able to have contact with people. In his time Litvinov was sent away[8] and that was a good thing. That's what we need to do with Yakir and with Solzhenitsyn. In addition, Solzhenitsyn is a Nobel laureate, and bourgeois propaganda will of course use that against us to the fullest extent. Kuznetsov[9] stayed in England as you know, but Solzhenitsyn is not Kuznetsov. He is capable of doing us great harm.

As to Sakharov, I feel that we need to fight for him. He is a different type of person. We are not talking about Solzhenitsyn here. Comrade Keldysh[10] asked about this too, by the way. After all, Sakharov has three times been made a Hero of Socialist Labor. He is the creator of the hydrogen bomb. I feel that the discussion today at the session is very useful and it will help us fine tune our work.

Kosygin: I completely agree with the statements of my comrades. The Party has always taken the nationalities question quite seriously. As we were approaching 1941, the year World War II began, we were convinced in a most real way of the productive results of the tremendous work done by the

Party to create cohesion among our people. Even in the first years of the war the Soviet people demonstrated great cohesion and indestructible friendship. The victory in World War II was a victory of the Party's ethnic policies.

The question of Yakir, Solzhenitsyn, and Sakharov is an isolated matter. It needs to be resolved in the way that Leonid Ilyich Brezhnev said. The main thing, of course, is not a punitive policy but rather a political-educational approach. With Sakharov, it seems to me, we'll have to do some work. Yakir fancies himself a hero. He is Jewish, but has taken up as his weapon not Zionism, but nationalism. Solzhenitsyn has gone far beyond what we can endure, he has gone beyond the pale, and Comrade Andropov himself should decide how to handle these people in accordance with our available laws. And we will see how he resolves this question. If he resolves it wrongly, then we will correct him.

Andropov: That is why I am consulting with the Politburo.

Brezhnev: Apparently all the comrades present wish to speak, but judging by those who have already spoken, one thing is clear: that we are unanimous in our fundamental evaluation of this issue. So perhaps we will close on that note, unless the comrades insist otherwise. Which of the comrades insist on speaking?

Voices: We are fully "in favor" and the discussion may now be brought to a close.

Brezhnev: As regards Yakir and Solzhenitsyn, I agree with the opinions of the comrades. They must without question be removed from Moscow.

Podgorny: Regarding Yakir and Solzhenitsyn, I think that I, Comrade Andropov, and comrades from the Public Prosecutor's Office, the Ministry of Internal Affairs, the Ministry of Justice, and other organizations should go through the matter once again and make concrete proposals in accordance with the law and taking into account today's exchange of opinions.

Brezhnev: Correct. Let's do just that: we will entrust Comrades Podgorny and Andropov with the responsibility of going through the matter and making concrete proposals on the issue.

From the minutes of Politburo sessions for 1972. Original.

Notes

1. *Ivan Dzyuba was a Ukrainian rights activist who advocated Ukrainian independence; also a literary critic and member of the Communist Party of the Ukraine. In 1966, he sent a statement to the Central Committee of the Ukraine entitled "Internationalism or Russification" on behalf of a group of Ukrainian rights activists. In 1973, he was sentenced to five years of imprisonment for "nationalism and anti-Soviet activities."*

2. Pyotr Yakir (see Document 60, Note 2) had become a leading member of a group of dissidents who compiled and distributed the influential samizdat journal, *Chronicle of Current Events.* In June 1972, shortly after this discussion in the Politburo, Yakir was arrested, together with fellow dissident Victor Krasin, and subjected to prolonged interrogation about the *Chronicle.*

3. Presumably Abkhazia, a province of Georgia, was what the speaker had in mind.

4. "Russism" was a brand of Russian nationalism that began to be elaborated by certain dissidents during the late sixties and early seventies, associated with the samizdat journal *Veche* (Assembly).

5. *On 22 January 1969, First Lieutenant V.I. Ilyin shot sixteen times at a car on the Kremlin grounds carrying the spacemen G. Beregovoy, A. Leonov, V. Tereshkova, and A. Nikolaev. (He had believed Brezhnev was in the car.) In February 1970, he was sentenced by court order to compulsory treatment in a special psychiatric hospital. A report on the sentencing was published on 20 February 1970 in* Pravda.

6. Ion Yakir (1896–1937) was a celebrated Soviet army commander who was one of several senior Red Army officers arrested and killed during the purge of 1937. He was rehabilitated by Khrushchev and hence popular again with political leaders.

7. OUN—the Organization of Ukrainian Nationalists, the oldest and most militant of the Ukrainian separatist movements, had been fighting for the independence of Western Ukraine since 1939, first against the Germans and then against the Soviet regime. It was ruthlessly suppressed by Stalin and went underground, but surfaced again in the early sixties.

8. Pavel Litvinov, grandson of Foreign Minister Maxim Litvinov, was deeply involved in dissident activities. In addition to being one of the founders of the *Chronicle of Current Events* he had compiled and sent to the West two books of documents about the trials of fellow dissidents. In August 1968 he and six others staged an unprecedented demonstration in Red Square to protest the invasion of Czechoslovakia, for which he was sentenced to five years' internal exile and sent to Siberia (where he was at the time of this discussion). He emigrated to the USA in 1974.

9. The novelist Anatoly Kuznetsov caused a scandal in July 1968 by becoming the first Soviet writer to defect since World War II. He settled in London and published the first full version of his novel about Nazi atrocities in wartime Kiev, *Baby Yar,* which had been censored by the Soviet authorities for its sympathetic treatment of the Jews.

10. Mstislav Keldysh (1911–1978) was a celebrated mathematician and President of the Soviet Academy of Sciences from 1961–1975.

69 Politburo Resolution
"On Solzhenitsyn and Yakir"

No. P37 per minutes
30 March 1972
Top Secret

Comrades Podgorny and Andropov, with the participation of the appropriate ministries and agencies and taking into account the exchange of opinions at this session of the Politburo of the Central Committee, are charged with preparing proposals and presenting them to the Central Committee.

F. 3, *op.* 80, *d.* 645, *l.* 57. Excerpt from minutes.

70 Report of the Committee for State Security of the USSR Council of Ministers[1]

No. 854–A
3 April 1972
Special File
Top Secret

To the Central Committee:
The Committee for State Security has obtained surveillance information that Solzhenitsyn, who is still unaware that the Nobel Foundation Secretary Gierow has been denied entry to the USSR, is actively preparing for his arrival, which was planned for the purpose of delivering the Nobel Prize laureate's paraphernalia to Solzhenitsyn.

Solzhenitsyn's mistress Svetlova and her relatives are buying up dishes and food in large quantities for the guests invited to the reception to celebrate the award. Since the awards ceremony has been planned to coincide with the first day of the religious holiday of Easter on 9 April, the reception will also be organized to look like a religious celebration, for which appropriate foods are being prepared such as Easter cakes, dyed eggs, etc. Solzhenitsyn, who is living at Rostropovich's dacha, is busy memorizing the text of the so-called Nobel Prize laureate's traditional lecture.

It is assumed that Solzhenitsyn will give interviews to foreign correspondents who have been invited to this gathering. To prepare for the interview, Solzhenitsyn invited American correspondents Robert Kaiser and Hedrick Smith on 30 March for a four-hour conversation at his mistress's apartment. Solzhenitsyn submitted to the correspondents' twenty-five typewritten pages of answers he had prepared in advance, thus determining the kind of questions he would be asked.

At the very beginning of this conversation, Solzhenitsyn's mistress warned the correspondents that someone might well be eavesdropping on them, in view of which the rest of exchange was largely carried out by writing notes.

The materials obtained in the course of the conversation led to the conclusion that the interview will cover a broad range of questions. One of the correspondents had this to say about these questions: "I think this can be broken down into three parts. What they did against us, the hardships of life, your friends who were hurt because they knew you, etc." Apart from this, Solzhenitsyn will speak about his future literary plans and the Soviet writers and poets he regards as progressive. He will also speak in great detail about his life, in particular, about his imprisonment, his relatives, and, in this connection, about the articles in *Literaturnaya Gazeta*.

The conversation was taped by the correspondents. At the end of the talk, they took several photographs of Solzhenitsyn with his mistress and his son.

According to our information, Jackson, a UPI correspondent, intends to film the ceremony of the presentation of the laureate's certificates to Solzhenitsyn.

Chairman of the Committee for State Security
Andropov

F. 3, op. 80, *d.* 645, *l.* 66–67. Original.

Note

1. *The first page bears the signatures of M. Suslov, N. Podgorny, D. Poliansky, A. Kosygin, V. Grishin, A. Shelepin, G. Voronov, and F. Kulakov. A notation on the reverse of the page reads: "Comrade Kirilenko is on vacation; Comrade Mazurov is sick; Comrade Pelshe is on a business trip. V. Galkin, 4 April 1972."*

71 Telegram from the USSR Embassy in Sweden

Special No. 285
8 April 1972
From Stockholm
Classified
Copy No. 7[1]

RE: OUR NO. 281. FOREIGN MINISTER WICKMAN IN HIS PRESS STATEMENT STRESSED THAT THE POSSIBILITY OF PRESENTING SOLZHENITSYN WITH THE MEDAL AND THE DIPLOMA THROUGH THE SWEDISH EMBASSY IN MOSCOW STILL EXISTS. AT THE SAME TIME HE POINTED OUT THAT THE PRESENTATION COULD ONLY BE ORGANIZED IN SUCH A WAY THAT "THE EMBASSY WOULD NOT BE PART OF A POLITICAL DEMONSTRATION AGAINST THE HOST COUNTRY."

COMMENTING ON WICKMAN'S STATEMENT, THE PRESS NOTES THAT THIS IS AN INDIRECT ANSWER TO THE QUESTION THAT A DEPUTY OF THE PEOPLE'S (LIBERAL) PARTY, ALMARK, ASKED IN THE RIKSTAG CONCERNING THE READINESS OF THE GOVERNMENT TO ASSIST IN THE "PRESENTATION OF THE PRIZES TO NOBEL LAUREATES IN SWEDISH EMBASSIES IF THE LAUREATES GIVE THEIR CONSENT TO THIS."

THE PRESS, THE RIGHT-WING PRESS IN PARTICULAR, CONTINUES TO MAKE UNFRIENDLY REMARKS ABOUT US REGARDING THE CANCELLATION OF GIEROW'S VISIT TO MOSCOW. SOME NEWSPAPERS ATTACK SWEDISH AMBASSADOR JARRING AND THE GOVERNMENT IN AN ATTEMPT TO FORCE THEM TO CRITICIZE US. IN PARTICULAR, IT IS STATED THAT THE GOVERNMENT MIGHT FIND "AN OPPORTUNE OCCASION" TO EXPRESS ITS "REGRET" "UNOFFICIALLY" TO THE SOVIET REPRESENTATIVES ON THIS QUESTION.

IF THIS INDEED TAKES PLACE WE INTEND TO RECONFIRM OUR NEGATIVE ATTITUDE TOWARDS PARTICIPATION OF SWEDISH OFFICIALS IN THE CEREMONY OF PRESENTING THE NOBEL LAUREATE'S DIPLOMA AND MEDAL TO SOLZHENITSYN.

M. YAKOVLEV

F. 3, op. 80, d. 645, l. 79–80. Copy.

Note

1. F. Kulakov's copy.

72 Report of the Committee for State Security of the USSR Council of Ministers[1]

No. 942–A/OV
10 April 1972
Special File
Top Secret

To the Central Committee:
Measures taken by state security agencies have prevented certain Western circles from holding a ceremony for the presentation of the Nobel Prize laureate's paraphernalia to Solzhenitsyn, which was planned for 9 April this year.

According to a surveillance report, Solzhenitsyn became extremely nervous upon learning that Nobel Foundation Secretary Gierow was denied a visa to enter the USSR. He is reported to have said to his mistress: "Impudent dogs . . . they do whatever they want with me . . . we are too patient. . . ." With his friends he tries to behave in a calmer fashion. He stated that he would refuse to receive the laureate's paraphernalia at the Swedish embassy, and that he would accept them only from the Nobel Foundation Secretary Gierow himself.

On 9 April, Solzhenitsyn held a dinner party on the occasion of the religious holiday of Easter in his mistress Svetlova's apartment. The latter is beginning to play a more active role in various acts of provocation. Apart from the relatives of Solzhenitsyn's mistress, the dinner was attended by [Igor] Shafarevich, a corresponding member of the USSR Academy of Sciences, and Stolyarova, [Ilya] Erenburg's former literary secretary. These two fully share Solzhenitsyn's views and had assisted him in his preparations for the presentation of the laureate's paraphernalia.

On 10 April, two foreign correspondents (one of them Stig Fredrikson, a Swedish correspondent) came to Svetlova's apartment. They exchanged ideas (by writing notes) on the presentation of the prize and other questions we are still trying to determine.

According to our information, Rostropovich, at whose dacha Solzhenitsyn continues to live, visited US Ambassador Beam on 27 March. They had a two-hour discussion in the presence of some highly placed embassy employees. On 7 April, he visited the West German embassy. On 9 April, Rostropovich, together with his wife Vishnevskaya, spent five hours in the throne hall of the Zagorsk Ecclesiastical Academy where he observed the religious ceremony of prayer on the occasion of Easter.

Chairman of the State Committee for Security
Andropov

F. 3, *op.* 80, *d.* 645, *l.* 69–70. Original.

Note

1. *The first page bears the signatures of A. Kirilenko, A. Kosygin, A. Shelepin, M. Suslov, K. Mazurov, D. Polyansky, V. Grishin, G. Voronov, F. Kulakov, and N. Podgorny, and the following notation: "Comrade Brezhnev has been informed. K. Chernenko 14 July 1972"; a notation on the reverse of the last page reads: "Comrade Pelshe is on vacation. V. Galkin 18 July 1972."*

73 Memorandum from the USSR Foreign Ministry[1]

No. 739/GS
12 April 1972
Classified

To the Central Committee:
In his statement to the press, Swedish Foreign Minister Wickman said that the presentation of the Nobel Prize laureate's medal and diploma to Solzhenitsyn at the Swedish Embassy in Moscow still remains a possibility. (See telegram from Stockholm No. 285.)

The USSR Foreign Ministry believes that it would be advisable to make an appropriate statement to the Swedish Embassy in Moscow regarding this question.

A draft resolution is enclosed.
Please review.

A. Gromyko

F. 3, *op.* 69, *d.* 326, *l.* 15. Original.

Note

1.   *This memo was circulated among Politburo members as No. 40–45 on 12 April 1972 during the vote.*

74 Resolution of the Central Committee's Politburo

"On the Verbal Statement to the Swedish Embassy in Moscow"

No. P40/60
13 April 1972
Top Secret

That the draft of the verbal statement to the Swedish Embassy in Moscow shall be approved by the Politburo (see enclosure).
Central Committee Secretary

Enclosure
Re: Item 60 of minutes No. 40

Verbal Statement to the Swedish Embassy in Moscow
The USSR Foreign Ministry wishes to reconfirm the views of the Soviet Union conveyed to Sweden on numerous occasions regarding the fact that the Swedish Academy has awarded the Nobel Prize to Solzhenitsyn.

Commenting on this question, the Soviet government has stated firmly that the Soviet Union regards the decision to award the Nobel Prize to Solzhenitsyn and to present it to him as an unfriendly act against the Soviet Union. It was also pointed out that from time to time certain circles in Sweden have waged a hostile campaign against the USSR using Solzhenitsyn's name with the purpose of harming Soviet-Swedish relations.

Speaking on 7 December 1970,[1] the Swedish Foreign Minister stated that the Swedish government had nothing to do with the decision of the Academy regarding Solzhenitsyn and assured the Soviet Ambassador that the Swedish government would have no role whatsoever in matters concerning Solzhenitsyn's receiving the Nobel Prize.

In this connection one cannot help being surprised by recent pronouncements of certain officials in Stockholm that a presentation of the

Nobel medal and diploma to Solzhenitsyn at the Swedish Embassy in Moscow still remains a possibility.

I have been authorized to state that the Soviet Union proceeds from the assumption that according to the assurances provided by the Swedish government, the Swedish Embassy in Moscow will refrain from any participation in ceremonies to present the medal and diploma to Solzhenitsyn. It is also hoped that Sweden will take steps to put an end to hostile pronouncements instigated in Sweden against the USSR with regard to Solzhenitsyn. This would serve the interests of good relations between our countries.

F. 3, *op.* 80, *d.* 645, *l.* 76–77. Excerpt from minutes.

Note

1. *The date is incorrect. See Document 45.*

75 Report of the Committee for State Security of the USSR Council of Ministers[1]

No. 969–A
13 April 1972
Classified

To the Central Committee:
The information the KGB continues to receive about the intelligentsia's reaction to Jerzy Romanowsky's article "Alexander Solzhenitsyn's *August 1914*, or the Book and the Myth," which was published in *Trud* [Labor] and

Literaturnaya Rossiya [Literary Russia] on 7 April of this year shows that the intelligentsia is united in its support of this publication and in condemning Solzhenitsyn's antisocial views.

N.P. Smirnov, a prose writer and Writers' Union member, has this to say: "The article is intelligent and well-founded. . . ."

[Gap in the sequence of pages; page 240 is missing.]

Y.L. Akim, a poet, states: "The article was written in a very objective fashion. It is high time Solzhenitsyn was put in his place."

A.S. Nekrasov, a prose writer, said the following: "The article produces a powerful impression. It is especially good that it was published in *Trud*, the workers' paper. We should do something with Solzhenitsyn. He has failed to become a great writer, as the article points out; however, he has definitely shown his political face—he is obviously an enemy of our system."

A.N. Alexeyeva, assistant professor at the History and Philology Department of Gorky University, states: "In his *August 1914*, Solzhenitsyn actually spits on the Russian people. The book is yet another signal that we should no longer tolerate him on our soil. He should be kicked out to the West that he holds so dear to his heart."

[The original document contains more than 10 similar letters—Trans.]

The following Moscow writers also spoke with approval about this publication: G. Brovman, F. Kuznetsov, Y. Galperin, B. Zubavin, M. Ruderman, V. Zakharchenko, S. Mikhalkov, G. Mdivani, and V. Pertsov. The article was also supported by composer O. Feltsman, Leningrad television director Belinsky, and many others.

Solzhenitsyn responded as follows to the publication:

> I did not expect *Literaturnaya Gazeta* to go that far. What I cannot understand is why they have this system—making others do it. . . . They will never write anything themselves. Böll was right. We should not bark back, and try to react to everything. If things have gone so far that the entire world is reading this, they will bark from all directions, and from every lair. We should not pay any attention to this. Let them write. This will be settled by history.

Chairman of the Committee for State Security
Andropov

F. 3, *op.* 80, *d.* 645, *l.* 72–75. Original.

Note

1. *The first page bears the signatures of M. Suslov, A. Kirilenko, V. Grishin, F. Kulakov, A. Shelepin, K. Mazurov, D. Polyansky, G. Voronov, A. Kosygin, N. Podgorny, D. Ustinov, P. Demichev, and M. Solomentsev; on the reverse of the last page is the notation: "Comrade Pelshe is on vacation."*

76 From the Minutes of the Central Committee Meeting

14 April 1972
Top Secret

Chairman: Comrade L.I. Brezhnev
Present: Comrades Voronov, Grishin, Kirilenko, Kosygin, Kulakov, Mazurov, Polyansky, Suslov, Shelepin, Andropov, Demichev, Solomentsev, Ustinov, and Katushev

Questions Discussed off the Agenda
1. About Solzhenitsyn

Brezhnev: Solzhenitsyn is becoming more impudent. He writes numerous slanderous letters and speaks at press conferences. He is very bitter. We should take the most resolute steps to deal with him.

Andropov: It seems he should be stripped of his Soviet citizenship. Let the Swedes take him.

Brezhnev: At the last meeting we authorized Comrade Podgorny together with the Public Prosecutor's Office and the KGB to deal with this question. However, Comrade Podgorny is away.[1] That is why we may want to wait a few days until he comes back and together with the other comrades makes a proposal on this question.

Andropov: I would like to discuss the question of how we should deal with Yakir. We could certainly arrest him now and try him. But would it be the most opportune moment for this? Maybe we had better do this after the ratification of the treaties.

Kosygin: Solzhenitsyn is acting with impudence. All his actions go unpunished. That is why he carries on like this. I think he should be kicked out. Besides, we must somehow deal with Rostropovich. We should summon him and tell him to stop his tours abroad.

Brezhnev: Instead of touring Barnaul, for example, or other Soviet cities, he prefers to go to New York, Paris, and other cities abroad. We did tell them to stop Rostropovich from going abroad, but he continues to tour all over the world. In brief, we should deal with these persons the way we decided to at the Politburo meeting.

From minutes of the Politburo meetings in 1972. Original.

Note

1. *N. Podgorny was on an official visit to Turkey from 11 to 17 April 1972.*

77 Memorandum of the Committee for State Security of the USSR Council of Ministers[1]

No. 1707–A
17 July 1973
Top Secret
Special File

To the Central Committee:

The KGB recently obtained information giving grounds to state, without a shadow of doubt, that apart from anti-Soviet public literary activity and statements, Solzhenitsyn is also trying to carry out *illegal subversive acts* by drawing individual Soviet citizens into his hostile activities and instigating them to engage in unlawful actions.

On 19 June of this year, Solzhenitsyn spoke to Superfin (who was arrested for anti-Soviet crimes in July)[2] and his friend Borisov[3] about changing his tactics against the Soviet state and social system. He insisted that they should engage in active forms of hostile activities. He said: "Let us stop playing around with 'loony bins' and other things and get down to action."

On 16 June of this year, Solzhenitsyn had a similar conversation with the writer Korzhavin.[4] He said that it was necessary to organize opposition to the actions that state agencies take against the antisocial activities of certain personages.

His conversation with his stepson, Dmitry, on 2 July shows how bitter Solzhenitsyn has become. Speaking to this eleven-year-old child, he had this to say:

> For us life is a neverending struggle. There is no one in this country whom the government hates more than me. The government is all powerful. They have the world at their feet. And I am sitting right under their nose. But Mama and I have never given up anything without a fight. And we never will give up. We would rather die. That is why we will always be fighting to the very end. We will never compromise, since compromising has destroyed humanity. . . . If they (the KGB) get hold of you,

> you should know that there will be a fight on your account, a
> global and international fight. When you are there you must
> behave with dignity. Do not bend your knees before them,
> never ask them for mercy, nor try to kiss your way out of the
> situation, nor promise them anything. Be confident and tell
> them that they are bound to lose and to perish.

Trying to impose his anti-Soviet views on those close to him, Solzhenitsyn
has established contacts in different cities and works hard to expand them.
His supporters have been discovered in the Crimea region, in Ryazan,
Tambov, Novocherkassk, and other cities. Among Solzhenitsyn's contacts,
his friends from Leningrad are of particular interest; they include: E.G.
Etkind, a PhD in philology known for his anti-Marxist views, who wrote the
provocative so-called "Brodsky Letter to the Central Committee;" L.A.
Samutin, a retired person who was convicted for serving as a brigade
commander in the traitor Vlasov's Russian Liberation Army; E.D.
Voronyanskaya, a retired person; E.V. Ivanova, a music teacher; and others.
They are active supporters of Solzhenitsyn and his hostile views. All of them
make multiple copies of his works and always have them in their possession.[5]

In order to document Solzhenitsyn's criminal activities that are punishable
by law, the KGB has taken a number of measures that have resulted in the
collection of the materials confirming his hostility to the socialist system,
Communist Party policy, and the Soviet government. They also point to his
strict adherence to the views and ideas of the most reactionary circles in the
West. Of particular interest are documents in the possession of N.F.
Pakhtusova, a resident of Leningrad, born 1917, who before retiring used to
work as a chief geologist of the North-West Geological Department. In
particular Pakhtusova has in her possession Voronyanskaya's so-called
Memoirs, in which the author recounts the anti-Soviet contents of
Solzhenitsyn's *The Gulag Archipelago*. In Voronyanskaya's view, in this book
Solzhenitsyn showed ". . . The corruption of a nation 200-million strong.
The destruction of its better part, including half its Party members. The
murder of its intellect, conscience, and humane spirit. . . ." (More detailed
excerpts from the *Memoirs* are enclosed.)

After investigating Solzhenitsyn's close friends, we have discovered that he
provides material support to many of them, sometimes in the form of hard
currency.

Solzhenitsyn's anti-Soviet nature can be clearly seen in his literary works.
All the books he plans to write and those that he has almost finished (*October
1916*,[6] *Volunteers' Highway*[7]) are intended to debunk the ideas of the Great
October Socialist Revolution, discredit the history of the Soviet state, and
instigate antisocial activities.

Solzhenitsyn views his finished novel [sic] *The Gulag Archipelago* as the "summit" of his hostile works. The novel [sic], his cronies claim, is intended to show the Soviet public and the public abroad "the bloody extermination of the people, the suffering of millions, the hidden, unbearable convict's life of a good half of the Russian people during half a century of Communist rule." Solzhenitsyn himself says of *The Gulag Archipelago*: "It's a killer work, a real knockout blow!"

All the above signifies that Solzhenitsyn is a dedicated opponent of the Soviet state and its social system. He has deliberately embarked on the path of anti-Soviet struggle, employing Western propaganda machinery and the mass media to further his aims.

Solzhenitsyn's anti-Soviet views go back to his student years. At that time he produced a politically harmful manuscript and circulated it among his friends. In 1945 he was convicted for anti-Soviet activities and sentenced to eight years imprisonment. He completed his sentence, but in 1957 was rehabilitated. After the Twentieth Party Congress, Solzhenitsyn, masquerading as an opponent of the consequences of the personality cult and exploiting the Party Congress decisions in his favor, wrote *The First Circle* and *Cancer Ward* directed against communist ideology and the practice of socialist construction, claiming that socialism represented an unbridled exploitation of the people.

Considering that Solzhenitsyn's anti-Soviet activities are corroborated by the materials obtained, the KGB is taking steps to document them with the goal of *pressing criminal charges against Solzhenitsyn.*

Chairman of the Committee for State Security
Andropov

Enclosure
16 July 1973
Classified

Excerpts from the Memoirs of E.D. Voronyanskaya

The author describes in her *Memoirs* how Solzhenitsyn wrote *Arch* (referring to the unpublished work, *The Gulag Archipelago*), and also gives her views which were shaped under the influence of Solzhenitsyn's works.

Voronyanskaya writes as follows:

The corruption of a country of 200 million people. The weeding out of its better part, including half of its Party members. The elimination of its intellect, conscience, and its good will. The destruction of all Christian commandments. These are replaced by consumerism and stupefaction. Subtle and not-so-subtle messages: kill, steal, denounce, lie. Betray your mother and your father. Make an idol of your leader and you will reap the benefits. From now on, the Ministry of State Security is your church. Pray to nobody but the Ministry and its henchmen, and you will be rich and protected, and none of your crimes will be punished.

I know of some of Solzhenitsyn's contemporaries who have read *Arch* and, under its influence, not only began to think of the fate of their country, but also to notice things they used to pass by indifferently and to engage in public acts they had never thought of committing. Even the civic positions of Tvardovsky, Kaverin, Grigorenko, academician Sakharov, and other prominent figures and contemporaries of the writer were reinforced, or sometimes emerged for the first time, under the direct influence of S.'s mighty spirit and his uncompromising struggle.

While paying lip service to the right of national self-determination, not only did we keep throttling the peoples of our own Federation, but we sent tanks against 14 million Czechoslovak citizens. We crushed Hungary under our tanks as well. We need to write dozens of volumes in order to comprehend Russia's real history after 1917. Over this half-century, the Russian people and their kin have been subjected to a senseless, bloody, brutal extermination not by the thousands, not by the tens of thousands, but by the millions." (pp. 59–60)

Voronyanskaya paraphrases certain parts of the work and evaluates its importance.

This historic chronicle, *Arch*, narrates the bloody extermination of the people, its many tragedies, and the sufferings of millions. If the human race doesn't commit suicide in a fit of madness, *Arch* will be studied by historians, philosophers, economists, sociologists, art critics, painters, writers, composers, filmmakers, actors, and artists of all kinds and from all nations. Not one thinking person will pass by this Everest of Russian literature, which embraces the unfathomable suffering of the people, revealing the hidden, unbearable life of half the Russian people during fifty years of Communist rule. *Arch* poses a multitude of great and eternal questions, exposes the true dialectics of history and the false philosophy of dogmatists, the criminal nature of their deeds, and the contemptibility of their positions.

The author relates sincerely and truthfully how all this was born, how it blossomed, flowered, was hidden, made secret, what it ultimately turned into and what it has cost us.

We knew a lot. And still we did not know that our Soviet penal camps were more horrible than tsarist dungeons or fascist camps (there were escapes from fascist camps, after all); that we had the heroic Kengir and Ekibastuz[8] in the history of the camps. Our contemporaries were not aware of this, even if many of them had lost their fathers, husbands, brothers, or sons in these camps. I cannot find the right words to describe this book, which recites the most gruesome and bloody tragedy of our two hundred million–strong people in the many centuries of its existence.

Meanwhile, the written and oral stories of those who are still alive, the unpublished memoirs, prose, archival materials, clandestine leaflets, and confiscated books have continued to flow to S.'s mind and heart. During the year after *Arch* was completed, he accumulated a great deal of them. A different light was cast on the role of Korolenko[9] in the revolution, and his prophetic vision of pitch darkness beyond an illusory light.

Then there was the cowardly and dastardly role of Gorky. In 1967 and 1968 we read all the speeches and articles of Krylenko,[10] that apostle of Soviet jurisprudence. We met survivors from Vlasov's army. We recorded for Solzhenitsyn all that took place in Novocherkassk, all the details of the suppression of the people's rebellion in that city by tanks.[11] We continued to receive stories from those who had suffered, testifying to even more ghastly, brutal, and repugnant incidents. (pp. 60–64)

In her *Memoirs*, Voronyanskaya advances libelous contentions that the Soviet government is interested in infusions of foreign currency and will do anything to obtain them:

For hard currency the Soviet government is ready to sell not just its own father, but all of Marxism-Leninism with its three sources (not openly, of course, but in secret. . .).

. . . And it turns out that so long as *Arch* remained unknown (although, perhaps, they will swallow it as well?), S. could be an object of commerce, and they could think about how to transfer his earnings to the USSR and confiscate them 'for the construction of communism in the entire world.' (p. 89)

At the end of her *Memoirs*, Voronyanskaya writes as follows: "In *Arch*, he told us of the flame that consumed our country. Now he has decided to return to the sparks of this flame. How did this all catch fire, flare up, turn into a conflagration, and what was the spark that set off the blaze that devoured the country?" (p. 91)

(The author's style has been preserved.)

Faithful and true copy:

Department Head of the Committee for State Security of the USSR Council of Ministers
Bobkov

F. 3, *op.* 80, *d.* 646, *l.* 18–25. Original.

Notes

1. *The first page bears the resolution: "Send to all Politburo members for information. L. Brezhnev," and the signatures of A. Kosygin, A. Kirilenko, D. Polyansky, K. Mazurov, F. Kulakov, N. Podgorny, M. Suslov, A. Pelshe, A. Shelepin, A. Gromyko, A. Grechko, D. Kunaev, and V. Shcherbitsky. The reverse side of the last page has a note: "Comrade Grishin is sick."*

2. Gabriel Superfin is a young literary scholar who helped Solzhenitsyn with archival research for *The Gulag Archipelago*. He was arrested shortly before this KGB report was drawn up on suspicion of having sent the *Prison Diary* of Edward Kuznetsov abroad and being one of the editors of the *Chronicle of Current Events*. The following year (1974) he was sentenced to four years in the labor camps. He now lives in the USA.

3. Vadim Borisov is a church historian who became a friend and collaborator of Solzhenitsyn's in the early seventies. Among other things he contributed an article to Solzhenitsyn's anthology *From Under the Rubble*.

4. Naum Korzhavin (real name Mendel) is a poet who came to prominence during Khrushchev's "Thaw" in the late fifties and was allowed to publish very little until he emigrated to the USA in the mid-seventies.

5. Leonid Samutin was one of Solzhenitsyn's informants about conditions in the Vlasov army during World War II (see Document 6, Note 5), and afterwards helped him with secretarial work on *The Gulag Archipelago*; Elizaveta Voronyanskaya was his chief typist in Leningrad for *The Gulag Archipelago*; Ivanova was another assistant.

6. The sequel to *August 1914*.

7. Clearly a mistake. *Volunteers' Highway* (under that and other names) was an early work written while Solzhenitsyn was still in the labor camps (see Document 2, Note 20).

8. Kengir and Ekibastuz were two camps in which the prisoners rose up in rebellion against their guards and overseers. Solzhenitsyn, who had personally participated in the Ekibastuz rebellion, described them in detail in *The Gulag Archipelago*.

9. Vladimir Korolenko (1853–1921), a short story writer of the turn of the century, was well known for his humanitarian and liberal sympathies (he was twice arrested and banished during tsarist times). At first he supported the October Revolution, but just before his death turned against it.

10. Nikolai Krylenko (1885–1938) was Chief Public Prosecutor and then People's Commissar of Justice during the Stalin era and distinguished himself by leading the prosecution in the most notorious show trials of the twenties and thirties. He was denounced during the purge of 1937–1938 and shot as an enemy of the people. Solzhenitsyn devoted many pages of *The Gulag Archipelago* to an analysis of his career.

11. Novocherkassk was the capital of the Don Cossack region, where Solzhenitsyn had spent a brief part of his childhood and where his first wife, Natalia Reshetovskaya, came from. In *The Gulag Archipelago* he describes the unprecedented strike by factory workers that occurred there in June 1962. The strike was suppressed with tanks and rifle fire in which over fifty people were killed, but the whole incident was kept secret for many years afterward.

78 Report of the Committee for State Security of the USSR Council of Ministers[1]

No. 1902–A
10 August 1973
Top Secret
Special File

To the Central Committee:
On 17 July 1973 under No. 1707–A we reported that certain friends of Solzhenitsyn in Leningrad possessed documents proving that this author had written *The Gulag Archipelago*, an obviously anti-Soviet piece of work.

In order to document Solzhenitsyn's hostile activities, we obtained a warrant from the USSR Public Prosecutor's Office and on 4 August 1973 conducted a search at the apartment of Pakhtusova, one of Solzhenitsyn's contacts. During the search we discovered and seized 192 documents, most of them of an anti-Soviet and politically harmful nature. Among the documents we confiscated we found the *Memoirs* of Voronyanskaya, a friend of Solzhenitsyn, in which she summarizes the content of *The Gulag Archipelago*. (A copy of these *Memoirs* was enclosed with the previous memorandum). We also confiscated Pakhtusova's diary, where she gives the following assessment of this composition:

> No book like this has ever been written in the entire history of humankind, either in terms of content or in terms of its genre, which is impossible to define. This is not a literary genre or a work of literature, but life itself, condensed in a bloody cluster of anguish, despair, resignation, and rebellion. These are transmogrified screams. Pain, tears, sobs, rage, prayers, and the invocations of a prophet! This is the Gospel of the twentieth century! And this Gospel was created by a Prometheus, it is a political time bomb, and if by some miracle the entire people were able to read it without hindrance, it would lead to a revolt and barricades!
>
> It is impossible to read this book, your throat is constricted by a nervous spasm, you want to scream, to run somewhere, and finally to punch, to murder all those prospering, ruling bandits, those Stalin-like 'godfathers'!

Entries in Pakhtusova's diaries indicate that Solzhenitsyn's close contacts in Leningrad used to keep several typewritten copies of *The Gulag Archipelago*, but Solzhenitsyn instructed them to burn them. In the meantime, he prepared a third version of his work. In this regard, I would like to draw your attention to the following entry in Pakhtusova's diary:

> I had a visit from E. (Voronyanskaya). She was agitated and upset. She found out that A.I. (Solzhenitsyn) decided to publish. . . . I was also dumbstruck by this announcement. I wonder what has prompted A.I. to take such a desperate decision? Didn't he always say that this book would see the light of day only after his death? And I can understand that—if it were published in his lifetime, it would kill him at once. A trial. Camps, execution by firing squad, poison, an arranged hit-and-run accident—that's what awaits him after the publication of this book. Yet he is doing it. Why? Maybe he's afraid that Reshetovskaya (his former wife) will denounce him anyway and he will die for nothing and his creation destroyed? That must be the reason: if I have to die, let me die at least for a published book, which the KGB will not be able to confiscate or destroy, since it will have been published abroad. Those are the questions that trouble us. The book will be published in 1973, but, perhaps, A.I. is plotting another move: to leave the [US] SR with his family, ie, to force the government to expel him from the country. In any event, it's obvious that he is getting ready for some decisive turn in his life. Such facts as the liquidation of . . . in its former versions and his request to have his correspondence returned testify to this. His visit this spring to bid farewell to his friends in Leningrad also fits this picture.

We also confiscated Pakhtusova's card file with information on personages who were repressed[2] from 1924–1954. Pakhtusova describes it as follows: "Our catalog of martyrs includes approximately 2,000 names of those who were repressed, although it is limited to victims of the thirty years of Stalin's tyranny . . . who were sentenced under Article 58[3] of the Russian Federation Penal Code."

Chairman of the Committee for State Security
Andropov

F. 3, *op.* 80, *d.* 646, *l.* 26–28. Original.

Notes

1. *The first page bears the resolution: "Send to all Politburo members for information. L. Brezhnev," and has the signatures of A. Kosygin, A. Kirilenko, D. Polyansky, K. Mazurov, F. Kulakov, N. Podgorny, M. Suslov, A. Pelshe, A. Shelepin, A. Gromyko, A. Grechko, D. Kunaev, and V. Shcherbitsky. The reverse side of the last page bears the notation: "Grishin is sick."*

2. "Repressed" was the official Soviet euphemism for government sanctions ranging from arrest and imprisonment to execution.

3. The catchall article directed against "anti-Soviet propaganda" that was most widely used in mass arrests during Stalin's time (see Document 2, Note 11).

79 Memorandum of the Committee for State Security of the USSR Council of Ministers[1]

No. 2036-A
26 August 1973
Special File
Top Secret

To the Central Committee:
Documents obtained by the Committee for State Security show that Solzhenitsyn still maintains his anti-Soviet attitude and more often than ever behaves as an undisguised enemy of the socialist system. For these purposes, he actively makes use of Western propaganda services and provides moral and material support to those Soviet citizens who display anti-Soviet tendencies.

Solzhenitsyn is finishing his novel *October 1916* and is ready to begin a new, third "knot" known as *February 1917*. He has already written several chapters of this book and submitted them to his friends for comments. At the same time, Solzhenitsyn, with the assistance of his associates, continues to gather information on personages sentenced in recent years for crimes against the state and on the conditions of their detention in corrective labor institutions, and he is also collecting facts regarding the authorities' allegedly unlawful actions against the dissidents. He composes them for the Western media in a biased fashion and deliberately distorts the actual state of affairs. For instance, speaking about the prisoner Galanskov,[2] who died in confinement, Solzhenitsyn contends that it resulted from the deliberate actions of his doctors.

Seeking to attract public attention to himself, Solzhenitsyn continues to produce provocative political documents in which he appeals to the Western reader by criticizing certain aspects of the socialist system. Such criticism is actively used by the enemy in its ideological subversion of the USSR. In these documents, Solzhenitsyn relentlessly raises the issue of the authorities' persecution of him, the alleged curtailment of his rights in the USSR, and his dire financial straits. In the most recent of such statements, he told Western correspondents about his letter to Comrade Shchelokov, USSR Minister of Internal Affairs. Its content, based on Solzhenitsyn's account, was reported by a number of bourgeois radio stations. A day later, Solzhenitsyn gave another interview to foreign correspondents on the condition that it would be published in the West on 28 August 1973.

Both Soviet and foreign media have repeatedly reported on Solzhenitsyn's status and his material well-being. The state provided Solzhenitsyn with a three-room apartment in Ryazan, where he still maintains his official residence. A two-story dacha near Moscow is registered in his name, and his second wife lives in a five-room apartment in the center of Moscow. He spends the summers with his family at a leased dacha in the village of Firsanovka in the Khimki District. Over the last two years, Solzhenitsyn has drawn 32,301 hard-currency rubles from foreign banks, which he used to buy Moskvich-412 passenger cars for Reshetovskaya, his first wife, and for Svetlova, the mother of his second child. As a rule, he buys hardware and food at the Beriozka hard-currency stores. In recent days, Solzhenitsyn has been preparing a new document for foreign audiences regarding the allegedly difficult position of Soviet literature and its most talented representatives. Solzhenitsyn has told foreign correspondents the following in explanation of the need for such a statement:

> You know what's happening now, you know Sakharov's situa-
> tion. In astronomy we have the concept of the nadir. The
> zenith and the nadir. Right now, we have a social nadir. I have
> been spending all my time writing my novel. On numerous
> occasions I was asked to speak out, yet I kept silent because I
> was busy writing the novel. At this point, though, I feel that I
> can no longer do it (abstain from speaking out). . . .

Solzhenitsyn has undertaken all this activity under the guise of demanding a lawful residence permit for Moscow.

Legally he does indeed have such a right. Yet there are many sides to this issue of Solzhenitsyn's residence permit in the capital. First of all, by residing in Moscow on lawful grounds, Solzhenitsyn, who personifies impunity, would become a natural magnet for all sorts of dissatisfied individuals.

Secondly, Solzhenitsyn even now uses his wife's Moscow apartment for meetings with foreigners. Once he gets a residence permit, he will hold such meetings more openly, since he already has many acquaintances and regular connections among foreign reporters.

Thirdly, the issue of his residence permit has a political dimension, since Solzhenitsyn has rejected all demands to clarify his position and to provide a proper appraisal of his participation in anti-Soviet campaigns conducted in the West, thus refusing to show respect for the opinion of the Soviet public and for the laws of the country where he lives.

Finally, we cannot ignore either the opinion of the USSR Writers' Union, which considers Solzhenitsyn's residence in Moscow undesirable, or numerous statements of the same nature made by a number of prominent representatives of the Soviet artistic establishment. These circles are still discussing, for instance, a speech by Khrabrovitsky, a well-known figure in the film industry, at a plenary meeting of the Filmmakers' Union, where he demanded not just a denunciation of Solzhenitsyn's anti-Soviet actions, but his expulsion from the country.

It is quite obvious that Western special services, especially in connection with preparations for the second stage of the European conference,[3] are placing certain hopes on the so-called "dissidents," and particularly on the anti-Soviet statements of such persons as Solzhenitsyn, planning to use them to enhance the positions of our ideological adversaries regarding the issues of "civil liberties" in the USSR and of information exchange.

It is true that from a formal, legalistic perspective, Solzhenitsyn is entitled to seek a permit for residence in his wife's apartment. Yet his behavior conflicts with the ordinance on residence permits in Moscow, and the satisfaction of his insistent demands would unavoidably cause political damage.

Since the USSR Ministry of Internal Affairs, in response to Solzhenitsyn's demand to grant him a residence permit in Moscow, has replied that this issue falls under the jurisdiction of the Moscow City Council, we think that if Solzhenitsyn applies to that body, it would be advisable to give him a reply along the following lines: "The Moscow City Council has reviewed your residence request and cannot give you such permission, since you have not ceased your anti-Soviet activities. Moscow is a city with a strict regimen, from which individuals who behave in this manner are evicted." Please review.

Chairman of the Committee for State Security
Andropov

F. 3, op. 80, d. 646, l. 30-33. Original.

Notes

1. *The first page bears the resolution: "Send to all Politburo members. A. Kirilenko" and the signatures of F. Kulakov, K. Mazurov, A. Kosygin, D. Polyansky, L. Brezhnev, and A. Gromyko. The last page bears the notation: "The KGB (P.P. Laptev) was informed of the approval. V. Galkin. 3 September 1973"; the reverse side bears the notation: "Comrades Grechko, Podgorny, Suslov, and Shelepin are on vacation; Grishin and Pelshe are sick."*

2. Yuri T. Galanskov, a dissident poet, editor, and human rights activist, was sentenced to seven years' hard labor in 1966 for his samizdat writings and compilations. He died in a labor camp in 1972 from lack of proper medical care.

3. *The Conference on Security and Cooperation in Europe (CSCE) took place from 1973–1975 in three stages. The first stage was held in July 1973 in Helsinki at the level of foreign ministers; the second stage was convened from September 1973–July 1975 in Geneva and consisted of working meetings to prepare the final political documents; and the third and concluding stage was held in Helsinki on 30 July–1 August 1975, and was a meeting of the leaders of thirty-three European countries, the United States, and Canada. The Final Act of the CSCE came to be known as the Helsinki Accords.*

80 Memorandum of the Committee for State Security of the USSR Council of Ministers[1]

No. 2045–A
27 August 1973
Special File
Top Secret

To the Central Committee:
As reported earlier, on 26 August 1973 Solzhenitsyn met, in Moscow at his wife's apartment, with correspondents of the US news agency Associated Press and the French newspaper *Le Monde*, and gave them the text of his latest interview. We discovered that Solzhenitsyn had prepared the entire text of the interview in advance. He personally wrote the text in the form of his own questions and answers.

The entire interview is constructed around Solzhenitsyn's slanderous contention that there are no civil liberties in the Soviet Union, and that the state allegedly takes systematic measures to suppress ideas in our country.

Solzhenitsyn writes, in part, in his interview:[2]

> Last year, in commenting on the award of my Nobel Prize, I tried humbly, though in vain, to call people's attention to two unequal degrees of assessment of the scope and moral significance of events, and to the fact that events in a country that determines the fate of the world cannot be treated as 'internal affairs.'
>
> Also in vain, I pointed out that the jamming of Western radio broadcasts in Eastern countries creates a situation resembling the eve of a disaster and undermines treaties and international safeguards. Everything has remained the same, as if nothing were said, and, perhaps it is useless to repeat myself today. You cannot explain the meaning of the jamming of radio broadcasts to those who have not experienced it, who have not lived through such jamming for many years. This is a daily dose of filth in your ears and eyes, this is insulting and humiliating. This is a degradation of adults down to the level of children. Even goodwill broadcasts during some of the most

friendly visits are often jammed. Such broadcasts are supposed to avoid even the slightest deviation in their assessment of events, in their comments or emphases, and everyone is supposed to perceive events in an absolutely identical way. And a great number of events occurring in the world must remain unknown to our population.

It is a paradox, but Moscow and Leningrad have become the most ill-informed capitals in the world. Their inhabitants try to obtain information from those who come to the city from rural areas. Out there, for economic reasons (this jamming 'service' costs our people a great deal) jamming is less frequent. Yet according to observations in various localities over the past few months, jamming has spread to cover new areas and has become more intense. I recall the fate of Sergei Khanzhenkov, who in 1973 came out of prison after having served a seven-year sentence for his attempt, or even intent, to remove a jammer in Minsk. And yet we cannot perceive this 'crime' in any other way than as an act of struggle for world peace.

The objective of the current suppression of thinking in our country may be defined as 'Chinesation,' as an implementation of Chinese ideals. But were not such ideals realized in the thirties already? All this has already been forgotten. How many people in the West in the thirties ever heard about Mikhail Bulgakov, Platonov, or Floransky [sic]?[3] Everything resembles China. Today we have thousands of dissidents, we have clandestine writers and philosophers, but the world will learn of them only after the passage of an entire epoch, in fifty or a hundred years' time, and very few of their works will escape merciless destruction. That's the ideal our rulers would like to recreate. Yet I state with confidence that a return to such a regime is impossible in our country. I will give you reasons. First of all, there is international information, the penetration and influence, in spite of everything, of ideas, facts, and the protests of human beings. We have to understand that the East is not indifferent to protests by the Western public. On the contrary, it is petrified by this threat. Only such protests, when we hear the unified powerful voice of hundreds of prominent individuals, the opinion of an entire continent, can make a dent in a progressive regime. When oppressors hear timid and isolated protests without any hope of success, accompanied by inevitable curtsies to the cases of Greece, Turkey, and Spain, that only makes them laugh. When the racial composition of a basketball team becomes a more important international event than daily injections that weaken inmates' brains in psychiatric hospitals, can we feel anything but aversion toward a civilization of egoism and myopia? In the light of worldwide publicity our prisons retreat and disappear.

Thus Amalrik, who was supposed to get a long prison term back in 1970, got three years in the beginning. Besides, the authorities were forced to send him to [exile in] Kolyma rather than to a political camp in Mordovia. Today, due to a new wave of international public opinion, they had to 'restrain themselves' once again to three years.[4] Under different circumstances, the result would have been far worse.

The Western world has used publicity to assist and save many of our oppressed people, who not only feel grateful for their defense, but also provide a shining example of perseverance and selflessness even when facing death or suffering in the torture chambers of murderous psychiatric hospitals. Here is the second and main reason why I am sure that Chinese ideals are no longer acceptable in our country. The unbending General Grigorenko needs far more courage than is needed on a battlefield when, even after four years in a psychiatric prison hospital, he continues to reject every attempt to force him to buy his liberation from suffering with the price of a retreat from his convictions.

Vladimir Bukovsky, who has spent all of his youth in psychiatric and ordinary prisons and camps, has not been defeated and has not taken advantage of an opportunity to live in freedom. Instead, he prefers a life of conscientious sacrifice for the benefit of others.[5]

Earlier this year, he was brought to Moscow and given the following offer—he could be freed and would be allowed to emigrate, provided that he would not conduct political activities. That was all. In addition, once abroad, he would be able to restore his health. According to contemporary Western standards, he could have paid far more for his freedom, for the deliverance from his suffering. Some American prisoners of war were known to sign any paper against their country, putting their precious lives above convictions, but Bukovsky deemed his convictions more precious than his life. This lesson is clear for everyone in the West, although, quite possibly it will remain useless. In response, Bukovsky advanced just one condition: release from psychiatric prisons those he has tried to defend in his writings. He was not satisfied that his liberation would not have been a payoff for personal cowardice. He did not want to run while leaving others in distress. And so he was sent back to the camp to serve his twelve years.

Amalrik had a similar choice in the spring of this year. He could have confirmed the testimony of Krasin and Yakir.[6] He was promised freedom in return. Yet he also refused and was sent to Kolyma to serve a second sentence. In addition, there have been many other instances, the details of which remain unknown to us, where pain and suffering are hidden from our view under the guise of state secrets.

If we know that a person has not given up, we can draw a certain conclusion that such a person is unshakeable in his convictions. A similar dilemma quite often faces those who live a more ordinary life, who have not been arrested, but who have to make a choice. Take, for instance, Gorlov, who was in the garden two years ago when the state security forces raided my dacha.[7] The only reason he was not arrested right away was because of his active resistance, which attracted public attention. Right now they are demanding that he remain silent, while threatening to destroy his scientific and professional career. Obviously this is not an empty threat, but, in spite of it, he has not succumbed to pressure to keep silent. Just that—keep silent.

This spirit of sacrifice is the beacon of our future. In addition, the human being possesses one psychological trait that constantly amazes me. When happy and careless, he dreads the most minute misfortunes and strives to remain ignorant of the suffering of others and of anticipated future suffering. He makes concessions in many respects, including important ones, with the sole purpose of extending his bliss. Yet suddenly, when that person is totally broke, destitute and free of everything he used to regard as central to his entire life, he finds the firmness to be tenacious until his very last step, sacrificing his life rather than his principles.

If mankind had only this first trait it would have never held on to the peaks it has reached. Yet because humans also have the second trait, they can rise up from any abyss.

It would be better if mankind, while still on top, could foresee the future fall awaiting us. The experience of the most recent generations has completely convinced me that only the indomitability of the human spirit, steadily directed against menacing danger, ensures the true defense of peace for one individual, for everybody, and for all of mankind.

Solzhenitsyn has scheduled the publication of the interview for 28 August 1973.

In the opinion of Western reporters, Solzhenitsyn, by giving this interview, pursues an objective of creating difficulties for the Soviet Union during the second stage of the Conference on Security and Cooperation in Europe.

Chairman of the Committee for State Security
Andropov

F. 3, op. 80, d. 646, l. 36–40. Original.

Notes

1. *The document is accompanied by the instruction: "Send to all Politburo members (code— Special File). A. Kirilenko"; it was sent to Politburo members and candidate members, and Central Committee Secretaries, on 28 August 1973 under No. P1630.*
2. For the full text of this interview see *The Oak and the Calf*, Appendix 26.
3. The modernist writers, Mikhail Bulgakov (1891–1940) and Andrei Platonov (1899–1951), were both attacked in the early thirties, and their best work censored and suppressed. It was not until the sixties that their works were rediscovered and published, first clandestinely and eventually openly. They are now acknowledged as two of the best Russian prose writers of the century. Pavel Florensky (1882–1943), a theologian and philosopher, was repeatedly arrested during the early thirties and eventually sent into administrative exile. Some of his writings were rediscovered and embraced by literary structuralists during the sixties, and he was hailed as a precursor.
4. Andrei Amalrik was sentenced to three years' exile in Siberia in 1965 for his surre-alist writings and his contacts with Western reporters, but stayed only a year, which he described in his *Involuntary Journey to Siberia* (Harcourt Brace, 1970). In 1968 he circulated and published in the West a brilliant essay, *Will the Soviet Union Survive Until 1984?*, for which, in 1970, he was sentenced to three years in the labor camps. (In 1976 he emigrated to the West, and died soon afterward in a road accident in Portugal).
5. Vladimir Bukovsky was a celebrated younger dissident who was in and out of labor camps and psychiatric hospitals for several years as a result of his highly public protests. In 1971 he caused a sensation by smuggling information to the West

about the incarceration of sane individuals (of whom he was one) in psychiatric prisons and their punishment with mind-altering drugs. In 1976 he was released from a high-security prison and sent to the West in exchange for a Chilean communist, and later described his experiences in his autobiography *To Build a Castle* (Viking, 1978).

6. Pyotr Yakir (see Document 60, Note 2, and Document 68, Note 2) and fellow dissident Viktor Krasin had both recanted after their arrest in the spring of 1973 and gave damaging testimony to the KGB about the editors of the *Chronicle of Current Events* and other activists. Their trial in August was turned into a show trial to which Western reporters were invited, but it did not have the desired effect of intimidating other dissidents, although it did damage the *Chronicle* and slowed the movement for a while.

7. See Document 52.

81 From the Minutes of a Politburo Meeting

30 August 1973
Top Secret

(Chairman: Comrade A.P. Kirilenko
Present: Comrades Y.V. Andropov, A.N. Kosygin, F.D. Kulakov, K.T. Mazurov, D.S. Polyansky, P.N. Demichev, V.I. Dolgikh, I.V. Kapitonov, and K.F. Katushev

Following the Politburo's meeting, Comrade Kirilenko said that a letter from scientists on the subject of Sakharov had played a major role.[1] But, if we stopped there and failed to support these scientists, we would not achieve the needed effect. Perhaps we should publish, in some form, materials voicing disapproval of Sakharov's behavior by other scientists, workers, and representatives of the intelligentsia as well. But we should preserve a strict proportion in this respect.

Kosygin: Our public doesn't know what Sakharov is and what he has written. That's why it would perhaps be worth publishing an article on Sakharov.[2]

Kirilenko: Maybe it would be worth preparing a brief for the Central Committee Secretaries of the Communist Parties of the Union Republics and of the territorial and oblast Party committees regarding Sakharov, Solzhenitsyn, and the trial of Yakir and Krasin.

The Politburo members approved this proposal.

Comrades Demichev and Kapitonov were instructed to review and resolve issues related to the publication of materials regarding Sakharov, keeping in mind the discussion at this meeting of the Politburo, and to prepare the text of a brief for the Central Committees of the Communist Parties of the Union Republics and the territorial and oblast Party committees.

Kosygin: We should take tougher measures with respect to Sakharov. Let Andropov think of further measures in this regard. Solzhenitsyn is also stepping up his activities.

Andropov: This is a fair observation. We have discovered that Sakharov is indeed mentally ill, but we need to talk directly with him. Maybe this should be done by somebody from the top ranks, for instance by Comrade Kirillin.

Kosygin: Comrade Kirillin is sick. He is in the hospital for surgery.

Andropov [to Kosygin]: Maybe you would do it, Alexei Nikolaevich?

Kosygin: Yes, I could talk with him.

Andropov: Solzhenitsyn is becoming more and more active in politics and serving as a unifying force for former prisoners and all malcontents. He gave an anti-Soviet interview to *Le Monde*'s correspondent. We managed to obtain a manuscript of his *Gulag Island* [sic]. It is a crude anti-Soviet piece of work written by Solzhenitsyn back in 1965 and intended for publication after his death. We will summon Solzhenitsyn and accuse him of a crime against the Soviet government.

I want to say a few words regarding the trial of Yakir and Krasin. The accused pleaded guilty on all counts. In their statements, they exposed a number of foreign figures and denounced Sakharov.

We plan to hold a post-trial news conference for foreign reporters to discuss the results. The news conference will take place on Wednesday in the Foreign Ministry building. It will be conducted by the Ministry's Media Department.[3] Deputy Public Prosecutor Malyarov will be there. We will invite all foreign reporters, but the room seats only 60 persons, so some correspondents will not be able to participate.

From minutes of Politburo sessions in 1973. Original.

Notes

1. *See* Pravda *of 29 August 1973.*
2. The reason for the Politburo's concern over Sakharov was that in June that year he had given a long interview to a Swedish correspondent reflecting extreme pessimism about the future of the Soviet Union and his disillusionment with socialism. On August 16, two weeks before this meeting, Sakharov had been summoned to meet the Deputy Public Prosecutor M.P. Malyarov for a formal warning, to which he had responded by calling an open press conference to denounce the authorities. The *Pravda* article (see Note 1), signed by forty members of the Academy of Sciences, accused Sakharov of antipatriotic activities and of jeopardizing détente.
3. See *Pravda*, 6 September 1973, for a Soviet report on the news conference.

82 Telegram from the USSR Embassy in France

Special No. 2232
30 August 1973
From Paris
Top Secret
Copy No. 26[1]

Recently the French media have considerably expanded the publication of materials of an anti-Soviet nature, using the statements of Sakharov, Solzhenitsyn, and others for these purposes.

Our French friends believe that this campaign is being instigated by official circles and reflects certain specific features of French politics at this stage.

Georges Marchais[2] told us that in his opinion, *ruling circles are becoming apprehensive of the further development of détente in international relations.* A segment of the French bourgeoisie is afraid that its interests may be affected in an environment of further détente. *There is a potential for the strengthening of the influence of socialist countries in Europe and in the entire international arena.* In France, there is a potential for the strengthening of the left, primarily of the Communist Party. That's why *this anti-Soviet and anticommunist campaign is an attempt of sorts to put brakes on the détente process, to sow distrust regarding* the policy of the Soviet Union, and to preserve certain elements of tension in the international climate.

Georges Marchais noted that our French friends are taking active steps to counter this campaign, with articles in *L'Humanité* and Comrade Marchais's news conference on 29 August, which were reported by TASS. Our friends intend to continue to act in the same fashion.

Comrade Marchais also expressed a wish that we, for our part, also take appropriate steps to expose this campaign, which is contrary to the interests of détente.

Kizichenko

F. 3, op. 90, d. 259, l. 61–62. Copy.

Notes

1. *F. Kulakov's copy.*
2. General Secretary of the French Communist Party at the time.

83 Telegram from the USSR Embassy in France

Special No. 2256
1 September 1973
From Paris
Top Secret
Copy No. 20[1]

I hereby forward a telegram from *Pravda*'s correspondent V. Sedykh.

I met with comrades Marchais, Fajon, and Plissonier. In our conversation, they confirmed the assessments previously expressed to us by Comrades Lorand, Vieghe, and Poperin and set out in our previous telegram.

Comrade Marchais once again stressed the crucial significance of the Soviet peace program and visits by the Central Committee's Secretary General L.I. Brezhnev to the US, West Germany, and France for the cause of international détente. Marchais said that the French bourgeoisie is afraid of détente, which is conducive to the further strengthening of socialist forces and of the French Communist Party's position in the country. These factors are primarily responsible for the intensification of an anticommunist and anti-Soviet campaign in France. In this regard, Comrade Marchais inquired whether the Soviet Union intended to make appropriate representations to the French government in connection with the current anti-Soviet campaign in the bourgeois media. He especially emphasized the leading role of the French government's propaganda establishments in this campaign (Sakharov's interview with a correspondent of Agence France Presse, etc). Comrade Marchais stressed the need to intensify the ideological struggle against bourgeois propaganda under the current conditions. He noted that some of the French Communist Party's ideas in this regard have been described in his newly published book, *The Democratic Challenge*. In his turn, Comrade Plissonier confirmed the consent of our friends' leadership to an invitation of a delegation of the Socialist Party headed by Mitterand to the Soviet Union. In his opinion, this visit would help to "restrain" the Socialists during yet another anti-Soviet campaign in France and will promote the strengthening of the union of leftist forces. Comrade Plissonier noted that they were aware that Mitterand was trying to use the union of leftist forces to strengthen the position of the Socialist Party. This is natural, provided the Socialist Party grows at the expense of the 'Centrists' and other bourgeois parties, rather than to the detriment of the Communists.

Comrade Fajon, for his part, emphasized the significance of the upcoming *L'Humanité* festival for the French Communist Party as well as the importance of the participation of *Pravda* and other Soviet organizations and newspapers from other socialist countries in this festival. He informed me that the French Communist Party's leadership had entrusted him with preparations for the visit of the Soviet Communist Party's delegation to be headed by Comrade Zimyanin.[2] Comrade Fajon expressed his readiness to render the necessary assistance in order to arrange meetings of the delegation with the leadership of the French Communist Party's federation in the Bouche-du-Rhone Department and visits to communist-run municipalities in Arles, Nimes, and other cities. Comrade Fajon noted that they would be happy to be of service to the Soviet Communist Party's delegation. V. Sedykh.

Chervonenko

F. 3, op. 90, d. 259, l. 63–65. Copy.

Notes

1. *F. Kulakov's copy.*
2. *The Soviet Communist Party's delegation headed by M.V. Zimyanin attended* L'Humanité's *annual festival in France from 7–14 September 1973.*

84 Report of the Committee for State Security of the USSR Council of Ministers[1]

No. 2114–A
4 September 1973
Special File
Top Secret

To the Central Committee:
As previously reported to the Central Committee, on 4–6 August 1973 we conducted searches in Leningrad at the residence of E.D. Voronyanskaya, born 1906, retired, and at the residence of N.F. Pakhtusova, born 1917,

retired. As a result of the searches, we discovered and confiscated materials indicating their close ties with Solzhenitsyn.

Thus Voronyanskaya, who completely shares his views, edited and typed on her typewriter some of his works of an anti-Soviet nature, including *The Gulag Archipelago*. Pakhtusova, at Voronyanskaya's request, stored these books at her residence for a certain period of time. Pursuant to the results of the search, Voronyanskaya was subjected to interrogation. She told us about the nature of her relationship with Solzhenitsyn and about assignments that she had carried out at his request. She also gave a detailed account of the contents of *The Gulag Archipelago*. Upon returning home after the interrogation, Voronyanskaya tried to commit suicide, but her attempt was prevented. Voronyanskaya later explained that her action had been a result of her giving testimony against Solzhenitsyn. Voronyanskaya was hospitalized in order to bring her back to a normal physical condition. But as soon as she was discharged from the hospital on 23 August 1973, she returned to her apartment and committed suicide by hanging herself.

State security agencies and the Leningrad Public Prosecutor's Office took measures to contain any potentially undesirable consequences. On 30 August 1973, Voronyanskaya was buried by her relatives.

In connection with Voronyanskaya's death, Solzhenitsyn's friends in Leningrad have shown serious concern for her papers, especially because state security agencies got the opportunity to obtain a copy of *The Gulag Archipelago*. In their opinion, the discovery of this book is extremely dangerous for Solzhenitsyn's future.[2]

As a result of the measures taken we were able to discover and confiscate Voronyanskaya's papers, including the novel *The Gulag Archipelago*. We will file a special report regarding this book.

Chairman of the Committee for State Security
Andropov

F. 3, op. 80, d. 646, l. 43–44. Original.

Notes

1. The first page bears the resolution: "(To everyone). (informed) Suslov" and the signatures of F. Kulakov, A. Kosygin, K. Mazurov, A. Shelepin, D. Polyansky, A. Gromyko, A. Grechko, N. Podgorny, A. Pelshe, D. Kunaev, V. Shcherbitsky, and A. Kirilenko. The reverse side of the last page has the entry: "Grishin is on vacation. 13 November 1973."

2. The events leading up to the death of Elizaveta D. Voronyanskaya and the precise circumstances of her suicide have been a mystery till now, and this report goes some way toward clarifying the matter. Solzhenitsyn considered that Voronyanskaya had in effect been "murdered" by the KGB, either directly, or through the pressure exerted on her by incessant interrogations (see *The Oak and the Calf*, pp. 345–348). According to Solzhenitsyn, the body had been discovered in suspicious circumstances by an unreliable neighbor, and the family was not allowed to see it before burial. Solzhenitsyn did not then know of the earlier interrogation of Voronyanskaya's friend Pakhtusova (see Document 77), or of Voronyanskaya's erroneous conclusion (see Document 78) that Solzhenitsyn's request that all copies of the book be returned to him meant that he had decided to publish *The Gulag Archipelago* (which he hadn't). Similarly, the KGB reports included in this volume fail to indicate that it was Voronyanskaya who led them directly to the book, by revealing that a complete copy of the typescript was buried in the garden of Leonid Samutin (see Document 77, note 5). It was news of this development that so worried Solzhenitsyn's other Leningrad friends and caused them to send a warning to him in Moscow.

85 Letter from A. Solzhenitsyn to L. Brezhnev[1]

5 September 1973

Dear Leonid Ilyich,
Despite the plural title at the top [of the enclosed document], I have changed my mind about sending it to your colleagues and am forwarding this *single* copy to you alone through the Central Committee reception window. (There are two copies of the accompanying letter—I am sending one of them by regular mail.)

I think that any decisions will depend largely on you, and that you yourself will determine which of your colleagues you will wish to consult.

You will notice that I wrote my letter not with journalistic flourishes nor to reproach you, but rather with a strong desire to persuade you.

I am still hopeful that as a simple Russian man with a lot of common sense, you are quite capable of accepting my arguments, and if you do, it will be in your power to translate them into life.

If you do take this charitable action and embark on this path to save Russia, she will remember you often in the future with gratitude.

A. Solzhenitsyn

If you wish to discuss this letter with me in person, I am prepared.

Enclosure

[The enclosure consists of the text of Solzhenitsyn's *Letter to the Soviet Leaders*, published in English translation by Farrar, Straus, and Giroux in 1974. Owing to its length and easy availability it is not reproduced here.]

Note

1. *Chernenko's note attached to the letter reads: "Dear Leonid Ilyich: As per your request, I am forwarding Solzhenitsyn's letter addressed to you. Comrade Suslov first told me to inform all the members of the Politburo about this letter, but then he warned me that only Comrades Kosygin, Podgorny, and Andropov should see it. All of them have reviewed the letter in turn. Right now the original is with Comrade Podgorny. Best wishes. K. Chernenko. 28 September 1973." Also attached is a sheet with the signatures of M. Suslov, A. Kosygin, N. Podgorny, A. Kirilenko, Y. Andropov, and a resolution which reads: "To Comrade K.U. Chernenko. We have held several discussions about Solzhenitsyn at Politburo meetings. I think it essential that all the comrades should read his letter. 29 December 1973. L. Brezhnev."*

   The first page bears Brezhnev's instruction: "Show to Politburo members (in turn) 4 October 1973," and bears the signatures of A. Shelepin, D. Polyansky, A. Pelshe, A. Grechko, V. Grishin, A. Gromyko, P. Demichev, B. Ponomarev, M. Solomentsev, K. Katushev, V. Dolgikh, I. Kapitonov, K. Mazurov, F. Kulakov, D. Ustinov, G. Romanov, S. Rashidov, and V. Shcherbitsky.

86 Memorandum of the USSR Ministry of Foreign Affairs and the Central Committee's International Department[1]

No. 2175/GS
7 September 1973
Classified

To the Central Committee:
Recently the French bourgeois media have been playing an active role in the anti-Soviet campaign being pursued in the West. In addition to "independent" bourgeois newspapers and magazines participating in the campaign (in all probability, not without the knowledge of official circles), there are such French mass propaganda establishments as the Agence France Presse, and radio and television stations. Agence France Presse, for instance, has interviewed Sakharov; and *Le Monde*, along with the Associated Press (a US news agency), interviewed Solzhenitsyn.

In connection with the above, the Central Committee's International Department and the USSR Ministry of Foreign Affairs believe that it would be advisable to make appropriate representations to the French government, advising it that the anti-Soviet campaign being pursued in France runs counter to the French official line of developing friendly relations with the Soviet Union.

Our French friends (telegrams from Paris No. 2232 and No. 2256) also support the idea of such representations. It would be advisable to inform the leadership of the French Communist Party of their contents.

A draft resolution is enclosed.

Please review.

V. Kuznetsov
V. Zaglyadin

F. 3, *op.* 69, *d.* 789, *l.* 130. Original.

Note

1. Sent to Politburo members for a vote on 8 September 1973 under No. 103–105.

250

87 Report of the Committee for State Security of the USSR Council of Ministers[1]

No. 2176/Ch
8 September 1973
Special File
Top Secret

To the Central Committee:
On 6 September 1973, Solzhenitsyn invited Academician Sakharov and his spouse to his wife's Moscow apartment. Sakharov accepted the invitation. During the meeting that took place, he looked at some documents prepared by Solzhenitsyn. He [Solzhenitsyn] also approved Sakharov's antisocial activities, but advised him to suspend them on a temporary basis, and "to lie low for the time being." It is typical that lately Solzhenitsyn has been regularly trying to attract the attention of those who are known for their antisocial statements and actions.

As reported earlier, he encouraged the anti-Soviet activities of Superfin, currently under detention, and provided him with material assistance. He also influenced the antisocial statements of Korzhavin. We also know that he has maintained close relations with Ginzburg,[2] who served his sentence but has not changed his anti-Soviet attitudes.

Solzhenitsyn meticulously conceals his meetings with such persons and with certain foreign correspondents (as opposed to those to whom he gives interviews), and holds such meetings in secrecy.

The said facts are being taken into consideration by us in carrying out appropriate measures to constrain antisocial manifestations.

Deputy Chairman of the Committee for State Security of the USSR Council of Ministers
Chebrikov

F. 3, op. 80, d. 646, l. 45. Original.

Notes

1. *The document bears the signatures of M. Suslov, A. Kosygin, N. Podgorny, and A. Kirilenko.*

2. Alexander Ginzburg (together with Yuri Galanskov) had been arrested and tried in 1968 for compiling *A White Book on the Sinyavsky-Daniel Trial* and publishing a samizdat journal. Galanskov had been sentenced to seven years in the labor camps and had died there (see Document 79, Note 2). Ginzburg had served five years and had only recently been released.

88 Report of the Committee for State Security of the USSR Council of Ministers[1]

No. 2180/Ch
10 September 1973
Special File
Top Secret

To the Central Committee:
In his latest interviews with the Western media, Solzhenitsyn has threatened that if he were arrested or murdered, the world would learn of his most significant works of exposure, which constitute the main meaning of his life.

He evidently includes among these works *The Gulag Archipelago*, written in 1964–67 and kept a closely guarded secret.

This August, the Leningrad KGB carried out a number of operations that resulted in the acquisition of one copy of this composition, bearing the author's handwritten corrections.

The Gulag Archipelago has 1,104 typewritten pages and consists of seven parts, each containing from five to twenty-two chapters. The book is dedicated to "all those who did not survive to tell their stories. . . ." The author devotes his narrative to those years of Soviet rule when the "Gulag System," as the author calls it, was established in our country, which then systematically expanded, was filled with the victims of mass repressions, and finally developed into an entire "archipelago," with its own customs, laws, rights, and psychology.

The author attempts to recreate the history of the "archipelago," ie, of the corrective labor camps, and to describe the wanton violence and lawlessness that caused the deaths of a great number of innocent persons.

A summary of this composition of Solzhenitsyn's is enclosed. At the same time, we think it advisable to emphasize certain of the author's most important (in our opinion) contentions and conclusions.

Solzhenitsyn maintains that "the camps are not just a 'dark side' of our post-revolutionary existence," but a manifestation of the economic necessity of using forced labor, allegedly based on theories first advanced by Marx and Engels. He writes that "the main reason for the existence of serfdom and the Archipelago was the same—both were social instruments for the forced and unmerciful use of the unpaid labor of millions of slaves." The only difference was that in our time such labor was subordinated to the construction of socialism, and the camp system was created by the Communist Party with the direct involvement of Lenin.

That is why, continues Solzhenitsyn, all that has been done to restore the rule of law is just propaganda. Essentially, nothing has changed, since the problem is a product of the social system. In one of his chapters he slanderously asserts that "we still live in a nation without laws, without rights, and without a system of justice."

He sees only one solution—to publish dozens of "white papers" exposing the lawlessness that has allegedly reigned supreme in the nation since 1918 (after the exit of the left socialist revolutionaries from the Soviet government) and to hold a trial not so much of specific abusers of the law as of the crimes committed by the state, similar to the condemnation of the crimes of the fascist state in Germany.

It is characteristic that in this regard, Solzhenitsyn places his hopes on those who were or are imprisoned in corrective labor camps. In general, the author continually stresses in his composition the unfounded idea that as a result of the imprisonment in the "Gulag System" of a great number of individuals, our society supposedly contains a distinctive social category ("a nation") of prisoners ("zeks") with its own psychological traits, ideology, and even language. And they, too, must have their say. Therefore this work, as well as certain other works by Solzhenitsyn, gives us reason to conclude that he is not restricting himself to descriptions of the past, but aims to unite all former prisoners under the banner of the "struggle for justice." At the same time he does not conceal his view that justice can only be restored by changing the existing state and social system in our country.

Deputy Chairman of the Committee for State Security of the USSR Council of Ministers
Chebrikov

Enclosure
Classified

[The enclosure, consisting of a twenty-six–page KGB summary of Solz-henitsyn's *The Gulag Archipelago*, has been omitted from the American edition. It is signed as follows: "Faithful and true copy: Department Head of the Committee for State Security of the USSR Council of Ministers (Bobkov), 9 September 1973.]

F. 3, *op.* 80, *d.* 646, *l.* 47–81. Original.

Note

1. *The cover page bears the signatures of M. Suslov, A. Kosygin, N. Podgorny, and A. Kir-ilenko. A copy of the summary of* The Gulag Archipelago *was sent to the Central Com-mittee for a second time by Andropov on 3 January 1974 with forwarding letter No. 15–A and distributed to Politburo members and candidate members, and Central Committee Secretaries, on 3 January 1974 under No. P11.*

89 Politburo Resolution

"Regarding a Representation to the Government of France in Connection with the Anti-Soviet Campaign in the French Media"

No. P103/138
13 September 1973
Top Secret

1. The USSR Ministry of Foreign Affairs is hereby instructed to make a verbal representation to the Embassy of France in the USSR (enclosed).

2. The International Department of the Central Committee is hereby instructed to inform the leadership of the French Communist Party of this representation.

Central Committee Secretary

Enclosure
Re: Section 138 of Transcript No. 103
Classified

Verbal Representation to the Embassy of France in the USSR

The Soviet government would like to draw the attention of the French government to the fact that French media establishments have been actively participating of late in a campaign being waged against the Soviet Union by Western reactionaries. Articles and reports published in this regard flagrantly distort the intentions and actions of the Soviet Union on the international scene, as well as the domestic policy of the Soviet state. A number of French newspapers and magazines as well as radio and television stations have provided an outlet to so-called "Soviet dissidents." Their insidious inventions are used to stir up a fuss with obvious goals—to induce an unfriendly attitude toward the Soviet Union among the French public.

We are obliged to state that such a propaganda agency as Agence France Presse, the leading supplier of information to French newspapers, is playing an unseemly role in this campaign. For instance, the Moscow bureau of Agence France Presse at its own initiative recorded and published an interview with A. Sakharov that contains intolerable calls for interference in the Soviet Union's internal affairs and for an end to détente. An interview with Solzhenitsyn, distributed in particular by *Le Monde*, is similar in spirit. The Soviet public scornfully rejects the attempts of these individuals to sow distrust of the peaceful policies of the Soviet state, to slow down the process of détente, and to create obstacles to the strengthening of peace in Europe and the entire world. Soviet citizens are especially amazed that this hostile campaign is taking place in a country with which the Soviet Union has traditionally maintained friendly relations.

Nobody should have any doubt that the development of large-scale contacts and cooperation can be based only upon respect for the sovereignty of states and noninterference in their internal affairs.

In connection with the actions of the aforesaid French media establishments, we have the following questions: what are they striving for and whose viewpoint do they reflect in this case? For it is obvious that this anti-Soviet campaign is in patent conflict with the nature of Soviet-French relations and with the statements of the French government in this regard.

As to the Soviet Union, it firmly adheres to the spirit and the letter of Soviet-French agreements to develop a sense of friendship and mutual respect between the peoples of our two countries.

The Soviet government expects the French government to review the foregoing with appropriate care and to draw the necessary conclusions.

F. 3, *op.* 80, *d.* 646, *l.* 82–84. Excerpt from transcript.

90 From the Transcript of a Politburo Session

17 September 1973
Top Secret

Chairman: Comrade L. I. Brezhnev
Present: Comrades A.A. Grechko, A.N. Kosygin, F.D. Kulakov, K.T. Mazurov, D.S. Polyansky, M.A. Suslov, A.N. Shelepin, M.S. Solomentsev, V.I. Dolgikh, and I.V. Kapitonov

On the Matter of Sakharov and Solzhenitsyn

Brezhnev: Evidently we have been tolerating their anti-Soviet activities for far too long, and that is wrong. We should have stopped them right away. This, I think, is just our mistake, and they in turn are abusing our patience and probably consider it a sign of weakness. How else should we qualify the latest appeal of Sakharov to the US Senate?[1] This is not just an anti-State and anti-Soviet deed, but a Trotskyite deed. I think such actions would be prosecuted in any country. Some time ago we decided that Comrade Kosygin should speak with him. Maybe we should follow up on this decision.

Kosygin: I have no objection. We just have to think how to talk with him.

Brezhnev: He has to be told outright that he is following an anti-Soviet, anti-State line, and that if he doesn't discontinue such actions, we will be forced to take action in accordance with Soviet laws. Unlike him, we cannot violate our Soviet law. That's what he should be told.

Shelepin: Perhaps it's not worth involving the Politburo and, in particular, Comrade Kosygin in this dirty affair right now. As we know, he was seen by Malyarov, but that had no positive result. At this point, we should ask [Public Prosecutor] Rudenko to talk with him along the lines suggested by Leonid Ilyich [Brezhnev], and then decide what to do with them. In general, though, we have to take action.

Brezhnev: I have received Solzhenitsyn's letter to the Central Committee addressed to me. He writes in a slightly different manner compared to his previous letters but it's still nonsense. Let me ask Suslov to look into this matter and acquaint all Politburo members with the letter.

Suslov: I have not had time to look into this, but as soon as I do I will certainly pass this letter on to the others.

A decision was made: to set up a commission comprised of Suslov, Kosygin, Shelepin, Keldysh, Kuznetsov, Chebrikov, and Rudenko to prepare and submit to the Central Committee relevant proposals regarding this matter, taking into consideration the exchange of opinion at this Politburo session. The commission was authorized to take such prompt steps as might be required pursuant to the proposals offered at this Politburo session, to publicize this matter in the media, to conduct interviews, etc.

Brezhnev: Perhaps this commission should consider how to isolate this Sakharov. Perhaps we should exile him to the Siberian Division of the USSR Academy of Sciences.

Voices: We should send him to Narym. In Siberia he would continue to make trouble.

Brezhnev: To sum up, the commission should carefully study all these issues and make specific proposals.

From transcripts of Politburo sessions in 1973. Original.

Note

1. In early September 1973 the US Congress was debating the Jackson amendment to a bill proposed by President Nixon to grant the USSR "most favored nation" status. The amendment called for making such a status dependent on the Soviet Union introducing freer emigration policies for Soviet Jews. On September 14

Sakharov sent an open letter to Congress appealing to it to support the amendment. The letter was printed in full in capital letters in *The Washington Post* and was credited with influencing Congress to pass the amendment in the teeth of Nixon's (and Soviet) opposition.

91 Politburo Resolution
"Regarding Sakharov and Solzhenitsyn"

No. P104/VIII
17 September 1973
Top Secret

A commission comprised of Kosygin, Suslov, Shelepin, Keldysh, Kuznetsov, Chebrikov, and Rudenko shall prepare and submit to the Central Committee relevant proposals regarding this matter, taking into consideration the exchange of opinion at the Politburo session.

The commission is authorized to take such prompt steps as may be required pursuant to the proposals offered at this Politburo session (to publicize this matter in the media, to conduct interviews, etc).

Central Committee Secretary

F. 3, *op.* 80, *d.* 646, *l.* 92. Excerpt from transcript.

92 Memorandum of the Committee for State Security of the USSR Council of Ministers[1]

No. 2239–A
17 September 1973
Top Secret
Special File

To the Central Committee:
An analysis of materials in the possession of the Committee for State Security makes it possible to draw the conclusion that the enemies of détente have stepped up their struggle against Soviet foreign policy initiatives and are trying to change the course of international events in order to return to the "Cold War." In order to win over public opinion, they are attempting to use deception to discredit the Soviet social system and to sow distrust of it among those who do not have complete and objective information.

This struggle involves government officials and public organizations, as well as the media belonging to major monopolies and supervised by governments. Special [security] agencies are undertaking various inflammatory actions to provoke an uproar around the so-called issue of "civil rights in the USSR."

As these special agencies step up their activities and enemy propaganda gains in intensity, their main goal becomes more obvious—to employ all means of political pressure to bring about certain ruptures in the fabric of Soviet society, or, if that proves impossible, at least to create doubt with regard to further normalization of the relations between Western states and our country.

The hysteria surrounding the names of Sakharov and Solzhenitsyn that has been recently initiated in the West is directly subordinated to these purposes and is the result of a program which was prepared and coordinated well in advance.

Solzhenitsyn, who was already known in the West as a person of anti-Soviet tendencies, is being directly engaged by Western centers of propaganda, primarily on the basis of ideology, but also for large monetary rewards. The former writer is now trying to speak out as a political activist and an ideologist of sorts. In his latest documents he does not conceal his

259

desire to persuade mankind "of the unlawful nature of socialism" and of its ideology and practice.[2] In addition, it has become evident that Solzhenitsyn maintains clandestine relations with those who were previously imprisoned on political grounds. In his unpublished work, *The Gulag Archipelago*, Solzhenitsyn directly argues that such persons are ideologically and otherwise close to one another and hints at the possibility of uniting them.

Sakharov, who unlike Solzhenitsyn is more restrained in his attempts to prove "the unacceptable nature of the Soviet system," is nevertheless obviously descending to anti-Sovietism.

In essence both of them, while not formally united, act in a rather coordinated manner, playing up to the Western reactionary circles and, in a number of instances, carrying out their direct assignments.

It is natural that the imperialists, having found in Solzhenitsyn and Sakharov two persons who, due to existing circumstances, can continue to bark at the Soviet government with impunity, are doing their utmost to prolong this possibility for as long as possible. In turn, both Solzhenitsyn and Sakharov, encouraged by the response in the West, are becoming ever more insolent.

Here, it is important to note that both are not only firmly convinced of their impunity, but also strive to convince those closest to them of this fact. In his interview with a foreign correspondent, Solzhenitsyn stated directly: "You can be sure that not one hair will fall from my head."

The anti-Soviet activities of Solzhenitsyn and Sakharov that so far have gone unpunished are attracting more and more attention from the Soviet people. The absolute majority of them are indignant, but among the intelligentsia and youth one can occasionally hear such talk as: "Act bravely and openly, attract the attention of Western correspondents, rely on the support of the bourgeois media, and nobody will dare touch you." The development of such a trend is fraught with substantial negative consequences and forces us to contemplate more radical measures to put an end to the hostile pronouncements of Solzhenitsyn and Sakharov.

Today we have no real basis to believe that Solzhenitsyn and Sakharov will voluntarily abandon their hostile activities. Conversations with Solzhenitsyn at the Central Committee and the Soviet Writers' Union, and attempts to influence him with the help of public opinion and through the media, have borne no fruit. Conversations with Sakharov at the Presidium of the USSR Academy of Sciences and at the executive offices of institutes where he used to work have been equally fruitless. Sakharov's summons to the Public Prosecutor's Office to warn him against further anti-Soviet steps was used by him and those around him as a pretext to stage new hostile press conferences, during which he directly called upon the United States and other Western nations to abstain from the normalization of relations with the USSR unless they "squeeze concessions out of the Soviet leadership" for "the liberalization of the regime."

We have evidence that Sakharov and Solzhenitsyn intend to continue their meetings with representatives of the Western reactionary media in order to slander our country and to recruit accomplices among Soviet citizens.

Under these conditions, we deem it advisable to take a different approach with regard to the behavior of Solzhenitsyn and Sakharov.

1. Since we have documentary evidence showing that Solzhenitsyn's recent actions are not just the delusions of a writer, but the deliberate legal and illegal activities of a person who is deeply hostile to the Soviet system, it would be advisable, at a suitable time, to initiate criminal proceedings against him with the purpose of putting him on trial.

2. Since such a step would constitute an extreme measure, we think it possible to consider an intermediate solution, namely, to instruct the USSR Foreign Ministry, through its ambassadors in Paris, Rome, London, and Stockholm, to propose to the governments of those countries that they grant Solzhenitsyn the right of asylum, otherwise, under Soviet laws, he will have to be tried. This idea of ours could be legalized either directly or through special channels. The governments of those countries would be faced with a dilemma—either to grant asylum; to Solzhenitsyn or otherwise to give *de facto* consent to his trial. It is possible that given such circumstances, official circles in Western states would be less eager to provide direct encouragement to their propaganda establishments to incite passions regarding Solzhenitsyn and Sakharov.

3. It would be extremely important to have a meeting between Sakharov and one of the Soviet government's leaders.[3] We do not have much hope that Sakharov will change his behavior as a result of such a conversation (he is sick and feverish and overwhelmed by those around him). Yet such a conversation would pull the rug out from under those who are currently trying to reproach us that no member of the leadership has talked to such a "revered" person (a triple Hero [of Socialist Labor], an academician) and tried to bring him to reason. Such talk may be heard among good people abroad and even in our country. We have to keep in mind that Sakharov, while abusing his impunity, is very much afraid that he would be "stripped of his medals" or expelled from the Academy. As a preventive measure, he repeatedly confides these fears to Western reporters, who in their turn emphasize in the media that the Soviet leadership would never take such a step and does not have the right to do so. In light of the foregoing, the conversation might be used to tell Sakharov in definite terms that unless he discontinues his anti-Soviet pronouncements, he might lose the title of Academician and of a Hero of Socialist Labor (which would also entail the loss of 800 rubles a month, which he receives without having to do anything). As an alternative, Sakharov should be offered employment in Novosibirsk, Obninsk, or some other

closed locality in order to help him break away from a hostile environment, and above all from Western correspondents.

Such steps would naturally provoke a fuss in the West, perhaps a new ripple of anti-Sovietism and a certain amount of displeasure within some fraternal parties and progressive circles. There would also be talk among a certain (small) segment of the Soviet public. Yet none of this would have a lasting effect and would be of a purely temporary character.

If, on the other hand, we do not resolve the cases of Solzhenitsyn and Sakharov, they will be with us for a long time. Moreover, all of the aforesaid negative tendencies will manifest themselves one way or another, and the element of impunity would certainly work against us.

4. In order to limit the damage from our actions with regard to Solzhenitsyn and Sakharov, it might be advisable to prepare information concerning this issue for the leaderships of socialist countries and a number of fraternal parties.

5. Since the anti-Soviet campaign involves attacks against many features of the social and political structure, and the way of life of Soviet society, we consider it advisable for our propaganda to focus particular attention on this, and to provide additional theoretical materials explaining the nature of our state's policy and the multifaceted experience of the construction of a communist society. We have to reveal the essence of the democratic changes in our country, and, at the same time, use direct and indirect methods to discredit the views of Solzhenitsyn and Sakharov as the views of those who are alien and hostile to the achievements of socialism. We also deem it necessary to expand the use of various international forums and conferences to stage an active attack and to unmask the reactionary Western circles that are obstructing the normalization of the international situation.

Such materials should be more persistently distributed not just to the Soviet press, but also abroad, using the capabilities of TASS, Novosti Press Agency, and the State Television and Radio Committee. Perhaps we should prepare a single plan of action regarding this matter, even giving specific individual assignments to employees of public organizations and government agencies.

Since Sakharov and especially Solzhenitsyn in their latest documents try to cover up their anti-Soviet views and to attract the sympathies of various groups of the population by demagogical speculation on such issues as "the role of the Russian people in the Soviet state," "the status of women under socialism," the legality of "military service" in our country, the preservation of historical monuments, and in this regard the allegedly mistaken recon- struction of Moscow, etc, it would be advisable to pay particular attention to these issues in the media.

6. The Committee for State Security should use its capabilities to acquire and make available for propaganda and counterpropaganda purposes documentary evidence that exposes the ties between reactionary forces obstructing détente and the enemy's security agencies, the instigation by various imperialist intelligence services of anti-Soviet campaigns, and connections between such pariahs of our society as Solzhenitsyn, Sakharov, et al, and these services and foreign anti-Soviet centers.

Please review.

Chairman of the Committee for State Security
Andropov

F. 3, *op.* 80, *d.* 646, *l.* 85–91. Original.

Notes

1. *The first page bears the resolution: "For information purposes. L. Brezhnev" and has the signatures of M. Suslov, N. Podgorny, A. Kosygin, F. Kulakov, A. Gromyko, A. Grechko, D. Polyansky, K. Mazurov, and A. Shelepin; the last page bears the notation: "This issue was reviewed at the Politburo session of 7 January 1974. See No. P120/1 transcript." The reverse side of the document bears the notation: "Grishin, Kirilenko, and Pelshe are on vacation. 11 October 1973."*

2. A reference to an essay by Solzhenitsyn entitled "Peace and Violence," in which he proposed Sakharov for the Nobel Peace Prize (the nomination came too late for 1973, but was taken up in 1974).

3. *The planned meeting of M.A. Suslov with A.D. Sakharov never took place.*

93 Memorandum of the Committee for State Security of the USSR Council of Ministers[1]

No. 2487–A
19 October 1973
Classified

To the Central Committee:
The Committee for State Security reports that Sakharov and Solzhenitsyn, in spite of warnings, continue to engage in provocative behavior intending to discredit the foreign policy of the Soviet state. They are also broadening their contacts with foreigners and providing them with slanderous statements.

Sakharov has lately spoken out as an ardent advocate of Israel's aggressive policy, publicly accusing the Soviet Union and other socialist states of "one-sided support for Arab states," and demanding wide publicity for his appeals in support of Israel.

Bourgeois propaganda establishments have widely commented on Sakharov's pro-Israeli pronouncements, inciting US Zionists to show support for him and unambiguously letting it be known to Sakharov that, for their part, they are ready to assist him in his "mission" in the Soviet Union. Sakharov's associate, Glazov,[2] who left earlier for the United States, has told him over the phone that

> American Jews are, in essence, the only significant group here that understands the situation in the Soviet Union and is pre-pared to respond. These people are interested not just in Jew-ish affairs, as is so often the case, but in a broader context. You know that their feelings about you in particular are very well defined.

Last September Sakharov, in his conversation with Weizsäcker, the deputy chairman of the Christian Democrat faction in the West German Bundestag, asked him to provide assistance for the emigration of Soviet citizens of German origin to West Germany. When asked by Weizsäcker's assistant about the significance of the Great October Socialist Revolution for our country, Sakharov said: "I think history would have developed in a more favorable fashion without the October Revolution."

In that conversation Sakharov indicated his positive reaction to a resolution of the US Congress dealing with the issue of the emigration of Jews from the Soviet Union. "This is a very good resolution. It pertains not just to Israel, but to all issues of emigration. It must also pertain to Germans." He also expressed a desire that the Bundestag approve a similar decision.

Sakharov continues to spread slanderous statements regarding the use of psychiatric hospitals in our country to subdue "dissidents," and regularly sends relevant information to the West. In one of his telephone conversations Lower, a British psychiatrist, informed Sakharov of a forthcoming conference of British psychiatrists and read out to him the salient points that Sakharov had to cover in yet another appeal to the world public opinion regarding this issue.

To fulfill this assignment, Sakharov and other members of the so-called "Committee for Human Rights"[2] (Shafarevich and Podyapolsky) prepared and sent to the West an appeal regarding the alleged continuing use of psychiatric hospitals in our country for political purposes.

It is noteworthy that more and more often Sakharov indulges in hostile outbursts even in meetings with Soviet citizens. Thus in a conversation with [Viktor] Nekrasov, a Kiev writer, Sakharov, touching upon his appeal to Chile's military junta, said the following:

> I did not defend it in that letter. I defend it at this table. The junta is like Kornilov's rebellion,[3] but a successful one. If Kornilov had won, he would have shot five hundred Bolsheviks. . . . Or ten thousand, and would have saved the forty million people annihilated by the Bolsheviks. Unfortunately, Kornilov's rebellion failed.

Solzhenitsyn also makes use of foreigners' services for the transmission of slanderous information to the West, provocatively asserting that "being known abroad provides him with reliable protection against the Soviet judicial system."

Last September Solzhenitsyn, together with Barabanov (an employee of *Iskusstvo* publishing house who regularly sends slanderous materials to the West) prepared a provocative statement referring to a search in Barabanov's residence.[4] Solzhenitsyn gave this statement to Crepaud, an Associated Press correspondent, and insistently asked him to publish the statement abroad.

Explaining his request to Crepaud, Solzhenitsyn said that he considers it a crime when the authorities refuse to publish works which, in his opinion, are not in conflict with the country's laws.

They are going to put a person (ie, Barabanov) in jail. I think this is an issue meriting media attention, especially in the current situation when the issue of a European conference has come to the forefront, and also when the issue of trade benefits is being discussed in the United States.

Solzhenitsyn and his wife recently gave the foreign reporters Fredrikson and Stenholm (Sweden), and LaContre and Vishnevsky (France), biased information regarding certain aspects of political life in the USSR, in particular regarding the state of the so-called "democratic movement" since the trial of Yakir and Krasin.

Since Sakharov and Solzhenitsyn continue their provocations and have even stepped up the peddling of their services to reactionary imperialist, and particularly Zionist, circles, we would like to propose a review of the *recommendations prepared by the Commission headed by Comrade A.N. Kosygin, taking into account the considerations set forth in the Committee for State Security's memorandum* No. 2239-A, dated 17 September of this year.

Chairman of the Committee for State Security
Andropov

F. 3, *op.* 80, *d.* 646, *l.* 94–97. Original.

Notes

1. *Page 1 bears the resolution: "Circulate," and the signatures of M. Suslov, N. Podgorny, A. Grechko, A. Kosygin, K. Mazurov, F. Kulakov, D. Polyansky, A. Gromyko, A. Shelepin, A. Pelshe, D. Kunaev, V. Shcherbitsky, and A. Kirilenko; the last page contains the notation: "This question was reviewed at the Politburo session of 7 January 1974. See No. P120/1 transcript." The reverse side of the document contains the notations: "The KGB (Comrade Karpeshchenko) was informed that A.N. Kosygin's Commission had not yet submitted recommendations to the Central Committee. V. Galkin. 23 October 1973," and "Grishin is sick. 31 October 1973."*
2. *The Committee for Human Rights was established in 1970 by Valery Chalidze and included Sakharov, Igor Shafarevich, and others. The Committee was admitted to the International League for Human Rights (in the US) and the International Committee for the Defense of Human Rights (in France).*
3. General L.G. Kornilov led a military rebellion in September 1917 that was directed against the recently established Petrograd Soviet, the original seat of revolutionary unrest. But he also seems to have intended to overthrow Kerensky's Provisional

Government and establish a military dictatorship with himself at the head of it. Kerensky sided with the Petrograd Soviet, and the rebellion was defeated.

4. Evgeny Barabanov is an art historian who became friendly with Solzhenitsyn in the early seventies and collaborated with him in a collection of articles about Russia's future, *From Under the Rubble* (Little Brown, 1975).

94 Report of the Committee for State Security of the USSR Council of Ministers[1]

No. 2654–A
2 November 1973
Special File
Classified

To the Central Committee:
The Committee for State Security would like to inform you that Solzhenitsyn continues to maintain his hostile positions and is taking steps to unite antisocial elements and to provoke anti-Soviet statements by foreign public opinion.

At his meetings with Barabanov (as previously reported under No. 2484-A of 19 October 1973), Solzhenitsyn insistently recommends that any negative information regarding the internal situation in the USSR be immediately sent to the West. In his opinion, this would be a "guarantee of security" for Barabanov and his associates. Commenting upon Barabanov's provocative statement to the bourgeois media regarding the search of his residence, Solzhenitsyn said:

> You have done what any one of our fools and our dolts must know how to do. Just yesterday nobody knew your name, but today the entire world knows it. You are safe now. . . . You are now beginning to play the role that is needed, because, before

you, twenty million lives were lost. . . . You have achieved an absolute victory in your fight. Nobody will touch you now.

On 27 October 1973, Solzhenitsyn met V.V. Ivanov, an author known for his antisocial views.[2] He told Ivanov: "I consider it my duty to speak out for Sakharov once again, but in such a way that this statement would be not just in defense of Sakharov, but in defense of all of us. . . . I have to support him in a way which would not be interpreted as support for Israel." Solzhenitsyn and Ivanov discussed facts that could be used in his statement. After that he prepared the text, got Sakharov's consent, and sent the statement to the West.

Chairman of the Committee for State Security
Andropov

F. 3, *op.* 80, *d.* 646, *l.* 98. Original.

Notes

1. *The document bears the signatures of M. Suslov, A. Kosygin, and N. Podgorny.*
2. Vyacheslav Ivanov is a distinguished philologist, structural linguist, and specialist in poetics.

95 Memorandum of the Committee for State Security of the USSR Council of Ministers[1]

No. 3079–A
12 December 1973
Top Secret
Special File

To the Central Committee:
The Committee for State Security has evidence that as far as Solzhenitsyn is concerned, we are dealing with a political enemy of the Soviet state and social system. Solzhenitsyn's abomination of the Soviet government and his attempts to wage a struggle against it can be traced throughout his entire conscious life at any given moment, varying only in terms of his methods, degree of intensity, and the opportunity to disseminate his alien views of socialism.

Solzhenitsyn comes from a family of prominent landowners and cattle dealers. His grandfather, S.E. Solzhenitsyn, had more than two thousand hectares of land and nearly twenty thousand head of sheep. Following the Great October Socialist Revolution, the grandfather disappeared, and his fate is unknown; the father, an officer in the tsar's army, committed suicide.

Solzhenitsyn's mother, T.Z. Shcherbak, also hails from the family of a landlord who had a large estate in the area of the present-day Kubanskaya station.

Even as a student, Solzhenitsyn began to write compositions of an anti-Soviet nature and passed them around the small circle of his friends. During World War II, deprived of a proper environment in the army, he expounded his views in letters and diaries, and prepared a program to restructure socialist society, after which he attempted to organize an anti-Soviet group, for which he was sentenced in 1945 to eight years of imprisonment.

Solzhenitsyn's political credo is to deny that socialist revolution is a historically inevitable stage of social development and to affirm the advantages of the capitalist economy and of the bourgeois social system. This credo is reflected, for instance, in his latest book, *August 1914*, where Solzhenitsyn interprets the prerevolutionary situation in Russia and the significance of the October Revolution from hostile positions and writes the following:

> A reasonable person cannot support revolution because revolution involves a lengthy and mindless destruction. Any revolution

leads not to the renovation of a nation, but rather impoverishes it for a long period of time. The more bloody, the more protracted, and the more costly it gets, the closer it comes to the title of a Great Revolution.

Solzhenitsyn expresses such views among his associates. For instance he has said:

> The Soviet government ceased to exist on 6 July 1918. . . . The power of the Soviets was finished. . . . It was transformed into the dictatorship of a party. . . . Our rulers routinely falsified the results of elections in an absolutely brazen fashion. Everything was falsified, and more and more Bolsheviks were getting in. The truth lay with the people, not the Bolsheviks.
>
> I have no very great opinion of Lenin during the period of the revolution. . . . He was nothing but a serpent, a man totally without principles. He would literally tell you he was on your side, but when you went to the door, he would shoot you in the back. An absolute lack of principles.

Solzhenitsyn asserts that the construction of socialism in the USSR meant the unbridled exploitation of the people. Camps and convict labor without any legal protection were not accidental phenomena, but represented a deliberate system of exploitation of labor resources by the state. Such ideas are set forth in *The First Circle*, where Solzhenitsyn, for instance, asserts the following: "Convict labor was behind the creation of the national wealth, the conquest of scientific heights, the construction of power plants and new cities, the digging of canals."

Speaking about the Soviet government, Solzhenitsyn, in a conversation with his contacts, said the following:

> This is a government without prospects. They have no conveyor belts connecting them with ideology, or the masses, or the economy, or the world communist movement, or anything else. The levers of all the conveyor belts have broken down and don't function. They can decide all they want sitting at their desks. Yet it's clear at once that it's not working. They are paralyzed.

In his poem *Volunteers' Highway* he already writes:

> A Moscow-Georgian princedom, right by the capital's walls. Where medals and position decide, among the appointed few,

where they drink themselves to oblivion and dancers are on call. . . . Here's the Belorussky Station, and there's the Hunter's Row. Towering over the narrow street, the Commissariat's lights are aglow. Heap gunfire on it tomorrow, contort its concrete and steel, were it not for this fine theater, and the pity for its horses I feel.

To promote his anti-Soviet views, Solzhenitsyn chose the tactic of distributing his so-called "open letters" both within the country and abroad, as well as the texts of his interviews with foreign correspondents, which are actively exploited by Western propaganda in its ideological struggle against the USSR and other socialist countries.

In one such statement, an open letter to the Secretariat of the Russian Federation Writers' Union, he wrote:

> The blind leading the blind! You do not even notice that you are plodding in a direction exactly opposite to the one announced. In this time of crisis you cannot offer anything positive or kindhearted to our gravely ill society, but keep peddling your hatred and vigilance, your 'hold and never let go' position!
>
> What would you do without 'enemies'? You can no longer live without them, and hatred as strong as racism has become your environment where nothing can be nurtured. . . .
>
> What if the Antarctic ice melts tomorrow and all of mankind starts sinking? Under whose nose would you be poking with your 'class struggle'?

Lately, Solzhenitsyn has been attempting to act as an organizer and ideologist of certain persons hostile to the state and social system in the USSR. For instance, in one of their conversations, trying to convince Sakharov of the necessity of intensifying his antisocial activities, Solzhenitsyn said the following: "I have experience gained in encounters with the authorities stretching back to 1945, when they grabbed me, which tells me never to beg, but to stand your ground firm as a rock, and you will get what you want. . . ." Further, when trying to incite Sakharov to produce one of his routine travesties, Solzhenitsyn continued:

> That brief study you produced in a week and then published, in which you said that the absence of unemployment in the Soviet Union is an absolute lie, was excellent. We have unemployment for two reasons. Mass unemployment can be demonstrated economically. . . . We also have unemployment as a means of

political pressure. . . . Bang them for real, go over to the attack. Attack, but don't beg. . . . If you keep on banging them, these bastards will retreat! You can achieve something only if you talk ever more brazenly, apply more pressure. . . . Believe me. I've been battling them since 1945, and now it is 1973—that's 28 years—and each time I win and hold out only by being firm.

Solzhenitsyn's statements have acquired the character of a political platform aimed at the unification of kindred souls, primarily former prisoners, for the purpose of undermining the Soviet government. In particular, he said in his Nobel lecture:

An author is not an aloof judge of his compatriots and contemporaries. He is equally guilty of all the evil committed in his motherland or by his people. And if his fatherland's tanks spilled blood on the asphalt of another capital, brown stains would cling forever to the author's face.

In his interview with *Le Monde*'s correspondent, Solzhenitsyn stated the following: "I cannot agree that the murderous course of history is inexorable, and that a confident mind cannot influence even the most powerful force in the world. . . .

". . . It is time to act in order to respond to the increased persecution of Soviet dissidents."

The evidence of Solzhenitsyn's specific anti-Soviet and anticonstitutional activities provides all the necessary grounds to charge him under Article 70 of the Russian Federation Penal Code, which states as follows:

Agitation or propaganda for the purpose of undermining or weakening the Soviet government or the perpetration of certain especially dangerous state crimes; the spreading of slanderous fabrications discrediting the Soviet state and social system for the same purposes; or the dissemination, manufacture, or possession of printed matter of a similar content for the same purposes shall be punishable by imprisonment for a term of six months to seven years, with exile for a term of two to five years, or without such exile.

The institution of criminal proceedings against Solzhenitsyn would also have a positive effect in the sense that it would put an end to the impunity of his activities, which confuses Soviet citizens and gives rise to unwelcome rumors.

Nevertheless, in order to avoid various kinds of speculation, and taking into account proposals offered at various times by a number of prominent representatives of the Soviet public, *instead of taking such a measure we could strip Solzhenitsyn of his Soviet citizenship and deport him from the USSR.*

Inasmuch as the implementation of this option would require an entry visa to a foreign state, *we deem it advisable to instruct the USSR's ambassadors to Sweden, Switzerland, Denmark, and Lebanon to file official requests with the governments of these countries to grant Solzhenitsyn an entry visa.* In this connection, they should be directly told something like this:

> Solzhenitsyn, who used to be a writer, in recent years, under the influence of Western propaganda and especially since he was awarded a Nobel Prize, has started to act in a way that makes him liable under Soviet law, to prosecution under the relevant articles of the RSFSR Penal Code. Accordingly, the competent Soviet authorities will be forced in the near future to institute criminal proceedings against Solzhenitsyn with all the ensuing consequences.
>
> The Soviet government, guided by humane motives and keeping in mind that Solzhenitsyn is responsible for the support of four young sons, would consider the possibility of suspending his indictment under the Penal Code in favor of a deportation from the Soviet state. If requested by Solzhenitsyn, his family would be allowed to join him.
>
> We know that the press and television and radio stations of your country regularly and sympathetically promote Solzhenitsyn's views. That is why the Soviet government requests that you grant Solzhenitsyn and his family an opportunity to reside in your country. Otherwise, the Soviet authorities will be forced to act in accordance with the laws of the USSR.

We cannot rule out the possibility that such requests by our ambassadors will be unsuccessful. Yet even in the event that foreign countries refuse to grant Solzhenitsyn a residence permit, we would have indisputable advantages. First of all, this would once again demonstrate to world public opinion the humane attitude of the Soviet government toward Solzhenitsyn, even though he has engaged in criminal activities, and would give us an opportunity to use these circumstances in the event of his indictment. Secondly, once Solzhenitsyn finds out about this measure, being afraid of deportation from the USSR (he thinks he might be murdered in a foreign country), he may want to tone down his hostile activities and reduce his ties to foreign anti-Soviet circles.

This memorandum has been approved by Comrades A.N. Kosygin and M.A. Suslov.

Please review.

Chairman of the Committee for State Security
Andropov

F. 3, *op.* 80, *d.* 646, *l.* 99–104. Original.

Note

1. *The first page bears the resolution: "Send to all Politburo members and the Secretariat and then discuss. L. Brezhnev," with the signatures of N. Podgorny, M. Suslov, A. Kirilenko, K. Mazurov, A. Pelshe, V. Grishin, F. Kulakov, A. Grechko, A. Shelepin, D. Ustinov, P. Demichev, B. Ponomarev, I. Kapitonov, K. Katushev, D. Polyansky, and A. Kosygin, and the notation of A. Gromyko: "I think we should discuss this." The last page bears the notation: "This issue was reviewed at the Politburo session of 7 January 1974. See No. P120/1 transcript." The reverse side of the document bears the notation: "Dolgikh is on vacation. V. Galkin."*

PART IV
1974
EXPULSION

96 Memorandum from the Committee for State Security of the USSR Council of Ministers[1]

No. 2–A
2 January 1974
Top Secret

To the Central Committee:
As the Committee for State Security has reported several times, Solzhenitsyn has written a book entitled *The Gulag Archipelago*, the contents of which are absolutely anti-Soviet. A brief summary of this book was submitted to the Central Committee (No. 2180/Ch) on 10 September 1973. We stated in that memorandum that it was quite possible that several copies of this book were already abroad.

Despite measures taken by the KGB to withdraw the book, foreign propaganda outlets began publishing excerpts from it in late December 1973 wherein Solzhenitsyn most spitefully slandered the Soviet system, the Party's activities, and V.I. Lenin, our Party's leader.

Judging from publications already in existence, we can assume that foreign reactionary centers in different countries are simultaneously attempting to organize a widescale anti-Soviet campaign around Solzhenitsyn's book to discredit our country and Soviet foreign policy. In its memorandum of 15 December 1973,[2] which gives information about Solzhenitsyn's malicious anti-Soviet activities, the KGB proposed to take some steps regarding the possibility of forcefully deporting Solzhenitsyn from our country. In particular, it was proposed to instruct the Soviet Ambassadors in Sweden, Switzerland, Denmark, and Lebanon to make an official approach to the governments of these countries with a request to grant Solzhenitsyn an entry visa, and to state approximately the following:

> In the past, Solzhenitsyn occupied himself with literary activi-
> ties; in recent years, under the influence of Western propaganda
> and especially after being awarded the Nobel Prize, he has
> embarked upon a path of activity that by Soviet law falls under

the Criminal Code. Therefore, the competent Soviet authorities will be forced in the very near future to bring a criminal case against Solzhenitsyn with all the consequences that entails.

Guided by humane motives and bearing in mind that Solzhenitsyn has four young dependent sons, the Soviet government would consider it possible to deport him from the Soviet state instead of bringing a criminal case against him. If Solzhenitsyn so desired, members of his family could freely follow him.

In submitting this proposal, the KGB has not excluded the possibility that foreign governments could refuse our request to permit the entry of Solzhenitsyn. State security authorities have collected data indicating that special centers in the Western states are very interested in having Solzhenitsyn remain in the Soviet Union. Thus, one of the leaders of the NTS, in a meeting with our agent, said openly:

Solzhenitsyn will not come to the West because we will not allow it. We will not allow it because if he leaves the Soviet Union and comes to the Western world he will be forgotten in half a year. He is a poor writer whereas right now each of his statements sent here is of keen interest. There he is like a worm in an apple, while outside the apple, he is not worth a penny and becomes, so to say, nothing.

In light of the foregoing, we consider it advisable, in addition to addressing the governments of the countries mentioned above, to simultaneously sound out via specialized agencies the views of the leadership of one of the states friendly to us on the possibility of accepting Solzhenitsyn when he is deported from the Soviet Union.

In our opinion, it would be necessary in this case to deport Solzhenitsyn alone, without his family, but allowing him the right to reunite with his family at a later time in the country of his residence. We are proceeding on the basis that Solzhenitsyn will relocate to a country in Western Europe where he has considerable financial means.

In the event consent is given, Solzhenitsyn's deportation could take place through a decision of the Presidium of the USSR Supreme Soviet, and a brief statement could be published in the media.

Please review.

Chairman of the Committee for State Security
Andropov

F. 3, *op.* 80, *d.* 646, *l.* 105–107. Original.

Notes

1. *Page one of the resolution has the note: "It is necessary to discuss the proposed measures at a meeting of the Politburo. N. Podgorny," and the signatures of L. Brezhnev, A. Kosygin, and M. Suslov. On the last page is a note: "This issue has been discussed at the Politburo session of 7 January 1974 (see P120/1-protocol). V. Galkin."*
2. *Date is incorrect; see Document 95.*

97 Memorandum from the Committee for State Security of the USSR Council of Ministers

No. 4–A
2 January 1974
Classified

Enclosed find three xerox copies of one of the versions of *The Gulag Archipelago* by Solzhenitsyn.

According to reports in the bourgeois press, it has just been published in the West as a separate book.

Enclosure the as stated, to the distribution list only.[1]

Chairman of the Committee for State Security
Andropov

F. 3, *op.* 80, *d.* 657, *l.* 2. Original

Note

1. *A note is attached to the document from the manager of the Central Committee General Department: "At the request of Comrade Y.V. Andropov, and in coordination with Comrade M.A. Suslov, copies of Solzhenitsyn's 'works' were sent on 2/1/74 to Comrades Suslov, Podgorny, and Kosygin. 2/1/74. K. Bogolyubov."*

98 Resolution of the Secretariat of the Central Committee

"On Exposing the Anti-Soviet Campaign of Bourgeois Propaganda Regarding the Publication of *The Gulag Archipelago* by Solzhenitsyn"

No. St–108/4s
4 January 1974
Top Secret

Resolved:

1. To approve the text of the telegram to Soviet Ambassadors. (See enclosure.)

2. To publish articles in *Pravda* and *Literaturnaya Gazeta*[1] exposing the anti-Soviet, antisocialist nature of the malicious writings of Solzhenitsyn and the true goals of the propaganda hullabaloo around Solzhenitsyn incited in the West.

3. To instruct TASS, APN, and USSR Gosteleradio[2] to distribute materials in a timely fashion, stating the true political goals of Solzhenitsyn's writings and activities that are hostile to the cause of peace and socialism, and to expose the essence of the anti-Soviet campaign directed against the foreign policy achievements of the USSR, and its activity ensuring détente.

4. To require VAAP[3] to examine the possibility of applying legal penalties for Solzhenitsyn's violation of Soviet law, and to report to the Central Committee on this matter.

5. The mass media and the information channels are to step up their exposures of the antipopular nature of bourgeois democracy, racism, the amorality of bourgeois culture, and, in particular, bourgeois restrictions placed on prominent democratic activists.

Central Committee Secretary
M. Suslov

Enclosure
Classified
Re: jp. 4c, transcript 108

Berlin	Paris
Sofia	Vienna
Prague	Bonn
Ulan-Bator	Buenos-Aires
Budapest	London
Havana	New York
Warsaw	Brussels
Copenhagen	Rome

To the Soviet Ambassador:
Meet with one of the leaders from among our friends[4] and inform him of the following:

The reactionary press, primarily in the US and France, has, as you know, initiated a new anti Soviet campaign in connection with the publication of Solzhenitsyn's book *The Gulag Archipelago*. The timing of the publication of this book was quite clearly chosen so as to damage détente. Meanwhile, Solzhenitsyn's book, the nature of which is anti-Soviet and antisocialist, and is aimed at discrediting the October Revolution, socialism as a system, and V.I. Lenin personally, will be exploited by anti-communists to damage our movement and the interests of the revolutionary class struggle.

For our part, we will take political and propaganda measures in order to give a calm, well-argued response in the proper form to the slanderous campaign of the bourgeois press. We mean, in particular, to stress that Solzhenitsyn's book, this time more fully than ever before, discloses his White Guard views. It is directed not against certain facets of life in the Soviet Union, but against the socialist system as a whole, against the actual idea of the socialist revolution and the building of a new society.

Solzhenitsyn attempts to discredit the very idea of communism, and maliciously slanders Marx and Engels, and the founder of the Soviet state, V.I. Lenin.

When writing about the period of the Civil War, Solzhenitsyn makes much of the punitive measures taken by the Soviet government and 'forgets' to say that they were the response of

281

the people's regime to the mass White terror that constituted a component of the class struggle of the bourgeoisie and land-lords against the working people, and was supported by foreign intervention against Soviet Russia. As a result, hundreds and hundreds of thousands of communists and non-Party members who sided with the Soviet government were shot. Solzhenitsyn sneers at the heroic deeds of the Soviet Army during the Great Patriotic War, fully justifying those who went over to Hitler's side and fought with him against their own people.

Even the bourgeois press (for example, Agence France Presse) recognizes that Solzhenitsyn's book does not include any new facts and views except those widely used in his earlier publications. The facts of contemporary Soviet life do not pro-vide any support for those views. The Party, as is well known to comrades as far back as the Twentieth Congress, resolutely and decisively criticized violations of socialist democracy and law that had occurred in the 1930s and 1940s, and proclaimed that nothing like that would ever be permitted again. This is our principled position, which was confirmed at the Twenty-Fourth Congress, and is consistently implemented in practice.

Considering the above, we would like to draw the attention of friends to this new anti-Soviet campaign, and consider it advisable for your party to respond to it in a manner appropri-ate for you. We proceed on the basis repeatedly stressed in the documents of your party that the struggle against anti-Sovi-etism is the common cause of all Communists.

(For Paris only: Comrade Leirac's article in *L'Humanité* of 31 December 1973 was noted in Moscow with satisfaction. We think that the cooperation of our parties in this matter, as in many others, could play a decisive role in the struggle against the adversaries of socialism.)

Send telegram to confirm implementation.

F. 3, *op.* 80, *d.* 647, *l.* 1–4. Excerpt from transcript.

Notes

1. Pravda *published on 14 January 1974 an article by N. Solovyev "The Road of Treachery," and on 16 January, the* Literaturnaya Gazeta *published an article "Who Profits from this Anti-Soviet Ruckus?"*

2. TASS—Telegraph Agency of the Soviet Union; APN—Novosti Press Agency; USSR Gosteleradio—USSR State Committee for television and radio broadcasting.

3. VAAP—USSR Copyright Agency.

4. This formula presumably refers to the members of Moscow-oriented communist parties and other friendly (or front) organizations.

99 From the Minutes of a Politburo Meeting

7 January 1974
Top Secret

Presiding: Comrade L. I. Brezhnev
Present: Comrades Y.V. Andropov, V.V. Grishin, A.A. Gromyko, A.P. Kirilenko, A.N. Kosygin, N.V. Podgorny, D.S. Polyansky, M.A. Suslov, A.N. Shelepin, P.N. Demichev, M.S. Solomentsev, D.F. Ustinov, I.V. Kapitonov, and K.F. Katushev.

Re: Solzhenitsyn.

Brezhnev: According to reports from our representatives abroad and in the foreign press, Solzhenitsyn's latest work, *The Gulag Archipelago*, is being released in France and the US. Comrade Suslov has told me that the Secretariat adopted a resolution to instruct the press to expose the writings of Solzhenitsyn and the bourgeois propaganda being conducted in connection with the publication of this book. Nobody has read this book yet but its contents are already known. It is a contemptuous anti-Soviet lampoon. Because of this we have to take counsel as to how to act further. Under our law, we have every reason to sentence Solzhenitsyn to jail because he has encroached on everything that is most sacred: Lenin, our Soviet system, the Soviet government, everything that is dear to us.

At one time we jailed Yakir, Litvinov, and others, and after we sentenced them, the fuss ended. Kuznetsov, Allilueva,[1] and others went abroad. At first there was a bit of noise, and afterwards everything was forgotten. This defiant element, Solzhenitsyn, is on a rampage. He turns his back on everything and is heedless of everything. What shall we do with him? If we resort to sanctions against him now, will that be advantageous for us? How will bourgeois propaganda use it against us? I move that this issue be discussed. I want us simply to have an exchange of views, consult with one another, and arrive at a correct decision.

Kosygin: There is a memo from Comrade Andropov on this issue. The memo contains a proposal to expel Solzhenitsyn from the country.

Brezhnev: I talked with Comrade Andropov regarding this issue.

Andropov: I think that Solzhenitsyn should be deported without his consent. At one time Trotsky was expelled and nobody asked for his consent.

Brezhnev: Evidently, Solzhenitsyn will not give such consent on his own.

Kirilenko: He can be expelled without his consent.

Podgorny: Will there be a country that would take him without his consent?

Brezhnev: It is necessary to take into account that Solzhenitsyn didn't even go abroad to receive the Nobel Prize.

Andropov: When he was offered the opportunity to go abroad to receive the Nobel Prize, he raised the issue of guarantees for his return to the Soviet Union. Comrades, since 1965, I have been raising the issue of Solzhenitsyn. Today he has gone to a new, higher stage in his hostile activities. He tries to create an organization within the Soviet Union made up of former convicts. He opposes Lenin, the October Revolution, and the socialist system. His *Gulag Archipelago* is not a work of fiction; it is a political document. This is dangerous. There are tens of thousands of supporters of Vlasov, OUN, and other hostile elements. On the whole, there are hundreds and thousands of people among whom Solzhenitsyn will find support. Everybody is on the alert today regarding how to handle Solzhenitsyn, whether we apply sanctions against him, or leave him alone.

Not long ago comrade Keldysh called me and asked why we didn't take any measures regarding Sakharov. He says that if we remain inactive on Sakharov, then how will such academicians as Kapitsa, Engelgard, and others behave in the future?

All this, comrades, is very important, and we have to resolve these issues now despite the fact that the European Conference is in session.

I think that we have to take Solzhenitsyn to court, and apply Soviet law against him. Many foreign reporters are visiting Solzhenitsyn now, as well as other disgruntled people. He talks with them and even holds press conferences. Let's assume that we have a hostile underground and the KGB overlooked it. But Solzhenitsyn acts openly, acts impudently. He exploits the humane attitude of the Soviet government and carries out hostile activities with perfect impunity. Therefore, we should take all the measures that I wrote about to the Central Committee, ie, deport him from the country. First, we should ask our ambassadors to probe the governments of certain countries on the matter of whether they would accept him. If we don't deport him now, he will continue his hostile activities. You know that he wrote a hostile novel *August 1914*, wrote the lampoon, *The Gulag Archipelago*, now he is writing *October 1917*. The latter will be a new anti-Soviet work of literature.

Hence, I propose that we expel Solzhenitsyn from the country using administrative measures. We should instruct our ambassadors to make the appropriate inquiries in a number of countries, as I stated in my memo, with the goal of having them accept Solzhenitsyn. If we don't take these measures, then all our propaganda work will lead to nothing. If we publish articles in newspapers, speak about him on the radio, but don't take measures, it will be idle talk. It is necessary to clarify what we do about Solzhenitsyn.

Brezhnev: And what would happen if we deport him to a socialist country?

Andropov: This would hardly be acceptable to the socialist countries, Leonid Ilyich. It would mean that we are giving them such a fellow as a present. Maybe we should ask Iraq, Switzerland, or some other country? He could live abroad comfortably, he has eight million rubles in accounts in European banks.

Suslov: Solzhenitsyn has become impudent, he spits on the Soviet system and the Communist Party, he has encroached upon the holiest of holies, Lenin.

It is a matter of time in deciding what should be done with Solzhenitsyn: whether he should be deported or tried under Soviet law; in any case, it should be done. In order to take some measure in regard to Solzhenitsyn, our people should be prepared, and this could be done by initiating widescale propaganda. We were right about Sakharov when we carried out the appropriate propaganda work. In reality, we no longer receive malicious letters in regard to Sakharov. Millions of Soviet people listen to the radio, listen to broadcasts on these new writings. All this exerts influence on the people.

We should publish a series of articles and expose Solzhenitsyn. This must be done.

According to the decision adopted by the Secretariat, one or two articles are to be published in *Pravda* and in *Literaturnaya Gazeta*. The people should know of this book by Solzhenitsyn. Certainly, it is unnecessary to initiate a campaign around it, but several articles should be published.

Kirilenko: It would only draw attention to Solzhenitsyn.

Suslov: But it is impossible to keep quiet.

Polyansky: It is necessary to combine propaganda measures simultaneously with administrative measures.

Gromyko: Solzhenitsyn is an enemy, and I vote for the strictest measures in regard to him.

As far as propaganda measures are concerned, they should not be doled out in doses. They should be examined carefully. But we should not reject the steps suggested by Comrade Andropov. If we expel him from the country forcefully, it should be borne in mind that bourgeois propaganda could turn this against us. It would be good to expel him with his consent, but he would never give such consent. Maybe we should suffer a little more while the European Conference is still in session? Even if a country agrees, it would be unsuitable to expel him right now because widescale propaganda could be initiated against us and it would not help us at the conclusion of the European Conference. I have in mind to wait some three or four months, but once again, I say that, in principle, I support strict measures. Solzhenitsyn should be cordoned off to isolate him during this period so that people whom he could exploit for propaganda purposes would have no access to him.

The visit of Leonid Ilyich to Cuba is planned to take place in the near future.[2] And this is not advantageous for us either because a lot of different materials will be published against the Soviet Union. It is necessary to take propaganda measures inside the country exposing Solzhenitsyn.

Ustinov: I think it is necessary to start working on implementing the proposals suggested by comrade Andropov. At the same time, we should publish propaganda materials exposing Solzhenitsyn.

Podgorny: I would like to pose the question as follows. What administrative measure should be taken in regard to Solzhenitsyn: try him in accordance with Soviet laws inside the country, and make him serve a term here, or, as proposed by Comrade Andropov, deport him from the country? The fact that Solzhenitsyn is an enemy, an impertinent, vehement one, and that he leads renegades, is indisputable. That he does all that with impunity is likewise clear to all of us. Let's see what would be more advantageous for us, what measure: A court trial or sending him into exile? In many countries, in China, people are executed openly; the fascist regime in Chile shoots and tortures people; the British resort to persecution of the working people in Ireland, and here we have a vehement enemy and are passive when he smears everything and everybody with dirt.

I think our law is humane, but it is also merciless in regard to enemies. We should try him under our Soviet laws in our Soviet court, and make him serve his sentence in the Soviet Union.

Demichev: To be sure, there will be a fuss abroad, but we have already published several articles on Solzhenitsyn's new book. We have to expand our propaganda work further because it is impossible to remain silent. If Solzhenitsyn says in his *Feast of the Victors* that he is angry with the Soviet system, in *The Gulag Archipelago*, which he wrote in 1965, he speaks now with greater brazenness and candor against the Soviet system, and against the Party. Therefore, we should publish strongly worded articles in our press. To my mind, this would not affect détente and the European Conference.

Suslov: The Party organizations are waiting, the socialist countries are also waiting to see how we will react to the actions of Solzhenitsyn. And we cannot keep silent.

Katushev: We are unanimous in our evaluation of Solzhenitsyn's actions. He is an enemy, and we have to respond accordingly. Apparently, we cannot avoid resolving the issue of Solzhenitsyn now, but it should be resolved comprehensively. On the one hand, we must direct all our propaganda against Solzhenitsyn, and on the other we must take measures in accordance with Comrade Andropov's memo.

Obviously, it is possible by a Supreme Soviet resolution to deport him from the country and to publish a statement in the press. He has violated our sovereignty, our freedoms, our laws, and he should be punished for it.

The negotiations on deporting Solzhenitsyn will apparently take from three to four months, but I repeat that this issue should be resolved comprehensively, and the faster he is deported from the country, the better.

As far as our press is concerned, it is necessary to publish articles.

Kapitonov: I would like to discuss this issue as follows: If we deport Solzhenitsyn from the country, how would this act be understood by our people? There may, certainly, be all kinds of reservations, gossip, etc. What do we demonstrate by this: strength or weakness? I think that in any event we don't demonstrate our strength by doing it. We haven't yet exposed him ideologically, and have told the people practically nothing about Solzhenitsyn. It should be done. It is necessary, first of all, to start work on exposing Solzhenitsyn, to turn him inside out, and then any administrative measure would be understood by our people.

Solomentsev: Solzhenitsyn is a hardened enemy of the Soviet Union. If it were not for the foreign political activities currently being conducted by the Soviet Union, the issue could have been resolved without delay. But how would any such decision affect our foreign political activities? However, we must, in any case, tell the people everything that should be said. It is necessary to give a severe appraisal of his actions and his hostile activity. To be sure, the people will ask why no measures are taken against Solzhenitsyn. In the GDR, for example, an article has already been published on Solzhenitsyn and in Czechoslovakia as well, not to mention bourgeois countries, but our press keeps silent. We hear a lot over the radio on Solzhenitsyn, on his *Gulag Archipelago*, but our radio keeps silent.

I'm of the opinion that we should not remain silent anymore, people expect vigorous action. We must publish sharp articles in the press exposing Solzhenitsyn. Obviously, we must consult the communist parties of the capitalist states about the propaganda measures they should carry out in their own countries.

I think that Solzhenitsyn should be tried under our laws.

Grishin: Evidently Comrade Andropov should look for a country that would agree to accept Solzhenitsyn. As far as exposing Solzhenitsyn is concerned, it should be initiated immediately.

Kirilenko: Whenever we talk of Solzhenitsyn as an anti-Soviet propagandist and malicious enemy of the Soviet system, it always coincides with some important events, and we postpone the resolution of this issue. At one time it was justified, but now we cannot delay any further. What has been written about Solzhenitsyn so far is good, yet now we must write about Solzhenitsyn, as the comrades have said, more strongly and severely, with good arguments. For example, Krolikowsky, a Polish writer, wrote a very good article exposing Solzhenitsyn. Today Solzhenitsyn is becoming more and more insolent. He is not alone, he is in contact with Sakharov. He has contacts abroad with the NTS. Therefore, the time has come to tackle Solzhenitsyn properly and it should be followed by deporting him from the country, or by some other measures.

Andrei Andreyevich [Gromyko] says that this measure could backfire. No matter how it may turn against us, the issue cannot be left as it is. Enemies put spokes in our wheels, and we should not keep quiet about it. Even many bourgeois newspapers today speak out about Solzhenitsyn and state that he will be tried according to Soviet law, and that he is liable under the copyright convention that we joined.

I support the proposal advanced by Comrade Andropov.

Articles should be published in the newspapers, but they should be well argued and thorough.

Kosygin: Comrades, we are all of the same opinion, and I fully subscribe to everything that has been said.

For several years Solzhenitsyn has been attempting to take control over the minds of our people. We are somewhat afraid to touch him, yet the people would welcome any actions we take in regard to Solzhenitsyn.

If we speak of public opinion abroad, we should calculate as to where there is less harm: if we expose him, convict and imprison him, or if we wait another few months and then deport him to another country.

I think we'll have fewer losses if we act decisively now and sentence him under Soviet law.

Articles on Solzhenitsyn should be published in the press, but serious ones. Solzhenitsyn has been bought by foreign companies and agencies, and works for them. Solzhenitsyn's *Gulag Archipelago* is an unprincipled, anti-Soviet work of literature. I talked with Comrade Andropov on this issue. Of course, the capitalist states will not accept Solzhenitsyn. I support the idea that Comrade Andropov should sound out the capitalist states to investigate which one would accept him. However, we should not be afraid to impose severe measures of Soviet justice on Solzhenitsyn. Let's take England. Hundreds of people are done away with there. Or Chile, the same thing.

We must put Solzhenitsyn on trial and speak about him, and he could serve his sentence in Verkhoyansk. No foreign reporter would go there because it is very cold there. It should not be concealed from the people. Articles should be published in the newspapers.

Podgorny: Solzhenitsyn is engaged in active anti-Soviet activity. At one time we deported or tried less dangerous enemies than Solzhenitsyn, yet now we are unable to approach Solzhenitsyn and are looking for a way out. The last book by Solzhenitsyn offers no ground for mercy toward him.

Of course, this measure should not hinder the implementation of other actions. Solzhenitsyn has quite a number of followers but we cannot overlook his actions.

I think the people would support any action we undertake. Articles should be published in the newspapers, but they should be very convincing. Many know of him today and know also of his last book. The Voice of America, Radio Free Europe and other radio stations are broadcasting it. Here and abroad people are waiting to see what measures the Soviet government will take against Solzhenitsyn. He, apparently, is not scared and thinks that no measures will be taken.

I think that, despite the European Conference, we cannot refrain from taking measures to deal with Solzhenitsyn. Regardless of the fact that the European Conference is in session, we must take action against him, and let everyone know that we are conducting a policy of principle. We have no mercy for enemies.

I think we'll inflict great damage on our common cause if we don't undertake measures against Solzhenitsyn, despite the racket that will be kicked up abroad. Certainly, there will be all kinds of talk, but the interests of our people, the interests of the Soviet state, of our Party are above everything. If we don't take decisive measures, then we'll be asked why we didn't take such measures.

I want to support the idea of trying Solzhenitsyn. If we deport him, we'll demonstrate our weakness. We have to prepare for the trial, expose Solzhenitsyn in the press, indict him, conduct an investigation, and institute proceedings in court through the Prosecutor's Office.

Polyansky: Is it possible to arrest him before the trial?

Andropov: It is possible. I consulted Rudenko on the matter.

Podgorny: As far as deporting him to some other country is concerned, it is absolutely inadvisable to do so without the consent of the other country.

Andropov: We'll start the work on deporting him, and shall open a case and isolate him at the same time.

Gromyko: If we send him abroad, he will continue to harm us from there.

Andropov: I think it'll be worse if we delay the case in regard to Solzhenitsyn—it will be worse.

Podgorny: It is possible to prolong the case with Solzhenitsyn, to drag out the investigation. But he should be in jail the whole time.

Shelepin: When we gathered at Comrade Kosygin's three months ago and discussed measures to take on Solzhenitsyn, we concluded that administrative measures should be taken. At that time it was right. The situation is different today. Solzhenitsyn has openly opposed the Soviet government—the Soviet state. And I think it is advantageous for us to resolve the issue of Solzhenitsyn now, before the conclusion of the European Conference. It would demonstrate our consistent adherence to principle. If we conduct this action after the European Conference, we will be accused of not being sincere at the Conference; it will be said that when we made a decision we were already starting to violate that decision and so on. We must follow a clear and correct line. We'll not allow anyone to violate our Soviet laws. In my view it is not a suitable measure to deport him. I think we shouldn't entangle foreign states in this matter. We have a system of justice; let's start an investigation, and then trial proceedings.

Brezhnev: The issue of Solzhenitsyn is certainly not an easy one, it's very complicated. The bourgeois press tries to link the case of Solzhenitsyn with our major peace initiatives. What should we do about Solzhenitsyn? I think the best way is in accordance with our Soviet laws.

Everyone: Right.

Brezhnev: Our Prosecutor's Office can begin an investigation and prepare a charge, and then report on his offenses in detail. Solzhenitsyn has previously been in jail, has served a sentence for gross violations of Soviet law, and was rehabilitated. But how was he rehabilitated? He was rehabilitated by two people, namely, Shatunovskaya and Snegov. He should be denied communication with foreign countries under our law during the investigation. The investigation should be conducted in an open manner to demonstrate to the people his hostile, anti-Soviet activity in defaming our Soviet system, slandering the memory of V.I. Lenin, the great leader, founder of our Party and our state, defiling the memory of the victims of the Great Patriotic War, justifying counterrevolutionaries, and directly violating our laws. He should be tried according to the law.

At one time we were not afraid to stand up against the counterrevolution in Czechoslovakia. We were not afraid to let Allilueva out of the country. We have endured everything. I think we will survive this case too. We must publish articles giving a strict and clear response to the writings of such journalists as Alsop, and we must publish articles in other newspapers.

I have talked with Comrade Gromyko about the effect measures against Solzhenitsyn might have at the European Conference. I think the effect will not be great. Obviously, it would not be expedient to deport him because nobody will accept him. It was one thing when Kuznetsov and others ran away themselves, but it would be something else to deport someone administratively.

Hence, I deem it necessary to instruct the KGB and the USSR Prosecutor's Office to develop a procedure to bring Solzhenitsyn to trial in accordance with everything said here at this meeting of the Politburo in order to take legal measures.

Podgorny: We must arrest and charge him.

Brezhnev: Let Comrades Andropov and Rudenko draft the whole procedure of charging him, and everything should be done well, in accordance with our law.

I think it is necessary to instruct Comrades Andropov, Demichev, and Katushev to prepare information for the Secretaries of the fraternal Communist and Workers' Parties of the socialist countries and other leaders of fraternal communist parties on our measures in regard to Solzhenitsyn.

Everybody: Right. We agree.

The following resolution is adopted.

On Measures to Suppress the Anti-Soviet Activity of A.I. Solzhenitsyn

1. To bring A.I. Solzhenitsyn to trial for malicious anti-Soviet activity manifested in sending manuscripts of books, letters, and interviews to foreign publishers and information agencies, which contain slander against the Soviet system, the Soviet Union, the Communist Party of the Soviet Union, and their foreign and domestic policy; defile the blessed memory of V.I. Lenin and other figures of the Party and Soviet state and victims of the Great Patriotic War and German-fascist occupation; justify the activity of both internal and external counterrevolutionary elements and groups hostile to the Soviet system; and grossly violate the Resolutions for publishing his literary work in foreign publishing houses prescribed by the World (Geneva) Copyright Convention.

2. To instruct Comrades Y.V. Andropov and R.A. Rudenko to determine the course and procedure for conducting the investigation and legal proceedings of A.I. Solzhenitsyn in accordance with the exchange of views at this meeting of the Politburo, and to submit their suggestions on this issue to the Central Committee. To inform the Central Committee in a timely manner on the course of the investigation and legal proceedings.

3. To instruct Comrades Andropov, Demichev, and Katushev to prepare information for the first Secretaries of the Central Committees of the Communist and Workers' Parties of the socialist and some capitalist countries on our measures taken in regard to Solzhenitsyn in accordance with

the exchange of views at the Politburo, and to submit it to the Central Committee.[3]

4. To instruct the Central Committee Secretariat to determine the date when this information should be sent to the fraternal parties.

Minutes of Politburo meeting in 1974. Original.

Notes

1. Svetlana Allilueva is Stalin's daughter. In December 1966, Allilueva went to India to bury the remains of her husband who had died in Moscow. In March 1967, she moved from India to the US where she established permanent residence. Shortly afterwards she published a book highly critical of the Soviet Union, *Twenty Letters to a Friend* (Harper and Row, 1967).
2. Brezhnev's visit to Cuba took place from 28 January to 3 February 1974.
3. A different version of the decision was recorded in the transcript of the meeting of the Politburo session (see Document 100).

100 Politburo Resolution "On Solzhenitsyn"

No. P120/1—transcript
7 January 1974
Top Secret

Not to go beyond the exchange of views at the meeting of the Politburo on this issue.

Secretary

F. 3, *op.* 80, *d.* 647, *l.* 9. Excerpt from transcript.

101 Memorandum from *Pravda* Political Commentator Yuri Zhukov[1]

11 January 1974

To the Central Committee:
On 9 January 1974, when I appeared on television with replies to viewers' questions on bourgeois propaganda, I spoke in particular on the issue of how foreign radio stations, conducting anti-Soviet broadcasting in Russian, employ statements by Solzhenitsyn and Sakharov that in our perspective are hostile toward us and slander us.

I showed the TV viewers a large bundle of responses from Soviet people who are infuriated with the activity of Solzhenitsyn and Sakharov, and I said that I didn't intend to read them these letters because it could have given Solzhenitsyn and Sakharov the opportunity to pose as persecuted martyrs. However, I added that if foreign correspondents wished, I would gladly give them these letters for publication. At the same time I recalled that at one time, I had addressed foreign correspondents with a similar request regarding Sakharov's position but none of them responded to my invitation.

The next day, on 10 January, I was asked by reporters of *The New York Times*, *The Washington Post*, *The Baltimore Sun*, *Time* and *United Press International*, as well as by reporters of Scandinavian newspapers, with a request to show them the letters of Soviet people. I met with these reporters on 10 and 11 January and showed and read many of the letters to them. I told them that I received several hundred letters in total, the authors of which unanimously condemned the behavior of Sakharov and Solzhenitsyn and, in particular, the publication of Solzhenitsyn's *Gulag Archipelago*, excerpts of which have recently been broadcast by foreign radio stations.

Among the letters I showed to American reporters was a letter from A. Kontorshchikov, a veteran of the October Revolution, who lived in the city of Elektrogorsk. Comrade Kontorshchikov wrote that he had once undeservedly suffered repression, and was in the camps for seventeen years, but he preserved his faith in the Party and in the Soviet government, remaining a patriot devoted to his motherland. He rejected the attempts of Solzhenitsyn to make so much of the violations of law during the period of Stalin's personality cult, depicting the entire Soviet Union as one big concentration camp, and concluded: "It is necessary to protect the Soviet people, and our Soviet capital Moscow, against such counterrevolutionaries as Sakharov and Solzhenitsyn. Let ideological enemies of all breeds and foreign radio stations squeal, but the Soviet air will be clean."

During the discussion with the American reporters, I was telephoned by a TV viewer from Solnechnogorsk who said that he had listened to my TV broadcast and wanted me to send a response to "this skunk Solzhenitsyn." This comrade said that during the time of the personality cult he was unjustly repressed and spent eighteen years in the camps.

> Nevertheless, other comrades and myself, who were in the same situation, even in that hard environment, preserved our devotion to the Party, and did everything possible for the motherland. I remembered one instance. In 1943, a ship came to Nakhodka, where we were working, with the chassis of American Studebaker trucks that were to be delivered to the front. We had to manufacture the bodies, assemble the trucks, and send them to the West quickly. We convicts gathered together and resolved not to leave the shop till we manufactured all the bodies. We slept only three hours a day. And my team manufactured 365 bodies in ten days, and the trucks were shipped to the front ahead of schedule. What right does Solzhenitsyn have to exploit the subject of the camp?

I immediately told the American reporters sitting beside me everything that he had said. They looked quite miserable, like beaten dogs.

I made them write down excerpts from the letters, the names of the authors, and their home addresses.

Today, 11 January, for two hours I was reading to reporters from Sweden, Norway, and Denmark excerpts from other letters, from new mail, whose authors severely criticized Sakharov and Solzhenitsyn, and demanded the adoption of decisive measures against these slanderers.

I want to add that the authors of many letters I have received express their dissatisfaction with our, as they say, "too liberal attitude" in regard to Sakharov and Solzhenitsyn. The letter writers demanded the adoption of administrative measures against them, up to deporting them from the Soviet Union:

"If possible, could you state the reason for such leniency and tolerance in regard to Sakharov, Solzhenitsyn, and others who live in our country and slander us," comments Comrade A.I. Rybkin of Moscow.

"I'm greatly exasperated by the softheartedness that our government demonstrates toward such renegades as Sakharov and others," writes V. Chernikh from the city of Frunze.

"Our people are patient but our patience is coming to an end, and let the Sakharovs and Solzhenitsyns blame themselves when the people simply throw them out. For too long we have neglected to pay serious attention to them. And they have gotten the false idea that everything is permissible," writes T. Ryabova of Kaliningrad.

"I think that the time has come to ask these distorters of Soviet reality: do you love your motherland? If not, good riddance," writes Comrade Kotov of Murmansk.

I am attaching to this memorandum several letters that I have received.

Yuri Zhukov
Pravda Political Commentator

Enclosure 1

To Comrade Yuri Zhukov, Editor-in-Chief of *Pravda*:
I have been disabled since 1943; before that I was a healthy and cheerful Soviet man. In heavy fighting, retreating from Chuchuyev and down to the Shaumyan passes near Tuapse, I was wounded twice, but I didn't throw away my weapons entrusted to me by the Soviet government, and didn't surrender when breaking out of encirclement. I lost my comrades many times, friends and soldiers who loved life. And only near Tuapse was I taken to the rear of the country when I was heavily wounded the third time. The doctors and the nurses—our Soviet people—with their soul and heart, with their own blood saved me from death and preserved my life, and all that because they and I fought for the Soviet government, and the Soviet government did not forget me. I'm still alive due to the tireless care of our Soviet government and Party of Communists, of which I am a member.

How low did Solzhenitsyn have to stoop in order to smear the entire Soviet system? He is alive because twenty million people were lost so that he could live and learn, create something useful, not to glorify criminal scum, renegades, and traitors to the motherland, for whom a concentration camp or a jail are the locations of permanent residence in any state. It means that he is the same kind of traitor and betrayer of our motherland and a deliberate fellow traveler of fascism, he takes a long-range sighting of us and strikes us in the back. Why are our Soviet authorities still so humane with him, why are he and Sakharov walking around free and still playing the diplomats?!

On behalf of those killed in action for our Soviet motherland and those who are disabled and still alive, I demand the most severe measures of isolation and punishment against Solzhenitsyn, Sakharov, and another two hundred names that he mentioned in his lampoon. We, Soviet people,

295

building a new communist tomorrow, are 250 million people, and, if our society loses such parasites, the revolution will not suffer.

Group II Disabled World War II Veteran,
Andrei Ivanovich Yelfimov (Lvov)

Comrade Zhukov, I ask you to publish my letter of indignation in our *Pravda*.

Enclosure 2

Yuri Alexandrovich!
Recently the press reported on the anti-Soviet presentations of Sakharov and Solzhenitsyn to foreign bourgeois reporters, in which they slandered the foreign policy of the Communist Party and the Soviet government. Sakharov and Solzhenitsyn are damaging our state by their actions. All the progressive people of the world are condemning the fascist junta of Chile and the Israeli aggressors, and approving the position of the Soviet government in regard to these events. At the same time, Sakharov and Solzhenitsyn have spoken approvingly of the actions of the Chilean junta and Israeli aggressors, and denigrated Soviet policy. A legitimate question arises, Comrade Zhukov: Why aren't these cosmopolitans[2] and anti-Soviets, Sakharov and Solzhenitsyn, not made criminally liable under our law? Article 70 of the RSFSR Criminal Code provides penalties for persons who conduct agitation or propaganda for the purpose of undermining the Soviet government, or who with the same purpose disseminate slanderous fabrications that discredit the Soviet state and social system. These renegades should be isolated from society under this law in order to suppress their harmful activity.

Sakharov and Solzhenitsyn are not deluded people, they are malicious enemies, who, owing to their beliefs, deliberately speak out against the Soviet Union and the Soviet government's measures. They must not be allowed to try incessantly the patience of Soviet people, by whom the interests of our motherland are infinitely cherished. The Soviet people wholly approve and support the policy of their dear Communist Party and the Soviet government, and trust them to the utmost, while Sakharov and Solzhenitsyn attempt to undermine this trust. Nobody gave them this right and, therefore, there is no place for them in the ranks of the builders of communism, in the ranks of honest Soviet people.

P.I. Maximov (Kirov)

F. 3, op. 80, *d.* 664, *l.* 3–6. Original.

Notes

1. *A separate page bears the instruction: "Brief Central Committee Secretaries with it," and signatures of V. Dolgikh, K. Katushev, D. Ustinov, I. Kapitonov, B. Ponomarev, M. Suslov, and P. Demichev.*
2. A euphemism for "Jews."

102 Report from the Moscow City Party Committee[1]

No. 11
11 January 1974
Classified

To the Central Committee:
From information in the newspapers and broadcast by radio and TV, the working people of Moscow have learned with deep indignation of the release in the West of *The Gulag Archipelago*, the anti-Soviet publication by Solzhenitsyn.

The release of this publication is judged by Muscovites to be a new manifestation of the anticommunist campaign of bourgeois propaganda targeted against our country to undermine the socialist system and weaken the efforts of the Soviet Union to strengthen peace and détente. "The year 1973 will go down in history as a year of détente," said Comrade P.P. Bulichev, a communist-style worker, a lathe operator at the Lyublino foundry,

> as a year when, due to the efforts of our Party, the Leninist Politburo, and Secretary General L.I. Brezhnev personally, a significant step forward has been taken toward strengthening

world peace. We know that in the West there are individuals who detest this, that there are people in the world who wouldn't mind shifting the wheel of history into reverse, to fan the flames of the 'Cold War.' And publication of Solzhenitsyn's slanderous book in the West by the end of this year of détente is another anticommunist and anti-Soviet action. Evidently, the bourgeois propagandists are in bad shape if they resort to the aid of such renegades as Solzhenitsyn.

The publication of Solzhenitsyn's writings in the West, tarnishing our motherland and our people, incites the legitimate wrath of the whole people.

"The new racket stirred up in the West and associated with the publication of *The Gulag Archipelago*," said Comrade V.A. Kosolapov, Editor-in-Chief of *Novy Mir*,

> is aimed at impeding the cause of peace and détente. The Soviet writers' community has already expressed its attitude toward the activity of the renegade Solzhenitsyn, having expelled him from the Writers Union. His behavior is incompatible with the high status of a citizen of the Soviet Union.

Comrade A.I. Filippov, Candidate of Technical Sciences, sector chief at the Central Research Technological Institute, remarked:

> It is not by chance that the slanderer Solzhenitsyn is beloved by Western anti-Soviet circles. His seditious activities, which include defending the racist regime in South Africa, slandering Vietnamese patriots, and appealing to the West to prevent détente, are all to the advantage of the most frenzied reaction. The Soviet intelligentsia has long ago expunged Solzhenitsyn from its ranks. He should be expunged from the ranks of citizens of the USSR.

In numerous statements during discussions with propaganda specialists and political instructors, and in letters to the editorial offices of newspapers, the working people of Moscow speak of Solzhenitsyn as a renegade, an ideological saboteur, who slanders the Soviet state system, the Soviet people, and its heroic history.

"The 'assertions' of Solzhenitsyn in his lampoon," said comrade G.N. Krasnov, an engineer at the machine tool design bureau, "cannot withstand criticism. I wouldn't even want to argue with him because he doesn't deserve having anyone argue with him. All our Soviet reality, all our life provides a convincing rebuttal of the lies of Solzhenitsyn, and fully exposes him as an untalented scribbler."

Comrade V.F. Yelizarova, electric sewing machine operator and communist-style worker of the Smena Sewing Association, said:

> I'm an ordinary worker, a mother of two children, and I'm convinced daily of the concern of the Party and Soviet government for the Soviet people. We continuously experience the improvement of our well-being. We respond to the care of the Party and the government with shock labor, understanding that by doing so we strengthen the economic power and raise the authority of our motherland. My comrades and I are deeply indignant at the behavior of Solzhenitsyn and think that this scum should have no place on our Soviet earth.

"I'm offended, both as a citizen and as a historian, by the distortion of reality in Solzhenitsyn's book," said Academician B.A. Rybakov, Director of the Institute of Archeology of the USSR Academy of Sciences. "It is direct falsification of historical truth."

The working people of Moscow are indignant over Solzhenitsyn's judgments on the tsarist period of Russia as a "time of prosperity," with his attacks on the socialism that truly liberated millions of people from the oppression of exploitation, which contributed to the development of creative thinking in the people, and which supported the development of education, science, and culture, transforming a backward country into a leading economic and political power in the modern world. Solzhenitsyn's reasoning on the so-called "humanism" of the enemies of socialism, Hitlerite murderers, and traitors to the motherland, are perceived with a sense of deep indignation.

Comrade S. M. Khovansky, a fitter at the First Moscow Ball-Bearing Plant said:

> To please the darkest reactionary forces, Solzhenitsyn tarnishes and smears our socialist system, as well as our achievements with dirt.
>
> Everything that has been achieved by the work of Soviet people, everything that is sacred and cherished, is rejected by this renegade. My comrades at work and I think that Solzhenitsyn has lost the right to be ranked a citizen of our motherland, to eat our bread and walk on Soviet soil.
>
> We workers declare that we will not allow the defamation of our system, our people, and our Communist Party.

Indignant responses condemning Solzhenitsyn come from veterans of the Great Patriotic War who say that only a coward and deserter who doesn't care for the interests of his people, only a person who is alien to the word "motherland," can write so impudently and cynically about war.

Demonstrating unity in their views and judgments of *The Gulag Archipelago* and its author, the working people of Moscow ask the following kinds of questions: How long do we have to tolerate the anti-Soviet activity of Solzhenitsyn? Will Solzhenitsyn be answerable to Soviet law for publishing his book? Can the government of the USSR submit a protest to the UN against the activity of the publishing house that released Solzhenitsyn's book? Will more detailed information be given on the ideological damage of Solzhenitsyn's book *The Gulag Archipelago?*—and so on.

Many Muscovites suggest taking Solzhenitsyn to court or abrogating his Soviet citizenship and expelling him from the country.

Currently, the Moscow City Party Committee is organizing work to research questions that arise in regard to Solzhenitsyn and his book, and is taking measures to augment propaganda, lecturing, and mass political work in the collectives dealing with current issues of ideological struggle.

Secretary of the Moscow City Party Committee
V. Grishin

F. 3, *op.* 80, *d.* 664, *l.* 36–39. Original.

Note

1. Sent to members and candidate members of the Politburo and to Central Committee Secretaries on 14 January 1974 as No. P70.

103 Memorandum from the Central Committee International Department

"On Information for Fraternal Parties Regarding the Anti-Soviet Activity of Solzhenitsyn"[1]

No. 25–S–90
15 January 1974
Classified

To the Central Committee:
In accordance with instructions we submit information for the fraternal parties on the anti-Soviet activity of Solzhenitsyn. A draft of the Central Committee's decision is attached.[2]

F. 3, *op.* 69, *d.* 139. Original.

Notes

1. *Sent to members of the Politburo for voting on 16 January 1974 as No. P86.*
2. *Politburo decision No. P122/XVII was adopted on 17 January 1974 (see Document 109).*

104 Report from the Central Committee's Departments of Propaganda, Culture, and Science and Educational Institutions

15 January 1974
Classified

To the Central Committee:
The article in *Pravda* has provoked a wide response among all segments of the Soviet public. Workers, scientists, writers, artists, workers in theaters and cinematography, soldiers of the Soviet Army and the Navy, and students express their attitude toward the degenerate Solzhenitsyn in letters and verbal statements in *Pravda, Izvestia, Sovietskaya Kultura, Komsomolskaya Pravda, Literaturnaya Gazeta*, and on radio and television.

All are unanimous in appraising Solzhenitsyn as a traitor to the motherland and betrayer of the Soviet people, as a slanderer of Soviet reality, as a paid lackey of the enemies of socialism and the Soviet Union. All statements express anger that Solzhenitsyn is not punished for his ill-intentioned actions, which insult the highest and most sacred feelings of the Soviet people. The authors of the letters demand that urgent measures be undertaken against Solzhenitsyn in accordance with Soviet laws.

A list of statements received by the press is attached. The flow of letters of a similar nature continues.

Submitted for information.

Deputy Director Department of Propaganda
G. Smirnov

Deputy Director Department of Culture
Z. Tumanova

Deputy Director Department of Science and Educational Institutions
S. Shcherbakov

Enclosure

List of Most Characteristic Statements in Connection with the Publication in *Pravda* of the article "The Path of Treason:"

K. Fedin, writer:

"It is very good that *Pravda* has published a comprehensive article on Solzhenitsyn. It is high time to expose to the Soviet public the true face of this internal emigré."

M. Shaginyan, writer:

"I fully support the article in *Pravda*. I'm surprised by our tolerance regarding such scum. Solzhenitsyn remaining unpunished demoralizes our youth. And in general, he is not a writer. I said that in Hungary and in Switzerland."

V. Kozhevnikov, writer:

"Solzhenitsyn openly violates Soviet laws and behaves unconstitutionally. He supports the propaganda of war and opposes détente. We should make a calm firm decision to deport him from the USSR."

S. Babaevsky, writer:

"I'm very angry over this business. He shouldn't be coddled. He should be treated differently. . . . It's a total outrage! The article in *Pravda* was very politically correct. He is an internal emigré, a person who profits from anti-Sovietism."

The article in *Pravda* has been fully supported, and indignation in regard to the anti Soviet activity of Solzhenitsyn has been expressed by the following writers: Y. Bondarev, P. Brovka, Y. Martsinciavicius, E. Maltsev, A. Barto, A. Salynsky, A. Rekemchuk, L. Karelin, A. Ananyev, A. Surkov, V. Bokov, S. Shchipachev, L. Leonov, S. Ostrovoy, V. Firsov, and others.

The letters and telegrams sent to *Pravda* express a wish to discuss the article in the writers' organizations so that it would be possible, as they write, to influence more actively those who haven't yet taken a clear ideological position. Suggestions are being made for the publication of a confidential selection of characteristic excerpts from the works of Sakharov and Solzhenitsyn that would help to arm ideological workers with concrete facts in their explanatory work.

Some letters also state that "if in the next few days the measures that are to be taken regarding Solzhenitsyn are not announced in *Pravda*, they will have a reverse reaction." *Pravda* will "not be trusted."[2]

Notes

1. *Sent to members and candidate members of the Politburo and to the Central Committee Secretaries on 16 January 1974 as No. P87.*

2. *The last paragraph of the document was crossed out by M. Suslov prior to distribution.*

105 Report of the Committee for State Security[1]

No. 119–A
15 January 1974
Classified

To the Central Committee:
Information received at the Committee for State Security confirms that members of the diplomatic corps, foreign journalists, and other foreigners temporarily residing in the USSR are very interested in the article "The Path of Treason," published in *Pravda* on 14 January 1974.

Their common view is that the publication of this article is timely, its contents are pointed, and it will apparently be followed by concrete measures aimed at terminating the hostile activity of Solzhenitsyn.

Perrinell, a representative of Satra Corporation, an American company, commented that he understood the wrath of the Soviet people who were indignant over the behavior of Solzhenitsyn who has smeared dirt on everything that the Soviet people have achieved and take pride in.

Teimur, Ambassador of Iran, concerning the publication in *Pravda*, stated: "Only a jackal takes food from man and is always his enemy." According to Teimur, no democratic society would have protected such people. "True, some in the West support such 'heroism' but they are those who don't care who they laud to the skies so long as they have a pretext to smear Soviet reality with dirt."

Late, a reporter for the West German newspaper *Ruhrnachrichten* ("Ruhr News") is of the opinion that the time has come for such an article and "it is very good that there is such a publication at last that dots all the i's." Late specifically stresses the calm, businesslike style of the article and notes that it does not threaten Solzhenitsyn with repression. In the journalist's opinion, the Western public will be positively influenced by the fact that in its exposé, *Pravda* very clearly limited itself to the state of affairs prior to the Twentieth Party Congress and to the present time. The article "The Path of Treason," according to Late, persuasively demonstrates that Solzhenitsyn, by his position and writings, insults the entire Soviet people, thereby placing himself outside Soviet society.

Malek, Ambassador of Algiers to the USSR, has spoken in support of the publication in *Pravda* because Solzhenitsyn and his ilk have played into the hands of imperialism, undermining the reputation of his country.

Dansas, an Agence France Presse reporter, stresses that the article in *Pravda* is the official view of the Soviet government. Therefore, Dansas considers it as the first step in a series of measures that will evidently be taken against Solzhenitsyn.

Grulow, a correspondent for the *Christian Science Monitor*, holds the same opinion, and states that, following the publication of the article "The Path of Treason," one can expect "quite harsh measures against Solzhenitsyn." Grulow thinks that the Soviet Union will try to exploit the fact that it joined the Geneva Copyright Convention. However, according to Grulow, this move would have a negative aspect: The campaign that would inevitably be initiated on this occasion by the Western press would be an advertisement for both Solzhenitsyn and his book.

Lundström, Cultural Attaché at the Swedish Embassy, has commented on the publication of the article in *Pravda* that "the ring around Solzhenitsyn is tightening." The Soviet government, according to Lundström, "from all accounts considers it insufficient to restrict the access of Western reporters to him and deport some of them from the USSR. Evidently, the government is ready to take more determined measures."

Tsyge, the Ambassador of Ethiopia, has said: "Solzhenitsyn is in serious conflict with society. But the Soviet government is strong and he'll not be able to undermine it. Most likely Soviet society will annihilate Solzhenitsyn himself."

Many foreigners agree that Solzhenitsyn will evidently be deported from the Soviet Union and his Soviet citizenship revoked, because it is "the easiest way to resolve the complex of problems associated with him."

Some foreign journalists assume that no punitive measures will be taken against Solzhenitsyn. They note the fact that "public opinion" in the West would denounce any attempt to persecute Solzhenitsyn, and some Western governments would exploit this incident as propaganda during the second stage of the European Conference on Security and Cooperation in Europe currently in session in Geneva.

Buist, a British *Reuters* reporter, comments that "If the Soviet authorities put Solzhenitsyn in jail, they inevitably will have to relinquish their political goals."

Chairman of the Committee for State Security
Andropov

F. 3, *op.* 80, *d.* 664, *l.* 48–50. Original

Note

1. *The first page of the resolution bears the inscription: "Recommend distribution to Politburo members. Kirilenko," and the signature of M. Suslov; it was sent to members and candidate members of the Politburo and to Central Committee Secretaries on 22 January 1974 as No. P127.*

106 Report of the Committee for State Security[1]

No. 139–A
16 January 1974
Classified

To the Central Committee:
The KGB continues to receive information indicating that members of the diplomatic corps and foreign reporters in Moscow are actively discussing the article "The Path of Treason" published in *Pravda*.

Speaking to American reporters in Moscow, Dobbs, the temporary Charge d'Affaires in the USSR, stated that Solzhenitsyn's last book "undoubtedly played into the hands of circles questioning the need for détente."

According to Vishnevsky, an Agence France Presse reporter, Solzhenitsyn sought publicity for himself and thinks that he is invulnerable. Vishnevsky said: "Solzhenitsyn's books vividly portray his anger against the existing order in the USSR."

Foreign reporters stress the low literary quality of Solzhenitsyn's works, and explain the hullabaloo surrounding them as politically motivated. Kuballa, a *Rheinische Post* reporter, commented in a private conversation:

> *The Gulag Archipelago* is no more interesting than a telephone book. It is packed with reference information mixed with actual and farfetched facts. *Pravda* is right that the racket kicked up in the West about this new book by Solzhenitsyn is explained not by its literary qualities but by purely political motives.

Mason, an Associated Press reporter, notes that the Central Committee's newspaper has for the first time on its own behalf denounced Solzhenitsyn. He considers the publication of the article "The Path of Treason" as the beginning of a widescale campaign against Solzhenitsyn. Grulow, a *Christian Science Monitor* reporter; Dillion, head of the Moscow bureau of Agence France Presse; Fredericksson, a reporter of the Joint Telegraph Agency of Scandinavia; and some other foreign journalists are of the same opinion.

The foreigners do not rule out the possibility that Solzhenitsyn will be stripped of his Soviet citizenship and deported from the USSR. In that case, according to the foreigners, it would be hard for the propaganda authorities in the West to involve him in anti-Soviet campaigns. Elaborating on this idea, Line, the Third Secretary of the Embassy of Great Britain, said: "Solzhenitsyn could not work in the West. He would be away from his country and, most importantly, he would not have material for his new works."

Chairman of the Committee for State Security
Andropov

F. 3, op. 80, d. 664, l. 52–53. Original.

Note

1. *Sent to members and candidate members of the Politburo and to Central Committee Secretaries on 17 January as No. P94*

107 Report from the General Department of the Central Committee

"On Workers' Letters in Regard to the Anti-Soviet Activities of A. Sakharov and A. Solzhenitsyn"[1]

16 January 1974

Numerous letters continue to be received by the Central Committee in which the working people angrily and indignantly condemn the hostile activities of Sakharov and Solzhenitsyn directed against the interests of the Soviet people. They demand that harsh measures be taken to suppress it, and that these people be severely punished.

The authors of a large number of statements, addressed to the Central Committee, brand Academician Sakharov with shame due to his latest statements to bourgeois newspapers, as well as Solzhenitsyn because of the publication in the West of his slanderous book *The Gulag Archipelago*. Workers and agricultural laborers, scientists and artists, and employees of Soviet institutions resolutely oppose the attempts of these presumptuous anti-Soviets to slander the socialist way of life and the foreign and internal policies of the Soviet state. They adamantly support the practical actions of the Central Committee in implementing the historic decisions of the Twenty-Fourth Party Congress.

The *Pravda* article "The Path of Treason" has initiated a response from Soviet people that exposes Solzhenitsyn as an enemy and a traitor. Commenting on the publication in the newspaper, the authors of the letters state that reactionary propaganda, speculating on anti-Soviet concoctions, will not be able to poison the atmosphere of international détente achieved thanks to the titanic efforts of the Soviet Union. [. . .][2]

The authors of some letters do not confine themselves to evaluating the actions of Sakharov and Solzhenitsyn. They try to establish the reasons behind these people's anti-Soviet behavior. The idea most frequently expressed is that apparently there is something wrong with the USSR Academy of Sciences. Thus, Comrade Bogolepov of Moscow writes: "Unlike the cowardly scoundrel A. Kuznetsov, Academician Sakharov 'defends' in every way his anti-Soviet beliefs. This makes him more harmful than all the defectors known to us."

Evidently there is this order at the Academy of Sciences, says Comrade Chernetsky. Some academicians are behaving like freelancers. The administration doesn't control them at all, doesn't know what they do, where, to whom, or for what reason they give interviews. Comrade Chernetsky comments: "Where did Sakharov and Solzhenitsyn come from, and how? Where were the collective and the Party organizations of the USSR Academy of Sciences, and others? How could such rotten stuff form there?" "It is high time to impose order and end this depravity. It is time to stop being liberal," states a letter from Moldavia.

Often in conferring degrees and titles our academic councils pay attention only to a person's purely professional characteristics, leaving aside such fundamental components of erudition as high moral qualities, principle, loyalty to the people and the Soviet motherland. Stating in his letter that Sakharov was given too much freedom, Comrade Gainiev, a worker, stresses that we live in a complicated time. Therefore, Party control in selecting and placing cadres in all the areas of our life should be more stringent. Particular attention should be given to the ideological education of scientists and writers. [. . .]

Some letters contain a request to publish the complete text of Sakharov's statements. The authors motivate their request by the need to have a clear understanding of the extent of harm inflicted on Soviet society. A letter from Moscow states: "As far as is known from foreign radio broadcasts, Academician Sakharov has raised several questions on the subject of social relations in our country. These questions concerned shortcomings in our educational system, health care, guarantees of human rights, etc. To my regret, nobody has had the guts to openly respond to Academician Sakharov on the issue of these shortcomings." The author of this letter comes to the conclusion that judgments about the activities of Sakharov seem one-sided if his statements are missing.

A letter from Kharkov states: "On the issue of Sakharov and Solzhenitsyn, permit me to express some criticism of the primitive organization of our fight against such phenomena. The campaign of 'condemning and exposing' Sakharov in our press instead of stripping this 'king' and decorating him with a dunce's cap has actually made Sakharov popular among certain circles of the population, and surrounded him with the halo of 'a sufferer' and 'a fighter.' We are losing, in this case, an exceptionally favorable opportunity to show this Christ naked to the people and the whole world. Perhaps it should be done by subjecting Sakharov to an interview with Soviet reporters and scientists on issues which would best expose his pretensions and demonstrate that he is outside his element when poking into politics. This type of interview could include specifically chosen questions on the nature of Sakharov's 'mixed economy,' on his attitude to events in Chile, on the freedom of the Soviet people to emigrate from the USSR, etc. There are many issues in which Sakharov would play the fool. The interview would be edited and we could show it not only to our own people, but also to the whole world. And in general,"the author concludes," it is necessary to be careful to dig out the roots that create the Sakharovs and Solzhenitsyns.[. . .]"

Submitted for consideration.

Head of the Central Committee
General Department
K. Chernenko

F. 3, *op.* 80, *d.* 664, *l.* 56–63. Original.

Notes

1. *A note is attached to the document: "Dear Leonid Ilyich! When discussing this issue at the Politburo, as you will recall, many Politburo members mentioned numerous letters coming to different organizations. Therefore, I'm sending you a memorandum on the letters that have come to the Central Committee on this issue. With regards, K. Chernenko 11/1/74." Also attached is L. Brezhnev's recommendation: "Send to the Politburo and the Central Committee Secretariat, and continue to inform the Politburo on letters regarding this issue. Evidently letters are written also to the Supreme Soviet. It is desirable to receive information on the letters to the Supreme Soviet. L. Brezhnev." The report was sent to Politburo members and Politburo candidate members, and to Central Committee Secretaries on 18 January 1974 as No. P100.*

2. Here and elsewhere in this document, and in some of the following documents, repetitions and variations on the same themes have been cut. The cuts are all indicated by omission marks [. . .].

108 From the Minutes of a Politburo Session

17 January 1974
Top Secret

Presiding: Comrade M.A. Suslov
Present: Comrades Y.V. Andropov, A.A. Grechko, A.A. Gromyko, A.P. Kirilenko, A.N. Kosygin, A.Y. Pelshe, N.V. Podgorny, D.S. Polyansky, B.N. Ponomarev, G.V. Romanov, D.F. Ustinov, I.V. Kapitonov, and K.F. Katushev

To fraternal parties on measures adopted in regard to Solzhenitsyn.

Draft decision is adopted. The first paragraph on page 6 is excluded.[1]

Politburo members ask whether many people write to the Central Committee on the issue of Solzhenitsyn.

Chernenko reports that many letters have been received, everyone is indignant over Solzhenitsyn's behavior.

Minutes of Politburo sessions in 1974. Original.

Note

1. The removed paragraph [states]: "Solzhenitsyn has gone beyond purely ideological or even literary/creative differences. He has taken the road of directly violating Soviet laws—the road of treachery. The Soviet public has long demanded the adoption of resolute measures to suppress the anti-Soviet activity of Solzhenitsyn."

109 Politburo Resolution

"On a Report to Fraternal Parties Regarding the Anti-Soviet Activities of Solzhenitsyn"

No. P122/XVII
17 January 1974
Top Secret

1. Approve with corrections the text of a telegram to Soviet Ambassadors (enclosure 1).
2. Approve the list of parties to whom the report shall be sent (enclosure 2).

Central Committee Secretary

Enclosure 1
Re: Item XVII Protocol No. 122
Classified

Meet with a representative of the leadership of friendly organizations and pass on the following:

> As you know, bourgeois propaganda organs are continuing to expand a clearly coordinated anti-Soviet and anticommunist campaign, employing to this end the simultaneous publication in some countries of Solzhenitsyn's book, *The Gulag Archipelago*.
> This book is not simply the usual anti-Soviet sort of writing by Solzhenitsyn; it is his political manifesto in which he directly and unambiguously expresses what he earlier put into the mouths of literary characters, to some extent camouflaged in the form of literature. The totality of writings, statements, and interviews by Solzhenitsyn make it possible to characterize the essence of his political position. Today it is reduced to the following essential points:

—A clearly expressed counterrevolutionary nature. "I understood the falsehood of all the revolutions in history," states Solzhenitsyn in *Gulag Archipelago*. In all his writings he depicts the issue in such a way that the socialist revolution and the socialist rebuilding of society were not, and could not have been, to the benefit of the people. Solzhenitsyn is particularly angered by the October Revolution. In his slanderous imagination, it caused suffering for the people, and oppression.

—Deliberate distortion of the very essence of the socialist system. Solzhenitsyn depicts it as a system based exclusively on violence and total lawlessness. He slanders the great revolutionary V.I. Lenin, the founder of the Communist Party and the Soviet state, asserting that Lenin created the system of violence and was the "original cause of all our troubles." The violations of legality in the 1930s and 1940s, that truly occurred and were openly condemned by the Communist Party twenty years ago already, were, in Solzhenitsyn's mind, not a deviation from the norm, but the norm itself, or, to quote him, "the crux" of the entire history of the Soviet state.

—Slander of the current situation in the Soviet Union. Despite the well-known facts, Solzhenitsyn claims that violations of legality and unfounded persecution have not been ended and continue in more refined forms. He writes: "There is no law. As before, we live as in a country without law, without rights, and without justice."

—Spiritual unity and solidarity with all enemies of the October Revolution and socialist system. Smearing true revolutionary Communists with dirt, he characterizes Hitlerites and their myrmidons [in a quite flattering manner], reactionary Prussian officers, Petlyurovites,[1] Trotskyites, and Kulaks.

—Approval of all the forms of struggle against socialism, including armed struggle. Solzhenitsyn justifies and approves the participation of Vlasov's followers in the war against the USSR and highly praises the subversive, underground activities of the Trotskyites. Solzhenitsyn takes a negative view of the results of World War II merely because it ended not with the defeat, but with the strengthening and enhancement of socialism, thereby raising the Soviet Union's international authority. He utters the following blasphemy: "This war revealed to us that, in general, to be a Russian is the worst thing on earth."

—Justification of the criminal activities of imperialism. Solzhenitsyn has never criticized the imperialist reaction, nor condemned American aggression in Vietnam, nor that of Israel against the Arab states, nor the crimes of the Chilean junta and other fascist regimes. He asserts that there is no class struggle in real life, that it "has been invented" only to create a situation of artificial tension.

—Appealing to international reaction, Solzhenitsyn calls on reactionary circles to exert pressure on the Soviet Union, to reverse the trend toward détente and further improvement of relations between states with different social systems. Solzhenitsyn virtually concludes with the platform of imperialists and Maoists. It is no accident that Maoist and bourgeois propaganda support him.

Thus, Solzhenitsyn's views coincide fully with the political positions of all the enemies of socialism, beginning with the counterrevolutionary White Guards and ending with the ardent anticommunists of today.

Solzhenitsyn's system of views was evidently already formed in the pre-war period. His outlook developed within a circle of people deprived of wealth and privileges by the October Revolution. He never accepted the Soviet system and the power of the working people, placing his own individuality above "the crowd," above the Soviet people, whom he characterized as a cluster of informers and frightened, reserved, and cruel people. In his writings at the end of the war Solzhenitsyn planned "a transition to action" with the goal of making a "resolute strike against the post-war reactionary ideological superstructure" of the Soviet Union.

On the way to this goal Solzhenitsyn changed only the tactics of his actions. At one time it was possible to assume that along with other Soviet men of letters, he advocated eliminating the consequences of the cult of personality, criticized only the violations of socialist legality. That was how literary society perceived some of Solzhenitsyn's writings at that time, thinking that the obvious faults in his works would be subsequently eliminated.

The manuscripts of his novels *The First Circle* and *Cancer Ward*, sent by Solzhenitsyn to publishing houses and magazines, were critically rejected by editorial boards because of their unacceptable ideological trend. The Writers' Union Secretariat, individual men of letters, and Party authorities worked patiently with Solzhenitsyn in an attempt to persuade him to normal, constructive cooperation in literary and social life.

314

However, all these efforts were to no avail because of Solzhenitsyn's completely intolerable position. Furthermore, he categorically refused to dissociate himself from anti-Soviet forces abroad, who at that time were exploiting his name and writings for their own interests.

Solzhenitsyn soon unmasked himself and took to the road of open political struggle. One after another his writings and statements revealed that he opposed the very foundations of the socialist system. Leaving aside hypocritical assertions that his writings were being published in the West without his knowledge, he resorted to active propaganda in favor of anti-Sovietism and anticommunism and direct cooperation with forces seeking to destroy real socialism and the entire communist movement.

It is no accident that all the anti-Soviet campaigns associated with the name of Solzhenitsyn are conducted in a surprisingly coordinated manner. They are dedicated to important events in the life of the Soviet state, and focal points in the Party's foreign policy program (the fiftieth anniversary of the October Revolution, the hundredth anniversary of the birthday of V.I. Lenin, etc). Solzhenitsyn and his likeminded accomplices abroad found it necessary to publish *The Gulag Archipelago*, written five years previously, just at the time when, by their calculations, it could most harm the process of détente consistently supported by the Soviet Union.

The forces of reaction abroad created a whole system to support Solzhenitsyn, including widely promoting his writings, filming, instigating letters and statements in his support, creating a legend of an "unselfish and persecuted fighter for an idea," and finally, funding his subversive activities. The awarding of the Nobel Prize to Solzhenitsyn was one of the forms of such political and financial support.

Solzhenitsyn has never had and never will have any support on Soviet soil; he is morally and politically in complete isolation. However, today he has the powerful system of bourgeois propaganda under his command, and has actually become its paid employee, one who is particularly valuable because he operates on Soviet territory. With the assistance of bourgeois propaganda he has gained the opportunity to damage the cause of socialism and the interests of the international communist movement.

Acting so as to discredit communist ideals and undermine

the socialist system, Solzhenitsyn slanders all and sundry. Distortions of history and slanderous depictions of Soviet reality are interwoven with fabrications about his own "grievous" circumstances. It is all clearly aimed to elicit compassion in the average man and to induce his patrons to come up with money. He actually makes a profit from his anti-Sovietism.

Bourgeois propaganda claims that Solzhenitsyn is supposedly a fighter against the consequences of the cult of personality and advocates enforcement of the law. This is false from beginning to end. At its Congresses the Party firmly condemned past violations of legality, has fully eliminated the possibility of repeating these mistakes, and continues to advance socialist democracy in the country. This policy has been followed in the past, is being followed now, and will continue to be followed in the future consistently and resolutely by the Party.

Solzhenitsyn's views could have remained his own business. But today we are dealing not with the views of an individual, but with his active and deliberate anti-Soviet activity. We are dealing with an appeal to overthrow socialism, with the propagation of hatred toward the Party, the Soviet state, and its leaders. We are dealing with a consolidated attack by the imperialist forces against Marxism-Leninism, and the communist movement with Solzhenitsyn's participation. We are dealing, ultimately, with a crystal-clear attempt to undermine the cause of détente worldwide, to reinforce the positions of reaction and aggression in the capitalist world.

Solzhenitsyn's views and activities have been properly criticized in the Soviet press (articles in *Pravda* on 14 January and in *Literaturnaya Gazeta* on 16 January), and in the press of other socialist states. Solzhenitsyn's activities and the new anti-Soviet campaign initiated by bourgeois propaganda have been condemned in the publications of the Communist parties of France, Italy, the US, West Germany, Austria, and other countries. Active denunciation of the position and activities of Solzhenitsyn, who is an obvious weapon in the hands of our class enemy, is considered by the Party to be a necessary component in the common cause of fighting imperialism, the forces of reaction and aggression, and anticommunism in all its forms and manifestations.

Send telegram upon implementation.

Enclosure 2
Re: Item XVII Protocol No. 122
Classified

List of Parties to Whom Information Shall Be Sent on the Anti-Soviet Activity of Solzhenitsyn

1. Bulgarian Communist Party
2. Hungarian Socialist Workers' Party
3. Working People's Party of Vietnam
4. Socialist Unity Party of Germany
5. Workers' Party of Korea
6. Communist Party of Cuba
7. Mongolian People's Revolutionary Party
8. Polish United Workers' Party
9. Rumanian Communist Party
10. Communist Party of Czechoslovakia
11. League of Communists of Yugoslavia

1. Communist Party of Austria
2. Communist Party of Argentina
3. Communist Party of Belgium
4. Socialist Unity Party of West Berlin
5. Communist Party of Great Britain
6. Communist Party of Venezuela
7. Communist Party of Germany
8. Communist Party of Greece
9. Communist Party of Denmark
10. Communist Party of Israel
11. Communist Party of India
12. Iraqi Communist Party
13. Jordanian Communist Party
14. Communist Party of Ireland
15. Communist Party of Spain
16. Italian Communist Party
17. Communist Party of Canada
18. Progressive Party of the Working People of Cyprus
19. Communist Party of Colombia

20. People's Vanguard of Costa Rica
21. Lebanese Communist Party
22. Communist Party of Luxembourg
23. Martinique Communist Party
24. Communist Party of Norway
25. Peruvian Communist Party
26. Portuguese Communist Party
27. Reunion Communist Party
28. San Marino Communist Party
29. Syrian Communist Party
30. US Communist Party
31. Communist Party of Turkey
32. Communist Party of Uruguay
33. Finnish Communist Party
34. French Communist Party
35. Communist Party of Chile
36. Swiss Party of Labor
37. Left Party—Communists of Sweden
38. Communist Party of Ecuador
39. Socialist Party of Australia
40. South-African Communist Party (Foreign Bureau)

F. 3, *op.* 80, *d.* 647, *l.* 46–54. Excerpt from transcript.

Note

1. Followers of General Petlyura, a Ukrainian White officer who opposed the October Revolution.

110 Report of the Committee for State Security of the USSR Council of Ministers[1]

No. 147–A
17 January 1974
Classified

To the Central Committee:
Information received by the Committee of State Security indicates that the Soviet people fully and completely approve the article "The Path of Treason," published in *Pravda* on 14 January this year, exposing Solzhenitsyn as an anti-Soviet and anticommunist, who has deliberately joined the camp enemies of democracy and socialism.

Representatives of the working class and collective farmers speak of Solzhenitsyn with feelings of wrath and contempt, expressing indignation with the anti-Soviet campaign initiated in the West around the name of this traitor.

According to currently available data, the antisocial nature of the Solzhenitsyn–Sakharov–Maximov–Galich[2] group, including some others, is actively disseminating fabrications on the danger presumably threatening Solzhenitsyn, and they are attempting to stir up an anti-Soviet campaign in the West, appealing for widespread dissemination abroad and in the USSR of the lampoon, *The Gulag Archipelago*.

Chairman of the Committee for State Security
Andropov

F. 3, *op.* 80, *d.* 664, *l.* 69–70. Original.

Notes

1. *Sent to Politburo members and candidate members, and Central Committee Secretaries, on 18 January 1974 as No. P98.*
2. Vladimir Maximov, the new name here, was the author of a censored novel, *The Seven Days of Creation*, and had moved into dissident circles around 1972 (he later emigrated to Paris and founded the literary journal *Kontinent*).

111 Report from the Moscow City Party Committee

"On Responses of Moscow Workers to the Article 'The Path of Treason' by I. Solovyev, Published in *Pravda* on 14 January 1974"[1]

No. 18
17 January 1974

Following the publication of the article "The Path of Treason" by I. Solovyev in *Pravda* on 14 January 1974, numerous responses from working people continue to be received at the Moscow city and district Party committees and to local Party organizations expressing full support for the ideas and opinions expressed in the article. Muscovites angrily condemn the traitorous and slanderous activities of Solzhenitsyn, as well as the anti-Soviet campaign in the bourgeois press in connection with the appearance in the West of *The Gulag Archipelago*.

The letters and responses from Moscow working people state that this propaganda fuss aims to tarnish the socialist achievements in our country, slander the Soviet people and the Communist Party's policy, and retard the trend toward peace and cooperation between peoples.

"We have learned with indignation of the new anti-Soviet campaign incited by bourgeois propaganda regarding the publication of this dirty lampoon," says Comrade S. Khovansky, a fitter at the First Moscow Machine-Tool Plant. "In order to please reactionary forces, Solzhenitsyn, without a twinge of conscience, smears our socialist system, our achievements, and everything that is cherished by us. Solzhenitsyn, by his *Archipelago*, has revealed himself to be an enemy of our country."

The statements of the working people of Moscow stress that our reality fully exposes Solzhenitsyn's assertions as groundless. Tremendous success has been achieved by the Soviet people in the development of the economy, science, and culture, and in the growth of the authority of our country in the international arena. Professor E. Vorontsova, Corresponding Member of the Academy of Pedagogical Sciences, says:

Joyous, bright feelings fill the hearts of Soviet people as we enter the new year 1974. They are proud of the successes achieved in 1973 in economic and cultural construction, they are ready to make their motherland happy with still greater achievements, they wish to participate more actively in the people's struggle for the triumph of communist ideals. How piteous are the malicious, false writings of Solzhenitsyn, indicating that their author has long broken all ties with his motherland, with the Soviet people, and transformed himself into a deliberate enemy of our state, an instigator and a provocateur.

Teachers of School No. 593 in the Voroshilovsky District of Moscow, having read and discussed I. Solovyev's article "The Path of Treason," unanimously support the condemnation of the anti-Soviet activities of Solzhenitsyn:

> We think that in the era of détente, which is a result of the activities of the Party, the Soviet government, and Secretary General Comrade L.I. Brezhnev, the creations of Solzhenitsyn are hostile to our reality and our plans. The fact that Solzhenitsyn vulgarizes and discredits our Soviet life makes us angry and indignant.

The working people of Moscow support the point in "The Path of Treason" that Solzhenitsyn has been and continues to be an anti-Soviet and an anticommunist, deliberately defecting to the enemies of peace, democracy, and socialism, that he has assumed the role of provocateur and agitator, appealing to imperialists to conduct a "policy of force regarding the USSR."

An Honored Navigator of the USSR, a World War II veteran, Comrade Rudich, said:

> Who is Solzhenitsyn counting on with his slanderous writing? Only upon renegades who are embittered by Soviet reality, by the successes of our country's working people who are building a bright future under the leadership of the Communist Party.
>
> We are proud of the Soviet Union's power as a stronghold of peace, freedom, and social progress for all the people of the planet, and we censure the slander and treachery of Solzhenitsyn. We are heartily in agreement with the conclusions of 'The Path of Treason' that Solzhenitsyn is a provocateur and traitor.

Comrade A. Puzikov, Editor-in-Chief of *Khudozhestvennaya Literatura*, a member of the Writers' Union, an Honored Worker of Culture, said:

> Solzhenitsyn's pathological bitterness is long known. There-
> fore, it is quite natural that his clamorous creations, letters, and
> appeals have always invoked justified indignation among the
> Soviet intelligentsia. This writer, who has opposed himself to
> Soviet society, removed himself from the ranks of men of let-
> ters, has degraded himself to a petit bourgeois politician, and,
> flouting the ideals of the socialist motherland, is subservient to
> the interests of the most reactionary, most vile circles of impe-
> rialism. Solzhenitsyn is a class enemy, and his last anti-Soviet
> act of sabotage proves it once again. There is no place for such
> a person either in the ranks of Soviet literary workers or in our
> society.

K. Simonov, a writer, said: "I'm deeply offended by Solzhenitsyn's books and behavior which advocated hostile class and anti-Soviet positions."

B. Yefimov, People's Artist of the USSR stated: "All Soviet people are unanimous in their assessment of the hostile, anti-Soviet activities of Solzhenitsyn."

This view is shared by other workers in Soviet literature and the fine arts: eg, by G. Radov, a writer; T. Salakhov, People's Artist; M. Shaginyan, a writer and Lenin Prize laureate; and E. Simonov, Chief Director of the E. Vakhtangov Theater and People's Actor.

The working people of Moscow stress in their responses that Solzhenitsyn has no right to bear the lofty title of a citizen of the Soviet Union, and demand that he be tried for his anti-Soviet activities, treachery, and for slandering our country.

D. Chernyavsky, senior engineer at the Moscow Design Department of the Cascade Association, and a World War II veteran, said: "I think that this slanderer should be brought to trial and forced to leave the Soviet land."

Due to the publication of "Path to [sic] Treason" in *Pravda*, the number of questions being asked about *The Gulag Archipelago* has reduced. At the same time, Muscovites continue to ask questions about what measures are necessary to repel this latest wave in the anti-Soviet campaign. Could the USSR lodge a protest with international organizations, dealing with press issues and the activities of foreign publishers who print literature aimed at disorienting the Soviet public? Could our information agencies and radio increase their activity in exposing fraud and slander about the Soviet Union? Which publishing house and publisher printed Solzhenitsyn's lampoon in the West? Is it possible to send letters of protest to the address of the publishing house?

The Moscow City and district Party committees and the Party organizations of the capital continue to explain the issues to the working people that arise in connection with the publication of Solzhenitsyn's anti-Soviet *Gulag Archipelago* in the West. Propagandists, lecturers, people who make regular reports on domestic and international events are providing answers to questions, and continue to work with the working people of Moscow to expose bourgeois propaganda.

Secretary of the Moscow City Party Committee
V. Grishin

F. 3, *op.* 80, *d.* 664, *l.* 72–75. Original.

Note

1. *A separate page has the instruction: "Brief Central Committee Secretaries" and signatures of B. Ponomarev, K. Katushev, V. Dolgikh, M. Suslov, P. Demichev, and A. Kirilenko.*

112 Report of the Committee for State Security of the USSR Council of Ministers[1]

No. 150–A
17 January 1974
Classified

To the Central Committee:
The Committee for State Security continues to receive reports on the responses of Soviet people to "The Path of Treason" published in *Pravda* on 14 January this year. The majority of responses indicate that the Soviet people condemn with wrath and contempt the anti-Soviet and slanderous Solzhenitsyn, branding him as a dedicated accomplice of reaction and the enemies of peace, democracy, and socialism, and regarding as unacceptable his provocative and defiant behavior that dishonors the title of a Soviet citizen.

The assessments of Solzhenitsyn given in the article "The Path of Treason," the renegade who collaborated for many years with foreign publishers and mass media that are hostile to the Soviet people, an advocate of landlord capitalist orders and restoration of the bourgeois system, a pathological hater of communism and socialism, an extremely immoral personality, and, as a result, all aforesaid incites true enmity toward Solzhenitsyn that is expressed in demands to take severe measures against him.

Sokolov, a metalworker at the Zhigulevsky Auto Transport Plant, said: "As a worker I think that Solzhenitsyn should have been arrested a long time ago." Kozyreva, a worker in Ryazan, said: "I would have choked this scoundrel with my own hands. You should not be too soft with our enemies." Fomkin, an operator at the Lipetsk Free Falcon Plant, said adamantly: "If it were up to me, you would find nothing left of Solzhenitsyn." Kochukov, a sculptor from Leningrad, Academicians Tselikov, Zurabashvili, and other citizens spoke of the necessity to curb the hostile activity of Solzhenitsyn.

Besides wrath and indignation, "The Path of Treason" provoked in many Soviet people a certain bewilderment because of Solzhenitsyn's impunity.[. . .]

Some Soviet people think that it would be politically disadvantageous to punish Solzhenitsyn under the code. Moreover, there are indications that domestic and foreign policies of the Party enjoy the unanimous support of all the Soviet people; it is considered that the hostile attacks of Solzhenitsyn and the like are not frightening to the mature Soviet society; references are made to the great successes of the USSR in the international arena and in the peaceful construction of communism and the healthy creative atmosphere manifested in Soviet society. Some maintain that prosecuting Solzhenitsyn would play into his hands because he hopes to provoke anti-Soviet hysteria abroad and promote himself as a martyr.[. . .]

Reshetovskaya, Solzhenitsyn's former wife, who lives in Ryazan, thinks that the article is a serious warning to Solzhenitsyn that he will soon be deported from Moscow. Kholopov, Secretary of the Board of the Leningrad Branch of the RSFSR Writers' Union and State Prize laureate, believes public opinion against Solzhenitsyn must be more actively shaped.

According to many citizens, Solzhenitsyn should be deported from the Soviet Union, and his Soviet citizenship should be revoked. This view, in particular, has been suggested by Ivannikov, an instructor in Tambov; also by Bobrov, a veterinarian in Voronezh; Grabakin, a worker at the Oryol Watch Factory; and Petrosyan, an Armenian writer.

Several hostile and antisocial individuals, who are under surveillance by the state security authorities, are justifying and defending Solzhenitsyn, and attempt to promote him as a fighter for justice and freedom; they disseminate fabrications about the likelihood of him being forcibly confined to a psychiatric hospital, or assassinated under the guise of an automobile accident, and similar provocative rumors. Sakharov, Azbel,[2] Chukovskaya, Kopelev, and some other individuals, well known for their antisocial activities, openly call for people to defend the "great writer."

Chairman of the Committee for State Security
Andropov

F. 3, *op.* 80, *d.* 664, *l.* 65–67. Original.

Notes

1. *Sent to Politburo members and candidate members, and Central Committee Secretaries, on 18 January 1974 as No. P105.*
2. Mark Azbel, a physicist and well-known Jewish "refusenik," emigrated to Israel in 1975.

113 Report of the Committee for State Security of the USSR Council of Ministers[1]

No. 157–A
18 January 1974
Classified

The Committee for State Security has received reports that the majority of Soviet writers resolutely condemn the anti-Soviet and anticommunist activities of Solzhenitsyn, and fully support "The Path of Treason" published in *Pravda* on 14 January this year. Thus, Radunskaya, a writer, said: "I'm always very careful in regard to labels, but Solzhenitsyn is an enemy, an accomplice of anti-Soviets abroad, and he deserves the most harsh punishment. After publication of the article many who are in doubt will review their attitude toward him." Khazri, an Azerbaijani poet, commented: "By his filthy slander of the Soviet Union and the Soviet people, Solzhenitsyn abets our enemies who are awaiting a favorable opportunity to incite public opinion abroad against our state." Chapchakov, a critic in Moscow, said: "He is our mortal and most malicious enemy. He hates us so much that he is ready to sacrifice himself to raise tension in the world." Gurguliya, a poet in Abkhazia, stated: "Solzhenitsyn has gone to work for the most vehement enemies of the USSR and openly discredits our policies." Markaryan, an Armenian publicist; Rudny, a prose writer in Moscow; Kopots, a man of letters in Moldavia; Serebrovskaya, a writer in Leningrad; Tevsadze, a Georgian poet; Kupriyanov, a playwright; and others make similar remarks.

In condemning and censuring Solzhenitsyn, Soviet writers declare that he should be held to account, or be deported from the USSR. Thus, Kostin, a Volgograd poet, said: "It hurts and it's shameful that for some time this black sheep has been in our ranks. It would be disappointing if there were no place for him in jail."

Petrosyan, an Armenian writer, said: "The Soviet literary intelligentsia has many times already angrily condemned Solzhenitsyn's lampoons, but he doesn't draw any conclusions and continues his anti-Soviet activities." Katanov, a writer in Oryol, noted: "Solzhenitsyn systematically violates the law and insults the Soviet people and their historical past and present. Such people should be called to account or deported from the country." Pankin, a writer in Tula, said: "It's perplexing that this scum, who has taken a hostile path, is not brought to trial." Chaly, Secretary of the Ukrainian Writers' Union, said: "The impunity of Solzhenitsyn is adversely affecting other writers. I think that Solzhenitsyn's Soviet citizenship should be rapidly revoked, and he should be deported from the USSR."

Some writers believe Solzhenitsyn should be exposed by mobilizing public opinion against him to criticize his anti-Soviet and reactionary positions in a well-reasoned way.

Some members of the Soviet Writers' Union—Chukovskaya, Kopelev, Stolyarova, Voinovich,[2] Kornilov,[3] Orlova (Moscow), Etkind (Leningrad), Nekrasov (Kiev), Urdzhumelashvili (Tbilisi), as well as Maximov and Galich, who were earlier expelled from the Union, have spoken in support of Solzhenitsyn. These individuals justified Solzhenitsyn, asserting that he had defended the writer's right to freedom of speech and criticism.

Chairman of the Committee for State Security
Andropov

F. 3, *op.* 80, *d.* 664, *l.* 77–78. Original.

Notes

1. *Sent to Politburo members and candidate members, and Central Committee Secretaries, on 21 January 1974 as No. P109.*
2. Vladimir Voinovich, author of the wildly successful but censored novel *The Life and Extraordinary Adventures of Private Ivan Chonkin* (Farrar, Straus & Giroux, 1977), had protested Solzhenitsyn's expulsion from the Writers' Union and was about to be expelled himself. He was forced into emigration in 1980.
3. Vladimir Kornilov, a novelist and poet, was a friend of Voinovich and a supporter of Solzhenitsyn.

114 Report of the Committee for State Security of the USSR Council of Ministers[1]

No. 174–A
19 January 1974
Special File
Classified

To the Central Committee:
On 18 January of this year Solzhenitsyn met Crepeau, an American correspondent, in his home and gave him the following provocative statement (a copy is attached) for dissemination in the West.

Solzhenitsyn's behavior of late, particularly since Soviet propaganda authorities began exposing his anti-Soviet activities, is becoming immoderate, and is characterized by obvious hostility. Solzhenitsyn is continuously encouraging the West to raise an anti-Soviet hullabaloo around his name, thinking that it will provide him with a guarantee of his security.

The Committee for State Security continues its surveillance of Solzhenitsyn.

Chairman of the Committee for State Security
Andropov

Enclosure

Statement by Solzhenitsyn

18 January 1974

The furious press campaign conceals the main thing from the Soviet reader: What is this book about? What is this strange word "Gulag" in its title? *Pravda* lies when it says that the author "sees with the eyes of those who hanged revolutionary workers and peasants." No!—with the eyes of those who were shot and tortured to death by the NKVD. *Pravda* asserts that in our country there is "unqualified criticism" of the pre-1956 period. So let them just give us a sample of their unqualified criticism. I have provided them with the richest factual material for it.

Even today—even today—this path is not closed. And what a cleansing that would be for the country!

When I published *The Gulag Archipelago*, I still didn't realize the extent to which they would renounce their own former weak confessions. The way in which our propaganda organs choose to behave is dictated by their animal fear of exposure. It demonstrates how grimly they cling to the bloody past and shows they intend to drag it with them like an unopened bag into the future, without saying a word even of moral censure of those who did the hanging, interrogating and informing.

Typically, as soon as Deutsche Welle announced that it would broadcast excerpts from *Archipelago* for half an hour every day, they rushed to jam it so that not a single word from the book would break through into our country.

As if it could go on forever! I'm sure that the time will come when everyone will read this book in our country openly and freely. And there will be people who remember or who are curious, who will wish to know: What did the Soviet press write when the book came out? Who wrote those articles? And in the torrent of curses they will not find the names of the authors. They are all anonymous and signed by pseudonyms.

That is the reason why they tell lies so easily and about anything: Thus, as if quoting my book, they write that "the Hitlerites were indulgent and merciful toward the captive peoples," that the "battle for Stalingrad was won by penal battalions." All of this is a lie, comrade writers of *Pravda*. I ask you to quote the exact page numbers! (You will see that they will not do it.) TASS reports: "In his autobiography, Solzhenitsyn admits his hatred of the Soviet system and the Soviet people." My autobiography was published in the book of 1970 Nobel Prize laureates. It is available to the whole world. See for yourselves how shamelessly the Telegraph Agency of the Soviet Union lies. But why talk about TASS now that it shamelessly spits in the eyes of those who were exterminated, claiming that their sufferings and deaths were described in my book only for the sake of hard currency.

Once again TASS has miscalculated: The price of the book, which is published in all languages, will be extremely low so that a greater number of people will be able to read it. The price is such that it will only allow for the payment of the services of translators and publishers, the costs of the paper, etc. If there is an author's honorarium I will use it to perpetuate the memory of those who were killed and to render assistance to the families of political prisoners in the Soviet Union. I appeal to all publishers to donate their profit to the same cause.

And now about the lie that was published in *Literaturnaya Gazeta*: That in my book, "Soviet people are villains," that the essence of the Russian soul is such that "a Russian is prepared to betray his father and mother for a bread ration." Liars, show us those pages! This was written to incite my uninformed compatriots against me: "Solzhenitsyn supposedly equates Soviet people with fascist murderers." A small correction: Yes, I equated fascist murderers with the murderers of the Cheka, the GPU, and the NKVD.[2] The *Literaturnaya Gazeta* deliberately writes about "all Soviet people" so that our own hangmen would be lost among them.

But what pages will they quote? From what book? *Literaturnaya Gazeta* has been caught red-handed, looting and stripping corpses: it quotes from a copy of the book that was stolen, parts four and five of *Archipelago* which have not been published yet anywhere. Thus, the "man of letters" (the pseudonym of the author of the articles in *Literaturnaya Gazeta*) wrote his article in an office of the KGB.

The fourth part will be published, and there you will read the phrase: "I understood the falsity of all the revolutions in history" (at the end of the first chapter) and there was this assessment not of "Russian man" but of "Soviet life outside prison" (Chapter 4) in the titles of the sections: "Constant Fear," "Secrecy and Distrust," "Degradation of the Soul," and "Betrayal as a Form of Existence.". . .

And they still dare to claim that the publication of *Archipelago* has been exploited by world reaction to damage détente. The book's publication was ordered by our state security (currently it is the "world reaction"). It was predetermined by their wish to steal the manuscript of the book. If they truly wished détente, then why for five days this past August did they by fair means or foul try to obtain the manuscript of the book from a poor woman? I see the hand of God in this: It means that the time has come when, as it is said in Shakespeare's Macbeth: "Birnam wood will come."[3]

A true copy: Deputy Chief of the Department Nikashin[4]
19 January 1974

F. 3, op. 80, d. 647, l. 56–59. Original.

Notes

1. *Page one bears the signatures of M. Suslov, L. Brezhnev, N. Podgorny, A. Kirilenko, and A. Kosygin; on the back of the document is a notation: "Comment of Comrade A.P. Kirilenko: This statement by A. Solzhenitsyn has been carried by TASS."*
2. *Cheka, GPU, and NKVD were acronyms for the secret police before KGB came into use.*
3. *See The Oak and the Calf, Appendix 31. The text in the Russian edition and translated here differs slightly from that in the English edition.*
4. *Sic. Nikashkin is correct.*

115 Report of the Department of Organizational and Party Work of the Central Committee

"On the Attitudes of Soviet People to the Publication Abroad of the Slanderous Writings of A. Solzhenitsyn"

21 January 1974
Top Secret

To the Central Committee:
The Central Committees of the Communist parties of the Union republics,

territorial Party committees, and regional Party committees report that the working people are profoundly indignant over the anti-Soviet sensation incited by bourgeois propaganda over the publication abroad of Solzhenitsyn's subsequent slanderous writing under the title *The Gulag Archipelago*. They view it as a new attempt by Western reactionaries to undermine the international authority of the Soviet Government, slander the socialist system before all humankind, and halt the process of détente. In response to the filthy insinuations of hostile propaganda, workers, collective farmers, and intellectuals express their patriotic feelings and state their devotion to the cause of communism as well as their full solidarity with the Communist Party and total support for its domestic and foreign policies.

The Soviet people have carefully studied "The Path of Treason" published in *Pravda*. They read with interest the article published in the *Literaturnaya Gazeta* on this issue, as well as the statements of political commentator Y. Zhukov and writer A. Chakovsky broadcast by the Central TV. They were very timely and affected public opinion positively. Their political activism and hard-hitting style are noted throughout. By general acknowledgment these commentaries really show Solzhenitsyn's true face, convincingly exposing the hostile, anti-Soviet nature of his malicious writings and provide a worthy rebuttal to the views he preaches. The working people fully share the conclusions about Solzhenitsyn's so-called creativity. Our people express their satisfaction that A. Solzhenitsyn's latest lampoon has been sharply criticized, as a matter of principle in the communist press abroad.

The *Pravda* article calls a spade a spade. We have been waiting for a review for a long time. The behavior of this so-called "writer" can only be characterized as treachery. Treachery always evokes simultaneous feelings of indignation and disgust. "How could we not condemn him if he slandered the Soviet Union in his books. And this is happening just as our Party has firmly embarked on the course of détente," said Comrade Lobarev in a discussion, a steel founder at Nizhny Tagil Iron and Steel Complex in the Sverdlovsk region.

Comrade Panfilov, a worker at the Norilsk Bear Brook Mine in the Krasnoyarsk Territory, a Hero of Socialist Labor, said:

> The enemies of our country go out of their way to belittle the successes of our Party's and government's foreign policy and denigrate socialism. In this filthy business they find the support of such despicable scum as Solzhenitsyn. I support *Pravda*'s conclusion that he deserves the fate of a traitor with all the ensuing consequences.

Solzhenitsyn's anti-Soviet concoctions invoke anger and indignation in the people. Representatives of all strata of the population brand him with shame and contempt as a lowdown traitor and malicious slanderer of our state and social system. Numerous statements emphasize that there is nothing sacred for this political renegade, blinded with hatred, who unscrupulously capitalizes on the motherland. Our people are most disgusted by Solzhenitsyn's attempt to whitewash the Hitlerite invaders and the accomplices of Vlasov in his new lampoon. Thus he defiles the memory of millions of Soviet people who became the victims of their bloody acts in the Soviet Union during World War II.

Comrade Kulakovsky, a Byelorussian writer, said:

> Not long ago I attended meetings of the UN Assembly in the US, and listened to different speeches. Some of them were quite frenzied, profascist, and anti-Soviet. However, I didn't hear even from the representatives of the extreme right imperialist circles such vile slander as Solzhenitsyn hurls at our Soviet people and our great motherland.

Comrade Koyushev, Party member since 1918, a recipient of a special pension in Komi ASSR, stated:

> Solzhenitsyn attempts to present the abuses of the time of the cult of personality as a norm of Soviet life. But that is sheer slander. I was persecuted despite my innocence in 1937 and was imprisoned for seventeen years. But all that time I never lost faith in the Party. When I was rehabilitated, I was immediately given a comfortable apartment and a special pension; I enjoyed all the rights of a Soviet citizen. Four times I was elected to Party executive offices. Solzhenitsyn attempts to claim that you cannot write and speak the truth in the USSR. It's a lie! I wrote many articles on the mistakes made during the years of the cult of personality and on the persecution of innocent people so as to restore their good names. And all the articles were published without any corrections.

All the letters note that throughout the years Solzhenitsyn's anti-Soviet activity has been consistent, and is deliberate and frankly hostile. Many writers note that Solzhenitsyn is, in fact, the ideological inspiration behind certain anti-Soviet–minded individuals and a motley assortment of political renegades. As a result, many express surprise that no measures have been taken against him under our law. Some statements stress that the impunity of A. Solzhenitsyn may cause negative consequences and negatively affect politically unstable people.

Comrade Kurmanaev, a metalworker at the Salavat Petrochemical Complex, said:

> We heard earlier of Solzhenitsyn's indecent behavior. We have learned recently from our press that this wretched traitor is again slandering his people and his country. Our indignation knows no bounds and we don't understand why he has not yet been isolated. He should be removed from our bright road as scum.

Comrade Kulikov, chief land improvement specialist at the State Farm Ushaky in the Leningrad region, stated:

> All the peoples of the world, and the Soviet people all the more, always despised traitors. The fall of Solzhenitsyn is the fall of a loner who, in his hatred toward the Soviet government, has gone so far as to forget where he lives and whose interests he represents. It is unclear to me why our government, to put it mildly, has been messing so long with this trash. A society, like a human being, is healthy when it washes off its dirt.

The working people are unanimous in their opinion that by his despicable activity Solzhenitsyn has long ago placed himself outside Soviet society. The workers, collective farmers, and intelligentsia demand that his harmful activity be terminated. There are many proposals to press criminal charges and try him to the fullest extent of the law. It is also suggested that Solzhenitsyn be stripped of his Soviet citizenship and deported from the USSR.

Comrade Eideman, senior researcher at the Riga Medical Institute, a son of a distinguished Civil War military figure who perished during the period of the cult of personality, said:

> Solzhenitsyn pretends to be a truth seeker. One may think that he knows nothing of our Party's resolute condemnation of the violations of socialist law during the period of the cult of personality. Denigrating everything Soviet, he has managed to find evidence of mercy in the Nazis who are cursed and hated by progressive humankind; the Nazis who spilled rivers of blood on our land. It's monstrous! To be a citizen of the USSR is a great honor, and Solzhenitsyn has long ago become unworthy of this honor. I think his Soviet citizenship should be revoked and he should be deported from our motherland.

Comrade Levishchenko, an instructor at the Kiev State University, said:

> Solzhenitsyn is a traitor to the Soviet people, and a traitor, as it
> is well known, should be severely prosecuted. How long shall
> we tolerate this renegade in our land and feed him with our
> bread? We need once and for all to get rid of this scum, to lib-
> erate ourselves from the continuous need to expose his fraud
> and slander of our country, party, and people.

Many others express similar sentiments.

The Ukrainian Central Committee reports that some politically unstable,
nationalistic, and Zionist individuals in the republic are making negative
statements in connection with the publication of Solzhenitsyn's slanderous
writing abroad, expressing their sincere sympathy for him and support for the
views that he preaches.

The Party organizations are conducting the necessary instruction among
the population to expose imperialism's hostile schemes against our country,
to strengthen the education of the working people in the spirit of Soviet
patriotism, and to maintain high political vigilance.

I. Kapitonov

F. 3, *op.* 80, *d.* 664, *l.* 80–83. Original.

Note

1. *Sent to Politburo members and candidate members, and Central Committee Secretaries, on
   21 January 1974.*

116 Report of the Committee for State Security of the USSR Council of Ministers[1]

No. 266–A
29 January 1974
Classified

To the Central Committee:
Politically damaging leaflets appealing to people to defend Solzhenitsyn and Sakharov were distributed on 26 January 1974 in Leningrad at metro stations and in public gardens.

The leaflets were stencilled, signed "Emelya," and reproduced by a color photocopier.

Two hundred and thirty-five copies of the leaflets have been removed from the sites where they were distributed.

The Committee for State Security has undertaken urgent measures to find the authors and distributors of the leaflets.

Chairman of the Committee for State Security
Andropov

F. 3, op. 80, d. 647, l. 64. Original.

Note

1. *The document bears the signatures of M. Suslov, A. Kirilenko, and P. Demichev.*

117 Report of the Committee for State Security of the USSR Council of Ministers[1]

No. 300–A
1 February 1974
Classified

To the Central Committee:
As a supplement to our memorandum No. 174–A of 19 January 1974, we are sending a photocopy of an autobiography written by Solzhenitsyn himself and published in the anthology *Nobel Prize Winners of 1970* (the anthology was published in Stockholm in 1971).

Chairman of the Committee for State Security
Andropov

Enclosure

A. Solzhenitsyn

I was born in 1918, on December 11, in Kislovodsk. My father, a student at the philology department of Moscow University, did not finish his course of studies because he volunteered for the war of 1914. He became an artillery officer at the German front, fought through the whole war, and died in the summer of 1918, a half-year before my birth. My mother raised me. She was a typist and a stenographer in Rostov-on-Don where I lived through the years of childhood and adolescence. I finished a secondary school there in 1936. Since my childhood I have sensed an inclination for writing that no one forced upon me. I wrote a lot of the usual childish nonsense and in the 1930s, I made attempts to be published but my manuscripts were not accepted anywhere. I tried to get a literary education, but there was nothing in Rostov-on-Don that I wanted, and I couldn't go to Moscow because my mother was alone and sick, and beside that, our meager means didn't permit it. Therefore, I entered the mathematical department of Rostov University: I was quite talented in math, it came easily to me, but it wasn't my life's calling. However, it played a favorable role in my fate and at least twice saved my life: most obviously, I would not have survived the eight years of camps if, as a mathematician, I had not been taken for four years in the so-called *sharashka;* in exile I was allowed to teach math and physics, which made my life easier and gave me the opportunity to do some writing. If I had obtained a literary education, I would hardly have survived my trials as I would have been subjected to even greater restrictions. It is true that later I started that education: from 1939 to 1941 I studied, in parallel, physics and mathematics at the correspondence department of the Moscow Institute of History, Philosophy, and Literature.

I graduated from the Physics and Math Department of Rostov University a few days before the start of the war. When the war began, I became a driver in a transport unit due to my poor health and was in that capacity in the winter of 1941–1942. Only afterwards, and again because of mathematics, was I transferred to an artillery school and graduated from its abridged courses in November 1942. After that I became a commander of a reconnaissance artillery battery, and I was in that position continuously through the war in the front lines until my arrest in February 1945. It happened in Eastern Prussia which was strangely connected with my fate: back in 1937, as a first-year student at the University, I chose for a topic the "Samsonov Catastrophe" in 1914 in Eastern Prussia. I studied materials relating to it and had travelled there in 1945 my own. (Just now, in the fall of 1970, that book, *August 1914*, has been completed.)

I was arrested on the grounds of censored excerpts in my correspondence with a school friend in 1944–45, mainly because of disrespectful comments about Stalin, although we called him by a pseudonym. Drafts of stories and ideas, found in my field bag, served as additional material for the charge. However, that was not enough for the "trial," and I was "sentenced" in absentia in July 1945 in accordance with the system widely applied at that time, ie, by a decision of the Special Conference of NKVD to eight years in labor camp (it was considered at the time to be a moderate sentence).

I served the sentence first in reformatory camps of the mixed type (described in the play "Deer and Shelter of Branches"). Then, in 1946, I was summoned from there as a mathematician into the system of research institutes of the MVD–MGB, and I served the middle of my term in these "specialized jails" (*The First Circle*). In 1950, I was sent to the new "special" camps, created solely for political prisoners. I worked in such a camp in Ekibastuz in Kazakhstan (*One Day in the Life of Ivan Denisovich*) as an unskilled laborer, bricklayer, and foundry worker. A cancerous tumor developed in me which was operated on but not healed completely (its nature revealed itself only later).

A month later, after an eight-year term, an administrative order came without a new sentence and even without a "decision of the Special Conference" not to free me, but to send me "to endless exile" in Kok-Terek (Southern Kazakhstan). It was not a special measure against me; it was a very widespread method at that time. I was in exile from March 1953 (on March 5, the day when the death of Stalin was announced, I was let out beyond the walls without an escort) until June 1956. My cancer developed rapidly, and by the end of 1953, I was almost on my deathbed, without the ability to eat or sleep, and was poisoned by the toxins of the tumor. However, after being released for treatment in Tashkent, I was cured in the cancer clinic in 1954 (*Cancer Ward, The Right Hand*). During all the years in exile I taught math and physics at a village school, and, totally alone, secretly wrote prose (in the camp, by memorandumry, I could only write poetry). I managed to preserve it and brought it with me from exile to the European part of the country where I continued to work, openly with teaching, and secretly with writing, first in the Vladimir region ("Matryona's Yard"), and later in Ryazan.

All the years until 1961, I was not only *confident* that I would never in my life see in print a single line, but hardly gave any of my close acquaintances anything to read, afraid of discovery. Finally, by the age of forty-two, this secret writing began to oppress me greatly. The main trouble was the impossibility of checking my writing with experienced literary readers. In 1961, following the Twenty-Second Party Congress and Tvardovsky's speech there, I decided to let it out: to submit *One Day in the Life of Ivan Denisovich*. This revelation, as it seemed to me at that time, and it wasn't groundless, was very risky: it could have led to the ruin of all my manuscripts, and myself. But everything went well: A.T. Tvardovsky, after applying many efforts, managed to publish my story a year later. However, almost immediately the printing of my writings was stopped, my plays were also held up as well as (in 1964) the novel *The First Circle*; in 1965, it was taken away together with my archive of many years, and it seemed to me at that time to be an unforgivable mistake to reveal my work too early, and that I wouldn't be able to finish it.

Even events that have happened to us we cannot assess and recognize immediately, by their imprints, and even still more unpredictable and amazing for us is the course of future events.

F. 3, *op*. 80, *d*. 647, *l*. 66–69. Original.

Note

1. *The document bears the signature of A. Kirilenko.*

118 Memorandum of the Committee for State Security of the USSR Council of Ministers and the USSR Public Prosecutor's Office[1]

No. 348–A
6 February 1974
Classified

To the Central Committee:

As is known, bourgeois propaganda, by making use of the hostile lampoon *The Gulag Archipelago* by Solzhenitsyn, has lately incited an uproar in many European countries and the USA against the USSR and its internal and foreign policies. This wave of anti-Sovietism is marked not only by slander of the Soviet Union but also by a striving to inspire hostile outbursts in our country, as well as against its representatives abroad.

An analysis indicates that this campaign is quite well coordinated and directed from one center. Having gained a certain propaganda advantage after the publication of the first two parts of *The Gulag Archipelago* (five more parts have not been printed yet), our enemies have noticeably cut back their statements citing this work in recent days. To a certain extent this has been due to our response and the rebuff that Solzhenitsyn has been given by the Soviet public. Not the least role in this respect has been played by apprehension on the part of our enemies' special agencies over the fate of Solzhenitsyn himself. The West is clearly attempting to prevent further aggravation of the situation in order not to incite for the time being any further actions against Solzhenitsyn.

This tactic may create for us a false atmosphere of calm in implementing measures planned in regard to Solzhenitsyn. It may, in particular, diminish the activism of those who express the need to deport Solzhenitsyn from the Soviet Union to the West.

In view of this, it would be advisable to summon Solzhenitsyn to the office of Comrade M.P. Malyarov, Deputy Prosecutor General of the USSR, to inform him that as a result of his anti-Soviet activities, the USSR Public Prosecutor deems it necessary to examine the materials pertaining to this matter. A signed statement should be taken from Solzhenitsyn requiring him to inform the Public Prosecutor of any changes in his place of residence.

It is obvious that following the summons, Solzhenitsyn will himself give one of his regular interviews to foreign correspondents, which will be used in the West for an anti-Soviet campaign. But if he doesn't do it, the KGB has the means to forward a statement on this issue to the Western press, keeping the above goal in mind.

Please review.

Andropov
Rudenko

F. 3, op. 80, d. 647, l. 70–71. Original.

Note

1. *Page one of the document bears the resolution: "Urgent. We must come to an agreement. M. Suslov," and the signatures of A. Kirilenko, N. Podgorny, and A. Kosygin. The last page has the following remark: "Comrade K.U. Chernenko informed of the agreement of Comrade Y.V. Andropov. 2.7.74. N. Novikov."*

119 Memorandum of the Committee for State Security of the USSR Council of Ministers

No. 350–A/OV
7 February 1974
Very important
Special File

To the Central Committee:
On February 2, W. Brandt, Chancellor of West Germany, speaking in Munich at the ceremony of the annual awarding of Theodor Heuss Prizes,

stated that Solzhenitsyn could freely and without restriction reside and work in the FRG because many in the West couldn't imagine the hardships the world renowned writer allegedly encountered in his country. In a demagogic manner, Brandt stressed the right of an intellectual to free expression of his ideas.[1]

This statement by Brandt provides the basis to deport Solzhenitsyn to the FRG, having first adopted the relevant Decree of the Presidium of the USSR Supreme Soviet on depriving him of Soviet citizenship (the draft Decree is enclosed). This decision would be lawful in light of the materials we possess pertaining to Solzhenitsyn's criminal activities.

To coordinate practical steps in this direction, it seems advisable to establish contact through unofficial channels with representatives of the governmental circles of the FRG. Concrete proposals on procedures for transferring Solzhenitsyn to West Germany will be offered at a later date.

The present proposals have been coordinated with the Public Prosecutor's office (Comrade R. A. Rudenko).

Please examine.

Chairman of the Committee for State Security
Andropov

Enclosure
Draft
(Not for publication in the press)

Decree of the Presidium of the Supreme Soviet of the USSR On Depriving A.I. Solzhenitsyn of Soviet Citizenship and Deporting Him from the USSR

Taking into consideration the fact that Solzhenitsyn systematically carries out actions that are incompatible with the possession of USSR citizenship and inflicts damage on the USSR by his hostile behavior,

The Presidium of the Supreme Soviet of the USSR *decrees*:

On the basis of Article 7 of the USSR Law of August 19, 1938 "On Citizenship of the Union of Soviet Socialist Republics," for actions defaming the title of citizen of the USSR, to deprive Solzhenitsyn, Alexander Isaevich, born 1918 in Kislovodsk, of USSR citizenship, and to deport him from the USSR.

Chairman of the Presidium of the Supreme Soviet of the USSR
Secretary of the Presidium of the Supreme Soviet of the USSR

Moscow, The Kremlin
1974

Package No. 367. Original.

Note

1. *In his speech W. Brandt said: "We, let there be no doubt about it, stand for free expression of ideas and for the freedom of a writer to speak by any means available to him. Solzhenitsyn could live and work without any obstacles here, in the FRG. Stating this doesn't mean, naturally, to interfere. Everybody knows that we have good relations with the USSR. Differences in what we call ideologies and systems continue to exist. Many in the West cannot understand the hardships that a world renowned writer encounters in his country. I'm afraid that certain authorities there don't understand how good it would have been for their international authority if they had reacted in a milder way to a description of state power without cosmetics." (Telegram from Bonn, February 5, 1974)*

120 Letter from Y. Andropov to L. Brezhnev

7 February 1974
Top Secret
Special File

Leonid Ilyich!
I'm sending you a report prepared by Comrades V.M. Chebrikov and F.D. Bobkov, who are dealing directly with the Solzhenitsyn problem. It follows from this report that this problem has currently gone beyond the framework

of a criminal issue, and has been transformed into a problem of no small importance, having certain political characteristics. It follows also from the information that the majority of Soviet people correctly assess the criticism of Solzhenitsyn. And it is just on this point that increasingly often and in a pointed manner the question is asked: "Why don't the authorities take measures against Solzhenitsyn who, following the criticism of his views, did not lay down his arms but continues to speak out against Soviet power in a still more brazen manner."

I'm particularly worried that this question is asked increasingly often by the military and by some workers in the Party apparatus.

On the other hand, the fact should be considered that the book by Solzhenitsyn, despite our measures to expose its anti-Soviet character, in one way or another evokes a certain sympathy in some representatives of the creative intelligentsia. Thus, for example, certain well-known writers, while condemning the anti-Soviet character of *The Gulag Archipelago*, say that the facts described in the book actually took place and that this work should serve as a warning to a Soviet leadership that is alleged to be conducting a process of "re-Stalinization." Some perceive the "usefulness" of Solzhenitsyn's book to lie in the fact that it "will inevitably attract the attention of the Central Committee to the intelligentsia, primarily to the creative intelligentsia."

Certain individual workers and students have been heard to say that Solzhenitsyn calls on the Soviet leadership to lower the prices for consumer goods, to terminate aid to Cuba and the developing countries in the interests of raising the standard of living of the Soviet people. These ideas are not found in *The Gulag Archipelago*, but, as you remember, they were in Solzhenitsyn's notorious "Letter to the Soviet Leaders." According to our information, Solzhenitsyn, having rejected the idea of publishing this document in the near future, is nevertheless making its contents public with the aid of those around him.

In view of all this, Leonid Ilyich, I think it impossible, despite our desire not to harm our international relations, to delay the solution of the Solzhenitsyn problem any longer, because it could have extremely unpleasant consequences for us inside the country.

As I reported to you on the phone, Brandt made a statement that Solzhenitsyn could freely live and work in the FRG. Today, February 7, Comrade Kevorkov is flying out to meet with Bahr[1] to discuss the practical side of deporting Solzhenitsyn from the Soviet Union to the FRG. If Brandt does not pull back at the last moment, and the negotiations of Kevorkov are successful, then by February 9–10 we could have a coordinated decision, and I would immediately inform you about it. If the stated agreement takes place, it seems to me that not later than February 9 or 10 it would be necessary to adopt a Decree of the USSR Supreme Soviet on depriving Solzhenitsyn of

Soviet citizenship and deporting him from the motherland (the draft decree is enclosed).[2] The operation itself of deporting Solzhenitsyn could be carried out on February 10 or 11.

It should all be done expeditiously because, as is clear from surveillance documents, Solzhenitsyn is beginning to guess at our intentions and may make a public statement that would put us and Brandt in a difficult situation.

If for some reason the measure to deport Solzhenitsyn fails, I think it would be necessary to institute criminal proceedings against him (arrest him) not later than February 15. The Public Prosecutor's Office is ready to do so.

Dear Leonid Ilyich, before sending this letter, we at the Committee once again thoroughly examined all the possible damage we might incur if Solzhenitsyn were deported (less damage) or arrested (greater damage). Either way there will be losses. But unfortunately there is no other way out, since Solzhenitsyn's impunity is causing us more damage within the country than would be caused internationally if he were deported or arrested.

Respectfully,

Y. Andropov

Enclosure
6 February 1974

Committee for State Security of the USSR Council of Ministers:
Surveillance reports continue to be received on the reaction of the population to Solzhenitsyn's anti-Soviet activities. Analysis of the information shows that the majority of the Soviet people are politically correct in their evaluation of Solzhenitsyn and are indignant over his slanderous statements and hostile acts against the Soviet system. This segment of the population has no doubt that Solzhenitsyn should be held criminally liable for his actions. If this question is raised at all, it is only in terms of what should be done with him and how long he should be permitted to test the patience of the Soviet government.

Many express outright criticism of the authorities for not taking measures against this vehement anti-Soviet. Discussions of this topic have taken place among different strata of the population, including the army.

At the same time, numerous facts indicate that the publication of Solzhenitsyn's writings in the West brings him support and sympathy from certain elements of the creative and scientific technical intelligentsia, particularly in so-called neoliterary circles. Statements have been made that no matter how harsh Solzhenitsyn's slanderous writings may be, there is a good deal of truth in them, which should force the authorities to recognize the need to improve their work with the intelligentsia. Despite the fact that Solzhenitsyn has shocked some anti-Soviet minded individuals by his unrestrained slanders and frank hostility, they continue to see in him a person whom they would wish to emulate. Certain people are motivated by a desire to receive royalty earnings in foreign currency, others would like to revive so-called "samizdat" activity.

Many anti-Soviet elements are carefully watching the fate of Solzhenitsyn, evaluating our attitude toward him through the prism of their anti-Soviet activities. One close acquaintance of Solzhenitsyn, Professor Etkind, a resident of Leningrad, has said openly: "If Solzhenitsyn is deported, we will have to start packing to leave for Israel, because the situation will change, and we will no longer be tolerated here."

Solzhenitsyn's hostile influence and his incitement of antisocial manifestations are expressed in different ways. In some cases he gives direct instructions on what statements should be made to the bourgeois press. Thus, for example, he called on Sakharov to prepare a document on the existence of allegedly hidden unemployment in our country. He gave corresponding advice to other individuals making slanderous statements (Barabanov, Chukovskaya, Borisov, and others). Solzhenitsyn's ideas have been used in other cases as well. In particular, materials were prepared under the influence of Solzhenitsyn for such illegally disseminated journals as the *Chronicle of Current Events,* *"Veche,"* and others. Antisocial elements gravitate to him in search of advice.

A number of incidents have been observed during recent months that have been directly caused by Solzhenitsyn's activity. In Moscow and Leningrad, in particular, leaflets were disseminated appealing for his defense and containing anti-Soviet statements. On a wider scale, the influence of Solzhenitsyn and his publications has led to the spread of unhealthy attitudes. Workers have been heard to say that he was against any lowering of prices, against exporting goods needed by the people to Arab states in the form of aid, and so on. These rumors indicate that Solzhenitsyn is gradually disseminating what he wrote in his so-called letter "Letter to the Soviet Leaders."

In this way, Solzhenitsyn and his books have become significant factors in uniting unbridled anti-Soviets with all kinds of malcontents, drawing in even politically uneducated individuals. The resulting number of people is quite large.

All these circumstances have been carefully examined by the state security authorities in Moscow and the provinces. Measures have been taken to prevent hostile statements and to localize the harmful consequences of Solzhenitsyn's activity, as well as negative manifestations provoked by his anti-Soviet writings.

By failing to resolve the issue of Solzhenitsyn's criminal liability, it seems we are creating an unfavorable situation for ourselves, encouraging unhealthy attitudes and, ultimately, allowing the formation of conditions that will allow hostile elements to become more active.

Chebrikov
Bobkov

Package No. 367. Original

Notes

1. Egon Bahr was Minister without Portfolio and Chancellor Willy Brandt's most trusted aid.
2. *The draft Decree of USSR Supreme Soviet was not enclosed.*

121 Memorandum of the Committee for State Security of the USSR Council of Ministers[1]

No. 388–A
9 February 1974
Top Secret
Special Folder

To the Central Committee:
I am submitting a report, prepared by Comrades V.M. Chebrikov and F.D. Bobkov, who are dealing directly with the issue of Solzhenitsyn. It follows from their report that this issue has now gone beyond the framework of a criminal case and has been transformed into a major problem that has taken on a definite political character. As can be seen from the report, the

overwhelming majority of Soviet people have correctly understood our criticism of Solzhenitsyn. But they are increasingly and more urgently posing the question: "Why don't the authorities take measures against Solzhenitsyn, who instead of laying his weapons aside as his views are criticized, now speaks out against the Soviet government in an even more brazen manner."

It is particularly worrisome that this question is being asked more and more frequently among the military and among workers in the Party apparatus. On the other hand, it should be noted that despite our measures to expose its anti-Soviet nature, Solzhenitsyn's book in one way or another is envoking a measure of sympathy in representatives of the creative intelligentsia. Thus, for example, some prominent writers, while condemning the anti-Soviet nature of *The Gulag Archipelago*, say that the facts described in this book actually took place and that the book should warn the Soviet leadership against its alleged attempt to introduce "re-Stalinization." Some see the "usefulness" of Solzhenitsyn's book in the fact that it "will inevitably draw the attention of the Central Committee to the intelligentsia, and primarily to the creative intelligentsia."

We have recorded the statements of individual workers and students about Solzhenitsyn's appeals to the Soviet leadership to lower the prices of consumer goods, to terminate assistance to Cuba and the developing countries in the interest of improving the Soviet people's standard of living. These ideas are not found in *The Gulag Archipelago* but, as is known, they were expressed in Solzhenitsyn's notorious "Letter to the Soviet Leaders." According to our information, although Solzhenitsyn has renounced his idea of publishing this document in the near future, he is nevertheless making its contents public through those around him.

Proceeding from the aforesaid, it is impossible to delay the issue of Solzhenitsyn any longer, for, despite our desire not to damage international relations, any further hesitation may cause undesirable consequences inside the country.

As is known, on February 2 Brandt made a statement that Solzhenitsyn "could live and work freely in West Germany." On 8 February our representative had a meeting with an official authorized by Brandt to discuss the practical issues related to deporting Solzhenitsyn from the Soviet Union to West Germany.

As a result of those discussions, the following solution was adopted at the suggestion of the West German representative. On 12 February, in the evening, the Soviet Ambassador to Bonn, Comrade Falin, will contact Under-secretary P. Frank (it has to be him) with a request to receive him on an urgent matter at 8:30 AM on 13 February.

On 13 February at 8:30 AM, Comrade Falin will be received by Frank, to whom he will make a statement in regard to the deportation of Solzhenitsyn.

(The text of the statement will be submitted separately in collaboration with the Ministry of Foreign Affairs.) The cabinet will begin its meeting at 10:00 AM. Brandt will instruct Bahr, Frank, and an official of the Ministry of Internal Affairs to adopt a positive decision. At the request of the West German authorities, the plane, carrying Solzhenitsyn should be a scheduled flight, arriving in Frankfurt by 5:00 PM local time on 13 February.

From the moment Solzhenitsyn leaves the plane, Soviet representatives will take no further part in the action.

In the interests of conforming strictly with the formalities of the law, it would be desirable for the USSR Public Prosecutor's Office to file criminal charges against Solzhenitsyn on 11 February (this has been coordinated with Comrade R. A. Rudenko). Then, on 12 February, a Decree of the Presidium of the USSR Supreme Soviet should be adopted on revoking Solzhenitsyn's Soviet citizenship and deporting him from the USSR (the text of the Decree and a statement to the press are enclosed).

On the same day, Solzhenitsyn will be arrested and delivered to the remand prison where the prosecutor will inform him that criminal charges are being brought against him for his anti-Soviet activities.

It is proposed that Solzhenitsyn not be allowed to go home, and that on 13 February he be informed of the Decree of the Presidium of the Supreme Soviet, which will be followed a few hours later by his deportation.

It is important to do this speedily because, as surveillance reports show, Solzhenitsyn may guess our intentions and issue a public statement that would place us, as well as Brandt, in an embarrassing situation. If at the last moment Brandt, despite his assurances, for one reason or the other, changes his decision, Solzhenitsyn will remain under arrest and the Public Prosecutor's Office will conduct an investigation of his case.

In submitting this proposal, the Committee for State Security once again has examined most thoroughly all the potential damage that could be incurred as a result of Solzhenitsyn's deportation. There certainly will be losses. But there is no other way out, because Solzhenitsyn's impunity is already causing far greater damage inside the country than would be caused internationally by his deportion.

Please review.

Chairman of the Committee for State Security
Andropov

Package No. 367. Original.

Note

1. *Page one has the following signatures: aye —M. Suslov, aye —N. Podgorny, aye—A. Kosygin, aye—A. Kirilenko, aye—D. Polyansky, aye —A. Shelepin, aye—A. Pelshe, aye— A. Gromyko, aye—V. Grishin, aye—K. Mazurov.*

122 Memorandum of the Committee for State Security of the USSR Council of Ministers and the USSR Ministry of Foreign Affairs[1]

No. 389–A
9 February 1974
Top Secret
Special File

To the Central Committee:
In connection with the resolution of the question of Solzhenitsyn's deportation to West Germany, we submit for review the draft instructions for the Soviet Ambassador in Bonn[2].

Y. Andropov
A. Gromyko

Package No. 367. Original.

Note

1. *The document has the following signatures and votes: aye – M. Suslov, aye—N. Podgorny, aye—A. Kosygin, aye—A. Kirilenko, aye—D. Polyansky, A. Shelepin, aye—A. Pelshe, aye—V. Grishin, aye—K. Mazurov.*

123 Politburo Resolution

"Report of the Committee for State Security of the USSR Council of Ministers 9 February 1974, No. 388–A"

No. P125/112
11 February 1974
Top Secret
Special File

1. Agree with the proposals of Comrade Andropov set out in his report of 9 February 1974, No. 388–A.
2. Approve the draft Decree of the Presidium of the USSR Supreme Soviet in regard to this issue (enclosed).
3. Confirm the text of the statement by TASS (enclosed).

Central Committee Secretary

Enclosure 1
Re: item 112 in transcript No. 125
Top Secret
Draft
(Not to be published in the press)

Decree of the Presidium of the USSR Supreme Soviet On the Revocation of A.I. Solzhenitsyn's USSR Citizenship and Deportation from the USSR

Considering that Solzhenitsyn systematically performs actions that are incompatible with USSR citizenship and is causing damage to the USSR by his hostile behavior, the Presidium of the USSR Supreme Soviet has decreed:

On the basis of Article 7 of the USSR Law of 19 August 1938 "On Citizenship of the Union of Soviet Socialist Republics," for actions dishonoring the title of citizen of the USSR to revoke the USSR citizenship of

Alexander Isaevich Solzhenitsyn, born 1918 in Kislovodsk, and to deport him from the USSR.

Chairman of the Presidium of the Supreme Soviet of the USSR
N. Podgorny

Secretary of the Presidium of the Supreme Soviet of the USSR
M. Georgadze

Moscow, The Kremlin

Enclosure 2
Re: par 112 in minutes No. 125
Classified
(Not classified after publication)

TASS Statement[1]
By Decree of the Presidium of the USSR Supreme Soviet, A.I. Solzhenitsyn has been deprived of his citizenship of the USSR for systematic actions incompatible with citizenship of the USSR and damaging the Union of Soviet Socialist Republics, and on . . . February 1974 he was deported from the Soviet Union.
   Solzhenitsyn's family may follow him as soon as they deem it necessary.

Package No. 367. Excerpt from transcript.

Note

1. Published in Pravda on 14 February 1974.

124 Politburo Resolution

"On Instructions to the Soviet Ambassador to Bonn"

No. P125/113
11 February 1974
Top Secret
Special File

Approve the text of instructions to the Soviet Ambassador in Bonn (enclosed).

Central Committee Secretary

Enclosure
Re: Item 113 in transcript No. 125
Top Secret
Special File

Bonn
Soviet Ambassador:
In connection with the adoption of a resolution to revoke Solzhenitsyn's Soviet citizenship and deport him from the USSR, and in accordance with an agreement with the West German government reached through unofficial channels, on the evening of 12 February you should telephone Undersecretary P. Frank and, with reference to some urgent and important information you are expecting to receive from Moscow, should ask for an audience with him at 8:30 AM on 13 February. You may say that you are still not aware of the nature of the matter.

When meeting with Frank on 13 February, inform him of the following:

> The USSR Public Prosecutor's Office has instituted criminal proceedings against Solzhenitsyn and he is criminally liable under Soviet law for anti-Soviet activities. However, proceeding from humane considerations, and on the basis of the state-

ment of Chancellor Brandt on 2 February to the effect that Solzhenitsyn could freely live and work in West Germany, and in consideration of the relevant provisions in the West German Constitution, the Soviet authorities have decided to deport Solzhenitsyn to the Federal Republic of Germany on 13 February this year on a scheduled Aeroflot flight.

Then, as if adding this on your own, mention that in light of improving relations between West Germany and the Soviet Union, we trust that the circumstances associated with the deportation of Solzhenitsyn will not be made public prematurely, and will not be used for propaganda purposes.

In conclusion state that we hope for a favorable attitude toward this question from the Minister personally and from Chancellor Brandt.

Report back on your implementation.[1]

Package No. 367. Excerpt from transcript.

Note

1. The Soviet Ambassador to Bonn, Valentin Falin, met with Paul Frank on the morning of February 14 and informed him that Solzhenitsyn would arrive on a scheduled Soviet flight to Frankfurt that same evening. Solzhenitsyn was escorted in a separate cabin (presumably first class) by KGB agents and was met in Frankfurt by, among others, Heinrich Böll, who took him to his country cottage in Langenbroich to stay for the night. Despite protesting against his enforced expulsion, Solzhenitsyn seemed relieved to be free, and a day or so later travelled by train to Zurich accompanied by his Swiss lawyer, Dr. Heeb. Soon afterward he rented a house in the city center, and was eventually joined by his wife and children at the end of March (see Document 139).

125 Decree of the Presidium of the USSR Supreme Soviet

"On the Revocation of A.I. Solzhenitsyn's Soviet Citizenship and His Deportation from the USSR"

No. 5494–III
12 February 1974
(Not for publication)

Considering that Solzhenitsyn systematically performs actions that are incompatible with USSR citizenship and is causing damage to the USSR with his hostile behavior, the Presidium of the USSR Supreme Soviet has decreed:

On the basis of Article 7 of the USSR Law of 19 August 1938 "On Citizenship of Union of Soviet Socialist Republics," for actions dishonoring the title of citizen of the USSR to revoke the USSR citizenship of Alexander Isaevich Solzhenitsyn, born 1918 in Kislovodsk, and to deport him from the USSR.

Chairman of the Presidium of the USSR Supreme Soviet
N. Podgorny

Secretary of the Presidium of the USSR Supreme Soviet
M. Georgadze

Moscow, The Kremlin

Package No. 367. Copy.

126 From Minutes of a Meeting of the Politburo of the Central Committee

14 February 1974

Chairman: Comrade M.A. Suslov
Present: Comrades Y.V. Andropov, A.A. Gromyko, A.P. Kirilenko, A.N. Kosygin, A.Y. Pelshe, A.N. Shelepin, P.N. Demichev, B.N. Ponomarev, M.S. Solomentsev, V.I. Dolgikh, and I.V. Kapitonov

On informing socialist countries of the measures taken against Solzhenitsyn.

Andropov: Considering that all this is already known in the socialist countries, and that we have provided the relevant information via our representatives in the socialist countries, I think it is unnecessary to prepare and send this information.

Suslov: Supports proposal of Comrade Andropov.

From minutes of Politiburo sessions in 1974. Original.

127 Politburo Resolution

"On Informing Our Friends Concerning the Actions Against Solzhenitsyn"

No. P125/7—To be minuted
14 February 1974
Top Secret

To consider it advisable to inform friends on this matter.
The Secretariat of the Central Committee to examine and approve the text of the relevant information.

Central Committee Secretary

F. 3, *op.* 80, *d.* 647, *l.* 78. Excerpt from transcript.

128 Decree of the Central Committee Secretariat

"On Informing Leaders of Fraternal Communist and Workers' Parties on the Solzhenitsyn Matter"

No. St–114/51gs
14 February 1974
Top Secret

To approve the enclosed text of instructions to Soviet Ambassadors in regard to this issue (see enclosed list).

Central Committee Secretary

Enclosure 1
Re: par 51gs, transcript No. 114
Classified

To The Soviet Ambassador:
Visit Comrade Muri (further according to the list) or anyone deputizing for him and convey to him the following:

We have already informed you of Solzhenitsyn's anti-Soviet activities, which have fully revealed a platform that is hostile to the interests of socialism and the whole revolutionary movement, and also his political image as a person speaking from the position of reactionary and aggressive forces. The relevant materials have been widely published in the Soviet and foreign press, including the press of fraternal parties.

For many years Solzhenitsyn, despairing to find any force within the Soviet society that would be prepared to support his platform, has been in regular contact with foreign publishers and the mass media, including the media of White emigrés hostile to the Soviet people. He has taken the route of direct cooperation with foreign centers which openly intend to destroy real socialism and the entire communist movement, with organizations that are overt branches of the imperialist intelligence.

With these organizations' help, Solzhenitsyn published abroad a number of writings against the Soviet people, writings that slandered Lenin and the October Revolution, and mocked the heroes of World War II. Furthermore, he has directly addressed foreign imperialist forces with an appeal to exert pressure on the USSR and to interfere in its internal affairs. He has not refrained from approving all forms of struggle against socialism, and has openly advocated following the example of traitors, accomplices of Vlasov, who fought against our country and against the antifascist resistance in other countries in alliance with the Hitlerite forces.

In other words, Solzhenitsyn has long ago overstepped the bounds of differences with Soviet society and has taken the route of violating the Soviet Constitution and Soviet laws—the road of treachery. We cannot help but note that the anti-Soviet propaganda campaign launched in the West over Solzhenitsyn's latest libelous squibs has been thoroughly coordinated with the major Western mass media in a number of capitalist countries, providing him with unprecedented public attention. This cannot be considered as mere chance. In reality we are speaking of a wide scale political and propaganda action within the framework of the imperialist strategy of resisting the improvement of the détente process and reverting to the methods of the Cold War. The champions of this strategy are the most reactionary circles, including those who fear that the normalization of relations between countries with different social systems and the dissemination of the truth about Soviet reality, will increase the attraction of socialism.

An important goal of the anticommunist campaign initiated in connection with Solzhenitsyn is to camouflage the monstrous oppression of the workers and peoples by reactionary forces occurring daily in the capitalist world. The imperialists support a person whose activities they themselves have controlled and actively utilized for their perfidious ends.

Solzhenitsyn attempts to present himself as a writer who has suffered because of his beliefs and his literary works. However, he is not being accused for his literary works, though they are of a clearly antisocialist nature. Rather, he is guilty of regularly committing actions that damage the state interests of the Soviet Union.

As far as violations of socialist legality in the past are concerned, Solzhenitsyn's position is absolutely false. At its congresses and in resolutions at its plenary sessions, the Party itself roundly condemned past violations of socialist legality. In its practical activity, the Party and the Soviet state have totally eliminated the possibility of a recurrence of these phenomena. Our program is one of consistently strengthening socialist legality and unswervingly developing socialist democracy. This is our firm and constant line, and we will not retreat one step from it.

The Soviet public has repeatedly warned Solzhenitsyn of the impermissibility of his behavior, which beswitches the title of a Soviet citizen, and has demanded that he renounces his struggle against the socialist system. The Public Prosecutor's Office, in carrying out its functions, established by law, has repeatedly indicated to Solzhenitsyn that his activity is incompatible with Soviet law and the duties of a citizen of the USSR. However, Solzhenitsyn did not heed these warnings; on the contrary, he continued to intensify his activities in opposition to the socialist system, the Soviet state, and the Soviet people.

Under Soviet laws, activity that damages state interests, and the crossing over to the side of the enemy, and the abetting of reactionary imperialist forces in their hostile activity against the USSR, are crimes against the state—high treason—and may be punished most severely.

However, the highest government body, the Supreme Soviet of the USSR, has been able to restrict itself in regard to Solzhenitsyn to revoking his Soviet citizenship and deporting him from the Soviet Union.

As far as Solzhenitsyn's family is concerned, they may follow him at any time.

The time chosen by Solzhenitsyn, and the bourgeois propaganda apparatus he serves, to intensify anti-Soviet hysteria is illustrative. The indestructible solidity of the Soviet system and the unprecedently high authority of Soviet foreign policy drive our adversaries mad and force them to resort to the most vile methods of provocation in their search for any means to discredit our country and its foreign policy line. At the same time, they can bring hesitation and discord into the ranks of democratic parties and movements by exploiting "human rights." The measures taken by the Soviet state will be a blow to all these calculations.

It is characteristic that more sober-minded bourgeois circles already understand the weakness of reactionary propaganda. Many representatives of these circles stress that the minimal possible measures have been taken against Solzhenitsyn, and that any state would apply sanctions against an individual who has twice refused to appear at the Public Prosecutor's Office, or against a person who states directly that he does not recognize the force of the Soviet or a trial of his person. They admit that Solzhenitsyn's activity is against the State and cannot remain unpunished.

We are convinced that the fraternal parties will understand our position correctly, and will actively support the measures we have adopted against Solzhenitsyn, who is serving as a direct tool of anticommunism and anti-Sovietism.

It is self-evident that our Party and Soviet state will not succumb to any provocations, and will firmly and consistently conduct its policy, a policy to ensure the utmost consolidation of the socialist system and the construction of communism, a policy of peace and détente. By cleansing itself of traitors, the people's power is only consolidating its positions, consolidating the basis for the development of true socialist democracy, and furthering the construction of a new society.

Cable on implementation.

Enclosure 2
Re: par 51gs, transcripts No. 114

List of Parties to which Information is to Be Sent on the Solzhenitsyn Matter

1. Communist Party of Austria
2. Socialist Vanguard Party of Algeria
3. Communist Party of Argentina
4. Communist Party of Belgium
5. Socialist Unity Party of West Berlin
6. Communist Party of Bolivia
7. Brazilian Communist Party
8. Communist Party of Great Britain
9. Communist Party of Venezuela
10. Communist Party of Germany
11. Communist Party of Denmark
12. Communist Party of India
13. Jordanian Communist Party
14. Iraqi Communist Party
15. Communist Party of Ireland
16. Communist Party of Spain
17. Italian Communist Party
18. Communist Party of Canada
19. Progressive Party of the Working People of Cyprus
20. Communist Party of Colombia
21. Lebanese Communist Party
22. Communist Party of Luxembourg
23. Martinique Communist Party
24. Party of Liberation and Socialism of Morocco
25. Communist Party of Mexico
26. Socialist Party of Nicaragua
27. Socialist Unity Party of New Zealand
28. Communist Party of Norway
29. People's Party of Panama

30. Peruvian Communist Party
31. Portuguese Communist Party
32. Puerto-Rican Communist Party
33. Reunion Communist Party
34. Communist Party of Salvador
35. San Marino Communist Party
36. Syrian Communist Party
37. Communist Party of the USA
38. Tunisian Communist Party
39. Communist Party of Uruguay
40. Finnish Communist Party
41. French Communist Party
42. Communist Party of Chile
43. Swiss Party of Labor
44. Left Party–Communist of Sweden
45. Communist Party of Ecuador
46. Socialist Party of Australia

F. 3, *op.* 80, *d.* 647, *l.* 79–85. Excerpt from transcript.

129 Telegram from the USSR Embassy in Sweden

Spec. No. 129
14 February 1974
From Stockholm
Classified
Copy No. 19[1]

EXPRESS
THE REVOKING OF SOLZHENITSYN'S SOVIET CITIZENSHIP AND HIS DEPORTATION FROM THE USSR HAVE PROVOKED WIDESPREAD COMMENTARIES AMONG POLITICAL AND SOCIAL CIRCLES IN SWEDEN THAT ARE MAINLY UNFRIENDLY TOWARD US.

PRIME MINISTER U. [sic] PALME, IN AN INTERVIEW WITH THE TV AND PRESS, NAMED SOLZHENITSYN "A SYMBOL OF UNCOMPROMISING SUFFERING FOR THE TRUTH," AND STRESSED THAT HIS ARREST AND SUBSEQUENT DEPORTION FROM THE SOVIET UNION SHOULD BE CONSIDERED AS "AN EXTRAORDINARILY PAINFUL DEFEAT FOR ALL THOSE WHO STRIVE TO AFFIRM THE PEOPLE'S RIGHT TO A PUBLIC DEFENSE OF THEIR POSITIONS ON SOCIO-POLITICAL AND CULTURAL ISSUES." U. PALME NOTED THAT "EACH INDIVIDUAL SHOULD ENJOY THE RIGHT TO WORK AND ACT IN HIS OWN COUNTRY," AND SPOKE ALONG THE LINES THAT THE MEASURES REGARDING SOLZHENITSYN ARE ALLEGEDLY "A CAUSE OF GREAT REGRET, BECAUSE THEY WERE TAKEN WHEN BOTH WEST AND EAST ARE STRIVING FOR DÉTENTE AND AN INTENSIVE EXCHANGE OF VIEWS AND INFORMATION."

FELDIN, CHAIRMAN OF THE CENTER PARTY, ALSO SPOKE IN SUPPORT OF SOLZHENITSYN, AS WELL AS BOMAN, THE LEADER OF A MODERATE COALITION RIGHT-WING PARTY, THE PARLIAMENTARY FACTION OF THE POPULAR LIBERAL PARTY, THE CHAIRMAN OF WHICH, HELEN, MADE AN ATTEMPT TO PERSONALLY SUBMIT "A DEMAND" TO THE SOVIET AMBASSADOR TO GRANT SOLZHENITSYN THE POSSIBILITY TO RETURN TO THE SOVIET UNION. WE DECLINED THIS ATTEMPT, AND THE LIBERALS' APPEAL SENT TO US BY MAIL, WAS RETURNED TO THEM.

HERMANSSON, THE CHAIRMAN OF THE LEFTIST PARTY OF COMMUNISTS OF SWEDEN, STATED IN AN INTERVIEW WITH CORRESPONDENTS THAT THE PARTY'S EXECUTIVE COMMITTEE ADOPTED A STATEMENT IN CONNECTION WITH THE DEPORTATION OF SOLZHENITSYN THAT IT INTENDED TO "SEND" TO THE CPSU. THE STATEMENT, PUBLISHED IN THE PRESS, NOTES IN PARTICULAR THAT "WHEN THE AUTHORITIES OF A SOCIALIST COUNTRY ACT IN THIS MANNER, WHICH SIGNIFIES RESTRICTION OF THE FREEDOM OF SPEECH AND OF THE PRESS, AS IN THE CASE OF ALEXANDER SOLZHENITSYN, IT CONTRADICTS OUR PARTY'S UNDERSTANDING OF DEMOCRACY. . . . IT IS NECESSARY TO FIGHT AGAINST REACTIONARY VIEWS IN THE COURSE OF FREE AND OPEN DEBATES, BUT NOT THROUGH CENSORSHIP AND POLICE INTERFERENCE. THE CAUSE OF SOCIALIST CONSTRUCTION REQUIRES FREEDOM OF OPINION AND ORGANIZATION."

HERMANSSON, SPEAKING ON THE TV, RADIO AND IN THE PRESS, CONTINUED HIS WELL-KNOWN LINE, AND SPOKE REPEATEDLY IN A SPIRIT UNFRIENDLY TOWARD US, STRESSING THAT "IT WAS NECESSARY TO CONDEMN SHARPLY THE DEPORTATION OF SOLZHENITSYN."

A. LEVENBORG, MEMBER OF THE LPC [LEFTIST PARTY OF COMMUNISTS] BOARD, A DEPUTY OF THE RIKSDAG, PUBLICLY SUPPORTED OUR DECISION REGARDING SOLZHENITSYN, AND GAVE A PRINCIPLED POLITICAL APPRAISAL OF SOLZHENITSYN'S "CREATIVITY" IN A TV INTERVIEW. AT A MEETING

ORGANIZED IN STOCKHOLM ON 13 FEBRUARY BY THE UNION OF SWEDISH-SOVIET SOCIETIES, HE STATED THAT HE UNDERSTOOD THE MEASURES ADOPTED AGAINST SOLZHENITSYN (MORE THAN 150 PEOPLE ATTENDED). COMRADE A. LEVENBORG AGAIN SUPPORTED OUR POSITION REGARDING SOLZHENITSYN. IT IS INTERESTING THAT ALL FIFTEEN SPEAKERS EXPRESSED THEIR UNDERSTANDING OF THE NEED TO DEPORT SOLZHENITSYN FROM THE USSR.

AS WE HAVE BEEN TOLD CONFIDENTIALLY BY COMRADE TAKMAN, A MEMBER OF THE LPC BOARD, HERMANSSON TRIED TO INFLUENCE COMRADE LEVENBORG AND OTHER COMRADES WHO HOLD POSITIONS OPPOSING THOSE OF THE PARTY'S CHAIRMAN, INCLUDING THAT ON THE ISSUE OF SOLZHENITSYN. THIS WAS NOT THE ONLY REASON FOR CONVENING A MEETING OF THE LPC FACTION IN THE RIKSDAG, WHERE HERMANSSON, WITH THE SUPPORT OF I. SWENSSON, K. QUIST, G. LORENTSAN, AND OTHERS, REFERRING TO THE PRINCIPLE OF DEMOCRATIC CENTRALISM, SECURED APPROVAL OF THE EXECUTIVE COMMITTEE STATEMENT. COMRADES I. TAKMAN, A. LEVENBORG, R. PETTERSSON, AND K. NORDLANDER SPOKE SHARPLY AGAINST THE STATEMENT DURING THE DISCUSSION.

THE RESOLUTION OF THE EXECUTIVE COMMITTEE, IN WHICH THE MAJORITY ARE SUPPORTERS OF HERMANSSON, AND ITS SUPPORT BY THE FACTION PROVIDED T. FORSHBERG, THE LPC SECRETARY, GROUNDS TO STATE ON TELEVISION THAT THE POSITION OF A. LEVENBORG DID NOT REFLECT THE POSITION OF THE PARTY.

OUR IDEOLOGICAL ADVERSARIES, WITH THE AID OF NEWS ORGANIZATIONS ARE STRIVING TO HEAT UP THE ATMOSPHERE IN CONNECTION WITH THE DEPORTATION OF SOLZHENITSYN. IN THIS RESPECT, THEY MAKE PARTICULAR USE OF SAKHAROV AND OTHER LIKE-MINDED INDIVIDUALS. SAKHAROV'S INTERVIEW, GIVEN BY PHONE TO A. MILITS, THE LOCAL CORRESPONDENT OF *POSEV*, AND BROADCAST ON 13 FEBRUARY ON TELEVISION, CONTAINED AN APPEAL TO ORGANIZE AN INTERNATIONAL COLLECTION OF SIGNATURES FOR THE "RETURN" OF SOLZHENITSYN, AND SO ON.

AT THE SAME TIME, COMMENTARIES ON THE SUBSTANCE OF THE ISSUE ARE THAT THE DECISION ADOPTED BY THE SOVIET GOVERNMENT IN REGARD TO SOLZHENITSYN IS THE MOST "INCONVENIENT" FOR OUR ADVERSARIES. IT IS STRESSED, PARTICULARLY ON TELEVISION, THAT HE IS LOSING HIS "POLITICAL" SIGNIFICANCE AS A RESULT OF THE MEASURES TAKEN AND IS TURNING INTO ONE OF THOSE ANTI-SOVIET EMIGRES WHOSE VOICES ARE VERY LITTLE HEEDED. THE CONVICTION IS EXPRESSED OFTEN WITH CONSIDERABLE IRRITATION, THAT THE CURRENT PROPAGANDA CAMPAIGN AROUND SOLZHENITSYN WILL BE OF ONLY SHORT DURATION.

OUR POSITION REGARDING SOLZHENITSYN WAS EXPLAINED IN DETAIL IN A DISCUSSION WITH S. ANDERSSON AND B. CARLSSON, SECRETARIES OF THE SWEDISH SOCIAL-DEMOCRATIC PARTY, AND IT WAS STRESSED THAT UNFRIENDLY STATEMENTS AGAINST US WOULD NOT BE IN KEEPING WITH THE ATMOSPHERE OF NEIGHBORLY COOPERATION BETWEEN OUR COUNTRIES. WE SAID THAT THE "HYSTERIA" SURROUNDING THIS FIGURE WAS OF A TRANSIENT NATURE. THEY NOTED THAT, DESPITE THE DIFFERENCES IN OUR VIEWS IN CONNECTION WITH THE ISSUE OF DEMOCRATIC FREEDOMS, THEIR REACTION TO THE MEASURES AGAINST SOLZHENITSYN WOULD HAVE BEEN MORE RESTRAINED IF NOT FOR THE STRONG PRESSURE FROM THE RIGHT ON SOCIAL-DEMOCRACY, WHICH AT PRESENT IS IN A VERY TRICKY POSITION. S. ANDERSSON AND B. CARLSSON STRESSED THE INTEREST OF THE GOVERNMENT AND THE SSDP IN PREVENTING ANY DAMAGE TO SOVIET-SWEDISH RELATIONS BECAUSE OF THE CAMPAIGN AROUND SOLZHENITSYN, AND SAID THAT IT SHOULD NOT WORSEN PARTY CONTACTS WITH THE CPSU. FOR OUR PART WE LET IT BE KNOWN THAT IT DEPENDED PRIMARILY ON THE LINE THEY TOOK.

IN DISCUSSIONS WITH SWEDISH OFFICIALS AND WITH PUBLIC AND POLITICAL FIGURES THE EMBASSY CONTINUES TO EXPLAIN THE POLITICAL CONTENT OF THE CAMPAIGN AROUND SOLZHENITSYN AND ITS HOSTILITY TOWARD US.

M. YAKOVLEV

F. 3, *op.* 77, *d.* 817, *l.* 124–128. Copy.

Note

1. *P.N. Demichev's copy.*

130 Report from the Central Committee of the CP of the Ukraine[1]

No. 1/25
14 February 1974

To the Central Committee of the CP of the Soviet Union:
The TASS communiqué on the revocation of A. Solzhenitsyn's Soviet citizenship and his deportation from the country have been received by the working people of the Ukrainian SSR with profound understanding and great satisfaction. Fully approving the measures of the Soviet government against the malicious slanderer, renegade, and traitor, whose actions are incompatible with citizenship of the USSR and damage our motherland, the workers, collective farmers, intelligentsia, and all the strata of the population in the republic state that the Decree of the Presidium of the USSR Supreme Soviet expresses the will of the entire Soviet people.

V. N. Pikhterev, a leader of the coal-face team at Abakumov Mine in the Donet Coal Combine and a Deputy of the Ukrainian Supreme Soviet, has stated:

> The miners at our mine have always despised Solzhenitsyn's writings. Lately we have not had a single lecture or discussion where the workers would not ask the question: when will this anti-Soviet be called to order? And, speaking sincerely as a worker, miners call Solzhenitsyn among themselves nothing less than scum and a traitor. He long ago betrayed not only Soviet literature but also the Soviet motherland. Nothing has ever been sacred to this person. Praising traitors of the Vlasov type and his ilk, Solzhenitsyn has exposed his true face. The Donets miners like literature and have a deep respect for literary expression; they respect the hard work of the writer. But as far as such "authors" as Solzhenitsyn are concerned, we have always despised them and will continue to do so. Someone who does not love the motherland and slanders it, does not deserve to be its son nor its citizen. This is the reason why we have accepted the Decree of the Presidium of the USSR Supreme Soviet on deporting Solzhenitsyn from our country with such satisfaction. His place is among those people without a name and without a motherland. He deserves this shameful fate because of his anti-Soviet scribbling.

V.A. Orlov, senior mill operator in the sheet metal shop of the Zaporozhe Steelworks, a Hero of Socialist Labor, said: "The decree on revoking Solzhenitsyn's Soviet citizenship and deporting him from our country reflects the will of the entire Soviet people. I enthusiastically support this decision on behalf of my team. Solzhenitsyn is a malicious enemy of our motherland. There is no place for him among people building communism."

F.F. Naukhatsko, a tractor driver at the Michurin Collective Farm in the Semyonov District of the Poltava Region, said:

> Like all workers at our collective farm, I fully and heartily approve the Decree of the Presidium of the Supreme Soviet of the USSR on revoking Solzhenitsyn's Soviet citizenship and deporting him from the USSR. He is a literary accomplice of Vlasov and is unworthy of eating our honest bread. Let those whom he serves feed this traitor. But even they only needed him while he had the opportunity to slander the Soviet people as a citizen of the USSR.

World War II veterans heartily approve the decree on deporting Solzhenitsyn, who insulted the most sacred feelings of the Soviet people. P. I. Kalynyuk, a machine operator at the Rossia Collective Farm in the Chemerovetsk District of the Khmelnitsky Region, said:

> Millions of our people gave their lives to defend our socialist motherland against all sorts of riffraff. I did not endure the whole war in my tank, shed my blood, lose my best friends and relatives so that all sorts of scum could slander the most sacred thing that we possess, and throw wrenches in our works. There is no place among us for a person who justifies the actions of fascists and Vlasov's accomplices.

Numerous responses come from writers, artists, composers, research workers and other representatives of the Soviet intelligentsia. Leonid Novichenko, Secretary of the Board of the USSR Writers Union and Corresponding Member of the Ukrainian SSR Academy of Sciences, stated:

> I fully and completely approve the decision of the Soviet government to revoke Solzhenitsyn's citizenship and deport him from the USSR. We have been waiting for this decision a long time. This renegade and traitor has no right to the title of citizen of the Land of the Soviets. He was convenient for his political bosses, the bosses of anti-Soviet propaganda, as a person

with a Soviet passport who could be presented as a representative of some "internal opposition" in the USSR. Now the game ended. The hireling of imperialism has been finally unmasked. Let him scram from our sacred land, let him rot among the stinking mobs of Vlasov's accomplices who were not finished off, and whom he joined ideologically a long time ago. Our Soviet air will be the cleaner.

The prose writer Anatoly Dombrovsky, who is Executive Secretary of the Crimean Branch of the Ukrainian Writers Union, stated:

We Crimean writers approve the Decree of the Presidium of the USSR Supreme Soviet on revoking Solzhenitsyn's citizenship and deporting him from the country. By his actions, he has put himself in the shoes of an emigré, impudently slandering his motherland and its people. All Soviet people will support the decision of the government. The deepest contempt awaits the traitor abroad and he will see it in the eyes of progressive people in all countries. He crawled his way to filthy fame and remains at the beck and call of those from whom he received his pieces of silver.

Professor F.F. Medvedev, Chairperson at Kharkov State University and a Doctor of Philology, stressed:

Solzhenitsyn is an adversary of Soviet reality, and his main goal is to continue to expand the Cold War. He is a person for whom the interests of the Soviet people and of peace are alien. He is a mortal enemy of socialism and communism, and in his writings glorifies tsarism as well as circles alien to the socialist system and the Soviet people. I think that our government's decision is correct, because it is the demand of the people, the voice of the people. I consider Solzhenitsyn to be a vile criminal, villain, and an enemy of all that is advanced and progressive, who deserves still greater punishment.

Revoking Solzhenitsyn's Soviet citizenship and deporting him from the country are exactly the measures that were being proposed by many communists and by the working people in our republic in their statements at meetings, in discussions and at lectures, as well as by delegates to district, city and regional Party conferences. At the same time, some statements underline the excessively humane character of Solzhenitsyn's punishment. Thus,

367

braider S.I. Devyatova at the Kiev plant of Ukrainian Cable, a Hero of Socialist Labor, expressed the following opinion: "I'm a worker, and I'm proud of my motherland and our dear Soviet government, and I resolutely condemn Solzhenitsyn and the like. I think the decree on deporting Solzhenitsyn from the Soviet Union is too humane. He has caused so much trouble and has been such a blatant traitor. Let him serve his punishment here first, in our country, and then have him deported."

Many express the views that the fate of Solzhenitsyn should make Sakharov and his ilk, those who have openly begun to fight against and slander our Soviet reality, think twice. And if they don't draw the right conclusions, then the same measure should be applied to them.

The following questions are being asked: Where was Solzhenitsyn living of late? What was the procedure for the deportation? Where was Solzhenitsyn deported to? Does he have accomplices, and, if so, what fate is in store for them?

Secretary of the Central Committee of the Communist Party of the Ukraine
V. Shcherbitsky

F. 3, *op.* 80, *d.* 664, *l.* 101–104. Original.

Note

1. *Sent to Politburo members and candidate members, and Central Committee Secretaries, on 15 February 1974 under No. P298.*

131 Report from the Committee for State Security of the USSR Council of Ministers[1]

No. 444–A
14 February 1974
Classified

To the Central Committee:

Bourgeois correspondents accredited in Moscow are animatedly commenting on the announcement concerning the revocation of Solzhenitsyn's Soviet citizenship and his deportation from the Soviet Union.

They are forced to acknowledge in their reports and in private discussions that the Soviet authorities have found the most reasonable and efficient resolution of the Solzhenitsyn problem.

[Tim] Parks, a correspondent of the American newspaper *The Baltimore Sun*, said: "The Soviet government's action against Solzhenitsyn is a wise compromise between the demands of Western and Soviet public opinions." [Hedrick] Smith, an American correspondent, stated that the Soviet government's actions resolve almost all the issues that only a few hours earlier were disturbing world public opinion and provoking sharp reactions in the US Congress. [Erik] De Mauny, a BBC correspondent, said that a prolonged court trial of Solzhenitsyn would feed an anti-Soviet campaign abroad; therefore, the decision to deport Solzhenitsyn was unquestionably the best way out of the situation.

Mayer, a correspondent of the West German wire service DPA, said that the Soviet government had found the only correct, bold, and unusual way out of a highly complicated situation. He thought that the public in Western countries would duly appraise the deportation of Solzhenitsyn as a gesture of goodwill on the part of the Soviet government, which had every reason to initiate criminal proceedings against him. Buist, a correspondent of the British wire service Reuters, discussing the probable motives for the Soviet government's decision, stressed that by rejecting a trial of Solzhenitsyn, the Soviet authorities had striven above all to preserve the atmosphere of détente in its relations with Western countries. The same view was expressed by Clemens, a German correspondent, and Dillon, a correspondent of Agence France Presse. Ikuta, a correspondent of the Japanese *Asahi* Newspaper, thought that the action of the Soviet government would contribute to a further reduction of international tension.

According to many reporters, one of the results of deporting Solzhenitsyn is that Western propaganda centers will be deprived of the opportunity to employ Solzhenitsyn actively for the organization of anti-Soviet campaigns in the press. Thus Smith, the American correspondent, said in a private discussion that from now on Sakharov and Solzhenitsyn's accomplices were the "only hope" of Western correspondents, but the Solzhenitsyn affair would undoubtedly have a restraining effect on them. The Japanese correspondent Ikuta said: "Western journalists who hoped to 'warm their hands' on 'the Solzhenitsyn Affair,' were disappointed to learn of his arrival in West Germany."

Crepeau, a correspondent of Associated Press, told one of his acquaintances of his intention to go to West Germany for further coverage of the "Solzhenitsyn Affair," because there was "nothing to do" now in the USSR. In line with Smith, an American correspondent, Crepeau asked the USSR Foreign Ministry Press Department for an exit visa to the FRG. They intended to deliver the personal belongings of Solzhenitsyn's wife, Svetlova, in the near future to Solzhenitsyn. This intention of Smith has been approved by the US Embassy.

Some Western correspondents think that the sensation around Solzhenitsyn's name over the revocation of his Soviet citizenship and deportation from the USSR will gradually subside. Thus Parks, the American correspondent, said in a private conversation that the Western press would continue to report for another two to three months on Solzhenitsyn, after which there would be no interest in him. Buist, the British correspondent, acknowledged in a confidential discussion that the West greatly overestimated Solzhenitsyn's talent as a writer, and his deportation from the Soviet Union would be the beginning of the end of the writer's career.

Western journalists and diplomats pay great attention to the legal side of the "Solzhenitsyn Affair." Journalists were told at the French and US Embassies in Moscow that, under the RSFSR Criminal Code, the judicial authorities had the right to forcefully subpoena persons if they were twice previously subpoenaed.

According to available information, the "Solzhenitsyn Affair" has provoked great interest and concern in West Germany. It is unclear to many why preference was given to West Germany in choosing where Solzhenitsyn should be deported. It is apparent that the decision on this issue was influenced by the recent statement of Chancellor Brandt on the readiness of West Germany to grant Solzhenitsyn political asylum, as well as by the wish expressed by Heinrich Böll to receive Solzhenitsyn at his home. The decision to deport Solzhenitsyn to West Germany had presumably been agreed upon at the highest level. Therefore, the presence of Solzhenitsyn in West Germany would not aggravate the improvement of relations between the

USSR and West Germany.

Seeger, a correspondent of *The Los Angeles Times*, who regularly informs the political section of the US Embassy in Moscow on the development of events in "the Solzhenitsyn Affair," informed him, citing diplomatic sources, that the American Embassy systematically sent reports on this issue to the State Department. According to Seeger, the appeals of Senator Jackson to terminate trade with the Soviet Union had lost their significance to a certain extent due to the deportation of Solzhenitsyn, but Nixon's opponents would undoubtedly try to exploit the situation for their own purposes.

J. Loreau, First Secretary of the French Embassy in Moscow, said in a confidential conversation that the employees of the Embassy had been given strict instructions to abstain from expressing views and commenting on the arrest and deportation of Solzhenitsyn. The statement of White House Press Secretary Warren to the effect that the USSR had the right to resolve its internal affairs independently is being discussed by American diplomats.

Chairman of the Committee for State Security
Andropov

F. 3, *op.* 80, *d.* 664, *l.* 112–115. Original.

Note

1. Sent to Politburo members and candidate members, and Central Committee Secretaries, on 14 February 1974 under No. P288.

132 Report of the Central Committee Department for Organizational and Party Work

"On Workers' Responses to the Deportation of Solzhenitsyn from the USSR"[1]

15 February 1974

To the Central Committee:

Working people everywhere unanimously approve the TASS statement that Solzhenitsyn has been deprived of Soviet citizenship and deported from the country by Decree of the Presidium of the USSR Supreme Soviet for actions incompatible with USSR citizenship and damaging to our motherland.

The reports from the Central Committees of the Communist Parties of the Union republics, territorial and regional Party committees state that the Soviet people have taken this decision with great satisfaction, as a totally logical and justified act of cleansing our land of a traitor who took the path of undermining the Soviet government and the entire socialist system. Workers, collective farmers, and the intelligentsia state that the deportation of Solzhenitsyn corresponds to their will and desires. The common view is that this renegade who slanders everything sacred to a Soviet person, defames the memorandumry of our people's finest sons and daughters, maliciously blackens the glorious pages of its history, and slanders Soviet reality, has no place in our society. The responses state that the sanctions that have been adopted against Solzhenitsyn are a logical consequence of his vile activity. It is noted that the sharp criticism has done him no good, nor the warnings of the Soviet public and state authorities.

Everywhere it is said that the preventive punishment of Solzhenitsyn's hostile activity was correctly chosen. In the opinion of many, the prosecution this traitor deserves would have promoted him as a martyr. Remarking on the humaneness of the decision adopted in regard to Solzhenitsyn and his family, our people stress that the deportation of this anti-Soviet from the country is a wise and farsighted measure that will undermine the potential manipulations of imperialist propaganda. From now on, the comrades state, the writings of

Solzhenitsyn will be perceived in the West not as the scribblings of "an eye witness," but as the fruit of the sick imagination of a malicious person who was rejected with scorn by the Soviet people and became a lackey of international reaction.

Active members of Party organizations express their satisfaction with the fact that the Central Committee has sent a critical analysis of Solzhenitsyn's *Gulag Archipelago* to leading Party executives in a timely manner. This analysis according to the comrades, helps them to fully understand the loathsome face of the author and vividly illustrates the full depth of his moral and political degradation.

The Party organizations are conducting educational work in regard to the TASS statement and are providing responses to questions coming in. The view is expressed that it is necessary to publish some materials in the press, without initiating a propaganda campaign on this subject. In particular, some responses by Soviet people should be published, as well as those by our foreign friends, and articles exposing the provocative uproar in the West.

Deputy Head of the Central Committee Department of Organizational and Party Work
N. Petrovichev

F. 3, *op.* 80, *d.* 664, *l.* 117–120. Original

Note

1. *Sent to Politburo members and candidate members, and Central Committee Secretaries, on 15 February 1974 under No. P302.*

133 Memorandum from the Central Committee International Department

"On Instructions to the Soviet Ambassador to Sweden"[1]

No. 25–S–371
22 February 1974

The Soviet Ambassador in Sweden reports (special telegram No. 129 of 15 February of this year) that K. Hermansson, the chairman of the Left Party–Communists of Sweden (LPCS), has criticized in the press and on television the measures taken against A. Solzhenitsyn, characterizing them as "a restriction of freedom of speech and the press." The statement of the LPCS Executive Committee's Board published in the press is in the same spirit (see text enclosed).

It has been learned that K. Hermansson and his supporters in the leadership of the Party have secured the adoption of a statement by the Executive Committee convening a special plenary session, on March 10–11, of the LPCS Board, where they intend to censure representatives of the healthy forces in the Party, in particular, A. Levenborg, a member of the LPCS board, and the newspaper of the district organization of the Party *Norrskensflamman*, who have spoken from internationalist positions and approved our action in regard to Solzhenitsyn.

In order to support the healthy internationalist forces in the LPCS, we consider it advisable to instruct the Soviet Ambassador to hand an appeal to the leadership of the LPCS on behalf of the Central Committee, outlining our evaluation of the statements by K. Hermansson and the statement of the LPCS Executive Committee.

The draft resolution of the Central Committee is enclosed.[2]

B. Ponomarev

Enclosure
(Translated from Swedish)

Statement of the Executive Committee Board of the Left Party–Communists of Sweden on 13 February 1974

The struggle for democratic rights and freedoms is of fundamental significance. Not the least of its concerns are freedom of speech and of the press. The Left Party–Communists of Sweden, unlike the government and the bourgeois parties, has been the sole party in parliament that fought against the violation of these rights and freedoms by the police and courts in connection with the case of the Information Bureau. We demand that violations of freedom of opinion and organization be stopped, and that democratic rights and freedoms under the constitution of our country be strengthened.

When the authorities in a socialist country act in such a manner as to abridge freedom of speech and the press, as in the case of Alexander Solzhenitsyn, it contradicts the understanding of democracy by our party. It is necessary to fight reactionary views in free and open discussion, not by means of censorship and police interference. The work of socialist construction requires freedom of opinion and organization.

Left Party–Communists of Sweden
Executive Committee

F. 3, *op.* 69, *d.* 1143, *l.* 127–128. Original

Notes

1. *Sent to Politburo members on 26 February 1974 for voting under No. 127–56.*
2. *The Politburo resolution was adopted on 28 February 1974 under No. P127/103 (see Document 135).*

134 Report from the Committee for State Security of the USSR Council of Ministers[1]

No. 553–Ts
23 February 1974
Top Secret

To the Central Committee:
An analysis of the information available indicates that the Soviet government's measures regarding Solzhenitsyn have struck a serious blow to the plans of those Western forces that were actively using him for their subversive activities in an attempt to discredit our domestic policies and weaken the growing authority of the Soviet Union in the international arena.

Representatives of governmental circles in the major Western countries are forced to recognize the legality of the actions of the USSR government in regard to Solzhenitsyn, who for a long time actually defied it, refusing to obey Soviet laws. Noting the prudence of this action, many Western state and political figures stress in their confidential conversations and official statements that [this action] will not significantly influence the development of bilateral and multilateral state relations with the Soviet Union.

This approach has been clearly demonstrated by the French government, which officially announced the forthcoming visit of President Pompidou of France to the Soviet Union. Prime Minister Bratelli of Norway, confirming his intention to carry out his planned visit to the USSR, stressed that "the expanding contacts between Norway and the Soviet Union would be of very little value if attention were focused upon issues on which the points of view are totally different."[2]

The government circles of some states are beginning to express their apprehension of the fact that a favorable attitude on their part toward Solzhenitsyn could inflict a certain amount of damage on mutual relations with the USSR. It is indicative that the governments of some countries are manifesting a certain restraint on the issue of granting Solzhenitsyn political asylum and citizenship. According to available information, the Brandt government learned with satisfaction of the rapid departure of Solzhenitsyn from West Germany. Prime Minister Trudeau of Canada, though he confirmed his invitation to Solzhenitsyn to visit the country, indicated that it was doubtful that Canadian citizenship would be granted to him.

Business circles in capitalist states, who are interested in continuing to expand commercial and economic ties with the Soviet Union, express their satisfaction with the deportation of Solzhenitsyn from the USSR. According to Weinwort, a representative of the Chase Manhattan Bank in Moscow, this action considerably deprives the opponents of expanding Soviet-American business contacts of the opportunity to employ the activity of Solzhenitsyn as a pretext for the creation of obstacles to the normal development of relations between the two counties.

Available information indicates that the "Solzhenitsyn Affair" has not attracted great attention in the majority of countries in Asia, Africa, and Latin America.

The considerable activity caused by the first report on the "arrest of Solzhenitsyn," has been replaced by confusion and disappointment in Western political parties of the social-democratic tendency.

Progressive forces in the West, primarily representatives of the majority of communist and worker's parties, understand and approve the action in regard to Solzhenitsyn. It is noted that this measure pulls the rug out from under those who attempted to initiate polemics among leftist forces on the issue of Solzhenitsyn. It is indicative that the process reevaluating positions on this issue has started even among representatives of parties that initially condemned the action of the Soviet government. Thus, according to Petersson, a Deputy of the Swedish parliament from the Left Party–Communists of Sweden (LPCS), the resolution of the LPCS leadership on the issue, which was hostile toward the USSR, has currently been condemned by a number of Party organizations which are sending letters to the executive committee, protesting against this resolution.

The anti-Soviet uproar around Solzhenitsyn incited by the mass media of the capitalist states is clearly on the decline. The largest bourgeois newspapers are publishing articles on Solzhenitsyn on the back pages.

The majority of the population in Western countries are losing their interest in the "Solzhenitsyn story." Statements on Solzhenitsyn as a new millionaire, who made "good business" out of anti-Sovietism, has, to a large degree, destroyed the myth of him as "an ideological fighter for the freedom of dissidents in the USSR."

The attitude toward Solzhenitsyn is changing also among the so-called "liberal" intelligentsia that showed such interest in him. After getting acquainted in greater detail with some of his widely publicized "creations," a large number of experts have expressed their doubts as to the real creative worth of his works. According to Engelman, Vice President of the West-German section of the International PEN Club, Solzhenitsyn gained popularity not as a talented writer, buy only as "an accuser" who was gradually transformed into a patent servant of "Cold War" advocates thirsting for sensation. The view is expressed more frequently in this respect that it will be very difficult for Solzhenitsyn in the position of an emigré to preserve "the fame of a great writer" that he was pronounced to be in the West, because his anti-Soviet statements will hardly add anything new to those of other emigrés.

Anti-Soviet forces in the West, including representatives of the intelligentsia, consider the deportation of Solzhenitsyn to be a serious blow to the "dissident movement" in the USSR, which has been deprived of the main figure around which is concentrated.

The inspirers of anti-Soviet campaigns understand that in the long run, Solzhenitsyn will not bring them the kind of dividends he offered when he was in the USSR. The analysis by the leading American "Sovietologist" Brzezinski is indicative in this sense, which holds that it will be possible "to play the Solzhenitsyn card with great effectiveness for only a half a year—or a year at most—because he doesn't present any interest to the Western public either as a writer, or a historian, or as a personality."

Considering that the adversaries of détente will attempt, particularly in the near future, to continue to use Solzhenitsyn actively for purposes hostile to the Soviet Union, the Committee for State Security is taking measures to head off and weaken the effect of potential actions in this regard.

Deputy Chairman of the Committee for State Security
Tsvigun

F. 3, *op.* 80, *d.* 647, *l.* 88–91. Original.

Notes

1. *Sent to Politburo members and candidate members, and Central Committee Secretaries, on 23 February 1974 under No. P368.*
2. *A working meeting between G. Pompidou and L. Brezhnev was held on 12–13 March 1974 in Pitsunda; the official visit of T. Bratelli, Prime Minister of Norway, was held on March 18–25, 1974.*

135 Politburo Resolution

"On Instructions to the Soviet Ambassador to Sweden"

No. P127/103
28 February 1974
Top Secret

To approve the text of the telegram to the Soviet Ambassador in Sweden (enclosed).

Central Committee Secretary

Enclosure
Unnumbered
Re: par. 103, transcript No. 127
Classified

Stockholm
To the Soviet Ambassador:
In connection with the speeches made by K. Hermansson and the statement of the LPCS Executive Committee on the issue of Solzhenitsyn, refer to instructions you have received and inform the LPCS leadership of the following:

> Press reports show that Comrade Hermansson, the chairman of the Left Party–Communists of Sweden, has made statements in which he addresses the issue of Solzhenitsyn from a position unfriendly to the Soviet Union and casts doubt on the correctness of the action of deporting him from the USSR. The same line is reflected in the statement of the LPCS Executive Committee on this issue published in newspapers.
> As is well known to Swedish comrades, the Communist Party of the Soviet Union, in its relations with fraternal parties, is guided by principles of proletarian internationalism, solidarity and mutual support, respect for independence and equality,

and noninterference in each others' internal affairs. We consider the speech of Comrade Hermansson and the statement of the LPCS Executive Committee to be opposed to these principles, because the representatives of the LPCS leadership publicly subjected the policy of the CPSU and Soviet state to groundless criticism, effectively supporting the anti-Soviet campaign incited by reactionary forces in the West.

The Central Committee has repeatedly informed the leadership of the LPCS and other fraternal parties of the basic nature of the issue in regard to Solzhenitsyn. The issue is that Solzhenitsyn for many years has spoken from positions that are frankly hostile towards socialism and the international revolutionary movement. He is overtly cooperating with the forces of imperialist reaction that act to destroy real socialism, taking the road of blatant violation of Soviet laws, the road of treachery.

Solzhenitsyn has exposed himself by his anti-Soviet actions as a person hostile to the cause of progress and socialism, the cause of peace and security of nations. Hence, the revocation of Solzhenitsyn's Soviet citizenship and his deportation from the USSR have received the full support of the Soviet people and a correct understanding on the part of fraternal Parties, including the Communist Parties of Northern Europe, as well as of international progressive public opinion.

Thus we are all the more surprised by the speeches of Comrade Hermansson and the statement of the LPCS Executive Committee. We resolutely reject statements that the deportation of Solzhenitsyn is a violation of socialist democracy. It is known that democratic rights and freedoms are guaranteed to Soviet citizens by the Constitution and Soviet laws, and unlike in bourgeois states, are imbued with real content in our socialist society, where the power belongs to the working people.

The CPSU and the Soviet State follow a consistent course of strengthening socialist law and continually improving socialist democracy. However, we communists cannot allow abuse by anyone of our democratic rights and freedoms in order to undermine the socialist system, which our people won and defended in ardent struggle and at the price of numerous casualties.

It is Solzhenitsyn who took the road of abusing freedom of speech and the press. The Swedish comrades apparently know that for some years he was disseminating malicious insinuations in regard to our Party, the Soviet state, and the Soviet people, and directly appealing to foreign reaction to exert pressure on the USSR, and to interfere in its internal affairs. He openly approved all forms of struggle against socialism, including underground subversive activity and armed struggle.

With regard to the statement of the LPCS Executive Committee concerning the need to exert influence on Solzhenitsyn by means of an open and free discussion, we have already informed you that the Soviet public and our writers tried to convince Solzhenitsyn for a long time in the hope that he would renounce his fight against socialism. However, he didn't terminate his anti-Soviet activities and, in effect, took the road of direct violation of the law by participating in actions hostile to the motherland, which under Soviet law is a state crime— high treason. Solzhenitsyn declared outright that he didn't recognize the power of Soviet law over him as an individual at all. That is why the need arose to apply certain measures against Solzhenitsyn. We hope that our Swedish comrades will pay attention to these considerations and will not allow themselves to be dragged into a reactionary, anti-Soviet campaign that is targeted against real socialism, as well as against the common cause of communists worldwide.

The entire experience gained in the development of our movement indicates that only the united action by fraternal parties and international solidarity among communists can reliably guarantee success in the common struggle for peace, democracy, and socialism.

For the Soviet Ambassador. You may acquaint Comrade Levenborg or his deputy with this message. If the Swedish comrades ask you to give them the text of this appeal in writing, you may do so.

Telegraph your implementation.

F. 3, *op.* 80, *d.* 647, *l.* 92–95. Excerpt from protocol.

136 Memorandum from the USSR Ministry of Foreign Affairs and the Committee for State Security of the USSR Council of Ministers[1]

No. 536/GS
1 March 1974
Classified

To the Central Committee:
A request from the Federal Government Office in Switzerland has been received at the USSR Embassy on 25 February this year to legalize the power of attorney from Solzhenitsyn wherein he instructs his wife, N.D. Solzhenitsyna, residing in Moscow, to receive from Vneshposyltorg author's royalties in the form of certificates transferred to him from the USSR Copyright Agency in January–February of this year in British pounds sterling and Finnish marks (taking into account the deductions—about seven hundred foreign currency rubles). The power of attorney has been certified with the required signatures and stamps of the relevant Swiss organizations.

There are no legal grounds to refuse to execute the request of the Swiss in regard to legalizing Solzhenitsyn's power of attorney document (legalization consists of examining the conformity of the document to be legalized with the laws in effect, and in verifying the authenticity of the signature on the document of the official, and in witnessing this signature). Our refusal to legalize the stated power of attorney document could be exploited by hostile circles for anti-Soviet purposes.

At the same time, out of political considerations, it would be undesirable for the USSR Embassy in Switzerland to be involved in settling Solzhenitsyn's property affairs.

In this connection, the KGB and the USSR Ministry of Foreign Affairs deem it advisable that the USSR Vneshtorgbank should transfer Solzhenitsyn's royalties to his account in the Swiss bank and neither deduct taxes nor commission fees.

In the latter case the USSR Embassy in Bern could return Solzhenitsyn's power of attorney document to the Swiss authorities and inform them that the issue of legalizing this power of attorney is moot, because when

Solzhenitsyn was deported from the USSR the money mentioned in this document was transferred to his account in the Swiss bank.

Please review.

V. Kuznetsov
S. Tsvigun

F. 3, op. 69, d. 1160, page 5. Original.

Note

1. *Sent to Politburo members and candidate members for voting on 1 March 1974 under No. 127–106.*

137 Politburo Resolution "On Solzhenitsyn's Royalties"

No. P128/23
5 March 1974
Top Secret

1. Instruct the USSR Vneshekonombank to transfer the sums of the royalties immediately without deducting taxes or commission fees to the account of Solzhenitsyn in the Swiss bank.

2. Instruct the USSR Ministry of Foreign Affairs to order the USSR Embassy in Switzerland to return Solzhenitsyn's power of attorney to the Swiss authorities and inform them that the issue of legalizing this power of attorney is moot because the sums mentioned in the power of attorney were transferred to his account in the Swiss bank.

3. Order USSR Vneshekonombank not to accept royalties in the future in the event that they are transferred from abroad to the name of Solzhenitsyn.

Central Committee Secretary

F. 3, op. 80, *d.* 647, page 96. Excerpt from transcript.

138 Memorandum from the Presidium of the USSR Supreme Soviet[1]

No. 154cc
20 March 1974
Top Secret

To the Central Committee:
A statement has been received addressed to Comrade N.V. Podgorny, Chairman of the USSR Supreme Soviet, from N.D. Solzhenitsyna (Svetlova) with a request to permit her to travel to Switzerland to join A.I. Solzhenitsyn, her husband, along with her four children and her mother. She also asks that she be allowed to take with her the library and archive of her husband. N.D. Solzhenitsyna and her mother, Y.F. Svetlova, ask to be granted exit visas effective for not less than one month.

In accordance with the instruction of Comrade N.V. Podgorny, the request was examined by the Secretary of the Presidium of the USSR Supreme Soviet with the participation of V.M. Chebrikov, the Deputy Chairman of the Committee for State Security of the USSR Council of Ministers, M. P. Malyarov, First Deputy Prosecutor General of the USSR, B.T. Shumilin, Deputy Minister of Internal Affairs of the USSR, and I.A. Glebov, Directorate Chief of the USSR Ministry of Internal Affairs.

In the TASS statement published in connection with the Decree of the Presidium of the USSR Supreme Soviet of 12 February 1974 on revoking Solzhenitsyn's citizenship and deporting him from the USSR, it was stated that his family could follow him whenever they considered it necessary. In this respect there are no issues pertaining to the competence of the Presidium of the USSR Supreme Soviet. Hence it has been considered advisable to send this request to the Committee for State Security and the USSR Ministry of Internal Affairs for resolution of the issue in accordance with established procedure.

It is presumed that the other issues raised in this request, or issues that might arise in connection with the request, might be resolved as follows.

Given that Solzhenitsyn has been deported from the USSR, the USSR Ministry of Internal Affairs and the USSR Ministry of Finance should not extract the state duty fee for exiting the USSR from the family members traveling to join him.

In the statement he wrote on the day of his deportation, Solzhenitsyn also asked to take out the library and archive "that consisted almost entirely of his novel *October 1916*, materials related to it, and to the next novel, *March 1917*. The Committee for State Security, the USSR Public Prosecutor's Office, and the USSR Ministry of Internal Affairs consider it possible to transfer the archive on the condition that it is thoroughly examined during customs inspection. There are no objections to the taking of the library.

Copies of the statement from N.D. Solzhenitsyna and A.I. Solzhenitsyn are enclosed.

Reported for information purposes.

M. Georgadze

Enclosure 1

To Comrade N.V. Podgorny, Chairman of Presidium of USSR Supreme Soviet:
The decree signed by you on 12 February 1974 to revoke my USSR citizenship has been read to me.

I can only leave with my whole family: wife—Solzhenitsyna, Natalia Dmitrievna; sons—Solzhenitsyns, Yermolai, Ignat, Stepan, and Tyurin, Dmitri; and mother-in-law—Svetlova, Yekaterina Ferdinandovna.

I ask you to give us the opportunity to gather together and to leave together.

In addition, I ask you to grant permission and the practical opportunity for my aunt, Irina Ivanovna Shcherbak (residing in Georgievsk, Stavropol Territory, Lineinaya Street, 93) to travel to the place of my new residence.

I ask also your permission for the unobstructed export of my library and my literary archive, consisting almost entirely of the novel *October 1916*, materials related to it and to the next novel, *March 1917*.

A. Solzhenitsyn
13 February 1974

Enclosure 2

To N.V. Podgorny, Chairman of Presidium of USSR Supreme Soviet:
Since the Decree of the Presidium on the deportation of Alexander Isaevich Solzhenitsyn has practically deprived his family of the possibility of living in their homeland, I ask you to implement the stated guarantees for our exit and the unobstructed transfer of A.I Solzhenitsyn's archive and library.

N. Solzhenitsyna
14 March 1974

F. 3, *op.* 80, *d.* 647, *l.* 99–102. Original.

Note

1. *The first page has the following resolution: "Circulate to the whole Politburo. It is possible to approve, show it to Kirilenko," and the signatures of A. Kosygin, K. Mazurov, A. Grechko, D. Polyansky, A. Shelepin, F. Kulakov, A. Gromyko, M. Suslov, and Y. Andropov. On the last page is the following notation "Comrade M. P. Georgadze has been informed. V. Galkin. 3.28.74." The following notation is on the reverse side: "Comrades Grishin—sick; Pelshe, Podgorny—on vacation. 4.29.74"*

139 Report from the Committee for State Security of the USSR Council of Ministers[1]

No. 1168–A
2 May 1974
Classified

To the Central Committee:
The Committee for State Security reports that Solzhenitsyn, having had his Soviet citizenship revoked and having been deported abroad, retains his hostile opinions and is hatching plans to conduct subversive activity against the USSR.

Residing in Zurich, he has established, in particular, contacts with representatives of the Czechoslovakian emigrés in Switzerland, with the assistance of whom he intends to arrange the illegal delivery of his writings and other materials of an anti-Soviet nature to the Soviet Union. Solzhenitsyn stated in a discussion with the Czechoslovakian emigrés that his future activities would be subordinate primarily to the interests of the "opposition inside the USSR." He stressed that the "dissidents (Sakharov, Shafarevich, Ginzburg, and others) are currently unable to conduct propaganda activity effectively, and it is necessary at this stage to organize and structure their movement."[2]

At this same time, Solzhenitsyn continues to make slanderous statements in the Western press. Thus, in April, he made two statements in support of Grigorenko, Nekrasov, and Ginzburg, who allegedly are persecuted by the Soviet authorities. In March, Solzhenitsyn agreed in principle to speak on Radio Liberty and to publish the second and third parts of his anti-Soviet lampoon *The Gulag Archipelago*.

According to available information, Solzhenitsyn's family is currently suffering serious hardships in everyday life.[3] For example, Solzhenitsyn's, wife stated in a phone call to her Moscow friends that the conditions of life for Soviet citizens in Switzerland are bad, and tried to persuade them "not to come here of their own will."

The Committee for State Security, in view of the developing situation, continues its observation of Solzhenitsyn and his accomplices who have remained in the USSR.

Chairman of the Committee for State Security
Andropov

F. 3, *op.* 80, *d.* 647, *l.* 114–115. Original.

Notes

1. *Sent to Politburo members and candidate members, and Central Committee Secretaries, on 5 May 1974 under No. P894.*
2. Evidently the KGB had succeeded in infiltrating the Czech emigré community in Zurich, either directly or with the help of the Czechoslovakian security service.
3. These "hardships" appear to have been of a psychological, rather than material, character, and refer to the difficulties almost all Soviet citizens experienced in adapting to life in the West. The KGB was naturally happy to hear of, and to seize on, any complaints of such a nature.

140 Report from the Committee for State Security of the USSR Council of Ministers[1]

No. 2035–A
24 July 1974
Classified

The Committee for State Security reports on newly received materials pertaining to Solzhenitsyn.

Having settled in Zurich, Solzhenlitsyn at first refrained from any public statements, but retained his hostile opinions and did not renounce subversive activity against the USSR. In a private conversation, he unambiguously said that he was subordinating himself to the interests of the "opposition inside the USSR," because the "dissidents currently were unable to conduct propaganda activity effectively and at this stage it was necessary to organize and structure their movement."

In March of this year, in a discussion with representatives of the Czechoslovak emigrés in Switzerland, with whom Solzhenitsyn has established and maintained regular contacts, he expressed his point of view on the so-called "democratic movement in the USSR." In his opinion, certain members of the "movement" erroneously maintain that to keep the struggle against communism active, it was necessary to rely primarily on international public opinion, whose pressure would allegedly force the Soviet government to retreat. According to Solzhenitsyn's statement, Sakharov was a supporter of that tactic. Criticizing the position of Sakharov, Solzhenitsyn held that it was necessary, first of all to influence groups among the Soviet intelligentsia and youth, and in this manner fight to change the state system in the Soviet Union. According to Solzhenitsyn, profound personal differences on this subject had developed between him and Sakharov, whom he called "a crazy and irresponsible person."

Taking practical steps to implement his plans, Solzhenitsyn has founded and registered in Switzerland the so-called "Russian Social Fund" to which "royalties from the sale of *The Gulag Archipelago* and his other works" will supposedly go to "assist the families of political prisoners detained in Soviet camps." At the same time, Solzhenitsyn has taken measures to complete the publication and conclude new contracts for the publication of *The Gulag Archipelago*, which he intends to ship illegally to the Soviet Union with assistance from the Czechoslovak emigrés in Switzerland. Available information also indicates that after Solzhenitsyn's deportation abroad, interest in him in the West is steadily on the decline.[2] In this respect, it is interesting to note, in particular, the reaction of certain Czechoslovak emigrés who participated in the meeting with Solzhenitsyn. In their view, Solzhenitsyn is "an arrogant tsarist chauvinist," who rejects the ideas of democracy and socialism, and "regards Czechs the same way as Latvians or Estonians," ie, as people from the Russian provinces.

Articles are appearing more frequently in the Western press on the contradictory nature and insolvency of Solzhenitsyn's political ambitions.

The Committee for State Security is taking measures to circumscribe Solzhenitsyn's attempts to conduct hostile activity, to compromise him further in the eyes of Soviet people and work public opinion, and to step up its surveillance of individuals who rendered Solzhenitsyn support when he lived in the Soviet Union.

Chairman of the Committee for State Security
Andropov

F. 3, *op.* 80, *d.* 647, *l.* 117–118. Original.

Notes

1. *Page one bears the resolution: "Circulate," and the signatures of M. Suslov, F. Kulakov, A. Kosygin, N. Podgorny, A. Shelepin, V. Grishin, B. Ponomarev, K. Mazurov, A. Kirilenko, A. Pelshe, P. Demichev, and D. Polyansky; on the reverse side is the notation: "Comrades Grechko, Gromyko on vacation. 7.29.74."*

2. This was decidedly wishful thinking on the part of the KGB. In March, Solzhenitsyn had released his *Letter to the Soviet Leaders*, which was reprinted in full in the *New York Times* and many other papers around the globe, and provoked worldwide discussion. Similarly, volume one of *The Gulag Archipelago* was having a phenomenal success in translation (two million paperbacks were printed in the USA alone) and Solzhenitsyn's fame was even greater than before his expulsion.

Part V
1975–1980
Exile

141 Memorandum from the Committee for State Security of the USSR Council of Ministers

"On *The Oak and the Calf* and the Further Compromising of Solzhenitsyn"[1]

No. 1437–A
6 June 1975
Classified

To the Central Committee:
The Committee for State Security reports that the publication of articles and documents advantageous for us in various organs of the bourgeois press have led to a certain re-evaluation of Solzhenitsyn's persona by the Western public. The decline of interest in his persona has forced Solzhenitsyn to make a series of intemperate statements and publications. In particular, Solzhenitsyn has published a book entitled *The Oak and the Calf* with YMCA Press (France), the manuscript of which, as he says, was taken out of the Soviet Union by the West German writer Heinrich Böll (the book and a brief review are enclosed). At the same time, Solzhenitsyn has announced "progress toward the end of work on his next 'knots'—*October 1916* and *March 1917*, which represent continuations of his lampoon *August 1914*.

To publicize the book *The Oak and the Calf*, Solzhenitsyn went to Paris where, on 11 April of this year, he took part in a TV program on this book. During the program, Solzhenitsyn expressed thoroughly anti-Soviet opinions and preached such reactionary views on certain issues that he caused consternation even among the representatives of the French bourgeois press who had been invited to the program. Solzhenitsyn, in particular, condemned Western countries for not providing real assistance to the regimes in Phnom Penh and Saigon in their struggle against "communist" aggression, and stated that "the victory of the popular liberation forces in Cambodia and South Vietnam was the worst thing that could happen to the people of those countries."

Solzhenitsyn's statement made an exceptionally unfavorable impression on the French public, and the organizers of the broadcast had to "elucidate" certain things in the press.

According to available data, Solzhenitsyn attempts to distort the role of V.I. Lenin during the Great October Socialist Revolution and tries to over-emphasize the role of Shlyapnikov, the leader of "the workers' opposition," in his sequels, *October 1916* and *March 1917*. Some of the factual material needed to write the aforesaid sequels Solzhenitsyn received from M. Yakubovich, a former member of the Union Bureau of Mensheviks. According to Yakubovich, Solzhenitsyn intends to falsify the material he obtained in order to give an incorrect interpretation of the role of certain figures in the revolution. As a result, Yakubovich has supplied us with additional information that makes it possible to expose Solzhenitsyn as a falsifier of history.

On the basis of materials received from Yakubovich, as well as on the basis of N. Yakovlev's book *August 1, 1914*,[2] we intend to prepare some appropriate articles. We think they will damage Solzhenitsyn, because both authors used factual material in their works that Solzhenitsyn included in his books *October 1916* and *March 1917*.

These articles will be distributed abroad through the channels of Novosti Press Agency.

Please review.

Chairman of the Committee for State Security
Andropov

Enclosure

Summary
of *The Oak and the Calf* by A.I. Solzhenitsyn, YMCA Press Paris, 1975, 629 pages[3]

The Oak and the Calf has a subtitle: *Essays on Literary Life*. It consists of a brief introduction, ten chapters, and an appendix that includes the so-called open letters of Solzhenitsyn, his statements, interviews, and some other materials.

Solzhenitsyn's book describes certain periods of his life from the moment *One Day in the Life of Ivan Denisovich* was being prepared for publication to his deportation abroad in February 1974. It reveals his relations with the government authorities, the editorial board of *Novy Mir* magazine, and representatives of the creative and scientific intelligentsia. The title of the book is allegorical. Solzhenitsyn tries to represent himself as "the calf" who hasn't enough strength to overcome "the oak" (the Soviet State).

Characteristically, throughout the entire story, Solzhenitsyn exposes himself with cynical frankness as an irreconcilable enemy of socialism and workers' power. The author's hatred of Marxist-Leninist ideology and the Communist Party of the Soviet Union runs through the entire book. Solzhenitsyn does not even try this time to conceal his contemptuous attitude toward the creative intelligentsia, which he blames for cowardliness and conformity, and toward the overwhelming majority of the newspapers and journals published by the creative unions. At the same time, because of his exaggerated self-conceit, he constantly draws the reader's attention to the "exclusiveness" of the role he supposedly played in the political and public life of the country in the 1960s and 1970s.

In the first chapter of the book Solzhenitsyn notes that he started to write his works with no hope of ever publishing them. However, soon after the Twenty-Second Party Congress and Tvardovsky's speech there,[4] according to Solzhenitsyn, "the long awaited moment of terrible joy had arrived—the moment when I had to lift my head out from under the water . . . it was impossible to let that precious moment . . . go by!"

Solzhenitsyn describes in the next chapters how he managed to give the manuscript of *One Day in the Life of Ivan Denisovich* to Tvardovsky. He gives an account of the history of its publication and his personal relations with Tvardovsky, with members of the editorial board of *Novy Mir* and the Secretariat of the USSR Union of Writers, and speaks of the preparation of *Cancer Ward* for publication. Especially noteworthy is the fact that, making a slight bow toward only five modern Soviet writers (Shukshin, Mozhaev, Tendryakov, Belov, and Soloukhin), Solzhenitsyn speaks of all the other representatives of the creative intelligentsia with extreme scorn and arrogance, and in some cases even insultingly. He considers the USSR Writers' Union to be "a sacrilegious bazaar in the temple of literature, deserving only of the leather scourge." Characterizing A.G. Dementyev, Tvardovsky's deputy, Solzhenitsyn writes: ". . . Dementyev, who in the terrible year of 1949 hadn't failed in the role of executioner and organization secretary of the Leningrad Writer's Organization, in the Khrushchev period became the commissar of the most liberal magazine . . . was he sent there to freshen it up a bit, to clean up its act a bit?—but not to let too much through either!" And further, talking of Dementyev's speech during a discussion of *One Day in the Life of Ivan Denisovich* at a meeting of the editorial board: "Dementyev resembled an excited ferocious boar toward the end of his monologue, and if a hundred and fifty pages of my story were placed in front of him at that time, he would have probably chomped them to bits with his fangs."

While speaking positively of Tvardovsky on the whole and recognizing his talent as a poet, Solzhenitsyn cannot restrain himself from continually drawing the attention of readers to his illness.[5] Describing his numerous arguments with the Editor-in-Chief of *Novy Mir*, Solzhenitsyn accuses him of compromising with the government. He cites Tvardovsky's membership in the Party as the main reason for these arguments and even his very illness:

> Himself strangled during those months, he helped to strangle me as well. . . . A poet cannot belong to the Party for so many years without damage to himself. . . . I understood one thing about Tvardovsky: What else, for thirty-five years, could relieve this frustrating, burning, shameful, and fruitless stress if not vodka?. . . Go ahead and throw stones at him.

Erasing the entire path of development of Soviet literature and distorting the facts, Solzhenitsyn slanderously claims that our literature is oppressed and censored, and Soviet writers are without rights.

Solzhenitsyn describes in several chapters how, playing on Tvardovsky's trust, and despite the latter's categorical ban, he actively distributed his writings in samizdat. The same chapters reveal a sense of hurt pride in the author, who bore a grudge because he was not awarded the Lenin Prize for literature. Thus, Solzhenitsyn writes: "Yes, I gave them out!! I wrote them and I'll give them out! To hell with all your publishing houses!—People fight for my book, read it and copy it at night, it'll be a literary fact before you manage to open your mouths! Let all those Lenin Prize laureates try to give out their manuscripts in this way!" And further: "When I finished the first part of *Cancer Ward* I knew, of course, that it would not be accepted for publication. My main hope was samizdat."

Solzhenitsyn does not conceal the fact either that by distributing his writings in samizdat, he was pursuing the goal of subsequently sending them to the West for publication.

But he did not distribute his sharpest anti-Soviet lampoons through samizdat, afraid of criminal liability, and passed them to the West personally through a completely secret channel: "I have the possibility now to reveal an almost unbelievable fact . . . that I accomplished all the transmissions to the West neither through intermediaries, nor through a chain of people, but myself, with my own hands!"

In an attempt to defame Lenin's idea of Party mindedness in literature and the principle of Socialist Realism in the arts, Solzhenitsyn tried to prove that there were insurmountable, antagonistic obstacles between the creative intelligentsia and the government, because "in our country it has been the government itself, since its earliest, bloodthirsty days, that has driven all of our literature through a political pipe that was crudely carved and had rough edges."

Solzhenitsyn's attitude toward the Soviet government and the dictatorship of the proletariat is charged with pathological hatred. The majority of the book's chapters contain open declarations to this effect: "I have been dreaming for a long time that some photographer would produce an album: *The Dictatorship of the Proletariat*. There would be no comments or text, just *faces*—two or three hundred sagging, obese, sleepy, vicious mugs, and pictures of them getting into automobiles, mounting rostrums, towering over their desks—no comments, just: *The Dictatorship of the Proletariat!*"

Urging that a struggle be waged against the Soviet government, Solzhenitsyn, knowing no bounds in his impudence, states that it is necessary to speak with the nation's leaders only from a position of force, and to create the maximum uproar possible in the West, but the fight itself has to be conducted in the Soviet Union proper. In this connection he writes:

> . . . show force. How well they understand this language! *Only this language! This language alone . . .* they respect the *fist*, nothing more, the harder you punch them, the safer you are. . . . I never once regretted it: I gave it to them good, said everything I wanted! Neither *these* leaders, nor the next ones will be able to deal with the thunderbolts I've unleashed on them for the next fifty years. . . . I published the *Archipelago*, in the best possible place—while still there! . . . If I had published it . . . while in the West—it would not have had half the killing power.

Playing the holy fool and appealing to religious notions, Solzhenitsyn even goes so far as to picture himself as some avenging sword: "I'm only a sword, well honed against evil spirits, and enchanted so as to slash and scatter them. Help me, oh Lord, not to break from the blows! Not to fall from Thy hand!"

In some chapters of the book, Solzhenitsyn describes his relations with his family members, commenting that his second wife—N. Svetlova—was not only a kindred spirit and faithful helper, but also suggested various courses of action, gave him advice, etc. One chapter in the book is dedicated to the award of the Nobel Prize for Literature to Solzhenitsyn.

In some chapters, the author does not stop short at blatant falsifications and slander, speaking of alleged "persecution" on the part of the KGB and other government agencies.

On the whole, the book offers extensive material for exposing Solzhenitsyn as a vehement class enemy, a staunch political adversary of the state and social system of the Soviet Union and of other socialist countries.

Chief of KGB Directorate
F. Bobkov

F. 3, *op.* 80, *d.* 663, *l.* 1–9. Original.

Notes

1. *The first page bears the signatures of M. Suslov, A. Kirilenko, and B. Ponomarev, and the notation: "The KGB (Comrade P.P. Laptev) has been informed that there are no comments."*
2. Professor N.N. Yakovlev, a historian, went on to become the leading academic expert on "ideological subversion" (see Documents 144 and 145). His chef d'oeuvre was *The CIA Versus the USSR* (1983) which traced a worldwide propaganda campaign by the CIA and posited complete CIA control of the dissident movement.
3. *The book was left at the Secretariat by Comrade M. Suslov. Reported by S. Avetisyan. 6.18.75.*
4. At the Twenty-Second Party Congress, held in October 1961, Tvardovsky gave a rousing speech in which he called on Soviet writers to "show the labors and ordeals of our people in a manner that is totally truthful and faithful to life, without varnishing, and without cunningly smoothing out all contradictions." It was this speech, and the strongly anti-Stalinist flavor of the Congress, that persuaded Solzhenitsyn to submit *One Day in the Life of Ivan Denisovich* for publication.
5. A euphemism for Tvardovsky's alcoholism, which increasingly became a problem toward the end of his life.

142 Report of the Committee for State Security of the USSR Council of Ministers

"On the Publication of an Open Letter by V.A. Tvardovskaya to Solzhenitsyn in the Italian Newspaper *L'Unita*"[1]

No. 1812–A
11 July 1975
Top Secret

To the Central Committee:
The Committee for State Security with the permission of the Central Committee (our No. 1437–A of 6 June 1975) is implementing measures to discredit Solzhenitsyn and his anti-Soviet writings in the eyes of the world public.

As a result, the Italian newspaper *L'Unita* published on 24 June an open letter (the newspaper and translation are attached) from Tvardovsky's daughter, V.A. Tvardovskaya, a researcher at the Institute of History at the USSR Academy of Sciences, in which she cites concrete facts to expose Solzhenitsyn as having distorted Tvardovsky's role in his destiny. Tvardovskaya also accuses Solzhenitsyn of exaggerated conceit and of attempting to interpret world events "through the prism of his own predestination."

According to available data, Tvardovskaya's letter has been well received by the Western public.

The Committee for State Security is continuing to implement measures to compromise Solzhenitsyn.

Reported for information purposes.

Chairman of the Committee for State Security
Andropov

Enclosure

Translation of the Article in the Italian Newspaper *L'Unita* of 6.24.75
Tvardovsky's Daughter Speaks in the Press About Her Father: Letter to Solzhenitsyn from Moscow

The letter rejects statements made (by Solzhenitsyn) about the former Editor-in-Chief of *Novy Mir* and about that period whose starting point—in the minds and memory of unbiased people—was the Twentieth Party Congress. These statements are superficial and primitive: "There is simplicity that is worse than robbery: this simplicity robs the soul and the mind, stripping them of historical perspective, without which the appeal to courage and truth are empty words."

From our Editorial Office, Moscow, June:
Solzhenitsyn's most recent book, published now in the West . . . deals at length with Alexander Tvardovsky, who passed away in 1971. This name is well known in Soviet poetry and is closely associated with a part of the history of the magazine *Novy Mir*, which Tvardovsky edited for sixteen years. The personality and work of Tvardovsky became particularly well known during the period following the turning point at the Twentieth Congress. *Novy Mir* was the magazine that published the first work by Solzhenitsyn, namely, *One Day in the Life of Ivan Denisovich*. Valentina Alexandrovna, the poet's daughter, writes that Solzhenitsyn is currently distorting the role Tvardovsky played among Soviet intellectual circles. To re-establish the truth, Valentina Alexandrovna decided to send Solzhenitsyn an "open letter" by way of the newspaper *L'Unita*, a newspaper that is much read and whose opinion is heeded by workers and the intelligentsia. Tvardovsky's daughter reminds us that her father knew and loved his country and its culture. He told us: "I hope you will not forget your civic, moral, and political obligations."

Valentina Alexandrovna Tvardovskaya lives in Moscow and works at the Institute of History at the USSR Academy of Sciences. Only recently, the publishing house Editori Reuniti in Italy published one of her books on the Russian populist movement.

One of Solzhenitsyn's recent points of view: the statement he made to an Italian neo-fascist magazine in which, among other things, he said: "The right anticommunist wing should make its last crusade, and I feel wonderful among these right-winged beliefs and civilizations."

Carlo Benedetti

400

Dear Alexander Isaevich,

You have decided to acquaint the world with your life in your homeland during the memorable years that started with the publications of *One Day in the Life of Ivan Denisovich*—a turning point not only for you, but also for numerous readers, our compatriots. After that, your life entered the public arena.

"I believe you will pass the test of fame," were the words you cited in your book by Alexander Trofimovich Tvardovsky, the man who discovered you—first for himself, and then for his readers—along with your character, your writer's world, which contained a whole stratum of human life in our century. He discovered and accepted it as something without which his own existence and the existence of other people seemed to him incomplete.

"This story," Tvardovsky wrote in his article "On the Occasion of the Anniversary" (the fortieth anniversary of *Novy Mir*, January 1965),

> had to exist, it seemed to have already been in existence, only waiting for the time of its publication. . . . Up until now, Solzhenitsyn has published only four small (if we count the number of pages) works, each of which has testified to the many-sided development of an author at the height of his literary powers. . . . A great, very promising road lies before us, on which there certainly will be difficulties and delays and miscalculations, but I trust there will be even greater successes and accomplishments.

What happened afterwards is fairly well known from the point of view of the facts, but nevertheless needs to be seriously studied and evaluated. As a historian, I realize how difficult this task is, regardless of extraneous considerations and obstacles. I do not even think of making this attempt given my own abilities, much less on the spur of the moment. But it is impossible for me not to react to your book. You gave my father too great a place in it. The "portrait" of Tvardovsky comprises the nucleus of your version of the development of Soviet literature and history during that large chunk of time, whose starting point—in the minds and memory of the majority of unbiased people—was the Twentieth Party Congress and the process it initiated of social and individual internal changes.

Having read the book, one is convinced how removed you are from comprehending the significance of that process, which is evidently fated to be long and hard and which, having started here in our country, has not been limited—in the most important universal sense—to our country alone. How far you are from understanding the irreversibility of the tremendous movement and changes that have filled the current century and particularly its last decades. You have your own timetable of events, your own division into periods—based on yourself. And of course, your own particular understanding of their meaning. Believing in your own path, predestined "from above," and your own almost mystical calling, you examine everything around you, including the fate of people who intersected with your life, and the events in your country and in the world, through the prism of your own predestination.

You tower over the whole gaunt of people who appear in the pages of your memoirs—the only one who always knew what to do and where to go. "I see better, I see farther, I have decided." These words in your book show you to me in your entirety, Alexander Isaevich, the way you were, and even more, the way you want to seem now, "straightening out" your own life in conformity with your pre-set purpose. And Tvardovsky, for you, is primarily a reflection of your life, only with a minus sign, so to speak, an anti-Solzhenitsyn. One cannot immediately pick out the thread on which you have carefully strung together all the facts, but once one has noticed it, one cannot help but follow it. The thread running throughout the book is the incompatibility of two principles. One is personified by you, Alexander Isaevich Solzhenitsyn, an integrated person, lacking any doubt or hesitation, always and everywhere "breaking through," consistently negating everything in our life that originates in the revolution, everything that proceeds from it and is therefore doomed to be incorrigibly evil, until Russia returns to its primordial patriarchal principles, albeit modernized under the guidance of ideology-free technocratic leaders. Not only socialism but even democracy, are, of course, beside the point here.

Tvardovsky is the embodiment of the opposite principle, a man who was devoted to revolutionary traditions, who did not separate himself from social movements and changes that filled this century here and outside Russia. Tvardovsky, for whom Marxism "was not simply literary ballast;" Tvardovsky, who did not perceive the world "without dividing it into capitalism and socialism;" "Tvardovsky with a Red Party membership card in his breast pocket against which beat his heart." This Tvardovsky is the anti-Solzhenitsyn, who in your vision is supposed to be ambivalent, inconsistent, weak, and with no grounds for his understanding of either the present or the future.

Tvardovsky's ambivalence is one of the cornerstones of your ideas. You see it in the fact that Tvardovsky did not shake off what you regard as the historical dust from his feet, didn't shake it off, although he agonized over those horrible events and misfortunes that were inseparable from a certain era in our country's history, and that only a coldly cynical or dead-ended doctrinaire view could perceive as simply "zigzags." But you too, Alexander Isaevich, are not far from a doctrinaire attitude, only turned inside out. You too crave simple solutions and uncomplicated formulas.

As I read your book, I keep thinking that the difference between you and A.T. was not only in views but in the very foundations of your personalities. You are a person for whom all the issues have been resolved once and for all. Everything that the world is pondering over and passionately arguing about, whether it be history or modern times, or Lenin and October, or the need for a social revolution despite its novelty in the current, post-war era, or the growing unity of the world even with its increasingly obvious diversity, both general and particular, or the war on Vietnam, or the Watergate affair— everything is clear to you from the very beginning, everything is simple for you. But as the Russian proverb has it, there is simplicity that is worse than robbery. It robs the soul and the brain, stripping them of a true historical perspective, without which the appeal to courage and truth are empty words, no matter how eloquent.

Tvardovsky did not have ready-made answers. He was open to questions, whether they dealt with the deepest issues of creativity, or the most complicated issues of civic life. Most open for him until the last days of his life was the issue of a historical, objective, uncompromising evaluation of his generation, the generation in whose consciousness, deeds, and destiny victories and defeats were so contradictorily linked, clarity and blindness, courage and weakness. I talked with my father countless times about this issue that gave him no peace. A.T. increasingly understood that the answer had to include the entire age without removing a part from it, without "any blank spots;" that the meaning of an age can be plumbed only through serious reflection that does not forget its responsibility both to oneself and to society, and is not prevented from developing ahead of time by facts and evasive "formulas." Hence he was concerned most of all to help new generations to think independently, respond critically, and remain faithful to themselves. Only in this did he see true Marxist socialist and democratic continuity, continuity in fact, a continuation and development.

No, he did not call on people to forget, repeating time and again: "Memory, no matter how bitter you are, be a benchmark for the century." Forgetting was physically impossible for him, suicidal. But memory for him was not simply an appeal to vengeance and repentance. "You cannot build anything solely on anger, on negation"—that is what he meant when he spoke about the differences between you.

In the past, in the nineteenth century, negation was called "the irony of history." While it is just in its deepest motivations, it also turns out to be helpless to liberate itself from many features of the moral and psychological habits of what is being negated. Your link with a past that has not been fully overcome is not your fault, it is your misfortune—but even an explanation is not a justification. "Rendering circumstances their due, we will not, however, let people hide behind them—people are facts, too, and they are responsible for their deeds." This was written by one of my father's most beloved writers, by one of the most perceptive and moral representatives of socialist thinking in Russia—Hertzen. The criterion he offered is even more imperative today, especially for those who consider themselves to be advocates of truth and justice.

"Life taught me the bad," you write, "and I believe in the bad more"—and that is no accidental admission for you. Reading your book closely, one begins to understand that in your soul you really do harbor belief in the bad, which allows you to look first of all for what's wrong with everyone you come in contact with in life, for ways in which they are damaged, their weaknesses and inferiorities—everything that degrades a person. I will not speak now about the impact of this belief in the bad, which is to be explained in some ways by the tragic circumstances of your life, on the moral meaning of your works that A.T. valued exactly for the opposite—for their continuation and renewal of the humanist tradition of Russian literature. By believing in the bad, you above all betray yourself, the creator of the image of Ivan Denisovich. But there is another aspect that calls attention to itself; the fact that your belief in everything bad is not an accidental or unconscious outcome of some dark feelings that you find it hard to subdue, but rather a world view that you control. The people that populate your book—and I have in mind not only those whom you deliberately consider your enemies—are all depicted in such a way that their flaws and weaknesses, imagined or real, serve as a contrasting background for you, as a kind of pedestal, upon which you tower, the Unique One. But I think you get the opposite result. Of course, no one may encroach on your right to depict your life as you yourself see it—all memoirs are subjective. However, when a person dares to make his life, its lessons and its meaning, public property, then features of his personality stand out very clearly that do not otherwise strike the eye. And no artistic talent can conceal them. On the contrary, it will make the personal stand out even more, and will reveal what is hidden. It is hard to imagine anything more instructive, in this sense, then the picture you have drawn of your relations with the magazine where you got your start as a writer. Your "strong-willed principles" are there revealed most vividly, your authoritarian nature and intolerance. It is just this intolerance towards ways of thinking that differ from yours that is the basis of your concept of Tvardovsky's failure as a poet and editor. While acknowledging the strengths of Tvardovsky's convictions, in the final analysis you always interpret differences with him to be the result of his inconsistency, his desire to ingratiate himself with the authorities, even unscrupulousness and cowardice. Your interpretation of the facts rests on the given that your opinions are true, while it is equally a given that Tvardovsky is always wrong, unable to rise to Solzhenitsyn's level. If

Tvardovsky had only listened to you, everything would have been different. What exactly would have been different? In reality, your program is not very great. The main point, if not the only one, is to publish absolutely all of your writings without delay. Above all, you blame A.T. for not doing so. Tvardovsky is now gone, and the history of *Novy Mir* has not yet been written, and it seems that this makes your task easier.

But where did you get the idea that Tvardovsky who, after all, in your expression, had his own "orbit," was obliged nevertheless to subordinate himself to your influence and follow you? And if he did not do that, if, while appreciating your collaboration a great deal, he could not and did not wish under any circumstances to sacrifice to it all *Novy Mir*'s prose (represented by the names that you yourself rate as the best of our country's literature, and by other names), then of course it had to be, because he was a bigwig, hogtied by his nomenclature status, clinging tightly to the armrest of his editor's chair. . . .

The well-known motto "Whoever is not with us is against us" has been translated to your own liking: "Whoever is not with Solzhenitsyn is against conscience and truth." And from that perspective there is practically no difference between *Novy Mir* and other magazines, including those clearly hostile toward him. The rating of *Novy Mir* as a magazine on the sidelines of literary and social life, as a magazine that "didn't rise from its knees," that "perished with a stooped back," is not founded on any serious analysis of the literary process. No matter how paradoxical it might seem, and despite the many pages you have devoted to *Novy Mir*, the magazine is actually absent from your *Sketches of Literary Life*. They speak only of a feeble, incapable editor and provide some caricatures of his employees who are toadies and cowards. But a magazine is not only a good or a bad Editor-in-Chief, not only the editorial board and the small collective of editors taken together. It is the much larger circle of active authors, diverse representatives of the literary world, scientists and journalists who are drawn to this magazine, and just as large a circle of reviewers, authors, and finally active readers who send the magazine their views, comments, wishes, and evaluations from all over the country, from large and small cities and from the villages. All this taken together is an essential part of what is commonly called public opinion, which, although it is hard to quantify, is nevertheless real and weighty.

There is nothing of this in your book, nor could there be—here you are simply not qualified, not up to date on matters you did not follow, but upon which you undertake to pass judgment. *Novy Mir*, which you admit you did not read, of course seemed unnecessary to you in the form it took in reality, not free of weaknesses, but having its strengths as well, reflecting in and of itself the movement of the times, and generally acknowledged to be shaping both its readers and its authors—individualists of every possible stripe

(Tvardovsky's credo was "we can use everything that's talented, everything that's artistically truthful").

I think that for your Western readers, who are unaware of the real facts of life, it will remain unclear why *Novy Mir*, in your words, "died" when it ought to have prospered, gaining advantage from its tendency to compromise. But it's only strange if we remain grounded in reality. If we follow your thread, however, as I said before, which runs through your whole memoirs, then we must acknowledge that what was pre-ordained occurred, the sentence of fact was passed on to those who did not listen to you, although you knew the true solution.

Authoritarianism coexists poorly with morality. And if additional proof is needed of this, you have offered it with your book, with your method of rewriting history.

Illustrating your concept of Tvardovsky's failure, his inability to hold the reins of the magazine, you picture him as a "lost, weak" person who had become a captive of his own ailment, bound hand and foot with his "nomenclature status, his official position as 'first poet of Russia,'" who surrounded himself with unprincipled "time servers," and, as a result, let *Novy Mir* slip from his "feeble hands." Without this Tvardovsky, the pedestal you erected for yourself obviously would not have been so solid and high as you would have liked, and your mission and exclusiveness, and the uniqueness of your judgments on the future would not have appeared so convincing as they seem to you personally.

However, there are elementary rules of morality, accepted by everyone regardless of their beliefs and their degree of development. Are you an exception to this as well? In asserting the primacy of morality over politics, you, in the name of your own political intentions, consider it possible to overstep all bounds of the permissible. You allow yourself to use unceremoniously whatever you overheard and spied on through the keyhole, you cite gossip that is not first-hand, you do not even stop at "quoting" A.T.'s delirium in the middle of the night, which you wrote down, as you assure us, verbatim. Appealing to people to "live not by lies,"[2] with the utmost cynicism, though sometimes with a certain coquetry, you describe how you made deception the rule when dealing not only with those whom you considered as enemies, but also with those who lent a helping hand, supporting you in times of need, trusting you. Surely you, who call yourself a faithful Christian, who writes the word God with a capital letter, understand the blasphemy of all this? And now, turning someone else's life inside out, arbitrarily disposing of information about it that came to you by mere chance, you treat yourself with extreme "personal care," you are sincere just as much as you need to be to gain the trust of the reader, and to justify in his eyes your right to intrude into the most forbidden areas of another person's life. But by no means are you inclined to reveal yourself with the fullness advertised in your book. Thus, interpreting in your own way A.T.'s struggle to get the Lenin Prize awarded to *One Day in the Life of Ivan Denisovich* (as if he wanted to get the prize for the cover of his magazine), you keep silent about your own readiness at that time to grab the prize with both hands. And who knows what the fate of Solzhenitsyn the Lenin Prize–holder would have been? Who knows how it would have turned out if you had managed to collaborate with the magazine that was polemicizing with *Novy Mir*, which you were trying to arrange behind A.T.'s back in a duplicitous fashion?

And how do you speak of yourself in the scenes when Tvardovsky was leaving *Novy Mir*? "Don't go, Alexander Trifonovich," you said persuasively, while thinking to yourself that he should have done so long ago. It is frightening to imagine you in the role of managing a magazine, or even as sole adviser to the Editor-in-Chief. The manners of a general and such double-dealing would have poisoned the magazine's life even without any external restrictions.

Yes, your memoirs are not a confession, they are the opposite in both the literal and figurative senses of the word. And still, the picture that emerges from the book obviously does not correspond to its original purpose. What, after all, did you oppose to in the "duplicity" you saw in Tvardovsky that so disillusioned you? Integrity or a turning of your back on all questions, a refusal of searches and doubts? Consistency or immobility? Faithfulness to oneself, but only to oneself, while permitting duplicity in relations with others? And do you think, Alexander Isaevich, that all of this is compatible with your high calling? Then what does it consist of today, in reality?

Challenging your portrait of Tvardovsky, digging into the details of my father's life, proving the opposite on the principle of "it wasn't like that," or "it wasn't completely like that," or "it wasn't like that at all," is a job, from my point of view, that is shaming and senseless. But you knew what you were doing, you had a definite goal, and the means you employed to reach it, apparently, exposes all the more its ideological and moral nature. Your memory, which became peculiarly selective, was subordinate to this goal. Everything that could disrupt the picture that you needed was forgotten, discarded, silenced, or denied. In some cases it was difficult to tell whether it was deliberate distortion of the truth or absolute lack of comprehension that guided your pen, but the sense of falsehood did not leave me even in the places where you were supposedly quoting A.T. verbatim. You recall, for example, that in a discussion with you, Tvardovsky could not cite any reasons in favor of the Revolution except one: "What would have happened to me, what would I have been if it had not been for the Revolution!" The fact that

A.T. was able to cite only this as reasonable grounds for the Revolution—let that, like many other things, remain on your conscience. But it is characteristic how you understood, or rather misunderstood, this phrase. For you it is proof virtually of selfish self-interest on the part of a person whom the social upheaval permitted to climb "to the top." For Tvardovsky his own fate was simply a part of the people's fate. You had to completely fail to know or understand the man to assume that he would base his attitude toward reality on his personal circumstances. And you will find this ignorance and misunderstanding at every step of the way. But it is not I who will testify to readers on your lack of truthfulness. You are contradicted by all that Tvardovsky left behind him—his own writings, the issues of the magazine that he edited for sixteen years, the tremendous correspondence with writers and readers, his living image in the memory of everyone who knew him. All this is not nocturnal delirium, nor conjectures and fabrications, nor gossip that could not be verified. This is reality, enshrining the very force that will refute your memoirs, and which with time will act all the more strongly against you.

V. A. Tvardovskaya

Chief of Directorate, Committee for State Security of the USSR Council of Ministers
Bobkov

F. 3, *op.* 80, *d.* 648, *l.* 1–14. Original.

Notes

1. *Page one bears the signatures of M. Suslov, A. Kirilenko, and B. Ponomarev.*
2. A reference to a public appeal issued by Solzhenitsyn on the eve of his expulsion from the Soviet Union, in which he called on his fellow citizens to "stop cooperating with the lie." The appeal was called "Live Not By Lies" and became the name of a samizdat collection of documents about the expulsion.

143 Memorandum from the Committee for State Security of the USSR Council of Ministers

"On Publishing Yakovlev's Article 'The Calf with a Blade' on Solzhenitsyn in *Golos Rodiny* (Voice of the Motherland)"[1]

No. 2337–A
30 August 1975
Secret

The Committee for State Security is sending the galley proofs of an article by Prof. N.N. Yakovlev written in connection with the publication of Solzhenitsyn's lampoon *The Oak and the Calf* in the West (report No. 1437–A on 7.6.75). It seems advisable to publish the article by Yakovlev in the newspaper *Golos Rodiny* [Voice of the Motherland] which is distributed abroad,[2] and to send it to the West through the channels of Novosti Press Agency.

Please review.

Chairman of the Committee for State Security
Andropov

"The Calf with a Blade"

"Blade" means knife or dagger in underworld slang.

This book is a chronicle (obviously with acknowledged and un-acknowledged omissions), a hagiography of the last twenty years of the greatest man of our time according to its composer, ie, the man himself. No, perhaps not even "man" is the right word—go higher. To wit: "What gladdens me and what reassures me is that I am not the one who plans it all and carries it out, I'm only a sword, well honed against evil spirits, enchanted so as to slash and scatter them. Help me, oh Lord, not to break from the blows! Not to fall from Thy hand!" (pp. 407–408)[3]

Since such intimate relations with god are announced so soon, the history of the book is no surprise. Everything that happened to him during those years Solzhenitsyn hastened to write down, then conscientiously hid the pages in his latest hiding place. Now in the West at happy leisure—"the sunny goblet of the Swiss mountains beneath the window of my mountain cabin" (p. 412)—he has collected the pages into a book, only 629 pages of fine print. He polished it up a bit, inserted a subtitle "Sketches of Literary Life," and published it in Paris.

Most likely, after accumulating his thick volume, the scribe suddenly flew into a tizzy: "Cursing myself for this boring thoroughness I'm wasting the readers' and my own time." But he immediately recovered himself: "There is nothing I can compare *the sheer relief of speaking out* to . . . of bellowing not from some rooftop, not to a square, but to the whole world." (p. 181) Then followed a cynical confession. From the pages of his own book his image rose indescribably fouled, and that solely by his own zeal.

What he is after is beyond comprehension. As a working hypothesis there is probably only one possible explanation: in the West, apparently this wretch found himself among like-minded scum who take his credo for granted and were not in the least shocked. To go one better than they, to draw attention to himself, he had to turn a stranger trick, and that's exactly what this ambitious climber did. And set to work energetically with his pen, like a crook with his knife. . . .

> There's a knife in my boot,
> But I cannot show it,
> else all will fail

That's how he was, Solzhenitsyn now acknowledges (p. 291), during his brief stroll among Soviet writers. There's no need to add or subtract anything here—it's a vile story. Some of our shrewd men of letters opened their arms in the late 1950s and early 1960s because an enormous talent surfaced from the depths of obscurity, and what a boulder! They forgot the folk wisdom which tells you exactly what floats to the surface. When *One Day in the Life of Ivan Denisovich* and its author were discovered and brought to *Novy Mir*, it was a day of great triumph at the magazine. A.T. Tvardovsky

> kept beaming more and more. It was one of his happiest moments, it was his birthday party, not mine. He looked at me with benevolence, almost overflowing into love. . . . I was asked about my life, past and present, and everybody was embarrassed and fell silent when I cheerfully replied that I made a living by teaching, earning sixty rubles a month, and that it was enough for me. (I didn't want a full-time salary because I needed more time, and since my wife was well paid, I didn't have to support the family.) . . . And I was dressed in accordance with

the level of my salary. Imperiously and happily, Tvardovsky at once gave instructions for a contract to be signed with me at the highest permissible rate (one advance equaled my salary for two years). I sat there as if in a trance, making a big effort so as not to say too much about myself. . . . As the fox said to the peasant: just let me put my paw on the cart, and I'll jump in by myself. That's what happened to me. (pp. 30, 32)

That was the debut of the sufferer in literature. The friendly handshakes of these terribly nice men of letters, however, hung in midair. He was far from frank with the bighearted individuals gathered around the long oval table of the editorial board. This newly minted sufferer for truth was deceitful to the tips of his fingernails. He had long ago learned the art of inducing tears of pity in people. By sheer oversight (there it is, the inexorable fate of graphomaniacs!) he forgot how, two dozen pages earlier, before describing the beautiful scene at *Novy Mir*, he had described how matters stood, for example, at the school. And not for the sake of the truth, but solely to stress his uniqueness: "It was not enough to have thirty hours of teaching at the school, counselling work, a lonely bachelor existence (p. 186) (because of the secrecy of my writing I couldn't even marry); even the underground writing was not enough. . . ."

Let us interrupt this confession to note: many hands of friendship and concern were extended to him at this time to put an end once and for all to the poor devil's hard years. Everything possible was done for him. The school principal could not match the level of *Novy Mir*'s payments, but any teacher could tell you what his help was worth, getting his duties down to thirty hours a week and paying the dear man more than one and a half times the monthly salary. Who's talking about dressing yourself on sixty rubles? But let us continue:

It was necessary now to learn the craft of hiding everything written. And another craft came on the heels of this one: making microfilms by myself of the manuscripts . . . then hiding the microfilms inside book jackets with two addressed envelopes: one to the USA . . . an acquaintance with somebody, through him another one, then a code phrase in a letter or a meeting, then a nickname, a chain of several people, and one fine morning you wake up to find: "Oh, my God, I've been a conspirator for a long time now!" (pp. 9–10)

We botched it and he, fine fellow, shuffled right off to the Union of the Soviet Writers to be greeted with sighs, the groans of simpletons, and abundantly splashed with tears of emotion. At the Writers' Union he shook himself and then it started! Well-wishers conversed with him about the high calling of a writer, expecting this engineer of human souls to get down to work directly, but with a certain surprise, at first slight, they noticed that he was not at all attracted to literary activity. You may be sure that within the wonderful community of writers they discussed the said phenomenon a lot, and with Solzhenitsyn himself as well. As to this rogue rated by those who wished him well out of their incorrigible intelligentsia-inspired weakness, and certainly confided in him as well, we will remain silent for the time being. It would be simpler for those who rushed to embrace the genius then to look deep into their hearts, and to recall and keep in mind for the future: the lampoonist had not shown all his cards yet. There's more to come.

The fragmented paragraphs of the book hold many names, events, and facts, some of which took place and some of which certainly didn't. This is not the work of an amateur, but of a professional. In 1945, Solzhenitsyn helped a very close friend of his childhood be sentenced to ten years in prison, thus rewarding him for the preceding eighteen years of friendship. However, that was only the first step, during the investigation. In the labor camp, when he turned into a paid informer under the code name "Vetrov,"[4] he had greater prospects. He regularly wrote reports on the other prisoners, but, as he confessed in the third part of *The Gulag Archipelago*, he was racked with remorse. "I used to sigh," Solzhenitsyn grimaces abroad, recalling those years. "I calmed myself with caveats and placed my signature under the sale of my soul. The sale of the soul to save the body" (*The Gulag Archipelago*, parts 3–4. Paris, 1974, p. 359). As far as sighs are concerned, he is going too far. Vitkevich, who met with Solzhenitsyn many years later and remembered his treachery, nevertheless kept silent; he did not want to discuss it because "knowing my friend, I had no doubt that he would consider himself in the right, and would say that his main task was to save a great writer for Russia" (*The First Circle*, Novosti Press Agency, 1974, pp. 141–142).

Solzhenitsyn-Vetrov was very angry with his former friend, who suspected him of having a hard heart. In his statement of 2 February 1974, he remarked that Vitkevich had taken the road of "slander and personal discreditation," while in *The Gulag Archipelago* revealed the depths of his sensitivity: "Vetrov. The six letters of this name are burned into my memory with shameful cracks. But I had wanted to die with people! I was ready to die with people! How could it happen that I had remained alive among the dogs?" (*The Gulag Archipelago*, p. 359) Let us say what Solzhenitsyn leaves unsaid: a stinking dog that is ready to destroy everything and everybody to save his scabby skin. But enough of that. Let us note only that in the thirty years since the first—or was it the first?—treachery, Solzhenitsyn-Vetrov's skills have improved greatly—now he is a veteran provocateur, which has a direct bearing on his literary affairs.

Those who were involved in his fate in the late 1950s and early 1960s did not notice that for him, Soviet literature, and consequently, its creators, did not exist.

> I had already recognized once and for all that this literature, its dozen thick magazines, two literary newspapers, countless anthologies, individual novels and collected works, and the annual awards and the radio dramatizations of the most boring works, was unreal, and I didn't waste time on them or irritate myself by following them, knowing ahead of time that there couldn't be anything worth while in them. (p. 13)

And if that was the case, then conversations with writers and with Soviet people in general were necessarily brief.

Let's take a meeting of the creative intelligentsia in the Kremlin. "I deliberately went there in my teacher's suit that I had bought in the Worker's Clothing store, that had been repaired over and over again, with patches of red leather on black, and terribly in need of a haircut. It was easier for me that way to keep myself to myself and play the simpleton" (p. 71). Where could he ever find red leather?! It's not easy. If you don't believe me, try asking a consumer services center. I'm sure this benighted holy fool must have run into an expensive private cobbler! Well, be that as it may.

The poor fellow crept into the hall, shut his mouth, and stuck out his patched shoes for everybody to see. Different circumstances, different behavior. He was summoned to the Secretariat of the Soviet Writers' Union with a high purpose: to explain to him clearly that it was unseemly to pass his work around secretly and publish lampoons about his country. "I entered like a stick with the head of a robot: no human movements, no human expression" (p. 187). Well-wishers, trying to steel Solzhenitsyn—why mince words about it—for the frank discussions ahead, wrung their hands: for God's sake don't worry. He responded: "I will explode, but only according to plan if we agree on it at the nineteenth minute, or however many times are necessary during the meeting. And if we don't agree, of course, I won't." (p. 200)

He began speaking in an "unctuous voice." The meeting was like any other—boring, people yawning, of course. The writers didn't realize that for Solzhenitsyn, it was the battle of Borodino, and suddenly "I fired a hundred-and-forty-four–gun salvo at them and sat down quietly in the clouds of smoke." (p. 202) I read to them from a special file that I had prepared long in advance, having written grandiosely on the cover: "The Union of Soviet

Writers and I." (p. 280) And we can be grateful that he didn't frighten them with another gambit: "fixing my eyes in a terrifying convict's stare I announced in a metallic voice. . . ." (p. 364)

But the distinguished writers were not ready at all for:

> The meeting ended on Friday evening. The weekend passed, and on Monday afternoon the British (the BBC) were already broadcasting news of my summons to the Secretariat and the sense of the meeting, and fairly accurately, too [from Solzhenitsyn's own words, but more about that later—N.Y.]. "I'm not a needle in a haystack, I'll not get lost now!" (p. 206)

Solzhenitsyn benefitted to the utmost degree from the heartfelt generosity and kindness of a wonderful man named Tvardovsky. After the first meetings at *Novy Mir* he writes: "We were close friends, we could cooperate! I didn't imagine our editorial boards to be like that." (p. 31) In regard to Solzhenitsyn "Tvardovsky undertook an enormous effort to push forward with the impossible." (p. 67) The seasoned provocateur grabbed the poet with both hands in a mortal lock, while they tried to extract a rational kernel from the lengthy opuses that Solzhenitsyn dragged to him to read. Tvardovsky found that in one of Solzhenitsyn's "novels" some parts were written "from Party positions," but insisted that a lot be removed. "'From Party positions' (in my novel! . . .)—that's significant," smirks Solzhenitsyn now.

> It was not the cynical formulation of an editor who was ready to force the novel through. This combination of my novel with 'Party positions' was the sincere, the deepest, the only possible approach, without which he, a poet, but also a communist, would not have been able to set himself the goal of publishing the novel. But he did set himself such a goal, and he announced it to me. (p. 89)

However, despite Tvardovsky's wishes, it didn't work. Solzhenitsyn stubbornly tried to transform *Novy Mir* into a rostrum for anti-Soviet preaching. The provocateur got a big punch in the nose. What a grand project collapsed, he laments now after so many years: "Why did I give it to Tvardovsky? . . . What did I want? Most likely a repeat of *Ivan Denisovich*: to transfer the responsibility for this work from me to him." (p. 90) Yes, Solzhenitsyn never stopped being Vetrov.

Tvardovsky was increasingly concerned by the question of who he was dealing with. The poet apparently believed that sooner or later this unreasonable, stubborn fellow would come to his senses. But he was facing a sworn enemy. But why—why could Tvardovsky never completely figure out what lay behind the other fellow's "creativity?"

The answer is simple: Tvardovsky was guided by universally accepted standards of relations between people, but was dealing with a person with the psychology of a criminal. Solzhenitsyn recounts mockingly: "He is open with me, I'm never open." (p. 263) "Not once, never could I be as sincere with him." (p. 58) Certain explanations intersperse the lengthy descriptions of almost all the discussions with Tvardovsky—"I was lying" (p. 228); "I pretended, of course" (p. 248); etc. The poet was by no means a naive person:

> 'When will this conspiracy end?!' he would exclaim in his editorial office. I could understand his irritation and even despair: How could he come to an agreement with me and work together with me? Most likely he vowed many times to bind me with a firm relationship, but I would appear, disarm him with my affability and friendliness, and he would be mollified, and would no longer insist on making firm agreements for the future. (page 247)

Solzhenitsyn, while continuously referring to Christ and his suffering crucifixion for the Truth, always followed this tactic. Even describing his last meeting with Tvardovsky, when it was obvious that the great poet had few days left to live, he commented: "Alas, even at this last meeting with him I had to be secretive, as so often in the past. . . ." (p. 344)

But why all this duplicity on the part of a person who had chosen, in his own words, the profession of a lover of truth? The answer is obvious: Solzhenitsyn would not have lasted a single minute next to the pure honesty of Tvardovsky if he had opened himself up to him. Far away in foreign countries, Solzhenitsyn relishes the thought: "Our disagreement reflected the parting of the ways between Russian [in his view—N.Y.] and Soviet literature, and wasn't at all personal." Tvardovsky was "a son of his Party" (p. 143), grits Solzhenitsyn-Vetrov through clenched teeth. That says it all.

Hatred of the poet-Communist consumed Solzhenitsyn, and hiding behind the mask of wishing him well, he literally baited him. However, he measured it out in doses: "If I reveal this to Tvardovsky now, his heart will break!" (p. 121) Solzhenitsyn created constant stress for Tvardovsky. At one point, the poet cast "new reproaches [at me], as if moaning" (p. 142); in another, he became "very frightened" (p. 248), and in desperation, "jumped up and shouted in rage." (p. 144) It meant it was necessary to back off: "I patted him softly on the back but he grew still more enraged—'I'm not nervous!'" (p. 229) And all for the following reason: "He could control only his main hurts. . . . 'I'm putting my head on the block for you and you. . . .'

415

Yes, I could understand him: after all, I never opened up to him, the entire web of my calculations and moves was concealed from him and would emerge unexpectedly." (p. 113) But when the hidden was revealed, unfortunately only a corner of the curtain was lifted and then "there would be violence at the editorial office, he would smash chairs and yell. 'Traitor!!'. . . . he once screamed down the telephone.—'It's an anti-Soviet pamphlet! It's a lie.'" (pp. 293–294) In any case, "no response came" to Solzhenitsyn's last letter to Tvardovsky. (p. 309)

And he who had defiled as much as he could the life of the great poet, assuring everyone, right and left, that he ardently believed in god, had the gall to come to the funeral, and for the ninth day write a hypocritical, blasphemous memorial speech dedicated to Tvardovsky. And this apostate saw in the portrait above the coffin "in all its radiance that childishly shining trust that he carried through his whole life." This apostate who had dishonestly and ruthlessly abused the trust of the deceased was bound to notice that first. . . .

And the book he concludes in a hard, frosty manner: "But I wanted too much from Tvardovsky!" (p. 293) Businesslike, without emotion.

Yes, he was always what he recently called himself in such a masochistic manner but concealed in the past when living on Russian bread: "I'm ideologically extraterritorial!" (p. 147)

The camp theme—the persecutions at the time of the personality cult that Solzhenitsyn stakes his reputation on—represented the blasphemous speculation of a villain. The theme was nothing more than the famous red patch on a black plot, ie, to attract attention, to occupy the position of a lover of justice and use it to try to defame and undermine the Soviet system. It is quite obvious today from his book: This theme, so painful for all Soviet people, was a temporary one for a hypocrite, a foundation on which he would erect his main work, his novel on the year 1917. He chose it in order to make a career out of subversion.

By the winter of 1966–1967 "I discovered that, in the forty-ninth year of my life, I would finish my No. 1 work, everything I intended to write in the course of my life, except the last and most important work—R-17.[5] For thirty years, ever since the end of tenth grade, I had been thinking about that novel which was the primary goal of my life, turning it in my mind, rearranging it, putting it aside and accumulating new material." (p. 167) Two years later he notes: "I just passed my fiftieth birthday, and it coincided with a new feature of my work: I wasn't writing any more about camps, I had completed all my other tasks, I was faced with an entirely new and tremendous job—a novel about 1917 (which I thought at first would take me ten years)." (pp. 317–318)

Solzhenitsyn announces this scribbling with the greatest pride, for he planned to transform first minds, and then the course of history. A prophet can do no less. "I see," he prophesies, "how I am making history." (p. 162) But how, in fact? "Why it all had to happen in such a manner, and how it got intertwined and interwoven beginning with the year 1917." (p. 14) It was the year of the Great October Socialist Revolution. For starters, we will strike a stunning blow against it and use lower-case letters to refer to the Revolution. No sooner said than done. (eg, p. 344) That makes things a little easier. Now let us attack along another line: we'll express ourselves not in the language used by the Russians who accomplished the Great Revolution, because "the socialists, more than anyone else, especially Lenin, ruined the Russian language in their sloppy pamphlets." (p. 135) So that's what the problem is! Otherwise one would be flummoxed by how Solzhenitsyn mangles words and invents new ones that are incredible and horrible. So there is a profound intent in all this, and not just verbal swindling. A principled struggle against Great October, and not an unprincipled contamination of the great Russian language.

One more discovery (at the appropriate location in the Swiss mountains): "They are *communists*, not Russians at all" (p. 138), and it is clearly visible from the height of the aforesaid mountains that "socialism is depraved *in and of itself.*" (p. 308) Having risen to such glorious heights (and long since, by the way), Solzhenitsyn got busy and set about knitting his first knot: *August 1914*. I mean knitting, not writing, because this work has nothing in common with literature. It is not even politics, it is elementary subversion. Those who muttered something about Tolstoyan scope in the description of the year 1914, familiarize yourselves with the author's revelations at first hand, and along the way with Solzhenitsyn's "Russian language:"

> It is not at all a writer's task, but a concentrated strategy. Books are like divisions and corps: sometimes they have to dig in, not shoot, and not stick their heads out; sometimes, in the darkness and silence, they have to cross bridges; and then, concealing their preparations until the very last piece of soil is shovelled, launch a concerted attack at a surprising moment and from a surprising side.

And the author, like a Commander-in-Chief, pushes some forward, or pushes others back to wait . . . twenty knots, one a year means twenty years. But it took two years to write *August*, does that mean forty years? Or fifty?

> Another decision ripened gradually. The criterion for it was the open appearance of Lenin. As long as he figured in only one chapter per Knot and was not connected directly with the action, these chapters could be left with gaps to conceal them, and the Knots could be published without them. That would

417

be possible with the first three Knots, but in Knot four Lenin would already be in Petrograd and acting vigorously, and to reveal the author's attitude to him at that time would be equivalent to publishing the *Archipelago*. So: write and publish three Knots, and then move everything else into the final attack. (pp. 338–339)

Well, well. Has he gone mad, or what? Oh no, he is in his right mind, but is very sly, and slyness, as is known, is the mark of the beast. Solzhenitsyn put out the rumor that he was working on a book on the year 1914. And then he started to hand out chapters right and left for people to read with the goal of eventual publication. As usual, writers were very kind. Tvardovsky "read twelve sample chapters of the Samsonov Catastrophe and was extremely pleased with them, praising them greatly, and as an editor was already relishing how I would finish—and everything would be passable, patriotic, and now no one would stop us, and Solzhenitsyn would be published in *Novy Mir*, and life would be wonderful! I did not tell him what thorns were still to come in *August 1914*." (pp. 287–288)

Elated by this apparent success he wriggled out of the trap and tricked them—Solzhenitsyn set his sights still higher. Grinning mockingly to himself, he knocked out an impudent letter to the Central Committee: "I can submit to you for publication my new novel *August 1914* that I will be finishing in a few days. This book will not meet any censorship troubles: it constitutes a detailed military review of the Samsonov Catastrophe in 1914, in which the selflessness and the best efforts of Russian soldiers and officers were made senseless and doomed by the paralysis of the tsarist military command. To forbid *this* book in our country as well would surprise everyone." (p. 545)

He sent it and lay low for a while, assuming that no one would guess his game. But these fox-like tricks were to no avail this time. And there was reason for that, because the name of Solzhenitsyn, at his own initiative as we shall see below, had started to be surrounded with myths in the West. He incited an infamous anti-Soviet campaign, noting with satisfaction: "The samizdat battalions were already on the march!" (p. 153) Samizdat was obviously too frail for "divisions and corps," and possibly this was the reason for his idea of switching to the printing machinery of the Soviet state. But the "know-it-all" made a big mistake. For reasons that he has not disclosed in Switzerland, *August 1914* could certainly not be published in the USSR. The reaction to the book and the anticommunist propaganda uproar around it is well known. Solzhenitsyn rashly stuck out his rear end for a beating. And he was beaten accordingly.

418

Our benighted strategist groans in Switzerland, picking at the wounds of those times:

> *August 1914* initiated the split among my readers, a loss of sup-
> porters, and fewer remained with me than left. I was accepted
> with enthusiasm while I seemed to be only against Stalinist
> abuses. . . . With my subsequent steps I was inevitably obliged
> to reveal myself; it was time to speak with more precision and
> go deeper. And I was bound to lose the reading public because
> of this, and to lose contemporaries in the hope of winning their
> descendants. But it was painful that I had to lose some who
> were close to me. (p. 352)

But what did you expect? It was your pen that scribbled what these some twenty or whatever Knots boil down to, that the bourgeoisie "is a con- centration of national energy: the greatest." (p. 269) "It was knocked on the head in 1917 in Russia, it is hounded today in many countries, and posterity will not turn away from this road. The mole of history digs deep."

Solzhenitsyn has grown insolent in his impunity. He voluptuously recalls his deeds in the USSR at the beginning of the 1970s (p. 283). He behaved "with insolent confidence" (p. 244) because "I became so brazen that I was no longer scared: I was beginning to sense my strength and the heights I had scaled." (p. 233) And what was that unknown strength? Why, it was unquestionably the West, which the erstwhile pretender to the role of writer of the Russian land now addresses without shame, and for which he was finding passkeys the whole of his conscious life.

Already by the mid-1950s,

> I had managed to reduce all my camp work to a size to insert
> into a book cover (the plays of Bernard Shaw in English).
> Now, if anybody would undertake to go to Moscow, meet a
> foreign tourist in the street and slip it into his hands, the latter
> would certainly accept it, could easily take it out of the coun-
> try, then would slit open the covers and go to a publisher who
> would be happy to publish the unknown Stepan Khlynov (my
> pseudonym), and . . . the world would certainly not remain
> indifferent!

But he couldn't bring himself to ask somebody to execute this mission because he was in absolute isolation. "When I went to Moscow myself in

1956 and looked for a Western tourist to whom I could slip the book," he simply lost his nerve. (p. 315)

From the very beginning, from the time Solzhenitsyn started to be published, his main target was the West. He took into consideration only the views of those who shaped opinion there, and hastened accordingly to satisfy the powerful in that other world across the Soviet border, whence he expected material and moral advantage. That is how it was: he lived in Russia but worked for the West. It may be said that this is an exaggeration and laying it on thick. Not in the least. When his first fat lampoon was published abroad, the writer was beside himself: it had come out "in the West! But what I had to worry about was not that it had come out, but how it would be accepted. It was my first real test as a writer!" (p. 225) Let us note in passing that this was written at a time when Solzhenitsyn's popularity had reached a peak in our country after the publication in *Novy Mir*, when shortsighted souls foretold a great future for the connoisseur of human psychology, etc, etc.

There are unavoidable questions. He goes into hiding, says he didn't hand over his manuscripts himself, and plays dumb on how they reached foreign publishers. "Well, it means it had to be, God's time had come." (p. 224) While refusing to admit that he secretly slipped his manuscripts abroad, Solzhenitsyn keeps rewriting and rewriting his required, and, of course, thoroughly false, denial: "Suddenly I was overcome by a pang of gray remorse inside, maybe I did something bad? Maybe I was too keen on the West." (p. 232) Not even three years pass and he grows more impudent:

> Publishing the completed *August 1914* in the West. The novelty of this step: openly, in a Western publication, in my own name, without any clever evasions to the effect that somebody had used my manuscript, distributed it without my knowledge, but I was powerless to stop it. . . . And with future publications in mind, I was not indifferent to how *August 1914* would be received in the West.

God forbid that he should anger book lovers there with the sharp turns of his "clever evasions." (p. 195)

It was by no means for self-expression or the satisfaction of his author's vanity, perverted as it was, that he sent one manuscript after another for publication by foreign publishing houses. He expected assistance and support in response, greedily gluing his ear to the radio set: "Not even during the deepest immersion in one's work is one totally protected against the present: it flows in daily through the radio (Western radio, of course, but that sums up our whole situation." (p. 386) The chorus of foreign radio voices sets him in the right mood: "Worked hard at the last revisions of *Archipelago*, relaxing in the evening by listening to Western broadcasts." (p. 221) God, about whom Solzhenitsyn is so solicitous, is far away, but Easter has to be celebrated and there's no time—"only the nightly broadcast of BBC can interfere with the all-night service." (p. 231) What incredible loyalty to the Christian faith!

Having exchanged God for the BBC he got what he was waiting for: his name was repeated more and more by the foreign announcers in their Russian broadcasts. But it wasn't enough, he needed more, and the required contacts had already been established. Solzhenitsyn was expelled from the Ryazan organization of writers. That same evening he went to an intercity pay phone and called the necessary number. The next day,

> at six in the morning, I woke up, turned on Voice of America as usual, and they were broadcasting what I had told them the night before. I jumped up. The information age! Instantaneously—no, I had never expected it!! They mentioned it in four brief news broadcasts, and four times in detail. Very good! (p. 286)

Nothing interests him in his own country, "the main thing was to see that the echo was heard abroad" about Solzhenitsyn. (p. 186)

Echoes through the air waves are impalpable, however, and something more substantial was needed; for example, the Nobel Prize. In all likelihood he did not conceal his thoughts, and by hinting he brought it about: "I need this prize! As a step in a position, in a battle! And the sooner I get it, the stronger I will strike! I will get to the Nobel rostrum and then I'll blow them up!" (p. 316) He served the West with double, triple fervor, defaming everything Soviet. One cannot but wonder at his fantastic capacity for work in the field of anti-Soviet activity. You can't deny it, it was his favorite work. But still, it wasn't so simple.

The book clearly depicts how the syndicate Solzhenitsyn and Co was formed, where not just one pair of dirty hands was laboring. The tireless laborer points directly to its existence:

> From afar it would seem: How is it I don't break down? How do I manage to hold on alone and get through such a gigantic amount of work, how do I find the time to dig into archives and libraries, find references, verify quotations, question old people, and write, and retype, and collate, and bind—one book after another published in samizdat (and a copy of each stored away in reserve)—through what strength and what miracle? And you can't skip over these explanations, but even more— you can't give them either. (p. 209)

Why not? Deported from the Soviet Union now, he could have told everything. But he keeps things hidden, and the reason is absolutely clear: The main parts of the Syndicate, without any doubt, are not in our country where he could not have had any support, but in his beloved West.

And what is the explanation? Here it is: "Only now, no, only today do I understand how amazingly God brought this task to its accomplishment" (p. 416). What is amazing rather, is that it turns out that to receive the Nobel Prize there was a certain cutoff point: "The year 1970 was the last year when I still needed the Noble Prize, when it could still have helped me. After that I would have started the battle without it" (p. 324). But "higher forces" intervened, and Providence displayed its grace exactly on time—the contestant duly received the prize sought for in that 1970. He should have been overwhelmed with joy because he was recognized in the beloved West as a writer. But other, nonliterary ideas entered the head of the Nobel laureate: "Now I can talk with the government as an equal. There is nothing to be ashamed of in that: I have attained a position of force and will talk with them accordingly. I will not retreat an inch, but will invite them to do so." (p. 326)

Indeed, a Giant of Thinking, and who are they: the State, only 250 million people. "Yes, yes, of course, everybody knows you can't puncture reinforced concrete towers with a vine stem. But here's a thought: what if they're made of straw?" (p. 15) But what about the armed forces? I've seen these commanders with my own eyes, those who won World War II. They came to a meeting of writers: Marshals of the Soviet Union G.K. Zhukov and I.S. Konev. Solzhenitsyn glanced at them from afar and knew for certain that the first was "a serf, like all marshals and generals" (p. 130), and the second was "a rather stupid, average sort of collective farm brigade leader." (p. 85) There is nothing to discuss here. In brief, "You're done for, Bolsheviks, no matter how you look at it." (p. 454) Gibberish, of course, a gigantic case of chronic megalomania. Urged on by the prize, Solzhenitsyn could find no peace, and kept pushing his lampoons, leaping into a fantastic new life that, since he was over fifty, was truly stressful and unhealthy for him. One cannot read about his adventures without a smile: "A Nobel Prize laureate, yet I took to darting down dark alleys at unlikely times, changing my hat (my usual one was in my knapsack), hiding at street corners with no lights—and making deliveries. *Not once* did they track me down, and not once did they catch me out!" And then he describes in detail the procedure of darting through gateways, slipping from one suburban electric train to another, etc, etc. (pp. 430–431) "They had enough, and more than enough, material for a criminal charge against me, ten times more than was needed." (p. 133) This is not serious; it's inappropriate and really silly. Apparently the great warrior couldn't get it into his head that they paid no attention to his escapades because, from the point of view of the Soviet state, they were no more than the petty intrigues of a wretch. Solzhenitsyn exclaims in one of the few truthful places in the book that when, in the summer of 1973, the announcers of various "voices" were sounding off with endless variations of his name, he complained to his diary: "The Western radios are buzzing ten times a day: Solzhenitsyn is being persecuted, Solzhenitsyn is being victimized, but I don't even notice this victimization." (p. 378) And that is how it really was.

However, all patience has a limit. Solzhenitsyn transgressed the bounds of the permissible in any organized society. Today, when the ice of the Cold War is being broken up, the provocateur Solzhenitsyn-Vetrov is aligned with those who strive to return to the hard frost. His appraisals of the outstanding achievements in international affairs of the last fifteen years, scattered about his book, correspond precisely to the concepts of anticommunists, and even more so, to their most extreme wing. The massacre of the Indonesian communists in the early sixties, for example, brought him "happiness." (p. 127) Whenever the reactionaries went on the offensive, it unfailingly offered him the greatest satisfaction. He was always in a hurry to keep pace with reaction.

What was he so anxious, almost bursting, "to discuss with the government?" He would grit through clenched teeth: "Revoke the ban on my old things, publish *August 1914*, and things will change not only in regard to me, but to the entire literary situation, and, not just literature either." (p. 327) Beyond that, Solzhenitsyn sees himself entering somewhere on a white horse. In other words, achieving what the entire might of imperialism couldn't manage; the single-handed overthrow of the Soviet government.

But the trouble was that nobody was in a hurry to listen to him, although "the West was virtually kneeling to him." (p. 232) So he had to break up that hateful détente, for in his overheated imagination Solzhenitsyn was above peoples and governments, and had formed an alliance in cahoots with a tiny group of renegades to campaign against détente.

He couldn't find words enough to define the place of this group in world history. Sakharov, "in September (1973), was an arbiter for European governments." (p. 405) How, in the eyes of Solzhenitsyn, had such a gigantic result been achieved? Let's quote an appropriate source, *The New York Times*, on the essence of his credo, which had led him to such cosmic conclusions: "A great writer in a country is like a second government" (*The New York Times*, February 9, 1974).[6] When a person places himself in the chair of the leader of 250 million people, then naturally he judges and rules on what we ordinary mortals want, namely, neither détente nor normal relations with foreign countries. This pitiful blind man insolently declares it as his policy, developed somewhere in one of his hideouts. In reality, messieurs Solzhenitsyn, Sakharov, and Co, by their shrill screams, summoned the dinosaurs of the Cold War from their caves, and galvanized for a short time all that had been discarded by sensible people in the West. And then events developed in accord with the tried-and-true canons of "psychological warfare." Even without any Solzhenitsyns, their experts know their foul business well. The provocateur is happy, he is glued to the radio set and writes continuously. He writes down the malicious insinuations against the country that was still his motherland. Already the whole week beginning August 24 (1973) "the dissidents in the USSR were the foremost topic of the entire European press. . . . The following week was still more heated: the first week of September. . . . The campaign of Western support, like a racing flywheel, was gaining speed." (pp. 379, 382) What for? Only to talk a lot more about our country?

No! The matter took on a practical dimension, foul words were used to substantiate even more immeasurable deeds. The visceral anticommunism offered by Solzhenitsyn was rationalized into hypocritical explanations of the wish not to retreat from Cold War times. Here is a description of the situation in his own book:

> On the 10th (of September 1973) was heard the voice of Wilbur Mills, who was sick and staying at his farm, the Chairman of the Budget Committee of the US House of Representatives: he was against expanding trade relations with the USSR until the persecutions of such people as Solzhenitsyn and Sakharov was stopped. It meant the Jackson Amendment was being expanded: from emigration to human rights in the USSR! And the discussion in his committee was just approaching the critical moment. (p. 381)

But now the uncooperative Sakharov let Solzhenitsyn (read "the second government") down, because he did not appreciate the great plan, and only spoke in support of the Jackson Amendment. And now Solzhenitsyn hurls invectives from his Swiss remoteness:

> It was a twist that was hardly noticed by observers of the battle, and in essence it broke our battle, depriving us of our main success. . . . *The Washington Post* published Sakharov's letter on 18 September in *capital* letters. And the Congress returned to Jackson's Amendment. . . . If *we* are asking only for emigration, then why should the US Senate worry about something bigger? (p. 404)

It is some kind of phantasmagoria, the ravings of a madman, and rubbish. Having proclaimed himself "the government" of our country, Solzhenitsyn encroaches also on foreign countries. He aspires to become one of the world rulers, no less. In any case, I am convinced that on Capital Hill in Washington, the 535 senators and representatives are obediently voting for legislation that is pleasing to a handful of renegades. No matter how you look at it, it is clearly a clinical case, insanity grounded in megalomania. But beyond that, it is a splendid testimonial to those in the West who take him as an ally.

Our hero has taken the bit between his teeth, and now he does not even need Sakharov, because "the clarity of Sakharov's actions was strongly shadowed by the splintering of his personal intentions." (p. 387) Stop fighting on foot, mount a battle horse, Vetrov!

> Here we are, on a horse, galloping, at a time chosen by me (that's what presentiment means—to begin a campaign when all seems peaceful and it's not necessary), with others galloping alongside [I suppose the cowboy, Senator Jackson—N.Y.], and we have only to veer a little to the side and then hack away!!! We failed—at a moment when whole historical masses were in motion, when Europe for the first time began to be concerned, and *our* people's hands were tied in expectation of American trade benefits and by the European Conference, and for several months spread out in front of us they would be imploring me to! (pp. 376–377)

That Solzhenitsyn fought against the Soviet state requires no additional proof, but, as it turns out, he takes the credit for much else as well—"the governments of Nixon and Brandt were in a difficult situation because our stance had foiled the whole game. Kissinger dodged hither and thither." (p. 385)

Solzhenitsyn chose his own road—to the squadron of the Jacksons, which he was able to join when he was deported from the USSR. Let him play the politician there, and hack away on behalf of the side to which he always belonged body and soul. But the reinforcement they have received is not very great.

Currently quarantined, and recalling the years when he was conducting subversive activity in the USSR (and making a fortune), he tries to raise his price in the eyes of his patrons, stressing his foxy slyness and resourcefulness, and is surprised by the Soviet people: "Didn't they understand that I was like a mined bicycle the Germans had dropped in the middle of the road: there it lies, accessible, unprotected, but just let yourself be tempted, reach for it— and a dozen are dead." (p. 449) Yes, we saw it all right, that's why we gingerly took the scum by the scruff of the neck, bundled him onto a plane, and got rid of him. Together with his archive, desk, and all the rest.

Nevertheless, it slips through in some places in the book: He's ready to return to the USSR on a white horse to teach the Soviet people sense. But it won't work; the border is locked for Solzhenitsyn.

Apparently he also understands that these are castles in the air, and settling comfortably on his money bags, belches with contentment: "The warrior is not he who wins, but he who survives." (p. 241) He has achieved his goal!

F. 3, op. 80, d. 648, l. 28–30. Original.

Notes

1. *The following instruction appears on a separate sheet: " Comrade I.S. Chernoutsan, Please give me your opinion. M. Suslov. 1 September 1975."*

2. *Voice of the Motherland* was a lavishly illustrated and produced propaganda magazine aimed at Russian emigrés who were deemed sympathetic to the regime. It was distributed exclusively outside the Soviet Union.

3. The page numbers cited by Yakovlev refer to the Russian-language edition of *The Oak and the Calf* published in Paris in 1975.

4. Here and below Yakovlev plays on the confession Solzhenitsyn made in *The Gulag Archipelago* that as a young and inexperienced prisoner, he had allowed himself to be browbeaten into agreeing to inform for a while. He soon gave it up, and was never paid, as Yakovlev asserts. Needless to say, the Soviet authorities seized on this piece of information with great glee, and in 1976 circulated a forged letter signed "Vetrov" purporting to show that Solzhenitsyn had been an informer right to the very end of his camp career, while in the special camp in Ekibastuz. The forgery was exposed, however, and this element of the campaign was later dropped.

5. "R-17" was Solzhenitsyn's code name for *August 1914* in the years when it was still in the planning stage but had not yet been started.

6. The citation attributed to *The New York Times* is actually from *The First Circle*, and was widely quoted by Solzhenitsyn's supporters and admirers.

144 Memorandum from I. Chernoutsan, Consultant, the Central Committee Culture Department, to M. Suslov[1]

9 September 1975
Classified
To M.A. Suslov, Secretary of the Central Committee

Dear Mikhail Andreyevich,
In accordance with the assignment I was given, I enclose my remarks on N. Yakovlev's article, "A Calf with a Blade," prepared for publication in *Golos Rodiny*.

Solzhenitsyn's book *The Oak and the Calf*, published in the West, is saturated with rabid hatred of Soviet reality; it is based on numerous distortions and falsifications, and all the statements made in it can be disproved with facts.

In my opinion, we should select and deride only the more slanderous examples from Solzhenitsyn's writings, in order to denounce him as a provocateur and a shallow trickster who has tried to disguise common or garden slander with a mask of apparent plausibility.

The *article* by Professor N.N. Yakovlev, a historian who has already published an earlier criticism of Solzhenitsyn (in the February 1974 issue of *Golos Rodiny*), *basically fulfills this requirement. However*, one should not overlook some shortcomings in the article, such as poorly argued points, and somewhat incorrect statements.

It goes without saying that many of Solzhenitsyn's evil fantasies do not deserve detailed academic analysis, and can be subjected to a newspaper-style derision instead—a device successfully used by Yakovlev in several instances. But one cannot limit oneself to the satirical style as the one and only polemical tool.

Serious doubts could also be expressed regarding the way Yakovlev writes about Tvardovsky and other writers who in their day (in the early 1960s) positively assessed *One Day in the Life of Ivan Denisovich*.

Tvardovsky, who in the beginning really unconditionally trusted Solzhenitsyn, of course, did not know the libellous writings already prepared at that time by this Judas. With all his mistakes, sometimes very serious, Tvardovsky remained a Communist to the end of his days, and never shared Solzhenitsyn's anti-Soviet positions.

I also find the article's tone unfair regarding writers who were wrong at first in their appreciation of *One Day in the Life of Ivan Denisovich*.

> "In the late 1950s and early 1960s," writes Yakovlev, "some of our shrewd men of letters opened their arms because an enormous talent had surfaced from the depths of obscurity, and what a talent! A rock! They forgot the folk wisdom which tells you exactly what floats to the surface. When *One Day in the Life of Ivan Denisovich* and its author were discovered and brought to *Novy Mir*, it was a day of triumph at the magazine."

From our current point of view, in the light of the accumulated experience, such philippics do not require any particular acumen or civil courage. The sarcasm is apparently aimed not only at Tvardovsky and members of the *Novy Mir* editorial board, but also at such "shrewd men of letters" as Simonov and Yermilov who published their articles respectively in *Pravda* and *Izvestia*, as well as many other writers and critics (see articles and books by A. Ovcharenko, V. Pankov, L. Fomenko, and others) whose writings appeared during the peak of the glorification of Solzhenitsyn, who was presented as an example for Soviet writers and workers of culture in Khrushchev's speech at the reception on 17 December 1962. Such things should be ignored and forgotten, but that does not mean that it is necessary to mention them in an article exposing a traitor.

Solzhenitsyn's slanderous writings provide so much material for irrefutable and convincing criticism that there is no need to stretch the point or give incorrect quotations. Unfortunately, there are quite a few such instances here.

In the last column of the article the author says, "Having proclaimed himself the government of our country, Solzhenitsyn aspires to become one of the world's rulers. . . . No matter how you look at it, this is clearly a clinical case, insanity grounded in megalomania." If only everything were so simple!

The scathing ending of the article depicts Solzhenitsyn comfortably sitting on a bag full of money and happily spouting, "The warrior is not he who wins, but he who survives." It seems to me that the portrait of Solzhenitsyn as a trickster who managed to "survive" only very approximately depicts the essence of the matter.

I have mentioned that this is Yakovlev's second publication in *Golos Rodiny*. Unfortunately, his first article was not free of simplifications either, and carried away by the spirit of exposé, he sometimes used clearly anti-Leninist concepts of war and revolution. Ignoring a principal difference between

World War I and World War II—unjust and predatory on both sides—
Yakovlev claimed that the Soviet soldiers who entered Eastern Prussia in
January 1945 took revenge for the defeat of Samsonov's Army. "Soviet
forces," he wrote, "marched along the same roads where, choking in dust in
August 1914, the soldiers of Samsonov's Army bore their cross." Yakovlev
emphasizes that in January 1945, Soviet soldiers "took over the same towns
for which their fathers had fought in August 1914," and that "in the icy
January of 1945, Eastern Prussia was shaken by the thousandfold echo of the
steps of Samsonov's soldiers, the martyrs of August 1914." A little further
Yakovlev quotes (in no way documented) words presumably uttered by Soviet
soldiers and officers who were filled with joy at the liberation of Königsberg
and other places in Eastern Prussia, for "much Slavic blood had been spilled
on that soil."

I do not know where Yakovlev was fighting at that time, but I was an
officer in the troops that stormed Königsberg and the other fortresses of the
Teutonic Knights, and I can witness that none of us ever thought then about
the tragedy of 1914. We were not fighting to "revenge Samsonov's Army," or
"restore the glory of Russian arms," but to destroy the fascist rascals and to
bring closer the victory over Germany.

I think that even considering the specific audience of *Golos Rodiny*[2] (though
the article was also published in *Literaturnaya Gazeta*), it was not worth
playing up to their tastes by viewing historical events from the position of "a
single tendency," or reviving Slavophile concepts that had been ruthlessly
ridiculed by Lenin and other Marxists of the Lenin school.

Yakovlev's articles, I repeat, have a sharp polemical edge and vigor, but
they are not profound enough; sometimes the essence of the matter is left
out, and in some instances arguments are substituted with often biting and
witty points which, nevertheless, prove little. I have tried to demonstrate how
it happens in Yakovlev's latest article and in his discussion of *August 1914*
where he claimed that even "from the point of view of Sovietology, the novel
has zero value because it is pure nonsense." But if it really were "pure
nonsense" with an obvious zero value, Solzhenitsyn probably could not have
become the leader of all the anti-Soviet and antisocialist forces, and indeed
there would have been no sense in spending precious time on polemics
against him—something about which, somewhat insincerely, Yakovlev
complains in the beginning of his article on *August 1914*.

The real situation is somewhat different. In his literary works, in falsified
memoirs (like *Calf*), and in his "Experiment in Literary Investigation" (the
subtitle given to *Gulag Archipelago*) Solzhenitsyn has accumulated the
essential kernels of the ideas of anti-Sovietism and antisocialism. That is why
we see similar ideas and situations, similar "lines of force," in all his works.

In view of the above, and while acknowledging the unquestionable value of Yakovlev's article, I consider it absolutely necessary to remove certain inaccuracies and farfetched statements, as well as such polemical devices as can only annoy friends in need of arguments for a serious and convincing debate.

An article about Solzhenitsyn should serve the consolidation of progressive forces and help them to see the true face of this political renegade and adventurer. I feel that Yakovlev's article in its present form is not quite equal to this task.[3]

I. Chernoutsan
Consultant, Culture Department, Professor

F. 3, op. 80, d. 648, l. 31–41. Original.

Notes

1. *The following note was appended to the memo: "To Comrade Y.V. Andropov: It would be good to modify Prof. N. Yakovlev's article, taking into account the remarks made by Comrade I.S. Chernoutsan —M. Suslov. 10 September 1975."*

2. Russian emigrés (see Document 144, Note 2).

3. *On 10 December 1975, a reworked text of Yakovlev's article was received by Suslov; the article was sent to Andropov for consideration. A note of 2 July 1976 from S. Avetisyan was enclosed with the document; it said that, according to information received from P.P. Laptev, it was decided, not to publish the said article.*

145 Report from the Committee for State Security of the USSR Council of Ministers

"On Solzhenitsyn's Hostile Activities and the Decline of Interest in His Person Abroad and in the USSR"[1]

No. 7–A
4 January 1976
Top Secret
Special File

To the Central Committee:
The KGB has analyzed materials concerning Solzhenitsyn received after his deportation from our country and the revocation of his Soviet citizenship.

Finding himself abroad, Solzhenitsyn took active steps toward the publication of his anti-Soviet lampoons (*The Gulag Archipelago, Letter to the Soviet Leaders, Prussian Nights*), written before his expulsion from the Soviet Union and sent to the West through illegal channels. At the same time, stage versions of Solzhenitsyn's "plays" have been produced—*Republic of Labor* (Federal Republic of Germany), and *Article 58*[2] (Canada), as well as a film version of his lampoon *The Tanks Know the Truth*[3] (France).

Influenced by the bourgeois mass media, a certain part of the Western public initially displayed interest in the personality of Solzhenitsyn. This situation was used by the most reactionary circles of the West for creating yet another wave of anti-Sovietism. The press and radio stations of the capitalist states, particularly Radio Liberty and Deutsche Welle, made attempts at discrediting the government and social system of the USSR and Soviet foreign policy, by launching an extensive slander campaign, linked with the publication of the lampoon *The Gulag Archipelago*.

To neutralize Solzhenitsyn's hostile activities, in 1974–1975 the KGB sent to the West materials and documents favorable to us, in which the true nature of the slanderer and the class roots of his hatred for the Soviet system were revealed. In this context, the following publications produced the strongest effect: "I Was Betrayed by Solzhenitsyn," by N. Vitkevich, in *The*

Christian Science Monitor, US; "Solzhenitsyn and the NTS" in the newspaper *Russkiy Golos* [Russian Voice], USA; "A Mercenary and a Simpleton," by Yakovlev, newspaper *Golos Rodiny*, France, USA; "My Husband, Solzhenitsyn," by N. Reshetovskaya, Italy, Japan; "An Archipelago of Lies," by Yakovlev; as well as televised interviews with N. Reshetovskaya, M. Yakubovich, A. Kagan, and N. Vitkevich, who knew Solzhenitsyn personally and at different periods shared his views.

The information compromising Solzhenitsyn divulged in the West has led to a certain reassessment of his personality, contributed to the provoking of doubts as to the truthfulness and historical accuracy of his "writings," and resulted in a series of positive publications and speeches by representatives of progressive Western public opinion. Thus in his article "Solzhenitsyn—An Exposed Liar Known to All," published in the magazine *Femina* (Switzerland), the well-known Swiss writer F. Arnau accused Solzhenitsyn of "intentionally pumping up the atmosphere of fear of communism among Western readers for the sake of receiving huge fees for slandering his motherland." Solzhenitsyn was harshly criticized by the popular Western writers Diggelman, Steiger, D'Arle, and others.

These measures have significantly reduced the impact of Solzhenitsyn's hostile writings and forced him to admit publicly his true political anti-Soviet platform. It is indicative that Solzhenitsyn is more and more open in his attempts to combine forces with representatives of right-wing opportunist circles of the Czechoslovak emigration whom he has planned to use for the promotion of his anti-Soviet writings. However, his attempts have not succeeded, because, in the opinion of several leaders of the Czechoslovak emigration, in the course of their contacts, Solzhenitsyn behaved like "an arrogant tsarist chauvinist. . . . [He] rejected the ideas of democracy and socialism," and treated Czechoslovakia "as a province of Russia."

In 1974–1975, reactionary circles organized public appearances by Solzhenitsyn in Sweden, Switzerland, France, Canada, and the USA, during which he continued to express his malice against communism, and often made absurd political statements that shocked even his supporters. For instance, in the course of a televised interview linked to the publication of his lampoon *The Oak and the Calf* in France, the views Solzhenitsyn was preaching were so reactionary that the organizers of the broadcast were forced to publish "explanations" of some of his statements in the press. The author of one such "explanatory" article, A. Besançon, admitted that Solzhenitsyn's words were not understood by many viewers, though he argued that it had happened because people in the West had no idea of the realities of life in socialist countries.

Solzhenitsyn gave a particularly clear expression of his political "views" during his appearance at the Hilton Hotel in Washington, DC, organized by

AFL-CIO President George Meany. In the course of his speech, Solzhenitsyn particularly harshly criticized the administrations of Presidents Hoover and Roosevelt for providing economic aid to the young Soviet Republic, for establishing diplomatic relations with our country, and for the participation of the United States in World War II on the side of the anti-Hitler coalition. At the same time Solzhenitsyn attacked former President Nixon's and President Ford's administrations for their "concessions" to the Soviet Union. He accused the ruling circles of the US of insufficiently active interference in the internal problems of the USSR, and stated that "the Soviet people had been left to the mercy of fate."

"Interfere," insisted Solzhenitsyn, "interfere again and again, as much as you can." Further on, Solzhenitsyn accused the US government of "giving Vietnam away" to the Communists, and declared: "The victory of the people's liberation forces in Cambodia and South Vietnam was the worst thing that could have happened to the peoples of those countries."

According to informed sources, the response of the audience to Solzhenitsyn's speech at the Hilton Hotel was more than restrained. One hour after its beginning, many of the audience were seen to be leaving the auditorium. The American newspaper *The Washington Post* admitted that in the audience one could hear the following comments on Solzhenitsyn's statements: "This guy wants us to pick chestnuts out of the fire for him."

Not without interest is also the fact that after Solzhenitsyn's appearances in Washington, an opinion of his mental incompetence started spreading among the US general public and business circles. Thus a note in *The New York Times* of 3 July 1976[4] stated that, while considering the possibility of granting Solzhenitsyn an audience with President Ford, the latter's advisors who were against such a meeting, referred, among other reasons, to their doubts about Solzhenitsyn's "mental stability." *The Washington Star*, speaking of the fanatical nature of Solzhenitsyn's political propositions, noted, "Only a fanatic can give such recommendations as practical recipes for foreign policy, but fanaticism alone is not enough for foreign policy," and continued, "Stupidity does not cease being stupidity, even if it is spoken by Solzhenitsyn." The influential American commentator Joseph Kraft remarked in *The Washington Post* of 4 July 1976, that Solzhenitsyn's call for America to return to the Cold War should only convince the Americans that they must "listen to others' advice less, and live more by their own wisdom."

As an intransigent enemy of socialism and a professed adversary of international détente, Solzhenitsyn made a statement to *The New York Times* in July 1975, in which he called the participation of President Ford in the forthcoming Helsinki conference, "a betrayal of the peoples of Eastern Europe." In many of his speeches, Solzhenitsyn harshly criticized the countries of Western Europe and America claiming that, for the sake of their

433

own well-being and comfort, they were constantly yielding their positions in the international arena to the states with "totalitarian regimes."

These statements by Solzhenitsyn, his inordinate ambitions, arrant reactionary views, and at the same time his elementary political illiteracy have completely destroyed the myth of him as a "champion of democracy," and have alienated leading representatives of liberal circles, some politicians, and representatives of the scientific and creative intelligentsia of the West. This is further evidenced by the fact that, in spite of several attempts by Solzhenitsyn to obtain the citizenship of a Western country, the leaders of those countries have always found specious excuses to avoid making a decision. The Prime Minister of Canada, Pierre Trudeau, for instance, said to Solzhenitsyn that immigration matters "were outside the Prime Minister's competence."

A few leading statesmen in Switzerland have unequivocally expressed their desire to disassociate from Solzhenitsyn, and from his provocational activities. On 28 August 1976, at a session of the Foreign Policy Commission of Switzerland's Parliament, the President of the Swiss Confederation P. Graber replied to a deputy who had referred to the negative assessment of the Helsinki Conference by Solzhenitsyn; President Graber repudiated that reference and stated sharply that the Swiss "are perfectly able to assess the importance of the Helsinki Conference." On 16–17 September 1976, during debates at the National Council, the Chairman of the Foreign Policy Commission of the National Council of Switzerland's Parliament, W. Renschler, called Solzhenitsyn's speeches demagogic, while P. Graber, replying to G. Schwarzenbach, one of the few apologists of the slanderer, said in an irritated tone, "Schwarzenbach ought to read less of Solzhenitsyn . . . and pay more attention to Swiss writers."

Expressing its concern for the preservation of Switzerland's prestige as a traditionally neutral state, the influential bourgeois newspaper *National Zeitung*, in its issue of 30 July 1976, noted in an article analyzing Solzhenitsyn's activities that his behavior "does not contribute to the development of good relations between Switzerland and the Soviet Union."

Solzhenitsyn's political credo, his megalomania, his attempts to present himself as "a supreme judge" and "a prophet" have resulted in profound discord between him and a few persons who recently left the Soviet Union for the West (Sinyavsky, Maksimov, and Nekrasov).

Constantly feeling that the interest in his person is decreasing, not only in the West but also among his few supporters who have remained in the USSR, Solzhenitsyn has tried to restore his shattered "authority" by establishing the so-called "Russian Social Fund" to help persons allegedly persecuted in the Soviet Union for political reasons. However, for Solzhenitsyn the organization of the "Fund" was just another campaign for promoting himself, and the insignificant sums of money transferred to the addresses of several Soviet citizens, known for their antisocial activities (Ginzburg, Gorbanevskaya,[5] and others) were a pittance for the slanderous information they had supplied.

Solzhenitsyn's open and blatantly hostile activities, and his reactionary political platform expressed in his lampoons *From Under the Rubble* and *Letter to Soviet Leaders*, have provoked a negative response from the Soviet scientific and artistic intelligentsia, while the publication of the lampoon *The Oak and the Calf*, in which Solzhenitsyn allowed himself to launch insulting attacks against well-known Soviet writers and the creative intelligentsia as a whole, has contributed to the final discrediting of the slanderer even with the people who in the past furnished him practical assistance and support. In this context a characteristic document was an open letter from Tvardovsky's daughter condemning Solzhenitsyn, which was published in *L'Unita*, and met with the approval of well-known Soviet authors.

Literary circles in our country have harshly condemned Solzhenitsyn's latest public statements, which they regard, essentially, as a direct appeal to imperialist states to unleash a war against the USSR.

At present, only very few among Solzhenitsyn's former supporters living in the USSR maintain contact with him (Pasternak,[6] Ginzburg, Gorbanevskaya, Tyurin,[7] Bukharina,[8] Borisov). Solzhenitsyn's hostile activities have been condemned even by such well-known antisocial elements as Chukovskaya, Kopelev, and others who used to be Solzhenitsyn's closest friends.

It is indicative that if before, while Solzhenitsyn lived in the USSR, every publication on him in the Soviet press, as well as publication of his lampoons abroad, found a reflection here in certain antisocial actions (leaflets, graffiti, etc), now practically nothing like this happens.

Recently Solzhenitsyn has admitted that not only the Soviet people have an adverse attitude toward him but so does Western society. He has tried all sorts of ways of galvanizing a fuss around his name and for this purpose has been forced more frequently to resort to the help of the most reactionary extremist forces in the West, as well as diverse anti-Soviet and White emigré organizations (the Popular Labor Alliance, the Organization of Ukrainian Nationalists, and others).

The Committee for State Security along with interested institutions and agencies is continuing measures to further compromise Solzhenitsyn.

Reported for information purposes.

Chairman of the Committee for State Security
Andropov

F. 3, *op.* 80, *d.* 648, *l.* 43–50. Original.

Notes

1. *Sent to Politburo members and candidates members 4 January 1976 under No. P30.*
2. There is no play by Solzhenitsyn known by the title *Article 58*. It sounds as if the play in question was *The Tenderfoot and the Tramp*.
3. *The Tanks Know the Truth* was an original screenplay by Solzhenitsyn about events during World War II.
4. *There is a mistake in the document here and following. The reference is to 1975.*
5. Natalia Gorbanevskaya was a poet and human rights activist, and had taken part in the demonstration on Red Square to protest the invasion of Czechoslovakia, as a result of which she was briefly interned in a psychiatric clinic. Her book *Demonstration in Red Square* circulated in samizdat and was published in the West. She emigrated to Paris in 1976.
6. Evgeny Pasternak, one of Boris's sons.
7. The first husband of Natalia Svetlova.
8. Bukharin's widow, Anna Larina [Bukharina].

146 Memorandum of the Committee for State Security of the USSR Council of Ministers

"On the Revocation of N.D. Solzhenitsyna's Soviet Citizenship"[1]

No. 2302–A
12 October 1976
Top Secret

To the Central Committee:
Natalia Dmitrievna Solzhenitsyna (last name Svetlova before her marriage to A.I. Solzhenitsyn) born 1939 in Moscow, of Russian nationality, graduated from the Moscow State University (Department of Mechanics and

Mathematics) and completed postgraduate studies in 1970; at present she lives in the USA with her husband Solzhenitsyn.[2]

Before her departure from the USSR, Solzhenitsyna took an active part in organizing various antisocial events. She contributed to the anti-Soviet activities of Solzhenitsyn, helping him to collect materials for his slanderous writings and to copy and distribute his works.

After her departure from the Soviet Union, Solzhenitsyna, together with her husband, continued her active involvement in hostile activities against the USSR. In particular, it was upon her initiative that the so-called "Russian Social Fund," whose income was "intended to provide help to Soviet political prisoners and their families," was established in Switzerland. In 1974–1976, Solzhenitsyna transferred significant sums in Swiss currency from the above-mentioned Fund to the addresses of her former allies (Ginzburg, Grigorenko, Gorbanevskaya, Dremlyuga,[3] and others). Solzhenitsyn and his wife have designated Ginzburg as the "authorized" representative of the Fund; Ginzburg, who in the past was tried for anti-Soviet activities, is using the received funds to encourage criminal actions by antisocial elements.

Solzhenitsyna attempts to acquire biased information from the Soviet Union to use it later in anti-Soviet actions. In the case of Solzhenitsyn's book *The Oak and the Calf*, published in the West, saturated with hatred for the Soviet system and Marxist-Leninist ideology, certain chapters were prepared personally by Solzhenitsyna.

At present Solzhenitsyna admits to work on a book on "the persecution of dissidents in the USSR," that she intends to bring out in reactionary foreign publishing houses, and later, to organize its shipping to the Soviet Union.

Solzhenitsyna's behavior since her departure from the USSR proves that she has become intensely involved in the anti-Soviet activities of her husband, while formally maintaining Soviet citizenship. This situation can be used by the Solzhenitsyns to a purpose most undesirable for us, because Solzhenitsyna can apply for an entry visa to the Soviet Union with provocative purposes. The resolution of this problem would certainly involve certain difficulties for us. In view of the above, it seems advisable to consider the issue of revoking Solzhenitsyna's Soviet citizenship. The drafts of a Central Committee resolution and a decree of the Presidium of the USSR Supreme Soviet are enclosed.

Please review.

Chairman of the Committee for State Security
Y. Andropov

F. 3, *op.* 70, *d.* 237, *l.* 5–6. Original.

Notes

1. *The document was sent to Politburo members on 13 October 1976 for voting under No. 29–105.*
2. Solzhenitsyn and his family had moved from Zurich to a house near Cavendish, Vermont, in the summer of 1976, after touring Europe and the United States to give a series of public lectures and interviews. After settling in Vermont, he became a virtual recluse, and concentrated on continuing his series of historical novels (begun with *August 1914*) on the events leading up to the Russian Revolution.
3. Vladimir Dremlyuga was one of the relatively few working-class members of the dissident movement. He was a participant in the 1968 demonstration in Red Square against the invasion of Czechoslovakia and was sentenced to three years in the labor camps. He continued his dissident activities after his return to Moscow.

147 Politburo Resolution
"On Revoking N.D. Solzhenitsyna's Soviet Citizenship"

No. P3O/8
17 October 1976
Top Secret

To approve the draft of a Decree of the Presidium of the USSR Supreme Soviet[1] on this matter (draft enclosed).

Central Committee Secretary

Enclosure
Re: point 8, minutes no. 30
Draft
(Not for Press Publication)

Decree of the Presidium of the USSR Supreme Soviet
On Revoking N.D. Solzhenitsyna's Soviet Citizenship

Considering that N.D. Solzhenitsyna has systematically performed actions that damage the prestige of the USSR and that are incompatible with the possession of Soviet citizenship, the Presidium of the USSR Supreme Soviet resolves:

On the basis of Article 7 of the Law of the USSR of 19 August 1938, "On Citizenship of the Union of Soviet Socialist Republics," for actions defaming the title of a citizen of the USSR, to revoke the Soviet citizenship of Solzhenitsyna, Natalia Dmitrievna, born 1939 in Moscow.

Chairman, Presidium USSR Supreme Soviet
N. Podgorny

Secretary, Presidium USSR Supreme Soviet
M. Georgadze

Moscow, The Kremlin

F. 3, *op.* 80, *d.* 648, *l.* 51–52. Excerpt from minutes.

Note

1. *The Decree of the Presidium of the USSR Supreme Soviet No. 4640–IX of 19 October 1976.*

148 Report from the Committee for State Security of the USSR Council of Ministers

"On the Publication of a Manuscript About Solzhenitsyn"[1]

No. 87–Ts
17 January 1977
Classified

To the Central Committee:

The KGB is continuing its activities to further discredit Solzhenitsyn in the eyes of the world and Soviet public. Among other measures serving this purpose, a manuscript of a documentary nature (enclosed) has been prepared, authored by the Czech journalist T. Rezac.

From 1968 to 1975, Rezac resided as an emigré in Switzerland, where he met Solzhenitsyn, and for a while translated his libellous writings into the Czech language and participated in Solzhenitsyn's negotiations with the leaders of the Czechoslovak emigrés. On returning to Czechoslovakia, Rezac[2] publicly exposed the connections between Czechoslovak emigrés and Solzhenitsyn, after which he was granted an opportunity to visit the USSR for gathering additional materials on Solzhenitsyn's personality and on the latter's hostile activities before his expulsion from this country. Based on documentary evidence, the author of the manuscript has exposed Solzhenitsyn as a rabid class enemy of socialism, of the policy of peaceful coexistence policy, and of international détente.

The KGB has taken measures to ensure the publication of this manuscript abroad. In particular, the appearance of the book in Italian is scheduled for March 1977, with French and English translations to follow in the future.

Submitted for information purposes.

Deputy Chairman of the Committee for State Security
Tsvigun

Enclosure

Summary of the Manuscript of the Book on Solzhenitsyn by the Czech Journalist T. Rezac

The KGB presents, for information purposes, a translation of the manuscript of Rezac's book on Solzhenitsyn, with the provisional title: "This is not a Writer's Biography but a Report on the Autopsy of a Traitor's Corpse." The KGB is taking steps to publish the manuscript abroad in 1977 in Italian, French, and English.[3]

The manuscript's author is a Czech journalist who lived as an emigré in Switzerland in the period between 1968 and 1975, was Solzhenitsyn's translator, and knew him personally.

The manuscript has 329 pages and several inserts, additions, and cuts. The concluding chapter is the author's afterward. The book has two parts—"Scars" and "Molds"—and eleven chapters: "Childhood Diseases," "Natalia, Natalia . . . ," "Victory Belongs to the Honest," "Moment of Truth," "A Martyr without Martyrdom," "The Fighter for Truth," "The Giant," "At Any Price," "The Prophet," and "Exile."

The author shows the true face of Solzhenitsyn as a provocateur, anti-Soviet activist, enemy of peace and progress, evil and shallow person, and coward and traitor by nature. As the author recounts in the manuscript, he met Solzhenitsyn in person several times and talked to people who used to know Solzhenitsyn at school and at university, during the labor-camp period of his life, and after his release, and has used his personal impressions of Solzhenitsyn.

The book shows that Solzhenitsyn's choice of treachery, anti-Sovietism, and anticommunism was not accidental—it was a deliberate, well-thought-out decision born of base personal goals, with the aim of obtaining, at any price, world fame and the title of a great Russian writer ("the Tolstoy of the twentieth century").

On the basis of reminiscences of people who used to be close to Solzhenitsyn, Rezac shows that Solzhenitsyn, from his youth on, displayed a pathological megalomania bordering on hysteria (p. 30), that he was a deft and cunning opportunist, "a perfect intriguer," and a "resourceful hypocrite." (pp. 26, 28) He always wanted to be first, strove for the fame of a great writer, and tried to become a celebrity by any means possible, trampling all human standards of ethics and propriety on his way. To reach his goal he employed all possible means: lies, juggling of facts, intentional distortion of the truth, etc.

As the author of the manuscript states, Solzhenitsyn has more than one betrayal of those close to him to account for, among them his friends, his wife, his mother, etc.

An important place in Rezac's manuscript is given to the chapters in which Solzhenitsyn is characterized as a provocateur and intriguer.

Based on the admission made by Solzhenitsyn himself in *The Gulag Archipelago* that he was a secret informer for the labor-camp administration under the nickname "Vetrov," the author explores this story and proves that Solzhenitsyn was a paid informer, and that he was implicated in peoples' deaths. (pp. 183–187) The book quotes from the testimonies of Solzhenitsyn's former schoolmates (the well-known Soviet surgeon, Professor Simonyan, and Assistant Professor Vitkevich of the Bryansk Teachers' Institute), who stated that they had been shown transcripts containing Solzhenitsyn's denunciations of them, dating from 1945 and 1952. (pp. 150, 151, 153, 154, 168, and ff.) The manuscript presents many facts which characterize Solzhenitsyn as a clever time server who has always managed to create an advantageous and privileged position for himself. At school he was an "A" student, but in order to avoid an undesirable mark he would pretend to have seizures. At university he was awarded a Stalin Prize for excellent progress in his studies and active participation in public affairs. Although he was the scion of a big landowner and White Guard officer, Solzhenitsyn deftly concealed his family past, as well as his own political views and philosophical position. (pp. 38–40)

The chapter "A Martyr without Martyrdom" contains facts disproving the myth of inhuman sufferings that Solzhenitsyn endured during his arrest, investigation, and camp imprisonment. Using excerpts from Solzhenitsyn's books, Rezac shows the true situation. At the Lubyanka Prison, during the investigation, he lived in a cell with a good, clean bed, down pillows, chess, books, newspapers, a tea table, and a clean parquet floor. (pp. 149–150)

Solzhenitsyn also began serving his sentence for the criminal activities of which he was convicted during war time not in the North, but in Moscow, at the construction site of an apartment building as a parquet-floor layer, and then in Marfino (outside Moscow) in a special institute for acoustical research. Everywhere he was well fed, had access to books, was able to write, and did write. He served the last years of his sentence in Ekibastuz camp, where he also had a privileged position, working in the library. He paid to eat at the cafeteria and went to the movies twice a week. (pp. 182–183)

Exposing the lies heaped by Solzhenitsyn in his writings on the Soviet way of life, death camps along the lines of Hitler's and the torture of prisoners during investigation, the author cites the testimonies of people imprisoned with Solzhenitsyn to refute his fabrications. Of the people questioned by the author, not a single one confirmed that he had been subjected to torture and abuse. Not even Solzhenitsyn confirmed it in a confidential conversation with the author. All the former prisoners stated that despite their guilt before the Soviet people, revenge was not sought against them, only persuasion was used and only one thing demanded of them—honest work. (pp. 192–200)

In the manuscript, the author exposes Solzhenitsyn's version of the story of his arrest seized on by Western bourgeois propaganda. He states that Solzhenitsyn was pathologically afraid for his own life and was haunted by the horror that he might be killed at the front. It was he himself who calculatingly and deliberately implemented the idea of sitting things out in the rear at any cost, even that of arrest. (pp. 124, 130–140, 149–150) The book describes how Solzhenitsyn in late 1943 and early 1944 sent provocative letters containing anticommunist statements and harsh words about Stalin to various addresses by field courier, which was reviewed by military censorship. At the same time, together with his childhood friend, Officer Vitkevich (now an assistant professor at Bryansk Institute), he composed "Resolution No. 1," which indulged in anti-Soviet attacks and criticism of Stalin. (pp. 135–138) He kept books from the 1920s in his car (by Trotsky, Bukharin, and Zinoviev) and a German book with a portrait of Hitler. In Rezac's opinion, Solzhenitsyn expected his correspondence to be intercepted and that he would be removed from the front to the rear for interrogation and investigation of a group "conspiracy."

The author says that Solzhenitsyn himself confirms in his *Gulag Archipelago* that he indirectly begged Smersh, the counterintelligence agency: "Arrest me, take me away from the mines and the grenades to a safe place in the quiet of a prison at the rear." (p. 216) Solzhenitsyn's miscalculation, as the author explains, was that, when planning this provocation, he hoped for an amnesty which would be announced after the victory. The amnesty, however, did not include traitors and turncoats.

The second part of the manuscript, "Molds" (pp. 201–329), describes the masks under which Solzhenitsyn has hidden his true nature as an inherent informer and traitor. The chapter presents the facts of Solzhenitsyn's hypocrisy and bigotry, and his malicious jealousy of such authors as Sholokhov and Tvardovsky.

In this chapter the author explores the political reasons which encouraged certain Western circles to nominate Solzhenitsyn for the Nobel Prize, and describes the fuss raised by the anticommunist propaganda machine around the issue of Solzhenitsyn's "persecution" in the Soviet Union. Rezac exposes the falsehood of Solzhenitsyn's claims to indigent conditions and poverty: Solzhenitsyn traveled a lot; he acquired a car for his aunt; went to concerts, theaters, etc. He had many female admirers whom he did not neglect, and the number of his love affairs grew like an avalanche. (pp. 291–296)

In his chapter "The Prophet," the author describes the provocations designed and carried out by Solzhenitsyn in order to force the Soviet government to "expel" him from the Soviet Union. He did not want voluntary emigration, he wanted "expulsion," so as to present himself to his Western anti-Soviet friends with the halo of a martyr who had suffered for the truth. (pp. 305–308)

In his concluding chapter, "Exile," the author describes his own impressions of Solzhenitsyn, whom he met in Switzerland. He speaks of Solzhenitsyn's claims to the position of leader of the emigrés, of his prophecies and hysterical forecasts, of his attitudes and his threats against Russia and the Russian people, of his demand addressed to the Russian people to "repent" before the world for the sins of the revolution. The same observations are included in the author's preface to the book. The author describes Solzhenitsyn's pathological prophecies, and his appeal to peoples to repent that he launched in the circle of Czech political emigrés. Russia should repent for the revolution and return to its original borders, "the borders of the era of Ivan IV, the Terrible." To give up the Baltic Republics, the Black Sea, and "its lands in Soviet Asia." (p. 6) The Czechs must repent for the Hussite wars and the Taborites (p. 10), and the Germans—for peasant wars and for Karl Liebknecht (not for fascism and Hitler). (p. 9)

As demonstrated by Rezac, in his obscurantist preaching Solzhenitsyn goes so far as to declare the Russia of the Romanovs "the great and free Russia." (p. 9)

The author comes to the conclusion that Solzhenitsyn has failed as a writer, and that Western readers have long lost interest in him. For the moment he is needed only by the promoters of anti-Sovietism: he is supported by them, and he works for them.

F. 3, op. 80, *d.* 649, *l.* 3–9. Original.

Notes

1. *This information was sent to Politburo members and candidate members, and Central Committee Secretaries, on 24 January 1977, under No. P117.*
2. Tomas Rezac was, on the surface, a young Czech journalist who had emigrated from Czechoslovakia in 1970, a year after the Soviet invasion, out of disgust over the new regime, and he caught Solzhenitsyn's attention by the fluency of his Russian. In reality, he had been trained in a Soviet counterespionage college and seems to have been sent to Switzerland as an agent. It was probably he who sent reports back to the KGB about Solzhenitsyn's meetings with Czechoslovak emigrés in Zurich. In 1975 he vanished from Zurich, leaving a wife and a mountain of debts behind, and surfaced in Prague, after which he was invited to the Soviet Union by the KGB to write a specially commissioned biography of Solzhenitsyn.
3. So far as is known, the book never appeared in English.

149 Memorandum of the Committee for State Security of the USSR Council of Ministers

"On Publication of the Decree of the Presidium of the USSR Supreme Soviet on the Revocation of N.D. Solzhenitsyna's Soviet Citizenship"[1]

No. 423–A
2 March 1977
Classified

To the Central Committee:
For systematic activities damaging the prestige of the Soviet Union and incompatible with being a Soviet citizen, the Soviet citizenship of Solzhenitsyna, Natalia Dmitrievna, born 1939 in Moscow, at present residing in the US, was revoked by the Decree of the Presidium of the USSR Supreme Council of 19 October 1976.

At that time it was decided not to publish the said decree, but to invite Solzhenitsyna to the USSR Embassy and to withdraw her Soviet passport from her. However, Solzhenitsyna has ignored all invitations to come to the Embassy.

In view of the above, the KGB considers it advisable to publish the decree of the Presidium of the USSR Supreme Soviet on revoking Solzhenitsyna's Soviet citizenship in the *Vedomosti Verkhovnogo Soveta SSSR* [Proceedings of the USSR Supreme Soviet].

A draft Central Committee resolution is enclosed.

Please review.

Chairman of the Committee for State Security
Y. Andropov

Note

1. *The memorandum was sent to Politburo members for a vote on 3 March 1977, under No. 48–42.*

150 Politburo Resolution

"On Publication of the Decree of the Presidium of the USSR Supreme Soviet on the Revocation of N.D. Solzhenitsyna's Soviet Citizenship"

No. P49/23
5 March 1977
Top Secret

To publish in the *Vedomosti Verkhovnogo Soveta SSSR* the Decree of the Presidium of the USSR Supreme Council of 19 October 1976 on revoking N.D. Solzhenitsyna's Soviet citizenship (text of the Decree enclosed).

Secretary of the Central Committee

F. 3, *op.* 80, *d.* 650, *l.* 1. Excerpt from minutes.

151 Memorandum of the Committee for State Security of the USSR Council of Ministers[1]

"On Publication of a Book on Solzhenitsyn in the Russian Language"

No. 1432–A
5 July 1977
Classified

To the Central Committee:
On 17 January 1977, the KGB sent a report (No. 87–TS) on measures taken to arrange publication abroad of the book by the Czech journalist Rezac, entitled *The Spiral of Treason* containing materials discrediting the personality of Solzhenitsyn and his lampoons.

In June of the current year, an abridged version of the above book was issued by the Italian publishers, Teti & Co. Some cuts in the book were made in order to adapt the material for foreign readers. Measures have been taken to have the book accepted by publishers in other countries.

The KGB considers it advisable, in order to further discredit Solzhenitsyn in the eyes of the Soviet public, to publish the complete text of Rezac's book in Russian, for restricted distribution, using the facilities of the USSR State Committee for Publishing, Printing, and the Book Trade. The matter has been discussed with this State Committee (Comrade I I. Chkhikvishvili).

The draft of a Central Committee resolution is enclosed.

Chairman of the Committee for State Security
Y. Andropov

F. 3, *op.* 70, *d.* 673, *l.* 69. Original.

Note

1. *The memorandum was sent to Politburo members for a vote on 7 July 1977 under No. 62-55.*

448

152 Politburo Resolution
"On Publication of a Book on Solzhenitsyn in the Russian Language"

No. P63/31
11 July 1977
Top Secret

1. To accept the proposal of the KGB concerning the publication of a book by the Czech journalist Rezac.
2. To assign the publication of Rezac's book in Russian, for restricted distribution, to the USSR State Committee for Publishing, Printing, and the Book Trade (Comrade Stukalin).

Secretary of the Central Committee

F. 3, *op.* 80, *d.* 650, *l.* 5. Excerpt from minutes.

153 Report from the Committee for State Security of the USSR Council of Ministers
"On Solzhenitsyn's Attempt to Found a So-Called 'All-Russian Memoir Library'"[1]

No. 2439–A
11 November 1977
Classified

To the Central Committee:
The KGB has been informed that, concerned by the abrupt decline of interest in his person and in his lampoons in the West, Solzhenitsyn is trying

to attract the attention of the bourgeois mass media. Thus, in October of the current year, he published his so-called "Appeal to the Russian Public," concerning the founding of the "All-Russian Memoir Library," which is widely used by enemy propaganda centers for conducting hostile ideological actions directed against the USSR.

From Solzhenitsyn's "appeal" it is obvious that the purpose of the above "library" will be the concentration of various anti-Soviet, slanderous, and other materials related to the prerevolutionary and Soviet periods of our country's history. It is indicative that Solzhenitsyn emphasizes his interest in receiving materials from members of the so-called "second generation of Russian emigrés"—that is, from persons who witnessed the events of the twenties and the thirties, as well as the period of the Great Patriotic War.

The KGB is taking measures to contain and neutralize the above enemy action.

This memorandum is sent for information purposes.

Chairman of the Committee for State Security
Andropov

F. 3, *op.* 80, *d.* 650, *l.* 9. Original.

Note

1. *An instruction is enclosed on a separate sheet of paper: "Inform the Central Committee Secretaries, as well as Comrade Tyazhelnikov," signed by V. Dolgikh, Y. Ryabov, M. Zimyanin, M. Suslov, I. Kapitonov, A. Kirilenko, K. Rusakov, and K. Chernenko.*

154 Memorandum from the USSR State Committee for Publishing, Printing, and the Book Trade and from Novosti Press Agency

No. 0500
8 August 1978
Classified

To the Central Committee:

The State Committee for Publishing and Novosti Press Agency propose to publish the book *Solzhenitsyn's Spiral of Treason*, by the Czechoslovak writer and journalist Tomas Rezac, in Russian, with a press run of 100,000 copies.

Through the channels of Novosti Press Agency, the book was published in Italy by the Milan-based Teti Editore in 1977, and was received positively by readers. The author of the book used extensive factual materials to reveal the deep class roots of Solzhenitsyn's hatred of socialism, and to expose the practice of using such apostates by reactionary Western circles in their subversive ideological activity against socialist countries. This is a spirited, controversial, and talented book.

In 1978, Progress Publishers issued Rezac's book in an authorized translation, for restricted distribution. The Soviet public, which showed great interest in the book, is now suggesting that the book be printed in a mass edition.

We ask for your approval of a new edition of the book *Solzhenitsyn's Spiral of Treason* in Russian, by Progress Publishers. At the same time we ask you to instruct the State Committee for Publishing, Novosti Press Agency, and the All-Union Copyright Agency, to take appropriate measures for publishing and distributing this book by foreign publishing houses and book-trade companies.

Chairman of the USSR State Committee for Publishing, Printing, and the Book Trade
B.I. Stukalin

Chairman of the Board
Novosti Press Agency
L.N. Tolkunov

F. 3, *op.* 78, *d.* 16, *l.* 105. Original.

155 Memorandum of the Central Committee Propaganda Department and of the Department for Political Propaganda Abroad

"On Rezac's Book *Solzhenitsyn's Spiral of Treason*"

18 September 1978
Classified

To the Central Committee:
The State Committee for Publishing (Comrade Stukalin) and Novosti Press Agency (Comrade Tolkunov) have made a proposal concerning the distribution of *Solzhenitsyn's Spiral of Treason* by the Czechoslovak writer Tomas Rezac, in Russian and major foreign languages.

Rezac's book, published in 1977 in Italy by Teti Editore, in cooperation with Novosti Press Agency, met with a positive response. The reviews prove that the author managed, in a sharp, polemical form, to show the disgusting character of Solzhenitsyn and the counterrevolutionary essence of his activities, and to expose the schemes of international reactionaries to use similar apostates for subversive ideological activities against Socialist countries.

In 1978, Rezac's book was printed in Russian by Progress Publishers, in an edition of ten thousand copies.

A major part of the press run (seven thousand) was handed over to the KGB. The remaining copies were sent out through the mailroom of the Administration of the Central Committee to members of the Central Committee; candidate members of the Central Committee; members of the Party's Central Control Commission; heads and assistant heads of departments of the Central Committee; section heads, heads of consultants' groups, and consultants for the departments of administrative Party work, of propaganda, science, and educational institutions, of Culture and International Departments of the Central Committee, and of the Department for Political Propaganda Abroad; educators in the Central Committee Propaganda Department; Secretaries of the Central Committees of the Communist Parties of the Union Republics, of the regional and provincial Party committees, and of the Moscow, Leningrad, and Kiev City Party Committees; the heads of departments for propaganda, science, and educational institutions; the heads of educators' groups; the provincial and regional centers for political education (including Moscow, Leningrad, and Kiev); the Head of the Political Office of the Soviet Army and Navy, and his assistants; the Committee for Party Control at the Central Committee (the Chairman, his assistants, and the members of the Committee); the Editors-in-Chief and members of editorial boards of the Central Committee newspapers, magazines, and publishing houses; as well as to the heads and staff of other central ideological institutions, according to a list approved by the Central Committee Department for Propaganda, Department for Political Propaganda Abroad, and General Department.

In view of the above, further publication of the book in Russian seems inadvisable. The USSR Committee for Publishing, Novosti Press Agency, and the All-Union Copyright Agency are instructed to take measures for exporting the book to foreign countries through foreign publishers and companies.

Comrades Stukalin, Tolkunov, and Pankin have been informed.

Deputy Department Head
Central Committee Propaganda Department
V. Sevruk

Deputy Department Head
Central Committee Department for Propaganda Abroad
V. Falin

F. 3, *op.* 78, *d.* 16, *l.* 103–104. Original.

156 Telegram from A. Solzhenitsyn To K. Chernenko[1]

20 December 1979

Moscow, Staraya Ploshchad
To Politburo member Konstantin Chernenko, in person.
The Soviet Embassy in Washington has informed me of the categorical refusal to issue a visa to my only relative—my aunt, Irina Ivanovna Shcherbak, to visit me in the United States.

Could it be that all your past public shame is not enough, so that you now must tyrannize over a ninety-year-old, blind, deaf, crippled, and illiterate old woman?

Please give the necessary orders, let the old woman go, and don't force me to go public.

Alexander Solzhenitsyn

F. 3, *op.* 80, *d.* 650, *l.* 12. Copy.

Note

1. *The document bears the notations: "To Comrade N.A. Shchelokov. K. Chernenko."*
   "Urgently, to Comrade B.K. Yelisov. Decide with the KGB after coordinating with the relevant departments. N. Shchelokov. 12.28.79."
   "Approved."

157 Memorandum of the USSR Ministry for Internal Affairs

"On the Matter of Solzhenitsyn's Telegram"

No. 1/703
6 February 1980
Classified

To the Central Committee:
In accordance with the assignment, we report that Solzhenitsyn's telegram has been discussed with the KGB of the USSR.

It is considered advisable to refuse an exit visa to the Soviet citizen I.I. Shcherbak, who is a distant relative of the telegram's sender. This decision has taken into account the fact that when Solzhenitsyn was expelled from the USSR, all his requests concerning exit visas for members of his family and relatives were completely satisfied, and that a decision was made not to maintain official contacts with this person any longer. It is also considered advisable not to provide any answer to Solzhenitsyn in connection with his request.

Enclosure: two sheets.

Minister N. Shchelokov

F. 3, *op.* 80, *d.* 650, *l.* 11. Original.

List of Documents Included in the Book

The ordinal number of the document is shown in parentheses.

I. Minutes of Politburo Meetings

From the minutes of the Politburo session, January 7, 1972 (61)
From the minutes of the Politburo session, March 30, 1972 (68)
From the minutes of the Politburo meeting, August 30, 1973 (81)
From a transcript of the Politburo meeting, September 17, 1973 (90)
From the minutes of the Politburo meeting, January 7, 1974 (99)
From the minutes of the Politburo session, January 17, 1974 (108)
From the minutes of the Politburo meeting, February 14, 1974 (126)

II. Politburo Resolutions

Politburo resolution, "Instructions to the Soviet Ambassador to Italy," July 17, 1967, No. P47/95. Enclosure. Text of the instructions to the Soviet Ambassador to Italy. (14)

Politburo resolution, "On a Verbal Communication to the Secretariat of the Ministry of Foreign Affairs of the Republic of Yugoslavia in Connection with the Publication of Solzhenitsyn's *Cancer Ward* in the Yugoslav Newspaper *Delo*," June 21, 1968, No. P87/7. Enclosure. Draft of instructions to the Soviet Ambassador to Yugoslavia. (21)

Politburo resolution, "On Instructions to the USSR Ambassador to the Democratic Republic of Vietnam," November 18, 1970, No. P183/134. Enclosure. Draft of instructions to the Soviet Ambassador to the DR of Vietnam. (38)

Politburo resolution, "On Instructions to the Soviet Ambassador in Stockholm in Connection with Awarding the Nobel Prize to Solzhenitsyn," November 27, 1970, No. P184/159. Enclosure. Draft of instructions to the Soviet Ambassador to Stockholm. (42)

Politburo resolution, "On the Statement Made to Sweden's Ambassador to the USSR in Connection with Awarding the Nobel Prize to Solzhenitsyn,"

December 4, 1970, No. P185/7. Enclosure. Draft of the statement to Sweden's Ambassador to the USSR. (47)

Politburo resolution, "A Question from the Committee for State Security and the USSR Public Prosecutor's Office (On Solzhenitsyn)," January 7, 1971, No. P187/XI. (49)

Politburo resolution, "On Instructions to be Given to the Soviet Ambassador in Stockholm, Regarding Solzhenitsyn's Nobel Prize," November 19, 1971, No. P26/44. Enclosure. Draft of instructions to the Soviet Ambassador to Stockholm. (57)

Politburo resolution, "On Solzhenitsyn and Yakir," March 30, 1972, No. P37/prot. (69)

Politburo resolution, "On the Verbal Statement to the Swedish Embassy in Moscow," April 13, 1972, No. P40/60. Enclosure. Draft of the verbal statement to Sweden's Embassy in Moscow. (74)

Politburo resolution, "Regarding a Representation to the Government of France in Connection with the Anti-Soviet Campaign in the French Media," September 13, 1973, No. P103/138. Enclosure. The text of the verbal representation to the Embassy of France in Moscow. (89)

Politburo resolution, "Regarding Sakharov and Solzhenitsyn," September 17, 1973, No. P104/VIII. (91)

Politburo resolution, "On Solzhenitsyn," January 7, 1974, No. P120/1—transcript. (100)

Politburo resolution, "On a Report to Fraternal Parties Regarding the Anti-Soviet Activities of Solzhenitsyn," January 17, 1974, No. P122/XVII. Enclosure 1. Text of the telegram to Soviet Ambassadors. Enclosure 2. List of the Parties to which the information is to be sent. (109)

Politburo resolution, "Report of the Committee for State Security of the USSR Council of Ministers of February 9, 1974, No. 388–A," February 11, 1974, No. P125/112. Enclosure 1. Draft of the Decree of the Presidium of the USSR Supreme Soviet, "On the Revocation of A.I. Solzhenitsyn's USSR Citizenship and Deportation from the USSR." Enclosure 2. The text of the TASS statement. (123)

Politburo resolution, "On Instructions to the Soviet Ambassador to Bonn," February 11, 1974, No. P125/113. Enclosure. The text of the instructions to the Soviet Ambassador to Bonn. (124)

Politburo resolution, "On Informing Our Friends Concerning the Actions Against Solzhenitsyn," February 14, 1974, No. P125/7–To be minuted. (127)

Politburo resolution, "On Instructions to the Soviet Ambassador to Sweden," February 28, 1974, No. P127/103. Enclosure. The text of the telegram to the Soviet Ambassador to Sweden. (135)

Politburo resolution, "On Solzhenitsyn's Royalties," March 5, 1974, No. P128/23. (137)

Politburo resolution, "On Revoking N.D. Solzhenitsyna's Soviet Citizenship," October 17, 1976, No. P3O/8. Enclosure. Draft of the Decree of the Presidium of the USSR Supreme Soviet, "On Revoking N.D. Solzhenitsyna's Soviet Citizenship." (147)

Politburo resolution, "On Publication of the Decree of the Presidium of the USSR Supreme Soviet on the Revocation of N.D. Solzhenitsyna's Soviet Citizenship," March 5, 1977, No. P49/23. (150)

Politburo resolution, "On Publication of a Book on Solzhenitsyn in the Russian Language," July 11, 1977, No. P63/31. (152)

III. Minutes of the Central Committee Secretariat Meetings

From a transcript of the Secretariat meeting, March 10, 1967. (8)
From a transcript of the Secretariat meeting, July 18, 1967. (15)
From the minutes of the Secretariat meeting, October 7, 1971. (54)
From the minutes of the Secretariat meeting, February 16, 1972. (62)
From the minutes of the Central Committee meeting, April 14, 1972 (76)

IV. Central Committee Secretariat Resolutions

The Secretariat resolution, "On Measures in Connection with the Act of Provocation of Awarding the 1970 Nobel Prize for Literature to A. Solzhenitsyn," October 9, 1970, No. St–112/gs. Enclosure 1. Memorandum of the Central Committee Culture and Propaganda Departments of October 9, 1970. Enclosure 2. The text for publication: "A Dishonorable Game (On the Award of the Nobel Prize to Solzhenitsyn)." (26)

The Secretariat resolution, "On Exposing the Anti-Soviet Campaign of Bourgeois Propaganda Regarding the Publication of *The Gulag Archipelago* by Solzhenitsyn," January 4, 1974, No. St–108/4s. Enclosure. The text of the telegram to Soviet Ambassadors. (98)

The Secretariat resolution, "On Informing Leaders of Fraternal Communist and Workers' Parties on the Solzhenitsyn Matter," February 14, 1974, No. St–114/51gs. Enclosure 1. The text of instructions to Soviet Ambassadors. Enclosure 2. The list of the Parties to which information on the Solzhenitsyn issue is to be sent. (128)

V. The Decree of the Presidium of the USSR Supreme Soviet

"On the Revocation of A.I. Solzhenitsyn's Soviet Citizenship and His Deportation from the USSR," February 12, 1974, No. 5494–III. (125)

VI. Memorandums from Ministries, State Committees, Central Committee Departments, and Officials

Committee for State Security of the USSR Council of Ministers (KGB) and the USSR Public Prosecutor's Office memorandum, January 4, 1966, No. 6–S. (4)

KGB memorandum, October 29, 1970, No. 2945–A. (31)

KGB memorandum, November 14, 1970, No. 3125–Ts. (35)

KGB memorandum, August 16, 1971, No. 2067–A. Enclosure. Solzhenitsyn's open letter to Andropov, Chairman of the KGB, August 13, 1971. (52)

KGB memorandum, February 20, 1972, No. 421–A. (64)

KGB memorandum, July 17, 1973, No. 1707–A. Enclosure. Excerpts from E.D. Voronyanskaya's *Memoirs*. (77)

KGB memorandum, August 26, 1973, No. 2036–A. (79)

KGB memorandum, August 27, 1973, No. 2045–A. (80)

KGB memorandum, September 17, 1973, No. 2239–A. (92)

KGB memorandum, October 19, 1973, No. 2487–A. (93)

KGB memorandum, December 12, 1973, No. 3079–A. (95)

KGB memorandum, January 2, 1974, No. 2–A. (96)

KGB memorandum, January 2, 1974, No. 4–A. (97)

KGB memorandum, February 7, 1974, No. 350–A/OV. Enclosure. Draft of the Decree of the Presidium of the USSR Supreme Soviet, "On Depriving A.I. Solzhenitsyn's Soviet Citizenship and Deporting Him from the USSR." (119)

KGB memorandum, February 9, 1974, No. 388–A. (121)

KGB memorandum, "On *The Oak and the Calf*, and the Further Compromising of Solzhenitsyn," June 6, 1975, No. 1437–A. Enclosure. Summary of *The Oak and the Calf*. (141)

KGB memorandum, "On Publishing Yakovlev's Article 'The Calf with a Blade' on Solzhenitsyn, in *Golos Rodiny* (Voice of the Motherland)," August 30, 1975, No. 2337–A. Enclosure. Yakovlev's article, "A Calf with a Blade." (143)

KGB memorandum, "On the Revocation of N.D. Solzhenitsyna's Soviet Citizenship," October 12, 1976, No. 2302–A. (146)

KGB memorandum, "On Publication of the Decree of the Presidium of the USSR Supreme Soviet on the Revocation of N.D. Solzhenitsyna's Soviet Citizenship," March 2, 1977, No. 423–A. (149)

KGB memorandum, "On Publication of a Book on Solzhenitsyn in the Russian Language," July 5, 1977, No. 1432–A. (151)

The KGB and the USSR Ministry of Foreign Affairs memorandum, November 16, 1971, No. 1924/gs. (56)

The KGB and the USSR Ministry of Foreign Affairs memorandum, February 9, 1974, No. 389–A. (122)

The USSR Ministry of Foreign Affairs and the KGB memorandum, March 1, 1974, No. 536/GS. (136)

The KGB and the USSR Office of the Public Prosecutor memorandum, November 20, 1970, No. 3181–A. Enclosure. Draft of the Decree of the Presidium of the USSR Supreme Soviet, "On the Revocation of A.I. Solzhenitsyn's Soviet Citizenship and Deportation from the USSR." (40)

The KGB and the USSR Office of the Public Prosecutor memorandum, March 27, 1972, No. 778–A. Enclosure. Drafts of the Central Committee resolution, "A Question from the KGB and the USSR Public Prosecutor's Office," and of the Decree of the Presidium of the USSR Supreme Soviet, "On the Revocation of Solzhenitsyn's Soviet Citizenship and His Deportation from the USSR." (67)

The KGB and the USSR Office of the Public Prosecutor memorandum, February 6, 1974, No. 348–A. (118)

The USSR Minister of Foreign Affairs memorandum, December 3, 1970, No. 2235/GS. (45)

The USSR Ministry for Foreign Affairs memorandum, April 12, 1972, No. 739/GS. (73)

The USSR Ministry of Foreign Affairs and the Central Committee's Department of Relations with Communist and Workers' Parties of Socialist Nations memorandum, June 16, 1968, No. 1506/GS, 15–D–887. (20)

The Central Committee International Department and the USSR Ministry of Foreign Affairs memorandum, November 23, 1970, No. 2147/GS, 25–S–1993. (41)

The USSR Ministry for Foreign Affairs and the Central Committee International Department memorandum, September 7, 1973, No. 2175/GS. (86)

The Central Committee International Department memorandum, July 10, 1967, No. 25–S–1014. (13)

The Central Committee Culture Department memorandum, "On the Writer A. Solzhenitsyn Regarding the Publication of His Works Abroad," January 22, 1969. (22)

The Central Committee Culture Department memorandum, "On Solzhenitsyn's Letter," October 27, 1970. (30)

The Central Committee Culture Department memorandum, "On Solzhenitsyn," November 11, 1970. (34)

The Central Committee Department of Relations with Communist and Workers' Parties of Socialist Nations and the Central Committee Culture Department memorandum, "On Instructions to the USSR Ambassador to the Democratic Republic of Vietnam," November 17, 1970. (37)

The Central Committee Culture Department memorandum, "On the Publishing of Materials on Solzhenitsyn," November 20, 1970. Enclosure. Texts of the materials for publication: "A Necessary Explanation," "Our

Opinion." (39)

The Central Committee International Department memorandum, "On Information for Fraternal Parties Regarding the Anti-Soviet Activity of Solzhenitsyn," January 15, 1974, No. 25–S–90. (103)

The Central Committee International Department memorandum, "On instructions to the Soviet Ambassador to Sweden," February 22, 1974, No. 25–S–371. Enclosure. The LPCS statement. (133)

The Central Committee Propaganda Department and the Central Committee Department for Political Propaganda Abroad memorandum, "On Rezac's Book, *Solzhenitsyn's Spiral of Treason*," September 18, 1978. (155)

The USSR Writers' Union Secretariat memorandum, December 12, 1967, No. 812. Enclosure 1. The text for publication, "Regarding Solzhenitsyn's Letters." Enclosure 2. Solzhenitsyn's letter, December 1, 1967, to the USSR Writers' Union Secretariat. (18)

The Presidium of the USSR Supreme Soviet memorandum of March 20, 1974, No. 154cc Enclosure 1. Solzhenitsyn's statement, February 13, 1974. Enclosure 2. N. Solzhenitsyna's statement, March 14, 1974. (138)

The USSR State Committee for Publishing, Printing, and the Book Trade and Novosti Press Agency memorandum, August 8, 1978, No. 0500. (154)

The USSR Ministry for Internal Affairs memorandum, "On the Matter of Solzhenitsyn's Telegram," February 6, 1980, No. 1/703. (157)

N. Shchelokov's memorandum, "On the Solzhenitsyn Question." (53)

The *Pravda* political columnist Y. Zhukov's memorandum, January 11, 1974. Enclosure 1. A.I. Yelfimov's letter. Enclosure 2. P.I. Maximov's letter. (101)

Memorandum from I. Chernoutsan, Consultant, the Central Committee Culture Department, to M. Suslov, September 9, 1975. (144)

VII. Reports from Ministries, State Committees, Central Committee Departments, and Officials

KGB report, October 5, 1965, No. 2275–s. (2) Enclosure 1. Memorandum based on surveillance information on the writer Solzhenitsyn's attitudes. Enclosure 2. An annotation of A.I. Solzhenitsyn's novel *The First Circle*. (2)

KGB report, October 5, 1965, No. 2285–S. (3)

KGB report, January 14, 1966, No. 81–S. (5)

KGB report, May 17, 1967, No. 1197–S. (9)

KGB report, July 5, 1967, No. 1740–B. Enclosure. Report on A.I. Solzhenitsyn. (11)

KGB report, July 5, 1967, No. 1756–A. (12)

KGB report, September 14, 1967, No. 2338–A. Enclosure 1. Solzhenitsyn's letter to A. Tvardovsky of September 12, 1967. Enclosure 2. Solzhenitsyn's letter to the USSR Writers' Union Secretariat of September 12, 1967. (16)

KGB report, January 31, 1968, No. 218–A. (19)

KGB report, November 28, 1970, No. 3249–TS. (43)

KGB report, December 3, 1970, No. 3271–A. (46)

KGB report, December 28, 1970, No. 3511–A. (48)

KGB report, June 25, 1971, No. 1630–A. Enclosure. Solzhenitsyn's *August 1914* (an annotation). (51)

KGB report, October 27, 1971, No. 3720–A/OV. (55)

KGB report, November 23, 1971, No. 2953–A. Enclosure. The translation of the article "A Boorish Family," published in *Stern* magazine. (58)

KGB report, December 25, 1971, No. 3256–Ts. (59)

KGB report, December 31, 1971, No. 3318–A. (60)

KGB report, February 22, 1972, No. 438–A. (65)

KGB report, March 11, 1972, No. 601–A. (66)

KGB report, April 3, 1972, No. 854–A. (70)

KGB report, April 10, 1972, No. 942–A/OV. (72)

KGB report, April 13, 1972, No. 969–A. (75)

KGB report, August 10, 1973, No. 1902–A. (78)

KGB report, September 4, 1973, No. 2114–A. (84)

KGB report, September 8, 1973, No. 2176–Ch. (87)

KGB report, September 10, 1973, No. 2180–Ch. Enclosure. An annotation to Solzhenitsyn's *The Gulag Archipelago*. (88)

KGB report, November 2, 1973, No. 2654–A. (94)

KGB report, January 15, 1974, No. 119–A. (105)

KGB report, January 16, 1974, No. 139–A. (106)

KGB report, January 17, 1974, No. 147–A. (110)

KGB report, January 17, 1974, No. 150–A. (112)

KGB report, January 18, 1974, No. 157–A. (113)

KGB report, January 19, 1974, No. 174–A. Enclosure. A statement by Solzhenitsyn. (114)

KGB report, January 29, 1974, No. 266–A. (116)

KGB report, February 1, 1974, No. 300–A. Enclosure. Solzhenitsyn's biography, published in the collection *Nobel Prize Winners of 1970*. (117)

KGB report, February 14, 1974, No. 444–A. (131)

KGB report, February 23, 1974, No. 553–Ts. (134)

KGB report, May 2, 1974, No. 1168–A. (139)

KGB report, July 24, 1974, No. 2035–A. (140)

KGB report, "On the Publication of an Open Letter by V.A. Tvardovskaya to Solzhenitsyn in the Italian Newspaper *L'Unita*," July 11, 1975, No. 1812–A. Enclosure. Translation of V. Tvardovskaya's article. (142)

KGB report, "On Solzhenitsyn's Hostile Activities and the Decline of Interest in His Person Abroad and in the USSR," January 4, 1976, No. 7–A. (145)

KGB report, "On the Publication of a Manuscript About Solzhenitsyn," January 17, 1977, No. 87–Ts. Enclosure. Summary of the manuscript of the book on Solzhenitsyn by the Czech journalist T. Rezac. (148)

KGB report, "On Solzhenitsyn's Attempt to Found a So-Called 'All-Russian Memoir Library'," November 11, 1977, No. 2439–A. (153)

The Chief Directorate for Preservation of Government Secrets in the Press report, October 13, 1970, No. 988s. (27)

The Central Committee Culture Department report, January 29, 1966. Enclosure. A. Surkov's review of Solzhenitsyn's works. (6)

The Central Committee Culture Department report, "On the Discussions in the Soviet Writers' Union Regarding Solzhenitsyn's Conduct," October 4, 1967. (17)

The Central Committee Culture Department report, "Writers' Responses to the Expulsion of Solzhenitsyn from the Soviet Writers' Union," November 13, 1969. (23)

The Central Committee Culture Department report, "On the Responses of Writers to Solzhenitsyn's Antisocial Activities," November 18, 1969. (24)

The Moscow City CPSU Committee report, November 20, 1969, No. 328. (25)

The Central Committee Culture Department report, "On the Reaction of the Writers' Community to the Awarding the Nobel Prize to Solzhenitsyn," October 15, 1970. (29)

The Moscow City CPSU Committee report, January 11, 1974, No. 11. (102)

The Central Committee Propaganda Department, Culture Department, and Science and Educational Institutions Department report, January 15, 1974. Enclosure. A list of most characteristic statements in connection with the publication of the article "The Path of Treason" in *Pravda*. (104)

The Central Committee General Department report "On Workers' Letters in Regard to the Anti-Soviet Activities of A. Sakharov and A. Solzhenitsyn," January 16, 1974. (107)

The Moscow City CPSU Committee report, "On Responses of Moscow Workers to I. Solovyov's article 'The Path of Treason' published in *Pravda* on January 14, 1974," January 17, 1974, No. 18. (111)

The Central Committee Organizational and Party Work Department report "On the Attitudes of Soviet People to the Publication Abroad of the Slanderous Writings of A. Solzhenitsyn," January 21, 1974. (115)

The Ukraine CP Central Committee report, February 14, 1974, No. 1/25. (130)

The Central Committee Organizational and Party Work Department report, "On Workers' Responses to the Deportation of Solzhenitsyn from the USSR," February 15, 1974. (132)

V. Lebedev's report of March 22, 1963. (1)

Report from M. Zimyanin, Editor-in-Chief of *Pravda*, No. GL–124. Enclosure. M. Rostropovich's open letter to the Editors-in-Chief of the newspapers *Pravda, Izvestia, Literaturnaya Gazeta,* and *Sovetskaya Kultura,* October 31, 1970. (32)

VIII. Telegrams from the USSR Embassies in Sweden and in France

Telegram from the USSR Embassy in Sweden, November 15, 1970. (36)

Telegram from the USSR Embassy in Sweden, December 1, 1970. (44)

Telegram from the USSR Embassy in Sweden, April 8, 1972. (71)

Telegram from the USSR Embassy in France, August 30, 1973. (82)

Telegram from the USSR Embassy in France, September 1, 1973. (83)

Telegram from the USSR Embassy in Sweden, February 14, 1974. (129)

IX. Letters and a Telegram from Solzhenitsyn and Other Persons

K. Simonov's letter, "On Solzhenitsyn's Novel *The First Circle*," February 1, 1966. (7)

S. Toka's letter to the Central Committee, June 1, 1967, No. 63. Enclosure. Solzhenitsyn's letter to the Fourth Congress of Soviet Writers (in lieu of a speech). (10)

Solzhenitsyn's letter to M. Suslov, October 14, 1970. (28)

A. Chakovsky's letter to the Central Committee, November 11, 1970. (33)

Solzhenitsyn's letter to the Chairman of the USSR Council of Ministers, February 18, 1971. (50)

E. Furtseva's letter to the Politburo, February 17, 1972. Enclosure. Solzhenitsyn's letter to E. Furtseva, February 12, 1972. (63)

Solzhenitsyn's letter to L. Brezhnev, September 5, 1973. Enclosure. Solzhenitsyn's letter to the leaders of the Soviet Union. (85)

Y. Andropov's letter to L. Brezhnev, February 7, 1974. Enclosure. KGB report. (120)

Solzhenitsyn's telegram to K. Chernenko, December 20, 1979. (156)

INDEX

A

Abakumov, Viktor, 16, 37, 40, 47
Abashidze, I., 63, 105, 119, 123, 179
Abdumonunov, T., 63
Adamovich, Georgi, 134, 137
Aitmatov, Chingiz, 75, 78
Akhmatova, Anna, 46, 47
Akim, Y.L., 220
Alexeyava, A.N., 220
Allilueva, Svetlana, xxxi, 283, 290, 292
Alsop, Joseph, 290
Amalrik, Andrei, 238–240
Andrei Rublev, 112
Andreyev, Leonid, 162
Andropov, Yuri, xxv–xxxiv, 41, 153, 185,
    221, 242, 284, 285
Andryushchenko, G., 186
Antokolsky, Pavel, 103, 104
"Appeal to the Russian Public," 452
Aragon, Louis, 111
"An Archipelago of Lies," 434
Arbuzov, Alexei, 87, 91
Arkhangelsky, V., 107
Arnau, Frank, 434
"On the Artistic Mission of A.I.
Solzhenitsyn," 29
August 1914, xxvii, 101, 109, 156, 157, 173,
    177, 219, 220, 269, 337, 419, 421
Azbel, Mark, 326

B

Babel, Isaac, 47
Bahr, Egon, 343, 346, 348
Baklanov, Grigori, 167
Bannikov, A., 107
Barabanov, Evgeny, 265–267, 345
Baruzdin, S., 63
Beam, James, 216
Beria, Lavrenty, 20, 37, 40, 47
Berzer, Anna, 190

Blagoveschensky, I., 166
Bobkov, F.D., 53, 160, 176, 228, 254, 342,
    346, 398
Bokov, Viktor, 304
Boffa, Giuseppe, 98
Böll, Heinrich, 111, 190–193, 220, 353, 370,
    393
"A Boorish Family," 171–176
Borisov, Vadim, 223, 228, 345, 435
Brandt, Willy, xxxiv, 340–344, 346–348,
    353, 370, 425
"Breathing," 26
Bratelli, Trygve, 376, 378
Brezhnev, Leonid I., xvii, xix, xxi, xxiii,
    xxviii–xxxiii, 199, 202, 210, 221, 222, 256,
    257, 284
Brodsky, Joseph, 112, 193
"Brodsky Letter to the Central Committee,"
    224
Brovka, Petrus, 63
Brzezinski, Zbigniew, 378
Bukharina, Anna Larina, 435, 436
Bukovsky, Vladimir, 238–240
Bulgakov, Mikhail, 46, 47, 237, 240
Bunin, Ivan, 46, 162

C

"The Calf With A Blade," 411–426, 427
"The Campfire and the Ants," 27
Cancer Ward, xxii, xxv, 41, 48, 60, 61, 64–66,
    68, 69, 71–73, 75, 77, 79, 81, 83, 101, 105,
    112, 114, 118, 120, 132, 133, 161, 225,
    338, 396
Candle in the Wind (also see *The Light That Is
    in You*), 14, 49, 50
Chaikovsky, Boris, 112
Chakovsky, Alexander, 85
Chebrikov, 257, 346
Chernenko, Konstantin, xxxiii, xxxviii
Cherny, Sasha, 112

Chukovskaya, Lydia, 91, 92, 156, 190
Chukovsky, Kornei, 75, 78
"The City on the Neva," 27
"The Collective Farm Rucksack," 27
Crepeau, 327, 372

D

Daniel, Yuli, xxii, xxv, xxviii, 35, 36, 58, 59, 163
Dante (Alighieri), 15
One Day in the Life of Ivan Denisovich, xx, xxiv,
    12, 34, 36, 61, 75, 114, 117, 125, 161, 194,
    208, 337, 338, 395
"Deer and Shelter of Branches," 337
Delo, 79, 81, 82
Dementyev, Alexander G., 108, 395
Demichev, Pyotr N., 42, 58, 153, 164, 185, 207
Doctor Zhivago, 112, 162
Dostoevsky, Fyodor, 46
Dremlyuga, Vladimir, 437, 438
"The Duckling," 26
Dyakov, Boris, 75, 78
Dzyuba, Ivan, 200, 203, 204, 209, 211

E

"The Elm Log," 26
"Essays," 10, 11
Essays on Literary Life (subtitle; see *The Oak and
    the Calf*)
Etkind, Efim, 192, 193, 224, 345
"Experiment in Literary Investigation"
    (subtitle; see *The Gulag Archipelago*)

F

Fajon, 244, 245
Falin, Valentin, 347, 353
Feast of the Victors, xix, xxii, xxv, 23, 24, 26, 34,
    41, 48, 63, 64, 105, 116, 132
"Some Features of the Rhythm System and
    Composition on the Poem About Ivan
    Denisovich," 29
February 1917, 177, 232
Fedin, Konstantin, 63–65, 67, 75, 85, 103, 129
Firsov, Vladimir, 303
Firsova, 107
The First Circle (*Sharashka*), xx, xxii, xxiv, xxv, 7,
    11, 12, 15–21, 26, 36–39, 48, 73, 83, 118,
    120, 132, 138, 195, 225, 270, 337
Fischer, Louis, 8, 9, 25
Florensky, Pavel, 237, 240
Ford, Gerald, xxxv, 433
Frank, Paul, 347, 348, 352, 353
Fredrikson, Stig, 216
Fromm, Ullrich, 180

G

Gagarin, Yuri, 133
Galanskov, Yuri T., 233, 235, 252

Galich, Alexander, 192, 193
Gierow, Karl Ragnar, 130, 212, 214, 215
Ginzburg, Alexander, 251, 252, 435, 437
Glazov, 264
Gorbachev, Mikhail, xxiii
Gorbanevskaya, Natalia, 435–437
Gorky, 133
Gorlov, xxvii, 158–160, 239
Graber, P., 434
Granin, Daniil, 87
Grechko, A.A., 126
Grigorenko, Petro, 166, 167, 226, 238, 437
Grin, Alexander, 47
Grishin, V.V., 42, 153, 203
Gromyko, Andrei, xxix, 147, 285
Grossman, Vasily, 47
Guerra, A., 55–57, 98
The Gulag Archipelago, xviii, xxiv, xxv, xxx–xxxii,
    12, 13, 138, 224–228, 231, 242, 247,
    252–254, 260, 277, 279, 281, 283, 312, 313,
    328, 329, 347, 387, 389, 397, 429, 431
Gumilev, 46

H

Heeb, Fritz, 144, 145, 178, 353
Hegge, Per, 144
Hermansson, K., 362, 374, 379, 380
"His Goal—Man's Struggle Against the
    System," 135
"His Works and His Misfortunes," 98
Hoover, Herbert, 433

I

"I Was Betrayed by Solzhenitsyn," 431
"The Ideological Struggle: The Responsibility
    of the Writer," 84, 114, 120
Ilyin, V.I., 205, 211
"Incident at Krechetovka Station," 117
Isaev, Yegor, 85
Ivanov, Vyacheslav V., 268
Ivanova, E.V., 224

J

Jackson, Henry M., 371, 425
Jarring, 147, 168, 170, 214
July 1941, 167

K

Kabalevsky, Dmitri, 179
Kaiser, Robert, 213
Kapitonov, I., 58
Kapitsa, Pyotr, 41, 42
Katerina Ismailova, 112
Katushev, K., 164, 287
Keldysh, Mstislav, 209, 211, 257
Kerbabaev, B., 63
Khanzhenkov, Sergei, 237

Khlynov, Stepan (pseudonym for Solzhenitsyn), 21, 421
Khrushchev, Nikita, xix–xxiii, 3–5, 161, 204, 206, 208
Kirilenko, A.P., 153, 206, 207, 241, 242
Kirsanov, Semyon, 86
Kissinger, Henry, 425
Klyuev, Viktor, 46
Kobzev, I., 107
Kochetov, V., 89, 91, 111
Kohout, Pavel, 141
Kolman, E.Y., 156
Konenkov, 162
Kopelev, Lev, 91, 92, 156, 178, 190, 191, 193
Koptaeva, Antonina, 85
Korneychuk, A., 63, 65
Kornilov, Vladimir, 326
Korolenko, Vladimir, 227, 229
Korolev, 133
Korzhavin, Naum, 223, 228, 251
Kosmodemyanskaya, Zoya, 132
Kosygin, Alexei, xxvii, xxviii, 154, 209, 221, 242, 256, 257, 288
Kozhevnikov, Vadim, 63, 65, 85
Kraft, Joseph, 433
Krasin, Viktor, 239, 242
Kreps, V., 179
Kropotkin, Pyotr, 65, 67
Krylenko, Nikolai, 227, 229
Kulakov, F. 58
Kunaev, D., 202, 203
Kuprin, Alexander, 162
Kuznetsov, Anatoly, 209, 211, 257

L

"Lake Segden," 26
Lakshin, 178
Lebedev, Vladimir, xx
Lenin, Vladimir I., xxxvii, 8, 9, 270, 394
Leonov, Leonid, 87, 179
Letter to the Soviet Leaders, xxx, 249, 343, 345
Levashov, A., 107
Levenborg, A., 365
The Life of Lenin, 8, 25
The Light That Is in You (see *Candle in the Wind*)
"A Literary Wonder," 75
Litvinov, 209, 211
Longo, Luigi, 56, 57

M

Malyarov, 242, 243, 257
Malyshkin, V., 166
Mandelstam, Ossip, 46, 47
March 1917, 385, 386, 394
Marchais, Georges, 243–245
Markov, G. M., 61, 63, 65, 129, 153
Marshak, Samuel, 66

Martov, Georgi, 157
Maslennikov, A., 186
Matrosov, Alexander, 132, 137
Matryona's Yard, 114, 117, 338
Mauriac, François, 111
Maximov, Vladimir, 319
Mayakovsky, Vladimir, 46, 50
Meany, George, 433
Medvedev, Roy, 106, 178, 190
Medvedev, Zhores, 106, 138, 144, 156
"A Melancholy Tale" (see "A Sad Tale")
Memoirs (Voronyanskaya), 224–228
"A Mercenary and a Simpleton," 432
Mikhailovsky, 65, 67
Mikhalkov, Sergei, 64, 103, 104
Mikoyan, Anastas, 206
"Miniatures" (also known as "Miniature Stories"), 48, 119
Mints, K., 179
"Mode of Transport," 27
Mozhaev, Boris, 90, 92
Musrepov, G., 63
"My Husband, Solzhenitsyn," 432
Myaskovsky, N., 112
Mzhavanadze, 208

N

Narovchatov, Sergei, 87
Nekrasov, A.S., 220
Nekrasov, Viktor, 265, 326, 387, 434
The New York Times, 88, 121, 133, 423, 433
Nilsson, T., 143, 146, 147, 150, 168, 170
Nixon, Richard M., 257, 258, 427, 435
"The Nobel Prize for Solzhenitsyn," 98
Nobel Prize Winners of 1970, 336
Novichenko, L., 63, 65

O

The Oak and the Calf (Russian title: *The Calf Butted the Oak*), xxiv, xxv, xxxiv, xxxv, xxxvii, 393–398, 427, 437
October 1916, 156, 177, 178, 224, 385, 386, 394
Okudzhava, Bulat, 192,193
"The Old Bucket," 27
open letters, xxix, 88, 134, 159, 160, 195, 196, 271
Orlova, Raissa, 190
Ozerov, Vitali, 63, 73

P

Pakhtusova, N.F., 224, 230, 231, 246, 247
Palme, Olof, 362
Pasternak, Boris, xxv , xxviii, 46, 47, 111, 112, 162
Pasternak, Evgeny, 435, 436
"The Path of Treason" (also known as "The Road of Treachery," "The Road of Treason"), xxii, 302-308, 319–326

Petlyura, (General), 318
Pikhterev, V. N., 365
Pilnyak, Boris, 46, 47
Pimen, (Patriarch) 196
Platonov, Andrei, 46, 47, 237, 240
Plissonier, 244, 245
Podgorny, Nikolai, 208, 209, 210, 287, 290
"A Poet's Ashes," 26
Polevoy, Boris, 64, 85
Pompidou, Georges, 376, 378
Ponomarev, Boris, 164, 205
"Prayer," 27
"On Priorities," 122
Prussian Nights, 431
Prokofiev, Sergei, 111, 112
Pushkin, Alexander, 46

R

R-17 (code name; see *August 1914*), 416
Ramzin, Leonid K., 17, 25, 34, 35
Rasputin, Grigori, 177
Reed, Dean, 187
"A Reflection in the Water," 26
Remizov, Alexei, 35, 36
Renschler, W., 434
The Republic of Labor, xix, 21–23, 26, 63, 195
Reshetovskaya, Marla, 52
Reshetovskaya, Natalia (Natasha), xxvii, xxxiv, 52, 108, 109, 140, 175, 176, 178, 432
Reshetovsky, Alexei, 52, 53
Rezac, Tomas, 441–445, 448, 449, 451–453
"The Right Hand," 49, 339
"The Road of Treachery" (see "The Path of Treason")
"The Road of Treason" (see "The Path of Treason")
Romanowsky, Jerzy, 219
Roosevelt, Franklin D., 433
Rostropovich, Mstislav, 101, 102, 109, 110–113, 125, 156, 164, 216, 222
Rudenko, Roman, xxv, xxix, 257
"For the Russian-Language Edition Published Abroad in 1971," 156
Ryurikov, B., 63–65

S

"A Sad Tale" (also known as "A Sorrowful Tale" and "A Melancholy Tale"), 24, 26
Sakharov, Andrei, xxiii, xxix, xxx, xxxii, 41, 190, 210, 226, 241–243, 245, 250, 251, 255–257, 259, 260–266, 268, 389
Salinsky, A., 63, 66
Samsonov, (General), 166
Samutin, Leonid A., 224, 228
Sartakov, Sergei, S., 61
Savinkov, Boris, 133, 137
Schwarzenbach, G., 434

Sedykh, V., 244
Semichastny, Vladimir, xxv, 41, 42
Shafarevich, Igor, 215
Sharashka, xx, xxii, 11 (See *The First Circle*)
"Sharik," 27
Sharipov, A., 63, 65
Shauro, V.F., 41, 153
Shchelokov, Nikolai, xxviii, xxix, 161, 164, 233
Shcherbak, Irina, 171–176, 385, 455, 457
Shcherbak, Roman, 173–175
Shcherbak, Taisa (see Solzhenitsyna)
Shcherbak, Zakhar, 173
Shebalin, V., 112
Shelepin, Alexander, 257, 290
Shevchenko, Taras, 76, 79
Shlyapnikov, 394
Sholokhov, Mikhail, 64, 67, 75, 76, 85, 89, 111, 444
Shostakovich, Dmitri, 111, 112
Shtein, A., 91
Shtok, Isidor, 179
Simonov, Konstantin, 36, 39, 63–66, 73
Sinyavsky, Andrei, xxii, xxv, xxviii, 35, 36, 58, 59
Sketches of Literary Life (subtitle; see *The Oak and the Calf*)
Smirnov, Nikolai P., 220
Smirnov, Sergei, 85
Smith, Hedrick, 213, 369, 370
Sobolev, Leonid, 61, 88
Solomentsev, M. 41, 59, 287
Solovyov, Vladimir, 65, 67
Solzhenitsyn, Dmitri (see Tyurin, Dmitri)
Solzhenitsyn, A Documentary Record, 138
"Solzhenitsyn—An Exposed Liar Known to All," 432
"Solzhenitsyn Has Been Awarded the Nobel Prize," 99
Solzhenitsyn, Ignat, 385
Solzhenitsyn, Isaaky (Isai), 173, 174, 176
"Solzhenitsyn and the NTS," 432
"Solzhenitsyn, Nobel Laureate," 98
"Solzhenitsyn Receives the Nobel Prize," 99
Solzhenitsyn, S.E., 269
Solzhenitsyn, Stepan, 385
Solzhenitsyn, Yermolai, 385
Solzhenitsyna, Natalia Reshetovskaya (see Reshetovskaya)
Solzhenitsyna, Natalia Svetlova, xxvii, 145, 148, 151, 156, 178, 212, 216, 382, 384, 386, 397, 437–440, 446, 447
Solzhenitsyna, Taisia Shcherbak, 173–175, 269
"Solzhenitsyn's Appeal Cannot Remain Unanswered," 55–57
Solzhenitsyn's Spiral of Treason, 448, 451–453
"Alexander Solzhenitsyn's August 1914, or the Book and the Myth," 219
"A Sorrowful Tale" (see "A Sad Tale")

Stalin, Joseph, xix, 16, 20, 40, 231
Starikov, D., 179
Starodubova, V., 107
"Starting the Day," 27
Stein, A., 107
Steiner, Dieter, 172, 173, 176
Stolyarova, Ilya, 215
Suchkov, Boris, 87
Superfin, Gabriel, 223, 228, 251
Surkov, Alexei, 33–35, 63–65, 85, 103
Suslov, Mikhail A., 59, 100, 102, 153, 164, 205, 257
Svetlova, Natalia (see Solzhenitsyna)
Svetlova, Yekaterina Ferdinandova, 384

T

Tabidze, 47
Tanks Know the Truth, 48, 431
Tarkovsky, Andrei, 112, 113
Tarsis, Valery, 35, 36
The Tenderfoot and the Tramp, 3, 4, 48
Tendryakov, Vladimir, 90–92
Teush, Veniamin L., xxii, xxiii, 7, 25, 27, 29–33, 71
"This Is How We Live," 106, 122
Tikhonov, Nikolai, 87, 103, 129
Timofeyev-Ressovsky, 9
Toka, S.K., 44
Tolstoy, Leo N., 157, 161
"Travelling Along the Oka," 27
Trukhin, F., 166
Tsvetaeva, Marina, 46, 47, 50
Tumanova, 58
Trudeau, Pierre, 376, 434
Tvardovsky, Alexander, xx, 3–5, 60, 63, 66, 75, 86, 108, 156, 181, 182, 226, 395, 396, 400–408, 414–416, 418, 427
Tvardovskaya, V.A., xxxv, 399–408
Tyurin, 435, 436
Tyurin, Dmitri, 387 (see also Solzhenitsyn, Dmitri)

U

Ustinov, D., 58, 59

V

Vasily Tyorkin, 181, 182
Vasilyev, Pavel, 47
Vassa Zheleznova, 133
Vesely, Artem, 47
Vishnevskaya, Galina, 112, 113
Vitkevich, Nikolai, xxxv, 53, 412, 432, 444
Vlasov, Andrei, 34, 35, 165, 166
Voinovich, Vladimir, 326, 327
Voloshin, 46
"Volunteers' Highway," xix, 270
Voprosy Literatury, 73

Voronkov, Konstantin, 61, 63
Voronyanskaya, Elizaveta D., xxx, 224–228, 231, 246–248
Vorotyntsev, 157

W

The Washington Post, 433
The Washington Star, 433
War and Peace, 112
"*We* Shall Never Die," 27
Weizsäcker, Richard V., 264
"What a Pity," 48
What Do You Want?, 89
"Where Does The Nobel Prize Committee Look for Writers' Talent and Fame?" 122
Wickman, Krister, 168, 169, 214, 217
Wimmer, 98
Wurmser, André, 98

Y

Yagoda, 47
Yakir, Iona, 182, 211
Yakir, Pyotr, xxix, 180, 182, 203–207, 209–211, 221, 239, 241, 242
Yakovlev, N.N., 394, 398, 409, 426–430
Yakshen, K., 64, 66
Yakubovich, M., xxxv, 394, 432
Yefremov, Oleg N., 3–5
Yeltsin, xvii
Yesenin, Sergei, 46, 50
"In Yesenin's Homeland," 27
Yevtushenko, Yevgeny, 91, 99, 108
Yezhov, 47

Z

Zabolotsky, 47
Zalygin, Sergei, 75, 78
Zamyatin, Yevgeny, 35, 36, 46
Zhukov, Yuri, 293–296
Zimyanin, M.V. 245, 246
Zoshchenko, 47